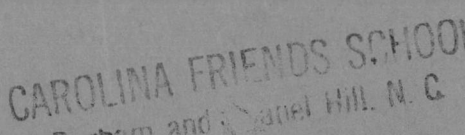

PRENTICE-HALL, INC., ENGLEWOOD CLIFFS, NEW JERSEY

Carolina Quest

THOMAS C. PARRAMORE

Department of History, Meredith College
Raleigh, North Carolina

Acknowledgments

The author is indebted to many of his colleagues and associates for their assistance in developing this volume. He extends his grateful appreciation to the staff of the North Carolina Department of Archives and History, particularly to Jerry Cashion, George Stevenson, Nancy Caroline Banks, Dick Lankford, and Walton Haywood. Also providing invaluable help were John Batchelor, Ruby Lanier, Michelle Lawing, and Jerry Cotton. Finally, I owe a debt of gratitude for the help and patience of my wife Barbara and daughters Lisa and Lynn.

Credits appear on page 510.

Photographic program by Michal Heron

Cover illustration by David Christensen

For description of cover events, see page 510.

Critic Readers

Mr. Jerry Cashion, Research Supervisor
State Department of Archives and History, Raleigh

Dr. Ruby J. Lanier, Department of History
Appalachian State University, Boone

Mr. John Batchelor
Northeast Junior High School, McLeansville

Library of Congress Cataloging in Publication Data

Parramore, Thomas C.
    Carolina quest.

    Includes bibliographies and index.
    SUMMARY: Traces the history of North Carolina from the arrival of the first settlers and the mysterious disappearance of the colony on Roanoke Island up to the present time.
        1. North Carolina—History—Juvenile literature.
[1. North Carolina—History] I. Title.
F254.3.P3   975.6   77-24119
ISBN 0-13-114900-8

Supplementary Material: Teacher's Guide

Carolina Quest
Thomas C. Parramore

10 9 8 7 6 5 4 3 2 1

Prentice-Hall International, Inc., London
Prentice-Hall of Australia, Pty. Ltd., Sydney
Prentice-Hall of Canada, Ltd., Toronto
Prentice-Hall of India Private Ltd., New Delhi
Prentice-Hall of Japan, Inc., Tokyo
Prentice-Hall of Southeast Asia Pte. Ltd., Singapore
Whitehall Books Limited, Wellington, New Zealand

PREFACE

The theme of this book is the ongoing search for a better community in the state of North Carolina. The quest began almost four hundred years ago and it continues today. The same light that shows us the path we have followed so far can also help us make out certain features of the road ahead. If we cannot see far ahead, at least we can have a good idea of what we hope to find. Everyone can join in the search and each of us can help chart the course for North Carolina and America.

On the pages which follow appear a Map and Art Portfolio. It consists of three full-color maps and a five page section of full-color photographs, ranging from early history to early twentieth century life in North Carolina. Pages 465-480, a North Carolina Album, continue the story with color photographs of present-day life in the state.

Each chapter tells about a part of the search as it has been made so far. Certain guides aid the quest through the chapters ahead. In each chapter, a map shows that part of North Carolina to which most attention is given. Historical locations appear in black, and present-day sites appear in color. "People in This Chapter" lists the main characters in the chapter. Unfamiliar terms are defined in the margins of the text. A "Chapter Checkup" at the end of each chapter serves for study and review purposes.

Most of the quotations throughout the text are from the author's research of primary sources. Acknowledgment of the major sources will be found on page 512. A complete list of the governors of the state, an index of the people in this book, and a general topical index will be found at the end of the book.

The author and editors hope you will enjoy your quest and that you will understand yourself and your state better for having made it.

Thomas C. Parramore
Raleigh, N.C.

CONTENTS

Physical Map of North Carolina

① The Mountain Region is part of the Appalachian chain. The highest mountains, on the Tennessee border, are the Great Smokies. Further east are the Blue Ridge. Clingman's Dome, in this region, is one of the tallest mountains in the eastern United States.

② Piedmont means foothills. In central North Carolina, rolling hills rise higher and higher as they approach the Blue Ridge. In time, the Piedmont became the state's main industrial region. It contains a large part of the state's people and wealth.

③ The Coastal Plain is low, flat country compared to the western area of the state. Historically, travel was difficult because of the many broad rivers. It is the state's chief farming area, a large producer of cotton, tobacco, soybeans, and peanuts.

④ The Tidelands is a wet, low-lying area that is affected by the ocean's tides. There are many swamps and marshes in this region. It was here that Europeans first settled in the sixteenth century. Most of the early history of the state was enacted here.

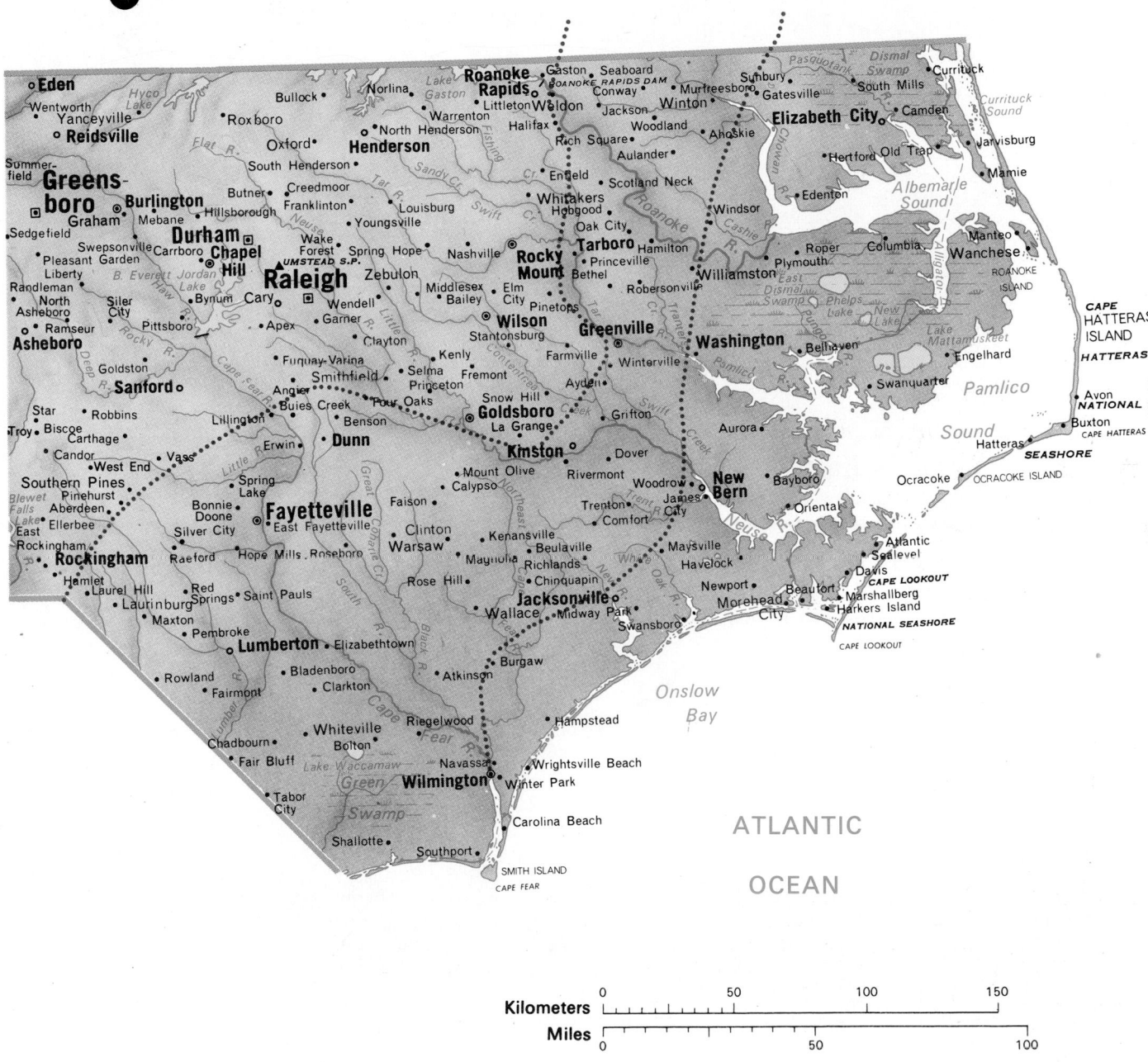

2   3   4

Eden
Wentworth
Yanceyville
Reidsville
Summer-field
Greens-boro
Burlington
Graham
Sedgefield
Swepsonville Carrboro Chapel
Durham
Pleasant Garden
Liberty
Randleman
North Asheboro
Ramseur
Asheboro

Bullock
Roxboro
Oxford
South Henderson
Butner Creedmoor
Mebane Hillsborough Franklinton
Wake Forest
Spring Hope
Nashville
Zebulon
Wendell
Bailey
Middlesex
Garner
Clayton
Kenly

Norlina
North Henderson
Louisburg
Youngsville

Henderson

Roanoke Rapids
Littleton Weldon
Warrenton
Halifax
Rich Square
Enfield
Whitakers
Hobgood
Oak City
Tarboro
Princeville
Bethel
Robersonville

Gaston Seaboard
Conway
Jackson Winton
Woodland
Aulander
Scotland Neck
Hamilton

Sunbury
Murfreesboro Gatesville
Ahoskie

South Mills
Elizabeth City Camden
Hertford Old Trap
Edenton
Windsor
Plymouth
Roper Columbia
Williamston

Currituck
Jarvisburg
Mamie

Albemarle Sound

Manteo
Wanchese
ROANOKE ISLAND

Siler City
Pittsboro
Goldston
Sanford

Raleigh
Cary
Apex
Fuquay-Varina
Smithfield
Angier
Buies Creek
Lillington
Benson
Erwin
Dunn

Louisburg
Selma
Princeton
Four Oaks
Goldsboro
La Grange
Kinston

Wilson
Stantonsburg
Farmville
Ayden
Snow Hill
Grifton
Dover

Greenville
Winterville

Washington
Belhaven

East Dismal Swamp
Phelps Lake
Lake Mattamuskeet
Engelhard
Swanquarter

CAPE HATTERAS
HATTERAS

Pamlico Sound

Avon
NATIONAL
Buxton
CAPE HATTERAS
Hatteras
SEASHORE

Star
Troy Biscoe
Carthage
Candor West End
Southern Pines
Pinehurst
Aberdeen
Ellerbee
East Rockingham
Rockingham
Hamlet

Robbins
Vass
Spring Lake
Bonnie Doone
Silver City
Fayetteville
East Fayetteville
Hope Mills Roseboro

Mount Olive
Calypso
Faison
Clinton
Warsaw
Magnolia
Kenansville
Beulaville
Richlands
Chinquapin

Rivermont
Trenton
Comfort
Woodrow
James City
New Bern
Bayboro
Oriental

Aurora

Maysville
Havelock
Newport
Morehead City
Beaufort

Atlantic
Sealevel
Davis
Marshallberg
Harkers Island
CAPE LOOKOUT
NATIONAL SEASHORE
CAPE LOOKOUT

Ocracoke
OCRACOKE ISLAND

Laurel Hill
Laurinburg
Maxton
Pembroke
Red Springs
Saint Pauls
Lumberton
Rowland
Fairmont
Bladenboro
Clarkton
Elizabethtown
Atkinson
Burgaw
Riegelwood
Hampstead

Jacksonville
Wallace Midway Park
Swansboro

Onslow Bay

Chadbourn
Fair Bluff
Whiteville
Bolton
Navassa
Wilmington
Winter Park
Wrightsville Beach
Tabor City
Shallotte
Southport
Carolina Beach
SMITH ISLAND
CAPE FEAR

ATLANTIC

OCEAN

| Kilometers | 0 | | 50 | | 100 | | 150 |
| Miles | 0 | | | 50 | | | 100 |

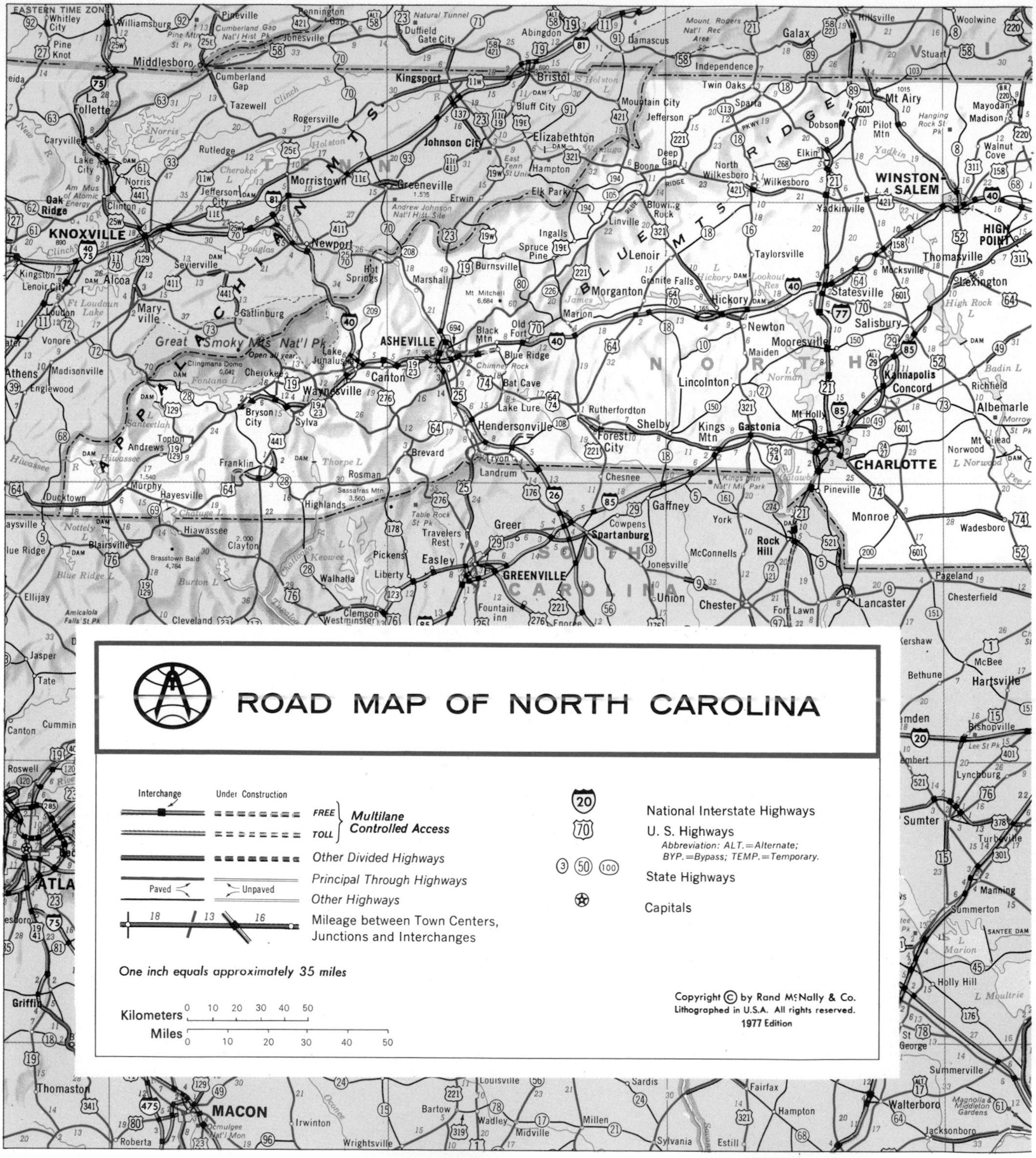

ROAD MAP OF NORTH CAROLINA
Interchange
Under Construction
FREE
TOLL
Multilane Controlled Access
Other Divided Highways
Paved
Unpaved
Principal Through Highways
Other Highways
18 13 16
Mileage between Town Centers, Junctions and Interchanges
One inch equals approximately 35 miles
Kilometers 0 10 20 30 40 50
Miles 0 10 20 30 40 50
20
National Interstate Highways
70
U. S. Highways
Abbreviation: ALT.=Alternate; BYP.=Bypass; TEMP.=Temporary.
3 50 100
State Highways
Capitals
Copyright © by Rand McNally & Co.
Lithographed in U.S.A. All rights reserved.
1977 Edition
KNOXVILLE
ASHEVILLE
WINSTON-SALEM
CHARLOTTE
GREENVILLE
MACON

Photographs from "North Carolina Album," pages 465–480

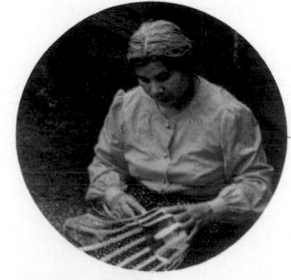

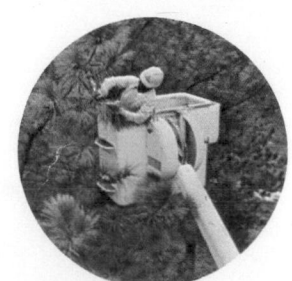

Martinsville · Ridgeway · Danville · Eden · Yanceyville · Reidsville · Prospect Hill · Roxboro · Oxford · Creedmoor · Henderson · Warrenton · Norlina · Littleton · Roanoke Rapids · Weldon · Jackson · Garysburg · Murfreesboro · Conway · Winton · Ahoskie · Rich Square · Scotland Neck · Hertford · Edenton · Windsor · Plymouth · Williamston · Columbia · Creswell · Elizabeth City · Sunbury · South Mills · Barco · Jarvisburg · Point Harbor · Kitty Hawk · Nags Head · Manns Harbor · Manteo

Burlington · Graham · GREENSBORO · DURHAM · Chapel Hill · Cary · RALEIGH · Wilson · Rocky Mount · Tarboro · Nashville · Spring Hope · Wake Forest · Zebulon · Apex · Clayton · Kenly · Farmville · Greenville · Washington · Belhaven · Swanquarter · Engelhard · Waves · Avon · Buxton · Hatteras

Asheboro · Ramseur · Siler City · Pittsboro · Sanford · Fuquay-Varina · Smithfield · Goldsboro · Snow Hill · Kinston · New Bern · Bayboro · Oriental · Aurora · Hobucken · Ocracoke

Troy · Biscoe · Carthage · Pinehurst · Southern Pines · Aberdeen · Lillington · Erwin · Dunn · Benson · Newton Gr · Mt Olive · Faison · Warsaw · Kenansville · Beulaville · Richlands · Maysville · Cherry Point Marine Corps Air Sta · Morehead City · Beaufort · Cape Lookout

Ellerbe · Rockingham · Hamlet · Raeford · Fayetteville · Spring Lake · Clinton · Roseboro · Harrells · Wallace · Burgaw · Holly Ridge · Jacksonville · Swansboro · Camp Lejeune Marine Corps Base

Cheraw · McColl · Bennettsville · Society Hill · Dillon · Latta · Laurinburg · Maxton · St Pauls · Red Springs · Lumberton · Clarkton · White Lake · Elizabethtown · Currie · Whiteville · Bolton · Delco · Wilmington · Wrightsville Beach · Hampstead

Darlington · Florence · Timmonsville · Effingham · Marion · Nichols · Green Sea · Tabor City · Chadbourn · Supply · Shallotte · Southport · Carolina Beach · Cape Fear

Olanta · Lake City · Hemingway · Kingstree · Greeleyville · Andrews · St Stephens · Jamestown · Moncks Corner · Awendaw · Mt Pleasant · CHARLESTON · Conway · Loris · Little River · Myrtle Beach · Murrells Inlet · Georgetown

Albemarle Sound · Pamlico Sound · Pamlico R · Raleigh Bay · Onslow Bay · Cape Fear · Atlantic Ocean · Wright Bros Nat'l Mem · Cape Hatteras Nat'l Seashore · L Mattamuskeet · Alligator L · L Waccamaw · Green Swamp · Whiteoak Swamp · Angola Swamp · Great Swamp

12 Forsyth County
Moravian settlements begin in 1753. (Ch. 6)

11 Buncombe County
Site of Biltmore and Biltmore School of Forestry. (Ch. 18)

10 Macon County
Cherokee Indian victory over British in the French and Indian War, 1760. (Ch. 6)

13 Gaston County
Textile mill strikes and violence, 1929. (Ch. 20)

14 Iredell County
Fort Dobbs built in 1756 to protect settlers from Indians. (Ch. 6)

15 Mecklenburg County
Gold found in 1828. (Ch. 11)

History in North Carolina

This map shows the location of the 100 counties in North Carolina. It also shows the larger cities found throughout the state. While all historic events cannot be shown on a map of this size, major events in the history of North Carolina are located for you. These events are explained in detail in the chapter indicated beside each event.

The map can be useful as you study this book by helping you locate routes traveled by various people. It can also help you understand relationships among different areas of the state.

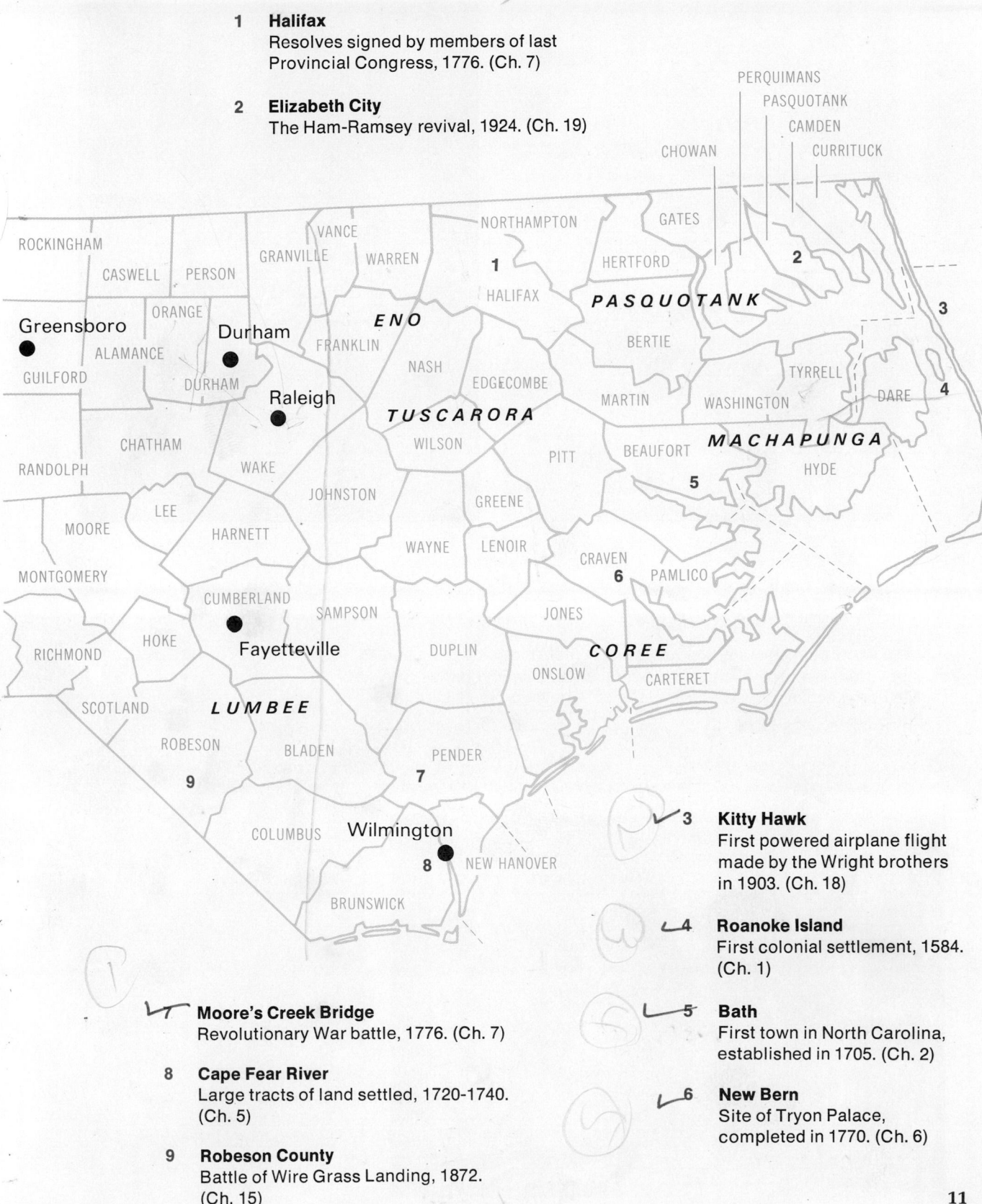

1. **Halifax**
   Resolves signed by members of last Provincial Congress, 1776. (Ch. 7)

2. **Elizabeth City**
   The Ham-Ramsey revival, 1924. (Ch. 19)

3. **Kitty Hawk**
   First powered airplane flight made by the Wright brothers in 1903. (Ch. 18)

4. **Roanoke Island**
   First colonial settlement, 1584. (Ch. 1)

5. **Bath**
   First town in North Carolina, established in 1705. (Ch. 2)

6. **New Bern**
   Site of Tryon Palace, completed in 1770. (Ch. 6)

7. **Moore's Creek Bridge**
   Revolutionary War battle, 1776. (Ch. 7)

8. **Cape Fear River**
   Large tracts of land settled, 1720-1740. (Ch. 5)

9. **Robeson County**
   Battle of Wire Grass Landing, 1872. (Ch. 15)

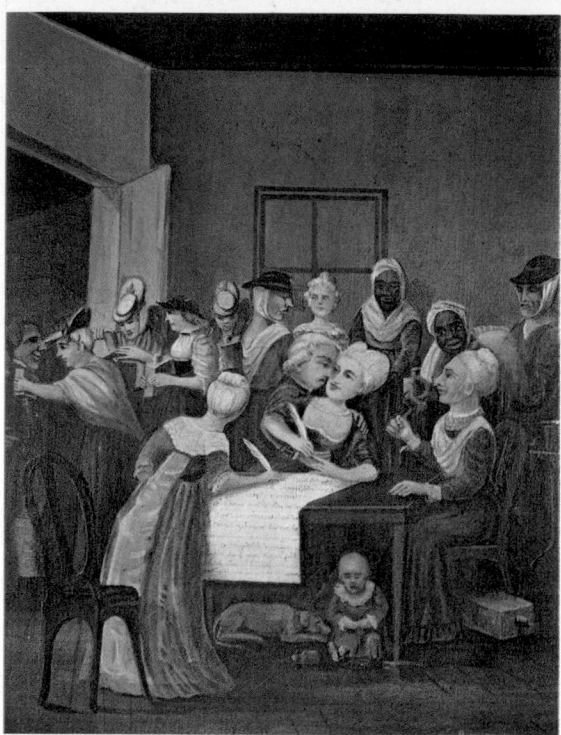

John White painted many scenes of Indian life. This painting (above left) is a copy of one of his watercolors. The Edenton Tea Party (above right) was a gathering of women protesting the British tax on tea in 1774.

Governor William Tryon and his troops face the Regulators in 1771.

Portraits of Dr. and Mrs. James Norcom (left), painted by Joshua Reynolds, express the style of dress in the early 1800s. The first North Carolina statehouse (upper right) burned in 1831. Elm Grove Seminary (lower right) was a private school of the early 1800s.

A sharecropper returns to his cabin after a hard day's work.

The naval attack in the Battle of Fort Hatteras, August 1861 (above).
Elizabeth City during the Civil War (below).

Parker D. Robbins (lower left), Union Army sergeant-major,
statesman, and inventor. Shucking corn after the harvest
(lower right), a post-Civil War scene by famed North Carolina
artist Mary Lyde Hicks Williams.

This scene shows the fall of Fort Fisher on January 15, 1865.
The loss of this fort was a serious blow to the Confederate
forces.

Mary Lyde Hicks Williams
painted many fine portraits
in the early twentieth
century. Here are two
examples of her work.

North Carolina has always been proud of its heritage.
This scene shows a part of Orton Plantation, one of the first
large estates in the Wilmington area.

The Palmer House at Bath
is a fine example of early
American style. Notice
the windows in the broad
chimney.

The Braun House at
Salisbury is one of many
restored historic homes
in North Carolina.

16

MAPS

PART ONE

Exploration and Settlement

1584-1715

The seashore off
Cape Hatteras

1580 Sir Francis Drake completes round-the-world voyage

1584 Explorers sent to America by Sir Walter Raleigh

1585 First colony settled on Roanoke Island

1587 Second colony settled on Roanoke Island

1588 Spanish Armada defeated by England

1590 John White returns from England to find colony gone

1607 Jamestown Colony founded

1620 Mayflower Compact signed
1621 Plymouth Colony founded

1642 Iroquois War begins

1650 Edward Bland's expedition to Hocamawananck

1660 Batts settles in Albemarle

1672 Batts visited by Quaker George Fox

1679 Batts' death
● 4,000 settlers in Albemarle

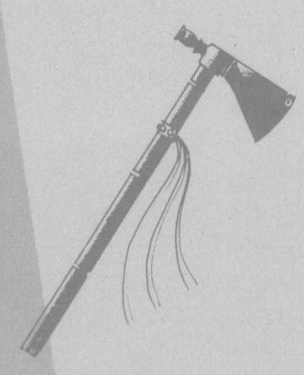

1

THE MYSTERY OF THE LOST COLONY

A Possible Solution

John White spent a sleepless night worrying about the colonists. They had remained on Roanoke Island three years earlier, in 1587, when White left for England. During the night just past he and his shipmates had called loudly to the shore, hoping for an answer. They had sung English songs and called out the names of some of the colonists. But Roanoke had been quiet through the night. White feared for what he might find on going ashore.

Now, in the fresh summer morning, there was some good news after all. As White and his party came across the beach they saw a tree with three letters carved on it: C-R-O. White guessed at once that this meant the colonists had left Roanoke. They had gone to the island of Croatan further south. A post by the gate of the deserted fort showed his guess must be right. On the post was the whole word: CROATOAN. The colonists had promised to leave some such sign in case they de-

John White, *an early settler and governor of the second colony*
Sir Walter Raleigh, *an explorer and founder of colonies*
John Smith, *founder of the Jamestown Colony*
Powhatan, *an Indian king*

Nathaniel Batts, *an explorer and fur trader*
Francis Yeardly, *an early settler at Albemarle*
William Strachey, *a Jamestown settler and writer*

Virginia Dare was the first white child born in English America.

cided to leave. They had not added the cross they had agreed to carve in case they were in danger. So John White could breath easily. His daughter, Eleanor Dare, and his three-year-old granddaughter, Virginia, were no doubt safe at Croatan with the others. Tomorrow, maybe next day, White would be happily rejoined with the friends and relatives he had not seen since he left for England.

One of America's greatest mystery stories thus began. John White never got to Croatan. Neither he nor any other Englishman ever saw the Roanoke colonists again. The one hundred nineteen people had vanished with scarcely a trace. No one to this day has been able to solve the riddle of their disappearance. But is the mystery entirely beyond solution? Some think it isn't.

The story of the Lost Colony goes back to the year 1584 when Sir Walter Raleigh sent two ships from England. He gave instructions for the captains to find a spot on the American coast for a military base. The idea was to use the base to make attacks against the Spanish in Florida and the West Indies. Spain was shipping huge amounts of gold and silver from its Central and South American colonies. The English were anxious to share in the loot. If Raleigh had a place from which his own ships could attack the Spaniards, he could gain great wealth for himself and power for his queen, the red-haired Elizabeth.

In the summer of 1584, the explorers reached Roanoke Island. They went ashore to investigate the place as a possible site for the fort. Captain Arthur Barlowe had already seen a good part of the world. But nothing quite compared with

Roanoke on this bright summer morning. The island, he declared, was

> so full of grapes, as the very beating, and surge of the Sea overflowed them, of which we found such plentie, . . . both on the sands, and on the greene soile on the hils, as also climing towards the tops of the high cedars, that I thinke in all the world the like . . . is not to be founde. . . .

A little farther along the beach, the English sailors were suddenly startled by "such a flocke of Cranes . . . , with such a crye redoubled by many Echoes, as if an armie of men had showted all together." Everything in this New World seemed wonderful beyond description. The cedars were "the highest and reddest in the world;" the "fatte Bucks, Conies, Hares, [and] Fishe the best of the worlde." They had come to look for a military base and stumbled instead upon a paradise.

The natives of paradise confirmed the first impression of the visitors. The English watched in awe from their ships when they first reached Roanoke Island. An Indian fisherman

Conies and **hares** are kinds of rabbits.

Eastern North Carolina, 1580

This and similar maps throughout the book pinpoint specific locations important to each chapter. These locations appear in black. Present-day sites appear in color.

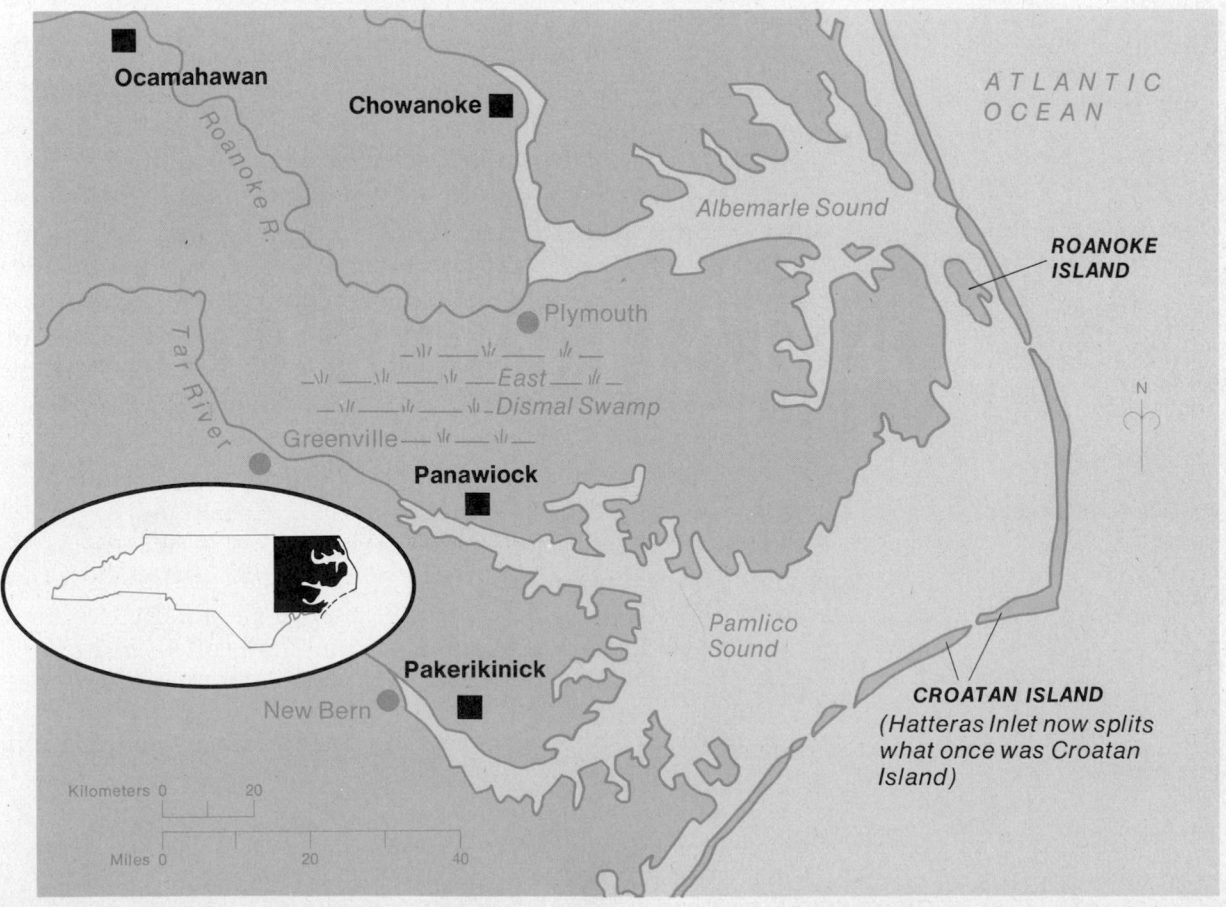

filled his canoe with fish in less than half an hour. He then gave all his catch to the sailors. Here on the island and on the mainland beyond, the natives were "most gentle, loving, and faithfull, . . . and . . . lived after the manner of the golden age." They would trade 20 valuable furs for an ordinary tin dish and 50 for a copper kettle. It was, said one of the Englishmen, "the goodliest soile under the cope of heaven."

A *cope* means a covering.

The explorers hurried back to England with enthusiastic reports for Sir Walter Raleigh. By September 1585, the first Roanoke colony was well established. The settlers, one hundred eight of them, were full of high hopes. Besides the gold and the silver they could steal from the Spaniards, the English hoped to find a water route across the American continent—a Northwest Passage they called it—to the Pacific Ocean. They hoped to find, as the Spanish had, gold and precious metals. The possibilities for wealth and fame seemed endless.

A *colony* is a group of people who leave their own country to form a new society ruled by their old country.

But nearly everything went wrong. The colony's leaders argued with one another. The men found that they had not brought enough supplies with them from England. Some began to grow grumpy and discouraged when they did not quickly find treasure waiting for them. There were some unpleasant dealings between the Indians and whites. There were rumors that one of the Indian leaders was plotting a massacre of the English.

A *massacre* is a mass killing.

In less than a year, the Roanoke colonists were back in England. Sir Francis Drake came by Roanoke on his way back to England after a raid against the Spanish. The colonists were glad to accept his offer of a ride home to England.

Walter Raleigh began almost at once to prepare for another colony. In the spring of 1587, he sent a new group, including women and children, to begin again at Roanoke Island. But soon the colonists began to worry about supplies. They asked their governor, John White, to return to England for tools, food, and other things they needed. At the end of the first summer, White left for England, promising to hurry back with the supplies.

A number of mishaps delayed White's return to Roanoke. The most important was the Spanish Armada. The great Spanish fleet, which sailed for England in 1588, was soundly beaten. However, not until the spring of 1590 could White get started for America. It was July before he finally reached Roanoke again. The colonists, it seemed, had run short of food and had gone to live with the Croatans. They must be either on Croatan Island, not far south of Roanoke, or else at some point about 50 miles up into the mainland. They had talked of going there before he left them.

An *armada* is a fleet of warships.

On the next day after reaching Roanoke Island, White

An engraving of part of a map drawn by John White, governor of the first Roanoke colony, shows Roanoke Island at center.

Sea dogs were pirates or experienced sailors.

A *plantation* is a large farm.

Founding means beginning.

and his men set out in their ship for Croatan. They expected to reach it before night. But the trip south was almost a disaster. The winds churned the water into huge waves. The crew struggled to keep the ship from being driven onto the beach. By the time they were halfway to Croatan, they had lost three of their four anchors. One more such loss and they might never see England again! With the weather, in White's words, growing "fouler and fouler," the attempt was given up. The English headed for the greater safety of deep water. They decided they would have to sail to Puerto Rico for repairs, returning next spring to Croatan.

In fact, they had left the New World forever. On the way to Puerto Rico, White's men realized their ship was badly damaged. It could only be repaired in England. Turning east, they made their way home to Plymouth harbor. They managed to arrive safely a few weeks later.

For the time being, Raleigh and the English had lost interest in building colonies. Dazzled by the feats of Drake and the other so-called "sea dogs," everybody was investing in raids launched directly from England against Spain and its shipping. When White found that no money could be raised to send another voyage to Roanoke, he retired to a plantation in Ireland. The "relief of my discomfortable company," he wrote, must be left "to the merciful help of the Almighty. . . ."

The English did not soon forget about their missing people on Roanoke Island. They later tried again to find them. The earliest clues to the fate of the Lost Colony were those noted by John Smith. He made reports to England, and in a book he later wrote about his travels. In the summer of 1608, a year after the founding of the Jamestown Colony, Smith learned from an Indian that the people he was looking for might be living at an Indian town to the southwest of Jamestown. The place was called Ocamahawan. The people who lived there were said to have tools of copper instead of stone. They were said to wear clothes instead of animal skins and to live in houses like those of the English at Jamestown.

The way to reach Ocamahawan, Smith learned, was either by traveling six days from Roanoke Island or else two days from Chowanoke, an Indian nation (and town) on Chowan River. Allowing perhaps 20 miles a day for inland travel at that time, Ocamahawan must have been about 40 miles north or west of Chowanoke, or on the other side of Chowanoke from Roanoke Island.

About the time that Smith received this earliest clue, he or one of the other Jamestown settlers drew a map that was soon afterward sent to England. It showed the village of Ocamahawan to be about as far to the northwest of Chowanoke as Jamestown was to the north, or maybe as much as 70 miles. Ocamahawan lay on the west bank of the Roanoke River well up from the river's mouth.

But the map showed a good deal more besides. On what seems to be the Neuse River, maybe 75 miles southeast of Ocamahawan, was a village called Pakerikinick. Written beside the name of the town were the words: "Here remayneth 4 men clothed that came from roonock to Ocanahowan." The mystery of the Lost Colony now seemed near solution.

Not everyone Smith talked with agreed that Ocamahawan or Pakerakinick were the best places to look for the missing Englishmen. The same map that showed these places also showed an Indian village called Panawiock, on what is probably the Pamlico River. At this place were written the words: "Here the King of Paspahegh reported our men to be and wants to go." The King of Paspahegh was a chief of the James River area. He was actually sent by Smith in 1608 with two white men to meet the whites at Panawiock. They were

Drawn in 1608, the writing on this Zuniga map is upside down. Writing at **A** says, "Pakerakinick here remayneth 4 men clothed that came from roonock to Ocamahawan." At **B,** "Ocamahowan" and "here the king of paspahegh reported our men to bee and wants to goe Panawiock." The map helps locate Ocamahawan which seems to be on the Roanoke River. Note also "Chawwan" (Chowan River) and "roonock" (Roanoke Island). The James River is near **C.**

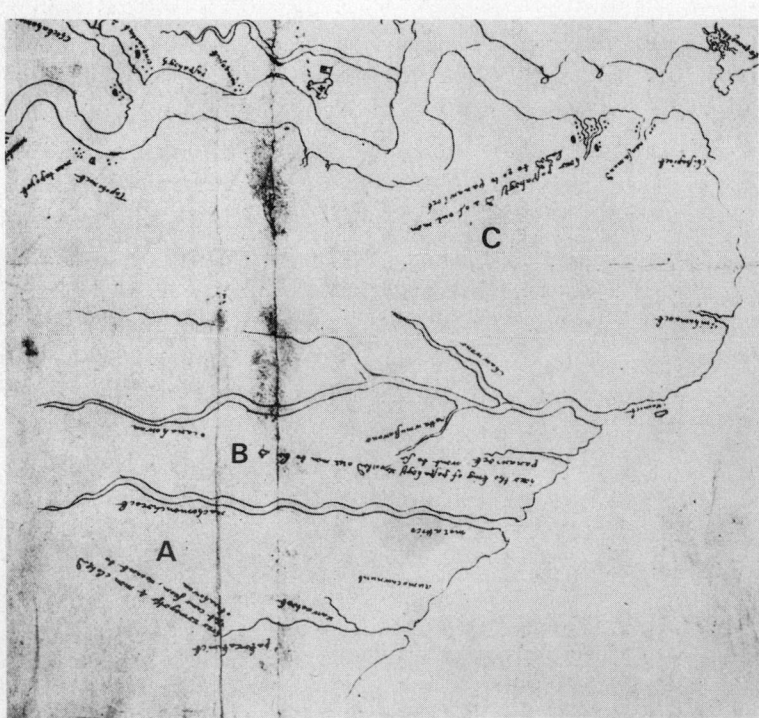

evidently some of the Lost Colonists. But the king did not get far. For some reason, he turned back and refused to make the trip after all. Later, Smith sent two more men on a visit in the same direction. But they came back to report that all the Lost Colonists were said to be dead. In the meantime, another scout had gone to the town of Chowanoke. He returned to tell Smith that he had found "little hope and lesse certantie" of the fate of the colonists.

When John Smith returned to England for good in 1609, he probably felt that all or most of the Roanoke colonists had been killed. An English historian soon afterward wrote that Smith had learned from Powhatan, most powerful of the Indian kings, that he had been present at the slaughter of the colonists. To prove it, Powhatan showed Smith some of their tools. But Smith himself reported that Powhatan had said that there were people at Ocamahawan who wore clothes. These sounded very much like survivors of the massacre.

The **Royal Council** were the advisors to the king.

Other rumors of the fate of some or all of the Lost Colonists continued to reach England. In 1609, King James' Royal Council sent orders to the leaders of the Jamestown Colony. They should make another search for the Roanoke people. Searchers were to go to "Ohonahorn," and from there to "Peccareccamicke." There they would find "four of the English . . . , lost by Sir Walter Raweley, which escaped the slaughter of Roanocke. . . ." But there is no evidence that such a search was actually made.

"Ohonahorn" and **"Peccareccarimicke"** seem to be the same as Ocamahawan and Pakerikinick.

Finally, there was one other report by a Jamestown resident. It contained clues about the missing colony. This was a book by William Strachey, who had lived at Jamestown from 1609 to 1612. From an Indian named Machumps, Strachey learned of the town of "Ochanahoen," where the people lived in two-story stone houses and raised tame turkeys. The Indians there had learned to build such houses, according to Machumps, from "those English who escaped the slaughter at Roanook."

"Ochanahoen" probably was the same as Ocamahawan.

Machumps also told Strachey of a place called Ritanoe. There a chief "preserved 7 of the English alive, fower men, twoo Boyes, and one young Maid, who escaped and fled up the River Chawanoke, to beat his copper, of which he hath certayn Mynes. . . ." Ritanoe had been mentioned by the first explorers sent by Raleigh to America in 1584. It was described by them as being southwest of Roanoke Island. They had said it had "a rich mine of Copper or gold" and that it was close to "certaine mountains lying West of Roanooc. . . ."

Strachey's book also suggests a reason why Powhatan was supposed to have killed the Roanoke colonists. As Stra-

A Secotan Indian village, visited by John White in the 1580s, stood in present Beaufort County, near the town of Bath.

chey understood it, some priests had come to Powhatan and warned him of danger. They predicted that a nation from the Chesapeake Bay area would rise and destroy Powhatan's empire. Hearing this, Powhatan, according to Strachey, made war on all who might attack him. It may have been in this war that he had some or all of the Roanoke colonists slaughtered. Up to that point, Strachey declared, the Roanoke colonists had lived peacefully among the Indians of the region for 20 or more years.

The problem with this is that the slaughter of the colonists seems to have taken place much later than other accounts suggested. If Strachey were correct, then the massacre must have happened just before, maybe even a little after, the arrival of the Jamestown colonists. Some historians have concluded that members of the Lost Colony, still living at Ocamahawan or some other town, may have heard in 1607 of the

This is the type of dwelling that served as a home for the first settlers at Jamestown in 1607.

A *sturgeon* is a large fish.

The *high-water mark* is a line showing highest tides or flood levels.

A stream, known at least since 1725 as Stonehouse Creek, rises in eastern Warren County and flows into the Roanoke River.

arrival of other Englishmen at Jamestown. They must have set out, so the theory goes, for Jamestown. They were met along the way and killed by Powhatan or his allies. If this were the case, maybe some survived the slaughter. Perhaps a few of the Lost Colonists never left Ocamahawan or whatever place they lived in.

To sum up, it seems clear that the Jamestown settlers thought that all or most of the Roanoke colonists had been killed. Some considered Powhatan the killer. Whether they thought the deed to have been done nearer to 1587 or 1607 is not certain. They also believed that some survivors might still be alive in 1609 or later at one or more of at least four different places in what is now North Carolina: Ocamahawan, Pakerikinick, Panawiock, and Ritanoe. Of these, only Panawiock seems to have been visited by the English. They were probably not sure of the location of the other three.

For later generations, the most helpful clue would be the stone houses thought to have been built at Ocamahawan. If the site could be located, and if sixteenth century English stone foundations or ruins could be uncovered there, the mystery of the Lost Colony would be at least partly solved. But where exactly was the mysterious town of Ocamahawan? The answer was not very long in coming.

In 1650, a party of Virginians was sent into the Roanoke River area. They were to open a trade with the Tuscaroras, a major Indian tribe. The traders were led by Edward Bland. Their trip took them to the falls of Roanoke, a part of the river that had probably not been visited before by Virginians. Bland later described the place he visited. It was the point on the river where the Indians killed sturgeon at the foot of the falls. The river here, he said, had high banks and a high-water mark of 45 feet. It is nearly certain that the place Bland described lies in or near the modern town of Weldon, North Carolina. The Tuscarora town here, according to Bland, was called "Hocomawananck."

The name and location of the Tuscarora town were nearly identical to the place shown on the Virginia map of 1608 as Ocamahawan. There seems little doubt it was the same town. Probably without realizing it, Bland had opened the way to a possible solution to the fate of some of the Roanoke colonists. He mentioned no stone houses there. But neither was he looking for any. The possibility remains that a search for stone foundations or ruins might prove that some of the Lost Colonists lived for a time at Ocamahawan. More than three and a half centuries later, however, no one seems to have followed up on Bland's important clue. This may be due to the doubts of scholars as to the exact location of the site of Ocamahawan.

The Permanent Settlement

The "south part of Virginia"—what is now North Carolina—was not permanently settled by the English until the middle of the seventeenth century. The Jamestown colony was plagued by troubles with the Indians, by disease, and other hardships. But it slowly and steadily took root and began to expand. Maps of the little-known country to the south gradually improved. The Virginia colonists sent expeditions in search of the Lost Colony or to explore the wilderness region.

Expeditions are search groups.

The growing settlement along the James pushed back the frontier beyond which trapping and hunting were best. It forced more and more settlers to strike out toward the Carolina sounds and the headwaters of the rivers. Several schemes for settling colonies in the region around Albemarle Sound came to nothing. But traders and explorers published reports describing the rich timberlands and farming country of the southern wilderness. The price of land was very low to people willing to go and settle there.

As it had in the 1580s, coastal North Carolina began to lure Europeans. Again as in the 1580s, writers painted beautiful but exaggerated word pictures of the southern wilderness. They made it sound easy to live there and to grow rich. They persuaded the poor and the unfortunate that here was the answer to their problems. It was the road to comfort and happiness. The reality, as many would find, was far different. As in the 1580s, many were being lured to their ruin.

A *sloop* is a small sailing ship.

Consider, for example, Nathaniel Batts. Mr. Batts was a young man who had been involved for several years in the fur trade of the Chesapeake Bay. He owned a small sloop and traded from the James River up into Maryland. He traded in the West Indies where his brother Richard lived and was a merchant. In the fall of 1653, Nathaniel Batts happened to miss getting aboard his sloop as it started on a voyage southward in search of furs. Hoping to find the sloop at Roanoke Island, he applied to Francis Yeardly, a well-to-do Virginian. He wanted a boat and supplies so he could search for his ship.

Francis Yeardly had evidently been waiting for a chance to invest in some land on the Albemarle frontier. Here was that chance. He not only furnished Batts with a boat and supplies but asked him to try to deal with the Indians of Albemarle for a tract of land there.

Whether Batts found his sloop is not known, but he turned his trip south into a fine adventure. He entered the sound region at Currituck Inlet, in company with three other Virginians. He explored the shores of Currituck and Albemarle Sounds, visiting some places that no white man had ever seen before. At Roanoke Island an Indian showed him the remains of the old fort built by the first Roanoke Colony 68 years before. He and his companions also made arrangements to buy a large tract of land on Pasquotank River from the Indians. They were to trade with the Indians in furs. He came back to Virginia with much new information for Yeardly about the Albemarle country. The two men seemed to have become, for a while, business partners.

As part of the deal to buy land from the Indians, it had been agreed that Yeardly would build an English house for the chief. He would provide it with English furnishings. Soon after Batts returned, Yeardly sent south a carpenter and five workmen. They stayed for five months. They not only built a house for the Indian chief but another for Batts as well. It stood on the western shore of Albemarle Sound between the mouths of Salmon Creek and Roanoke River. The house of North Carolina's first permanent white settler was a one-story frame building with two rooms and a chimney. It was a tiny place measuring 20 feet square. A more historic house was never built in North Carolina.

Nathaniel Batts probably did not spend long periods at his new house. He used it mostly during the trapping season when the Indians had plenty of furs to trade. In 1656, he married a Virginia widow and lived, when not away in Albemarle, at a plantation left to her by her first husband. Some-

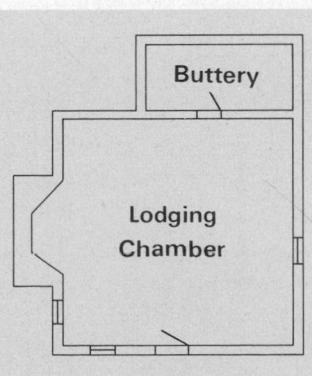

Buttery

Lodging Chamber

Nathaniel Batts' house was built in 1655 in present Bertie County. Batts is believed to be the first permanent settler in what is now North Carolina.

where around 1660 he seems to have moved to North Carolina for good, probably leaving his family behind in Virginia. In that same year, Batts bought a piece of land on Albemarle Sound from the chief of the Yeopim Indians.

There was much to learn about the business of trapping animals and dressing furs. Batts probably got a good deal of help and advice from the Indians. He found that the powerful tribes of old had mostly melted away. They had been hard hit by wars and the diseases introduced by the white people. The great Chowanoke nation was now reduced to a few miserable villages. Around the rim of the sounds lived the feeble remains of the Paspatank and Machapunga, the Neuse, the Yeopim and the Pampticough, all of them small and declining. Further up in the interior country lived the last of the Meherrins and Nottoways. Only the Tuscaroras, to the west of the Chowan and Roanoke Rivers, were still powerful enough to think of challenging the whites. In time, Batts became familiar

Dressing furs means preparing them for sale.

Pampticough was the old spelling for Pamlico.

This John White map shows the coastal area, Albemarle Sound, Roanoke Island, and the Roanoke and Chowan rivers.

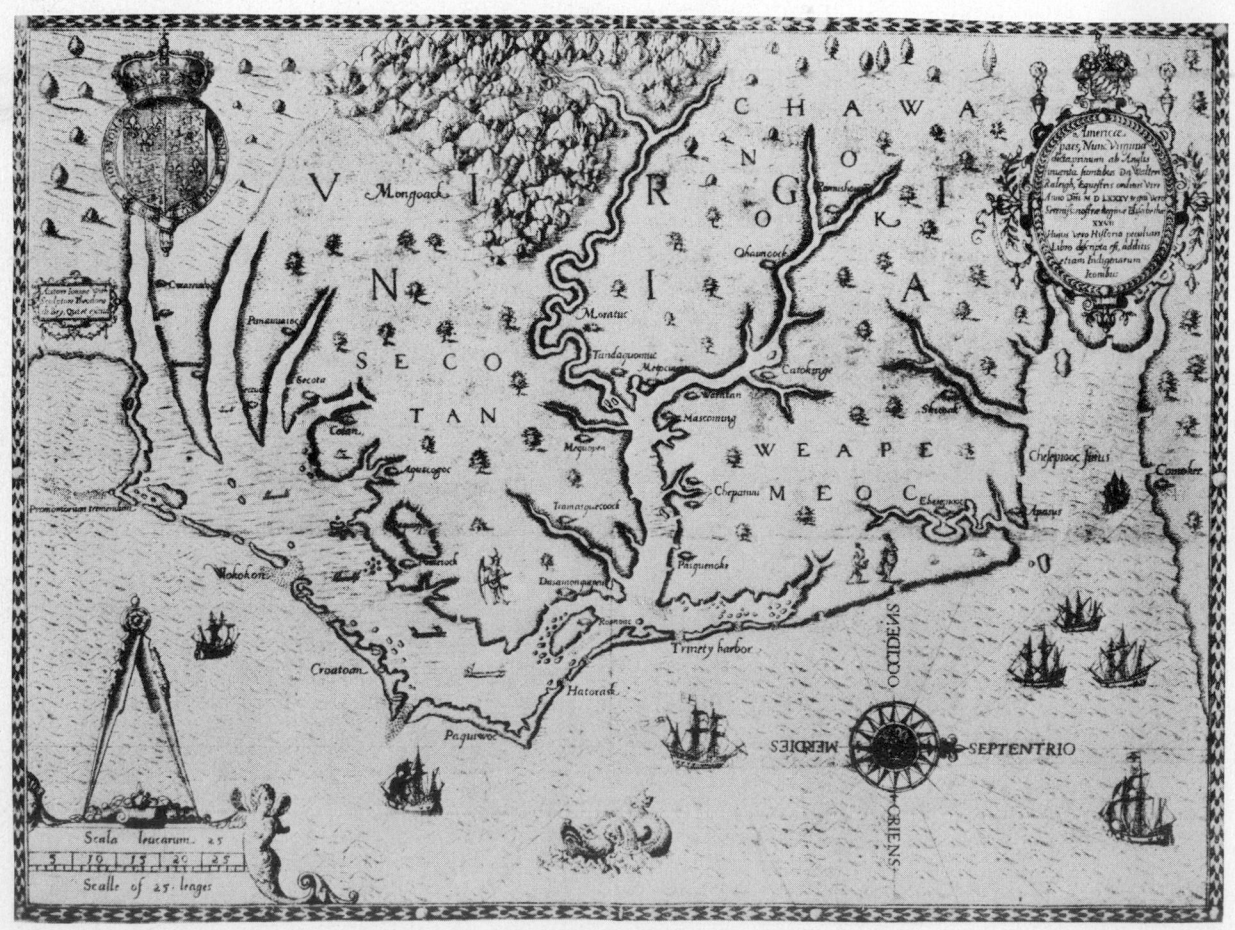

with the ways of all these tribes. He was, for several years, probably the only white settler there.

The fur trade must have been, at first anyway, all that Batts had hoped it would be. The forest yielded plenty of beavers, foxes, rabbits, minks, otters, and other common animals. But there were also buffalo, elk, panthers, and many other beasts that long ago disappeared from the forests of North Carolina.

Early settlers took up tracts of hundreds or thousands of acres each, so they lived well apart from each other.

In a country without roads, bridges, or ferries, Nathaniel Batts traveled almost everywhere by boat. The existence of his name at such widely scattered points as Batts Island (or Batts Grave) in Albemarle Sound, Batts Point on Pamlico River, and Batts Creek on the Neuse may show something of the nature of his travels. For a time he played a prominent part in promoting the settlement of the Albemarle area. A community of settlers grew up in the vicinity of his house. But somehow Batts was never able to fulfill his dreams of wealth and happiness.

The truth seems to be that the first white North Carolinian was something of a rascal. He got himself into debt often and sometimes used ugly tricks and illegal means to get himself out. He had to go to court in Virginia for refusing to hand over to his wife some property left to her by her first husband. Batts even charged her for boarding the children of her former marriage. Long after he was dead, North Carolina courts were still trying to straighten out problems caused by the illegal use of lands that did not belong to him.

A Quaker missionary named George Fox visited Batts in 1672. He found Batts to be "a rude, desperate man," though perhaps trying to reform. Batts put on airs for the visitor, calling himself the "former governor of Roan-oak." He used the title "Captain Batts." Well before his death in 1679, Batts had become a man of little property and less reputation. North Carolina's first settler must have found the country harsh and cruel. Many others were to share his sad experience.

The Continuing Quest

Quest means search.

Nathaniel Batts lived to see some four thousand people come to live on or near Albemarle Sound. Before his death, North Carolina had become an English colony with courts, churches, government, and other institutions. But it had not

Institutions are organized groups devoted to certain purposes.

This statue of Sir Walter Raleigh was erected in 1976 in Heritage Square in the city of Raleigh.

A *rude society* means one that is not well developed in rules and social manners.

A *utopia* is a paradise.

A *symbol* is something that stands for or represents something else.

yet become a community in which people could work together effectively for the common good. The white population grew very slowly. This gave time to the earliest settlers to develop a style of life which, like that of Nathaniel Batts, was individualistic and self-seeking. The settlers learned to seek their own frontier-style justice or do without. They learned to provide everything for themselves because little or no help could be found. Having learned to get along on their own and not look for outside help, they resented the arrival of sheriffs, judges, and tax collectors. Their lives might be hard and short, but they wanted no interference between themselves and the rugged land they had learned to cope with.

In some ways this was a good and wholesome style of life. It demanded much of the settlers but gave them a sense of pride in their own achievements. They had a spirit of freedom they could not have known elsewhere. But there were disadvantages as well. The case of Nathaniel Batts was probably much nearer the rule than the exception. The life of the frontier was brutal and lawless. It could not afford to pity the weak or help the unfortunate. By disease and storm, flood and famine, war and crime, it wore down the settlers until many were miserable and defeated.

Before North Carolina could become a civilized community, its people would have to learn the habit of cooperation. They would need to develop a sense of social discipline and many kinds of teamwork. They would have to overcome, somehow, their earliest and oldest tradition as a frontier colony, that of "every man for himself." But this would prove to be a very difficult tradition to outgrow.

In some ways the history of the people of North Carolina—red, black, and white—has been a struggle of more than three hundred years to find proper limits for the expression of their individual hopes and beliefs. One of the most challenging problems has been that of creating a society in which freedom can be preserved without preventing the cooperation and teamwork needed for common progress. Later chapters will follow the growth of the people of North Carolina from the rude society of Nathaniel Batts' day to the present. But the reader will find that North Carolinians are still—in some ways—shaped and affected by the attitudes and forces of Batts' generation.

The little group of colonists who set out in 1587 to find utopia on Roanoke Island, then, may well serve as a symbol for the continuing quest. Present-day North Carolinians still pursue the paradise of Sir Walter Raleigh and John Smith, of John White and Nathaniel Batts. They feel they are nearer to it than in 1587. But they know they haven't arrived there yet.

Chapter Checkup

PEOPLE

John White John Smith Francis Yeardly
Walter Raleigh Nathaniel Batts

PLACES

Roanoke Island Ocamahawan Pakerikinick Puerto Rico
Croatan Island Chowanoke Panawiock

FACT

What was the reason for the founding of the colonies on Roanoke Island?
How was it that Nathaniel Batts came to live in America?

INTERPRETATION

What do you think happened to the second Roanoke Island colony after
  John White left for England in 1587?
Why were the earliest settlers of Albemarle so independent-minded? How
  might such an attitude have helped and hindered the development of
  the colony there?
Why do you suppose the Indians were not afraid of the whites when they
  first met on Roanoke Island?
Why might Powhatan have wanted to kill survivors of the Roanoke colony
  around 1607?

VOCABULARY

Colony Individualistic

ACTIVITY

Using a modern highway map of eastern North Carolina, try to locate the
  sites of places mentioned on the White and Zuniga maps. Which ones
  have probably been heavily built over by modern towns?

SUGGESTED READING

Corbitt, D. L. *Explorations, Descriptions, and Attempted Settlements of
  Carolina, 1584–1590.* Raleigh: State Department of Archives and His-
  tory, 1953. Excerpts from accounts by Elizabethan voyagers.
Fletcher, Inglis. *Roanoke Hundred.* Indianapolis: Bobbs-Merrill, 1948. A
  novel about Roanoke colonies.
Robinson, Melvin. *The Riddle of the Lost Colony.* New Bern: Owen G.
  Dunn Co., 1946. Brief account of the mystery and possible solutions.

1663 Grant of Carolina
to Lords Proprietors

1665 New charter for Carolina
colony

1660 The Restoration begins
in England

1670 Peter Carteret becomes
governor; Albemarle divided
into four precincts

1670 Founding of Charleston
(Charles Town)

1675 King Philip's War begins

1676 Plantation Duty Act

1677 Culpeper's Rebellion
begins

1679 Sothel named governor;
Sothel captured by pirates

1689 Resignation of Sothel

1689 King William's War begins

2

CULPEPER'S REBELLION

The Rebellion Opens

Aristocrats are people of high
rank in society.

Proprietors means owners.

On the surface of things the fall of 1677 was one of the finest
seasons so far experienced by the settlers of Albemarle. The
acting governor, Thomas Miller, had come from England in
July. With him he brought a generous new set of regulations
from the Lords Proprietors, the eight English aristocrats who
owned the colony. The proprietors had agreed to lighten some
of the stricter laws and to try harder to promote the welfare of
the people of Albemarle. The inhabitants were assured that
Virginia would not be allowed to take control of Albemarle as
had often been threatened.

There were other promising signs too. The Chowanoke
Indians, following their uprising in 1675, had settled down, resigning themselves to life on the pitiful little reservation
granted to them by the whites. The latest hurricane season
had not damaged the crops as it had several times in the past.
The weather had been favorable to the production of good to-

Thomas Miller, *acting governor*
Thomas Eastchurch, *governor of the colony*
Zachariah Gillam, *a ship captain*
George Durant, *a leading citizen of Albemarle*

John Culpeper, *a rebel leader*
Peter Carteret, *a plantation builder and governor*
Seth Sothel, *a governor of Albemarle*

bacco and fat hogs. If the colony's leaders could settle their differences, Albemarle might soon begin to prosper.

The new governor, Thomas Eastchurch, had not yet arrived from England. He had left London in company with Thomas Miller but, stopping off in the West Indies, he had fallen madly in love with a rich widow. Appointing Miller acting governor, Eastchurch sent him on to manage things until he arrived. He then married the widow and the two of them were enjoying a long Caribbean honeymoon. Love and peace seemed at last to be the main influences in the affairs of the Albemarle colony.

On the first day of December 1677, the schooner *Carolina* arrived in Albemarle Sound and dropped anchor in the mouth of Pasquotank River. In spite of the scars and barnacles left on the hull by the seven weeks voyage from England, the *Carolina* was a fine-looking ship. Her captain, Zachariah Gillam—or "Old Zach," as some called him—looked forward eagerly to a few weeks ashore and a handsome profit from his share of the *Carolina's* cargo.

Like the outward appearance of harmony and well-being of the colony, the graceful hull of the *Carolina* concealed the sources of death and destruction. Stored in the dark spaces below the decks was an arsenal of flintlock guns, lead balls, powder, wicked cutlasses, and rum. In the wrong hands the cargo of the *Carolina* could bring a fiery and tragic end to the pleasant autumn in Albemarle.

Captain Gillam ordered out his longboat. He was rowed ashore to present his ship's papers to the Collector of Customs, who happened to be Mr. Miller, the acting governor. Miller greeted the captain and began to examine his papers with the fussy caution of someone who is looking for trouble. He asked the captain if he had carried any tobacco out of Albemarle last year when he left for England. Gillam replied

Cutlasses are short, heavy swords.

38

that he had. Had the captain paid the tobacco tax? Yes, said Captain Gillam, as soon as he reached England. But what about here in Albemarle before he left, as the law required? No, Gillam answered, for it would be unfair to have to pay the same tax in two places.

Zachariah Gillam and his longboat crew spent the night in Mr. Miller's uncomfortable jail. The acting governor, Gillam found, was a hard man who meant to put up with no more nonsense from these seafaring people. Thomas Miller knew very well that the New England shipmasters had been getting away for years with what amounted to robbery from the Albemarle government and the Lords Proprietors. They had slipped away in their little sloops and schooners time and time again with cargoes of tobacco on which they had paid no tax. What was worse, they were often aided in doing so by the tobacco planters of Albemarle. Many of them had no better liking for the tax than did the mariners. Zachariah Gillam must serve as an example to these northern tobacco pirates and a warning that the rule of law—Thomas Miller's law—had come to Albemarle.

During the first hours of Gillam's confinement, Thomas Miller took a closer look at the papers of the *Carolina*. He noted that it was carrying a passenger named George Durant. This was a name that Miller knew well. Durant was a leader in Albemarle and a man with a reputation for dissent from the government. In fact, he had gone to London in order to protest the appointment of Eastchurch as governor. Durant had been

Seafaring people are those who make their living on ships.

Mariners means sailors.

Dissent means protest.

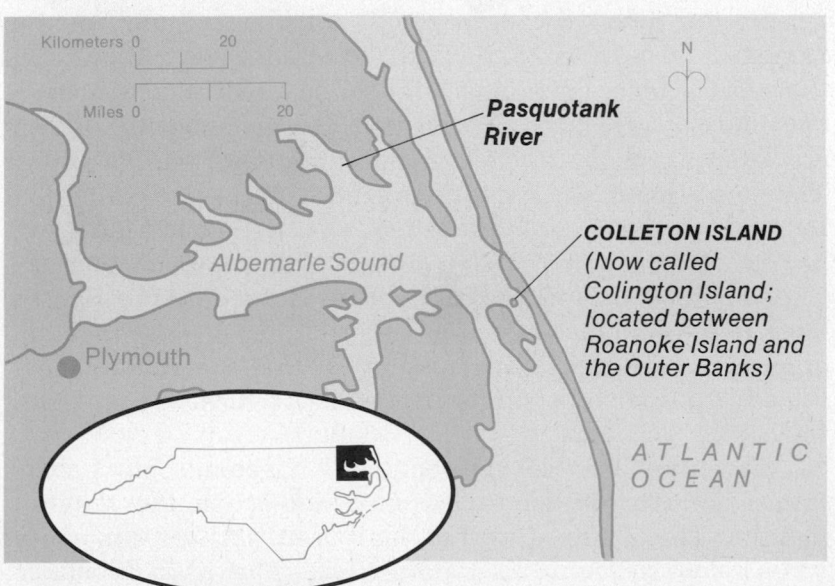

Albemarle Sound Area, 1675

This drawing shows William Miller boarding the *Carolina* to arrest George Durant, a leader in Culpeper's Rebellion.

there still when Miller and Eastchurch left for Albemarle. The combination of a cargo of weapons and a passenger such as Durant could easily lead to an explosion in the colony.

Armed with a pair of pistols, Miller rowed himself out to the *Carolina,* reaching it a little before midnight. He climbed onto the moonlit deck and pushed the cocked pistols into the chest of the surprised George Durant, informing him that he was under arrest. At that moment, some of the crewmen of the *Carolina* overpowered Miller. He was allowed, after a few hours, to return to shore, but word of the incident spread rapidly in the early morning hours.

By the time dawn broke over Albemarle Sound on December 2, "Culpeper's Rebellion" was under way. About 30 of the rebel leaders, including John Culpeper (whose name was somehow attached to the uprising), George Durant, and others, drew up a list of their main complaints against Miller. They were bitter about the treatment of Zachariah Gillam but there were other complaints as well. They charged Miller with having hurt the planters with a heavy and unjust tobacco tax. They claimed that he had denied to the people the right to have free elections, as well as other "Injuries, mischiefs and grievances hee hath brought upon us, that thereby an inevitable ruien is comeing (unless prevented) which wee are about to do. . . ."

The final lines of the complaint covered a great many things done by Miller to irritate colonists in the previous months. The acting governor had been accused, in earlier years before receiving his appointment, of being an unbeliever

A ***rebellion*** is armed resistance against the government.

in God, a traitor to the king, a heavy drinker, and other things. Since returning as acting governor he had, indeed, conducted an election that in some ways violated the constitution of the colony. He had led a campaign to persecute those who objected to his policies. There was also a serious question as to whether Eastchurch had the power to appoint Miller or anyone else as acting governor. In other words, there was some doubt over whether anything Miller ordered was legal.

The rebels, perhaps a hundred in number, hurried to arm themselves with weapons from the *Carolina*. Armed groups were sent in several directions to arrest Miller and other members of the Proprietary party. One by one, Miller and his supporters were rounded up and taken by the rebels to makeshift jails. Within a few days the rebel leaders were in control of the government of Albemarle. It remained to be seen whether they could hold onto it.

The Albemarle rebels were now in power but they were branded as enemies of the king and the Lords Proprietors. Unless they could find the right words and arguments to justify what they had done, they could expect that the strength of Great Britain would sooner or later be turned against them. It was agreed among the rebels that Miller ought to have a public trial so that the misdeeds charged against him could be proved. Such a trial, they hoped, would win for them the sympathy of the powerful men in England and insure that Miller would not hold office again.

The trial opened in mid-December at the house of George Durant. It was a comedy of fumbling inexperience—like a scene from *Alice in Wonderland*. After the rebels gathered at Durant's, someone pointed out that the trial would only be proper if led by members of the Governor's Council, that is, Miller and his fellow prisoners. The rebels handled this problem by holding an election on the spot and selecting a new council from among themselves. From the new officials a grand jury was chosen to go through the motions of deciding whether the evidence against Miller was enough to require a jury trial. If it wasn't, he would have to be set free.

The rebel sheriff and others, merrily drunk on the rum that Captain Gillam had given out along with the weapons, congratulated each other that Miller would hang before the sun went down. As the grand jury left the courtroom to consider its decision, John Culpeper whispered to the jury foreman that the decision must be "billa vera." This was a kind of pig Latin—a sign of Culpeper's ignorance of legal language—by which he meant "true bill," or a finding that Miller must be tried. When the grand jury returned after a few minutes, the

A **rebel** is a person involved in a rebellion.

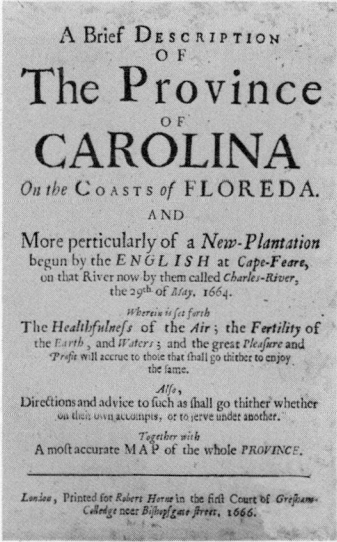

A pamphlet was designed to attract settlers to the new English colony, begun in May 1664 on the Cape Fear River.

Grand juries are groups that decide when there is reason to hold a trial.

foreman announced the words "bill of error," meaning that Miller must go free!

The court room became a scene of panic. Culpeper's Rebellion seemed to be on the verge of collapsing over the difference between "billa vera" and "bill of error." The grand jury became greatly confused amid the shouts and curses of the other rebels. It held a quick conference and changed the decision to true bill. But the trial had hardly begun when a messenger arrived with news that Governor Eastchurch had just landed in Virginia. He issued an order that the rebels lay down their arms and release the prisoners.

The trial of Thomas Miller broke up in alarm and disorder. Obviously the rebels had to find a way to prevent Eastchurch from returning to Albemarle. That would surely mean the end of the rebellion and grave danger to its leaders. A force of armed men was sent to the border points where Eastchurch might cross from Virginia into Albemarle. Eastchurch began recruiting a force of Virginians to help him smash the rebellion. He had not gotten far with this effort when he suddenly fell ill and died. For the moment the rebels were secure.

The Seeds of Revolt

A *civil war* is one between two sides belonging to the same country.

At the beginning of 1663, Albemarle, with its few dozen white familes and their black and Indian slaves, was not yet a colony at all. It was merely "the southern part of Virginia," a distant frontier that few wished to visit and fewer still to live there. In England, a long civil war, ending in 1660, had slowed immigration into Virginia to a trickle. With the return of peace, however, King Charles II needed ways of rewarding those who had helped him come to power. Grants of land in America was one of the least expensive ways to do this.

Early in 1663, some of the leaders who had aided Charles to become king proposed that he grant them a tract of American land on which to establish a colony. In March of that year, Charles agreed to a charter giving eight of his supporters a large region to develop for their own profit and England's power. It stretched all the way from the Atlantic to the Pacific and from Albemarle Sound south to what is now Charleston, South Carolina. Two years later he received complaints from the Lords Proprietors that the grant was still too small. The King generously extended the borders north to the present

Charles II was England's king from 1660 to 1685. The colony got its name from the Latin form of his name, *Carolus*.

The House of Burgesses was a body of elected representatives.

A *legislature* is a group of representatives who make the laws.

Virginia line and south midway down the Florida peninsula. The grant was probably the largest privately-owned territory in history.

The new charter of 1665 had some restrictions on the use of the grant by the Proprietors. They must allow the English inhabitants to have a role in making the laws. The laws must be similar to those that governed England. Also, the Proprietors must pay the king a small rent each year as well as a fourth of any gold and silver that might be discovered. Otherwise, the Proprietors could run things pretty much as they chose. They could enjoy whatever benefits they could get from the colony.

The Proprietors began by marking off their grant into three coastal counties, the northernmost being Albemarle. At first, the governor was to be in charge of everything. He would decide who would serve on the governor's council that helped and advised him. He could choose the judges and all the members of the legislature, called the House of Burgesses. For seven years the governors exercised one-man rule over the infant colony.

In 1670, with Peter Carteret as governor, the people of Albemarle finally gained a voice in the governing of the colony. Albemarle County in that year was divided into four precincts—Chowan, Currituck, Pasquotank, and Perquimans. The citizens of each precinct had the right to elect five representatives to the House of Burgesses. It was still up to the governor to decide when, where, and how often the House of Burgesses would hold its meetings. But, since it was the legislature that paid the governor's salary, he could be counted on to call it regularly into session.

This right of the legislature to decide how much to pay the governor and how the money was to be raised gave the people's representatives a good share of the power of the government. It also caused frequent squabbles in the legislature between the governor and his council (who were all members of the House of Burgesses) and the people's elected delegates. The same thing was true in all the colonies. It would create a tradition of tension between the representatives of the king (or Proprietors) and the people that would one day lead to revolution.

The Lords Proprietors recognized soon after 1670 that their Ashley River (South Carolina) settlement was much more favorable to the growth of a colony than was Albemarle. Large merchant vessels could trade directly from England with the Ashley River settlers. But only the smaller ships could safely cross the shallow inlets of Albemarle's Outer

Banks. For this reason, Albemarle colonists received less for what they sold and paid more for what they bought from abroad than any of their neighbors. Except through Virginia, the people of Albemarle had almost no contact with the outside world. The Virginians, resentful that Albemarle had been made part of a separate colony, charged heavily for handling the produce of the Albemarle settlers.

After 1670, the Proprietors gave their attention to their Ashley River settlement and gave little notice to Albemarle. This was keenly resented by many in Albemarle, who began to feel that the Proprietors were willing to let them rot. The Proprietors heard many complaints from Albemarle, but they pretended that the fault was in the laziness of the settlers. The colonists, unable to persuade the Proprietors, took out their anger on the governor and those he appointed to office. By 1676, Albemarle was wallowing in misery and was at the point of violent outbreaks. Many who might have settled there took note of the situation and wisely decided to stay away.

Many people shared the disappointments of Peter Carteret in trying to make a good life for themselves in Albemarle County. Early in 1663, four of the Proprietors decided to try to

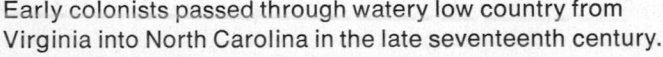

Early colonists passed through watery low country from Virginia into North Carolina in the late seventeenth century.

develop a large plantation in the Albemarle region. The idea was to spend a small amount of money at the beginning and use the quick early profits to build up a major business in grapes and winemaking. Pork and beef, which could be produced cheaply and quickly in Albemarle, would be sold in the West Indies. West Indian slaves would be brought in and used to build up the necessary vineyards and wine industry. Within a few years, the Albemarle plantation ought to become a bonanza for its owners.

In the summer of 1663, an agent was sent to Albemarle by the Proprietors. He was directed to look for a good place for the plantation. He chose Colleton Island in Roanoke Sound. He stocked it with cattle, had some land cleared for farming, and built a small dwelling house and a hog shelter there. Leaving an overseer to look after the place, the agent returned to England singing the praises of the plantation he had started.

To manage the plantation and its business, the owners chose Peter Carteret, an able and energetic young man. He was a cousin of one of the Proprietors. He was provided with several servants and appointed assistant governor of Albemarle. When he arrived at Colleton Island in late February 1665, Carteret found the farm already run down. A few hogs were running wild and there was no sign of the horses and cattle for which the agent had demanded payment from the Proprietors. With the permission of the Proprietors, Carteret moved what was left of the hogs over to Powell's Point on the mainland and started fresh. Here he cleared some more land and planted corn. But he was able to harvest little of the first crop because he and his servants all came down with the fevers that attacked every new immigrant from Europe.

The experience of Peter Carteret during the next five years was painfully summed up by him in a journal for the benefit of his sponsors. No doubt many others could have written much the same way he did:

A ***bonanza*** is a great gain or profit.

1666

Wee cleared fenced & planted what ground we could wee built a hog howse 80 foot Long & 20 broad . . . and got the hoggs there . . . but by the Last of October I had los neere a third of them. . . .

1667

Wee planted what corn and tob[acco] wee could . . . August ye 27th heere happened a great . . . harricane that destroyed both corne & tob[acco] blew downe the roof of the great hogg howse . . . carried away the frame & Boards of two howses. . . .

1668

Wee cleered more ground and repaired . . . fences planted both corne & tobacoe but such a great Drough[t] happened for about 3 month it burnt up all the tob[acco] & stented the corne. . . . Ye 30th July the raignes begane & continued untill the Later End of August soe that the great abundance of raignes did as much hurt as the drough[t]. . . .

1669

Wee repaired our fences planted corne & tob[acco] . . . ye 18th [August] a violent haricane . . . destroyed what tob[acco] was out broke & spoiled most of our corne. . . .

1670

Wee planted both corne & tob[acco]. . . . the 6th of August wee had a violent haricane that lasted 24 howers broke down timber trees blew down howses destroyed both corne & tob[acco] soe that it was Lick to be a famine amongst us. . . . it blew downe to the ground the hogg howse & a howse on the south side of the Inlette . . . & carried away a small howse On the North Pt of the Inlette where was 4 tunes of Corke ready trimed to putt in. . . .

So ended the Powell's Point plantation. Carteret, having served from 1670 to 1672 as governor of Albemarle, returned to England fully discouraged by the hard country and the growing political unrest haunting the colony. He made a final plea to the Proprietors for relief for Albemarle from high rents, its lack of sound defenses against the Indians, and the high fees placed on Albemarle goods passing through Virginia ports. But the minds of the Proprietors were elsewhere and no relief came.

The colonists who found it hardest to bear the misrule of the Proprietors were those who had lived in Albemarle since before the colony was formed in 1663. To them, Proprietary rule did not seem to offer advantages over earlier times when Albemarle had no government of its own. Some of these early settlers had come to Albemarle for the very reason that it had no public officials to interefere with their lives. The Proprietary agents seemed eager to take money from the pioneers but did little to make it seem worthwhile.

Another group who had no use for the Proprietors was the New England ship captains. The Albemarle trade was profitable to the sea-going merchants, but only if they could avoid paying customs duties on the products they bought there. To mariners and planters alike, the Plantations Duty

Act of 1673, which put a tax of a penny a pound on tobacco taken out of the colony, was a maddening injustice that threatened to wreck their trade.

When the mariners threatened to double the cost of articles they brought to sell in Albemarle if the tax was collected, the customs collector reduced it to a fourth of a penny a pound. By this time—1676—the Chowanoke Indians had risen in one last effort to rid themselves of white control. Settlers were uneasy about the few weapons they had to defend themselves. This was a new complaint against the Proprietors—that they had put so little money into defense of the colony. Tomahawks were no match for muskets, but it seemed clear that a few score well-armed men could take over Albemarle if they chose to do so.

A *musket* was an early kind of gun.

A *score* of men is twenty.

A map drawn by Nicholas Comberford in 1657 shows Nathaniel Batts' house at the fork of the Chowan and Roanoke rivers.

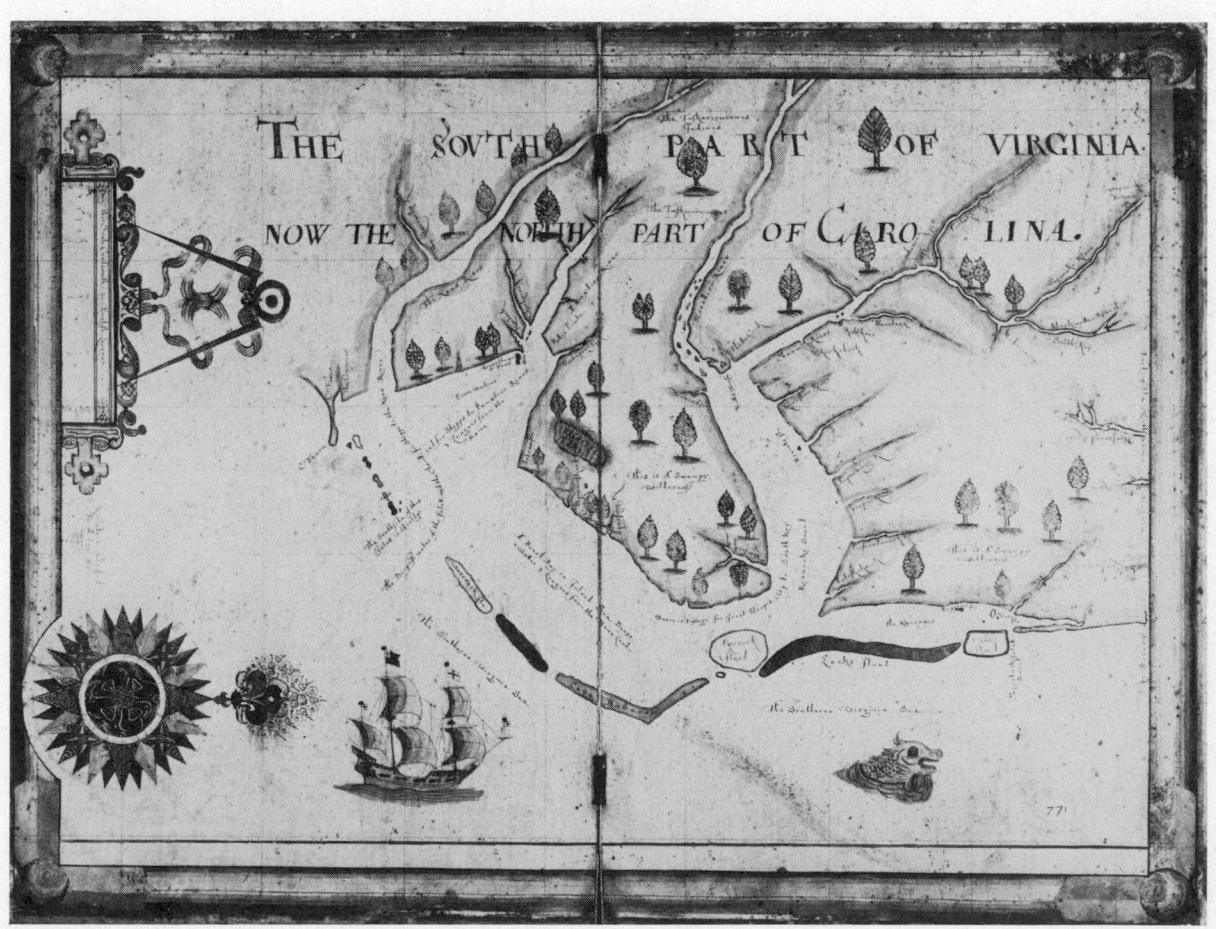

By 1677, rebellion was in the air in all the American colonies. The government of Virginia had been rocked by Bacon's Rebellion. It was a bloody war between wealthy planters and poor backwoodsmen. Bacon's rebels were defeated. But similar trouble arose in Maryland, South Carolina, and other colonies. The rebels in Albemarle included some who had joined—or would later join—in movements elsewhere against English officials. A small group of soldier-adventurers seemed to be wandering about the coastal settlements seeking to stir up—or at least profit from—local unrest wherever they could find or create it.

Before the end of 1676, Thomas Eastchurch, then acting governor, left for England to report on these troubles in Albemarle to the Lords Proprietors. He was especially concerned about the refusal of the customs collector to demand the full penny a pound tax on exported tobacco. But shortly behind Eastchurch came George Durant with another version of the trouble in Albemarle. Durant let it be known that he opposed the naming of Eastchurch as governor. He went so far as to declare that he would "turn Rebell" if that happened. Eastchurch, of course, was appointed governor and sailed with Miller for Albemarle.

When he reached Albemarle in July 1677, Acting Governor Miller promptly raised the tobacco tax to the prescribed penny a pound. Almost certainly, it was neither this act nor his later deeds as acting governor that led to arms being placed on board the *Carolina* before it left England. Gillam and Durant did not know Miller would be in power when they arrived. Nor was it the Indian uprising, which had been put down before the *Carolina* left Albemarle. It seems likely that the guns were intended for use against any government not acceptable to the discontented group in Albemarle. The circumstances suggest that Durant and Gillam may have left Albemarle in late 1676 with an understanding among leading conspirators that they were to buy arms unless the Proprietors appointed a governor acceptable to them.

Eastchurch did not have authority to appoint an acting governor and this is a point in favor of the rebels. But the governor's action was probably not the cause of the rebellion. Culpeper's own statement of grievances, composed at the start of the uprising, said nothing of Miller's claim to authority. The argument that Miller was not properly appointed does not seem to have occurred to the rebels until later. The rebellion was not against Eastchurch or Miller so much as against the Lords Proprietors.

Money was scarce in Proprietary North Carolina, but some coins were issued for the trade of the colony.

Conspirators are a group of people who plan a rebellion.

The Rebellion Fades

Culpeper's Rebellion dragged on through the years 1678 and 1679. Thomas Miller and other Proprietary agents wasted away in rebel jails and the rebel leaders happily shipped their tobacco abroad without worrying about taxes. The New England ship captains found business booming in Albemarle and made many profitable trips to the region. There was always a chance that forces from England or Virginia might suddenly appear and throw the rebels out of power, but month after month passed with no such result.

In distant London, the Proprietors spent these months struggling to sort out the conflicting rumors and reports they heard from the Albemarle. The rebels sent Culpeper and Gillam to present their side of the case to the Proprietors. But supporters of Miller also managed to send representatives to London. These included Miller himself, who had escaped from his log jail on Pasquotank River. Swayed first one way and then another, the Proprietors finally decided that both sides had behaved badly, but that Miller had never had proper authority to serve as acting governor. In a sense, there had been no rebellion because there had been no constitutional government to rebel against.

The vacant office of governor of Albemarle was filled by Seth Sothel, one of the Lords Proprietors. He was instructed to go to Albemarle and try to clean up the mess there. But the appointment was an unfortunate one. Sothel left England with a good reputation for fair and honest dealing but he arrived in Albemarle a desperate and ruthless man. He was to become one of the worst colonial governors.

The cause of Sothel's change of heart was no doubt his capture at sea on his way to America by Turkish pirates. He was taken to Algiers, in North Africa, and put to hard labor while his captors tried to collect a ransom for his release. He later reported that he was forced to work "with a heavy Chaine of nine links, each linke two inches and halfe thick upon his legg besides Bolt and Shackle." He was at last ransomed in 1681 for six thousand pieces of eight and two Arabs, Hadg Omar and another known to the English as "Buffolo Ball," who were prisoners in England.

Two years of slave labor must have poisoned the heart of Seth Sothel. He invented all sorts of illegal schemes to make

A *ransom* is a price paid for release of a captive.

This engraving was on a pamphlet urging people to settle in the region south of Jamestown. The region was pictured as a fertile Utopia.

himself rich at the expense of those he governed. He failed to send to England the rents collected for the Proprietors. He refused to carry out instructions to try cases arising out of Culpeper's Rebellion. When he heard that George Durant was saying critical things about him, he had Durant arrested and seized all his property for himself. In 1689, outraged settlers seized Sothel and made him take an oath to resign forever as governor and leave the colony. With his leaving, the rule of law at last came to Albemarle.

Several main leaders of the conflicts of earlier years came to sad ends. "Old Zach" Gillam was drowned in a Canadian river in 1682. Thomas Miller, perhaps brought low by his love for strong drink, died in debtors' prison in England three years later. John Culpeper faded into the mists from which he had risen. But George Durant, somehow surviving every swing of fortune's pendulum, died in prosperous old age in Albemarle in 1684. Durant's Neck in Perquimans County still bears his name.

Many men of Nathaniel Batts' generation longed for a mythical kind of "freedom" where each person may do only what one wishes to do. But this kind of freedom is one in which the strong can dominate the weak, in which might makes right. And that is freedom only for the few, not the many. There were settlers in Albemarle in the 1660s and 1670s who felt that the freedom demanded by John Culpeper was the wrong kind, but they may not have been in a majority. Fortunately, they soon would be.

Chapter Checkup

PEOPLE

Thomas Miller   Zachariah Gillam
Thomas Eastchurch   John Culpeper

PLACES

Colleton Island.   Pasquotank River.

FACT

Why did the Lords Proprietors pay more attention to their Ashley River settlement than to the one in Albemarle?

According to Peter Carteret's report, what were the main problems for those trying to start farms in Albemarle?

INTERPRETATION

Why would you say the rebels failed to complain to the Proprietors of Miller's illegal appointment as acting governor before they rose against him?

How did the powers of the early colonial legislatures help pave the way to revolution later on?

Should the Culpeper uprising be called a rebellion? (Was it the Lords Proprietors or only the local government in Albemarle that the uprising was directed against?)

Are laws necessary in order to protect freedom? Do more laws necessarily mean more freedom?

VOCABULARY

Proprietors	Legislature	Civil War
Rebellion	Conspirators	

ACTIVITY

Stage a trial for Thomas Miller, appointing counsels for defense and prosecution, grand jury, petit jury, and so on. Decide whether he was guilty or not—and of what.

SUGGESTED READING

Lefler, Hugh T. and Powell, William S. *Colonial North Carolina, A History.* New York: Charles Scribner's Sons, 1973. Pages 44–55. Brief account relates North Carolina disturbances with those of other colonies.

Rankin, Hugh F. *Upheaval in Albemarle: The Story of Culpeper's Rebellion, 1675–1689.* Raleigh: Carolina Charter Tercentenary Commission, 1962. Brief, reliable account of events and underlying causes.

1696   Bath County created

1698   French settlement
of Louisiana begins

1700   John Lawson sails
for Carolina

1701   Lawson settles in North
Carolina; Vestry Act passed

1702   Queen Anne's War begins

1703   New Vestry Act passed

1708   Glover's forces defeated
by Cary

1710   Founding of New Bern

1711   North Carolina separated
from South Carolina; Tuscarora
War begins

1713   Treaty of Utrecht signed

3

THE TUSCARORA WAR

The Murdered Man

Almost any young man living in London in the spring of 1700 would have had the same urge as John Lawson. He wanted to travel and see something of the world. London had long been the busiest place in Europe, home port of the world's largest fleets. Its miles of wharves groaned under the weight of tar barrels and tobacco kegs from Virginia and Maryland. There were boxes of ginger and pepper from the Spice Islands, and teas from the China coast. There were choice wares from a thousand places barely known even to Europe's mapmakers. Just this spring there was more than the usual commotion. Some Englishmen prepared to attend the Grand Jubilee of the Catholic Church at Rome.

John Lawson wanted to follow the pilgrims to Rome to see the wonderful places he had only heard or read about. His eyes and ears had carried him on journeys to the Arctic and to the rain forests of Africa. But his feet, so far, had not taken

The Grand Jubilee was a celebration held every 25 years in Rome.

53

John Lawson, *an explorer, writer, and settler*
James Petiver, *a druggist in England*
Christoph von Graffenried, *a Swiss nobleman*

Thomas Cary, *a deputy governor*
Edward Hyde, *a governor of the colony*
William Glover, *acting deputy governor*
Hancock, *a Tuscarora Indian king*

Yorkshire was a county in northern England.

The term "Indies" included both the East Indies (islands of the western Pacific near Southeast Asia) and West Indies (islands of the Caribbean Sea region).

The Plague was the bubonic, or black plague, a deadly disease.

The King's Evil was a name for scrofula, a disease thought to be curable by the touch of the king.

A *"seasoning"* was a case of malaria or other common fever contracted by almost all new arrivals in the southern colonies.

him beyond Yorkshire. His training to become an apothecary (druggist) had kept him tied down. Now he was free to wander. Surely the year 1700 was when he should turn his dreams into sails and visit some of the world beyond.

One day in the spring, as Lawson was thinking this way, he "accidentally met with a Gentleman"—so he later wrote—"who had been abroad, and was very well acquainted with the Ways of Living in both Indies. . . ." The man assured Lawson that the province of Carolina was the best country he had seen. Better yet, there was a ship at London on which Lawson might go there. A few days later, John Lawson watched the English coast sink behind the stern of this ship. The wide Atlantic opened for him the route to Carolina.

The man who told Lawson that Carolina was "the best Country" he could go to seems to have been a London druggist named James Petiver. Petiver was a kind of scientist. He was interested in the American colonies as sources for the roots, minerals, and other things that made up much of his stock of drugs and medicines. But most of the colonial realm was still unexplored. Who could tell what wonderful things might yet be found there? One might find cures for the Plague, the King's Evil, or the other awful diseases of Europe. With Lawson's own love for adventure, Petiver could picture the wonders awaiting him in the forests of distant Carolina.

The voyage to America was even more dangerous than usual. Winds and storms from the south battered Lawson's ship day after day, pushing it away from the Carolina coasts. In late July, the vessel finally reached New York harbor, far to the north of its destination. It took another month for Lawson to make his way to Charleston (then called Charles Town). He got there in its hottest season. Many were sick with fevers, including some of those already accustomed to the climate. But Lawson was young and strong and the "seasoning" fever seems to have had little effect on him.

By the end of the fall, Lawson was prepared for the great adventure for which he had come to Carolina. Before leaving England, or soon after reaching Charleston, he was hired by the Lords Proprietors to lead an expedition to the Carolina backcountry. The Proprietors still had not given up the dream of finding gold and silver. Priceless other things might also be found in the unknown regions toward the mountains. Lawson, with his good education and his gift for observing and describing things, was just the person to satisfy their curiosity.

On December 28, 1700, Lawson started up the coast from Charleston in "a large Canoe." With him went five other white men, four Indians, and a flop-eared Spaniel dog. Six days later the party reached and entered the Santee River. There they began their long adventure into the thinly-settled regions of the lower river and the wild country beyond.

In later years Lawson wrote a book about his adventure. It was one of the best accounts written about the early colonies. It was full of the kind of experiences the author had dreamed about at the London dockside. He would never forget, for instance, the Santee Indian hunter who stood seven feet tall, "the tallest Indian I ever saw." Then there was the old Congaree squaw who was said to be "above 100 years old." She looked at least twice her age in spite of her hearty appetite and her pipe of tobacco. How could he forget the incredible Indian doctor with no nose, who could quickly cure diseases that baffled the English physicians?

The **Congarees** were Indians of South Carolina.

The doctor with no nose had been a victim of yaws.

This four-foot-high wooden statue guarded the bodies of dead kings in the village of Secotan, near present Hobucken.

The hunting was marvelous. An Indian guide killed 15 turkeys from a flock that came out of a swamp to feed on acorns. There were skies full of pigeons. They swarmed so thickly "they sometimes split off the Limbs of stout oaks, . . . upon which they roosted. . . ." Even the smaller Indian villages kept a hundred or more gallons of pigeon's oil. This they used as the English did butter. The Congarees kept flocks of tame storks and cranes, some of the latter up to six feet tall. They bred them like chickens.

Most fascinating of all were the Indians themselves. The Waterees were as masterful "at picking of Pockets, as any, I believe, the world affords; . . . they will steal with their Feet." The King of the Enoes, awed by a book in Lawson's pack, begged him to teach the king's son "to talk in that book and Make Paper speak, which they call our Way of Writing. . . ." The Sewees, Lawson was told, had once built a fleet of large canoes. They set off in them to carry furs and skins for sale in England. But they met heavy storms and suffered many deaths before they could straggle back to their own coast. Lawson learned that the Flatheads were so named for binding

The **Waterees** were Indians of South Carolina.

The **Sewees** were Indians of South Carolina.

The **Flatheads** lived in the Waxhaw area on the border of North and South Carolina.

The Tuscarora Indian Region, 1700

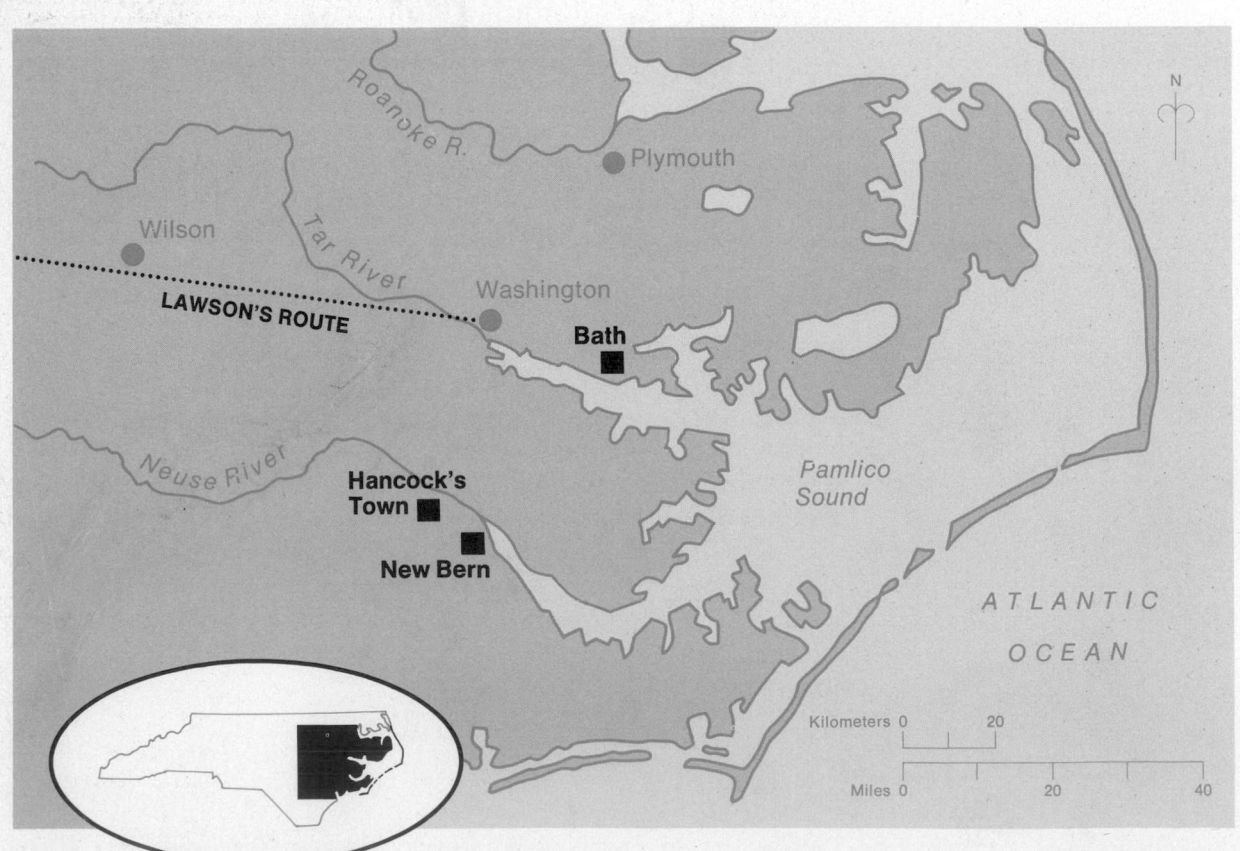

Pomeiock Village, located near present Englehard in Hyde County, was fortified by a circle of posts.

the heads of their infants in "a sort of Press." This made their eyes stand out from their heads. But they could see their game at great distances when hunting. The mystery of a town full of one-eyed Indians remained unsolved, however.

Having explored the country as far west as the Appalachians, the expedition turned east toward Roanoke Island. On February 23, 1701, 58 days after leaving Charleston, Lawson's journal noted that

About 10 o'clock, we met an Indian that had got a parcel of Shad-Fish ready barbaku'd. We bought 24 of them, for a dress'd Doe-Skin, and so went on, . . . finding, this day, the long ragged Moss on the Trees, which we had not seen for over 600 Miles. In the Afternoon, we came upon the Banks of Pampticough, almost 20 Miles above the English Plantation by Water. . . .

Next day . . . we . . . came safe to Mr. Richard Smith's of Pampticough-River, . . . where being well receiv'd by the Inhabitants, and pleas'd with the Goodness of the Contry, we resolv'd to continue.

In April 1701, Lawson wrote from Bath County to Petiver in London. He promised his friend that he would be "very industrious" in collecting specimens to study and send to England. Even now he was making plans to take a trip along the coast. He would look for curious shells, fish, insects and so on. His journal of the trip from Charleston was finished and would be sent "when you desire."

Lawson built a house for himself beside the Neuse River, where the town of New Bern now stands. There he settled down with an Indian friend and a bulldog. His talent for mathematics brought him work as a surveyor for the colony, into which more settlers were coming than ever before. There was much to be done in marking the boundaries of land grants and deeds as the pioneers pushed further south from Albemarle. But Lawson also needed time to explore and study and collect the specimens for which Petiver and others in England begged him. Then there was the book he wanted to write on the natural history of the colony, perhaps the first of several books.

Lawson had settled in the fastest-growing part of the region around the Carolina sounds. In 1696, the Proprietors created there the County of Bath. In 1705, they divided Bath into the precincts of Beaufort, Hyde, and Craven. By now there was talk of laying out a town on Pamlico River for the convenience of those who preferred the safety of town life. In that year, North Carolina gained its first incorporated town.

The idea seems to have been Lawson's. With two other men, he bought 60 acres along the lower Pamlico. They laid out lots and streets. The town was known from the beginning as Bath, and Lawson and his partners served as its first commissioners, or managers. Lots were quickly bought by some of the English and Irish settlers in the neighborhood. There were also some French Protestants—refugees from Catholic France—who came from Virginia to settle there. By 1708, Bath had a dozen or so houses and perhaps 50 or 60 white and black residents.

Land grants were tracts offered to people to encourage them to immigrate to the colonies.

As the colony developed there was increasing demand for Lawson's services and time. In 1709, Queen Anne ordered that the old border dispute between Virginia and Carolina be settled. The Virginians had argued for over 40 years that the dividing line should be the one authorized by the Lords Proprietors in 1663. It ran east through Albemarle Sound. The 1665 charter, moving the line northward by some 60 miles, was unlawful, claimed the Virginians. (This would have meant that such places as Edenton, Durham, Greensboro, and Winston-Salem would be in Virginia.)

Lawson was appointed, with Surveyor-General Edward Moseley, to join Virginia surveyors in the disputed region. He was to try to agree with them on where the boundary should be. Some measurements were made by both sides. But their figures did not agree and so the question was not settled. In the end, it took another 20 years to solve the border problem.

Gristmills are for grinding corn or other grain into flour.

While the border question lingered, Lawson was also busy with other things. During 1707 and 1708, he served as clerk of court and register for Bath Precinct. He helped establish a gristmill at Bath Town. In 1709, he sailed for England to arrange for publication of his book and to buy seeds, medicines, and other supplies. James Petiver was delighted with Lawson's book. Petiver encouraged him to continue the kind of studies he had begun so well. It was clear that Lawson was making a contribution to the progress of science. He was also helping persuade people to settle in Carolina. By the summer of 1710, Lawson was back at Bath, aflame with enthusiasm for new discoveries.

Baron de Graffenried was the founder and chief settler of the Palatine colony on the lower Neuse River in 1710.

His excitement was communicated to Petiver in a letter written in the autumn of 1710. He told Petiver that he intended—"If God prolongs my dayes"—to collect specimens of every plant in the colony. He wanted to gather specimens of every kind of beast, fish, insect, fossil, and mineral that he could find. He would study the habits of the Indians and the European settlers. He would gather information about mountains, valleys, springs, orchards, forests, and gardens. It would be a lifetime's work and more. But it would give Lawson the reputation of being one of the great scientists of the age.

Still another ambitious project occupied his days during 1710 and 1711—the founding of New Bern, the colony's second town. A Swiss nobleman, Baron Christoph von Graffenried, had become interested in finding a place in America as a home for Swiss and German Protestants who were badly treated in Europe. In 1709, he met Lawson in London. He decided to settle a community of Protestants in North Carolina. He bought a large tract on the Neuse and Trent Rivers from the

Proprietors. Graffenried gathered six hundred fifty settlers, acquired supplies, and sent them to Carolina in 1710.

The voyage was a nightmare in which half the crowded passengers died. A French warship robbed them of many of their belongings. The survivors finally reached Virginia and went on to Carolina. But for months they remained in a kind of shock from their tragic experience. At length they recovered and went to work. Lawson laid out a town where each family would have three acres of land along "very broad streets." They built a water mill and named the place New Bern after the Swiss town (Berne) where many of them came from. By the summer of 1711, New Bern was a neat and prosperous village. The leaders of the colony were pleased with their energetic and bright new community.

As the first light of dawn reached west across the Neuse Valley on the morning of September 22, 1711, the painted face of a Tuscarora warrior peered from the edge of a woods toward a cabin in the clearing beyond. The Indian clutched the tomahawk tightly in his hand. He motioned to others to start forward. At a nearby farm, at a trapper's house, at a river landing, and a tarburner's hut, other war parties begain to stir forward. And 70 miles upriver, in a part of the country never before visited by white people, the head of John Lawson stared into the early morning sky through sightless eyes. Its store of priceless knowledge was lost to humanity forever.

Evicting the Indians

A **deputy** is a person appointed as a substitute for someone else.

Charleston's fine harbor for ships was its main advantage.

For 20 years after 1691, North Carolina was governed by a deputy appointed by the proprietary governor, who lived at Charleston. The southern part of Carolina had grown faster than the northern part. It was more important as well as more profitable to the Lords Proprietors. After the overthrow of Seth Sothel in 1689, the leaders in the north were far more able and honest. They helped bring peace and prosperity to the Albemarle section. Settlers heard the good news and came in larger numbers to live there. They pushed south of Albemarle Sound and up the rivers and creeks that stretched into the interior.

Albemarle was not settled mainly by religious groups, like the colonies of New England. However, its government took a lively interest in religious institutions. The king and

Proprietors felt it was desirable to encourage some religious groups. But they discouraged or rejected others in the colonies, as was done in England. The Carolina Charter granted religious freedom in order to persuade people of all faiths to come to Albemarle. But the English leaders were mostly members of the Church of England. They tended to favor their own church over others.

As it happened, the first religious group to flourish in North Carolina was the Quakers. George Fox and other Quaker missionaries had visited Carolina as early as 1672. The congregations they started gathered strength in later years. By 1690, although members of the Church of England, called Anglicans, held most of the high offices in the colony, Quakers were gaining ground. In the Pasquotank and Perquimans River area, they were in the majority. At each new election they sent more of their own to the House of Burgesses.

Quakers are members of the church known as the Society of Friends.

During the 1690s, the Anglicans watched resentfully as the Quakers won control of the government of Albemarle. Anglican leaders sent complaints to the Proprietors. They wondered why the Church of England did not send missionaries to help build churches in Carolina. With help from England, the Anglicans could regain control.

In 1701, it must have seemed as if Anglican prayers were being answered. They pushed a Vestry Act through the legislature. The act divided the colony into Anglican parishes and demanded a tax from all citizens for support of Anglican preachers. An Anglican chapel, the first church building in the colony, was started at what is now Edenton. The Anglicans in Bath County received a gift of a thousand books from an English well-wisher. They were mostly religious, for the promotion of Anglican growth. It was the colony's first library.

A *vestry* is a governing board of an Anglican parish or district.

Quakers objected to the law of 1701 because it was aimed at crippling their development. It forced them to help pay the salaries of Anglican ministers. There was only one Anglican priest in the colony so far, but others could be expected. They could get to be expensive! The Proprietors, feeling that the act of 1701 was not strong enough, rejected it. But they agreed to another Vestry Act in 1703. This one provided that all members of the House of Burgesses must swear an oath that they were members of the Church of England. If they didn't, they could not legally hold office. When Thomas Cary became deputy governor in 1705, he found the colonists in an ugly mood. The Quakers, joined by a few Presbyterians, were bitter about the Act. Anglican leaders were determined to enforce it.

Cary was a Charleston merchant without strong feelings in the matter. But it seemed to him politically wise to enforce

Edward Hyde was Governor of the Carolina Colony, 1711-1712. He died there of yellow fever in 1712.

The Indians of coastal Carolina spread a mat on the ground and placed containers of food on it. When they ate, the men sat on one side of the mat, the women on the other.

the new law. He did so over the protests of the Quakers and others. When he went to visit Charleston, leaving William Glover as acting deputy, the situation became even worse. Glover bore down on the Quakers. There was talk of armed resistance, even though Quakers were understood to be opposed to violence. Cary, alarmed by Glover's actions, ordered him to resign, but he refused. The problem was settled briefly in 1708. Cary's supporters defeated those of Glover and Glover fled to Virginia. Cary appointed several Quakers to high office as a means of settling the conflict.

In the hope of providing more efficient government, the Proprietors, in 1711, separated North Carolina from South Carolina. Edward Hyde was sent over to become North Carolina's first governor under the new arrangement. Hyde used his authority to throw out the laws made during Cary's terms. When Hyde showed that he meant to support the anti-Quaker party, his opponents prepared for war.

"Cary's Rebellion" turned out to be a bomb without a fuse. Cary and the Quakers got hold of a six-gun ship and some muskets and attacked Hyde's forces. The attackers were beaten back. With help from Virginia, Hyde soon arrested Cary and those of his followers who were unable to flee from the colony. For the time being, Quaker opposition was silenced in North Carolina. Thirty years earlier, Cary might have succeeded, just as John Culpeper had. But the second generation of settlers had less taste for revolt. The government was often irritating, but there were peaceful ways of trying to discourage it from going too far. This seemed to be a sign of maturity and progress in the colony.

The Tuscaroras were the largest of the Indian tribes of eastern North Carolina. In 1711, they represented about four thousand of the five thousand coastal Indians in an area where fifty thousand had lived in the time of Nathaniel Batts. The Tuscaroras inhabited a large region between Roanoke and Neuse Rivers. But they were increasingly crowded by whites settling within their hunting and fishing grounds.

Smaller tribes could do little to discourage the white advance. But the Tuscaroras were a proud people. In his first meeting with them in 1701, John Lawson observed that they were "expert Hunters, yet they are too populous for one Range, which makes Venison (deer and bear meat) very scarce to what it is amongst other Indians, that are fewer. . . ." Ten more years of white immigration had further reduced the hunting ground. It made the venison on which the Tuscaroras depended even more scarce.

Indians tilled the soil with a hoe of fish bones on a wooden handle. Planting was done by the women.

The Tuscaroras were described by Lawson and others as being mostly tall and handsome, with black hair and hazel eyes. Most had yellow teeth from constantly smoking tobacco. They plucked their faces free of hair and walked with a stride that was "sedate and majestick." Lawson thought them "extraordinary Fellows" at running and leaping. He praised their ability to dance, night after night, "with the greatest Briskness imaginable, their Wind never failing them."

The Tuscaroras were a farming people in warm months. They grew Indian corn and tobacco, along with other vegetables and fruits. In winter they were hunters and trappers. They depended in all seasons on fishing to supply food. But life for them was not all work and food-gathering. They had a variety of sports, games, and celebrations. A popular game involved one player throwing pieces of split reed in front of another who tried to guess how many had been thrown. It was all done with quick motions of the hand and was played for high stakes. There were also various dice and ball games.

There was no government over all the Tuscaroras, though the villages often cooperated for common purposes. In general, each town had its own king or chief and a council made up of the best hunters and warriors. By 1711, the bow and arrow had mostly given way to the musket, purchased from the whites. But in a war, when there were not enough guns to go around, bows were still used.

An important experience in the life of a Tuscarora boy or girl was *husquenaw*. Near the end of each year, youths who were judged able to withstand it were herded together in a large specially-built cabin. Here they were left for up to six weeks in darkness, half-starved. They were given drugs to make them rave and howl. The little meat they received was rotten and mixed with filth. At the end of the period they were led out but kept under guard. Speechless and often reduced to skin and bone, they were guarded until thought fit to return to their families. Some even died from the ordeal. But once experienced, it was never to be repeated.

The point of it all was discipline. The Indians tried to achieve in a few weeks the social discipline that whites drilled into their young by years of schooling or apprenticeship. Indian children could not be spared for long from necessary tasks. *Husquenaw* accomplished much in a short time. Youngsters who withstood it became "obedient and respectful to their superiors," as one writer put it. They were able to bear "all manner of Fatigues and Hardships. . . ." Those who could not stand it would be of no use to the community.

"Fatigues" means tiring exercises.

At 16 or 17, the boys became hunters or warriors; the girls found husbands. Young men dropped their childhood names and took new ones, "some being called Eagle, Tyger, Panther, Alligator, or some such wild creature, esteeming nothing on Earth to give them a Name, but such kind of Wildfowl or Beasts." Women might fight beside the men in time of war. But generally they were employed dressing wild game, making reed mats and baskets, food-gathering, and in other domestic duties.

There had been occasional violence between whites and Indians since the arrival of the first colony at Roanoke Island. However, none lasted long or caused much bloodshed. Even so, the Indians, especially the Tuscaroras, had stored up a thousand reasons for hating whites. Smallpox and other European diseases killed Indians by the thousands. And there was the white man's rum, his cheating on trades, and his hunting and trapping on Indian lands. Now, in 1711, new swarms of whites were coming to settle at New Bern and other places. They helped themselves to the best land.

Cary's rebellion offered a chance that Hancock, greatest of the Tuscarora kings, could not allow to pass. Secretly, he sent agents to seek support from other kings among all the coastal tribes. Most agreed to attack. However, an important group of northern Tuscaroras under Chief Tom Blunt refused to have anything to do with it. A confederacy was formed and an army of five hundred was furnished with muskets, bows and arrows, and other weapons. It was agreed that they would attack a little before harvest time, when the most injury could be done to farms.

The Tuscaroras and their allies were making their final preparations for war in mid-September when two white men in a canoe appeared on the upper Neuse, far inside Indian territory. They were captured and brought to Hancock's Town. The Indians at first thought they had captured Governor Hyde, an official for whom the whites would pay dearly. But the captives turned out to be Baron von Graffenried and John Lawson. They claimed to be looking for a place to begin a new road to Virginia.

This was an awkward situation for Hancock. He had no particular quarrel with these two men. But it would be foolish to let them go on the eve of the Indian attack. A council was held to decide what to do with them. It was agreed to release both after the first assault on the white settlements. But Lawson angered some of the people from other tribes by arguing with them. They demanded his execution. Hancock, perhaps fearing the collapse of his alliance unless Lawson was sacrificed, gave the order to have him killed. The whites learned the story from Graffenried, who was later released.

This sketch shows the capture of Lawson and Graffenried by the Tuscaroras on the Neuse River in 1711.

A drawing by Graffenried shows Lawson, a black servant, and Graffenried about to be tortured by the Tuscaroras in 1711.

Victory and Defeat

Carolina Indians preserved the bodies of dead chiefs in a Quiokoson house. A priest (below) kept vigil night and day.

The Tuscarora War began with attacks on white farms and settlements on the lower Neuse on September 22. Within a few days the Indians had killed more than one hundred twenty settlers and captured others. New Bern, quickly fortified, was not attacked, but the outlying country was completely taken over by the attackers. Houses and barns were burned, crops destroyed, cattle killed and driven off, possessions looted. It was the worst disaster inflicted on whites in North Carolina's history.

For a few weeks it seemed that the Indians might succeed in driving the whites out of the colony. The colonists, panic-stricken inside their forts and settlements, did not know how to fight Indian fashion. They dared not venture out into the country. White leaders sent appeals to Virginia and South Carolina for help. It was proposed that the government of South Carolina raise a force of friendly Indians to attack the Tuscaroras. The South Carolina legislature voted the necessary money. An army of about five hundred Indians, led by white officers, marched north. These Indians were promised rewards and favors for their services.

The South Carolina force attacked the Tuscaroras at Hancock's Town and other places. They caused enough injury to force the Indians to agree to peace terms. These included a promise by the Tuscaroras to give up more of their hunting and fishing grounds. They were to pay a yearly tribute to the government of North Carolina. It was agreed that each side would exchange prisoners with the other. The army marched back to South Carolina. But the Tuscaroras, hearing that some Indians who had been captured were being sold into slavery, rose again.

A second army of South Carolina Indians was raised. This force smashed the Tuscaroras in battle, ending for all time their power as a nation. After killing or capturing some nine hundred fifty Indians, the South Carolinians left once more. Within a few months, smaller battles between whites and Indians broke up the remaining pockets of resistance. The Tuscaroras fled north to refuge with the powerful Iroquois Confederacy. It was the last time the whites in North Carolina would be gravely endangered by Indians.

The **Iroquois Confederacy** was an alliance of five Indian tribes or nations of New York.

John Lawson had been a victim of the terrible hatreds raised in Indian hearts by white mistreatment. The Indians were often cheated and abused by the whites. But the presence of the whites in the coastal region helps explain much of the antiwhite Indian feelings. In his book, Lawson wrote that "The Indians are very revengeful, and never forget an Injury done, till they have receiv'd Satisfaction."

But the Tuscaroras waited too long to settle their debt of vengeance against the whites. Although they were the strongest tribe in the region, they did not become leaders in a larger group of Indians. They could not defeat the whites alone. The downfall of the Tuscaroras cleared the path to the mountains for the onrushing Europeans. Within 50 years, white settlements would rim the base of the mountain barrier, the last obstacle to the conquest of the continent.

Chapter Checkup

PEOPLE

James Petiver
John Lawson
Christoph von Graffenried
Thomas Cary

Edward Hyde
Hancock
William Glover

PLACES

Approximate route of Lawson's journey of 1000 miles.
Area of N.C. claimed by Virginia in early 18th century.
Bath
New Bern
Hancock's Town

FACT

What was the reason for the founding of New Bern?
What was the main reason for making North Carolina a separate colony from South Carolina?
Why did the Tuscaroras practice *husquenaw*?
Why did the Tuscarora War begin in 1711 rather than earlier or later?
What became of the Tuscaroras?
Why did the Quakers oppose the Vestry Acts?

INTERPRETATION

What reasons can you think of for building the early North Carolina towns at the mouths of rivers?
Suggest reasons why Cary's Rebellion was less successful than Culpeper's.
Did the Tuscaroras have good enough reasons for attacking the whites?

VOCABULARY

Seasoning	Vestry
Land grants	Anglican

ACTIVITY

Study the plans of Secotan and Bath. How much can you tell about the difference between Indian and white cultures from the differences you see between the towns?

SUGGESTED READING

Lee, E. Lawrence, Jr. *The Indian Wars in North Carolina.* Raleigh: Carolina Charter Tercentenary Commission, 1963. Pages 14–38 contain good, brief account of Tuscarora War.
Rights, Douglas. *The American Indian in North Carolina.* Winston-Salem: John F. Blair, 1957. Detailed survey of Indian life and history in early N.C.
South, Stanley A. *Indians in North Carolina.* Raleigh: State Dept. of Archives and History, 1970. Brief survey of major tribes from prehistoric to recent times.

PART TWO

The Developing Colony

Oconoluftee—reconstruction
of a Cherokee Indian village

1715-1775

1713 Hyde dies of yellow fever

1715 North Carolina laws revised

1717 Blackbeard and Bonnet become partners

1718 Blackbeard settles at Bath; killed by Maynard's men

1718 French expansion on the Mississippi begins

1722 Death of Governor Eden

1724 Burrington becomes governor

1725 Everard replaces Burrington

1728 Boundary dispute with Virginia settled

1729 North Carolina becomes a royal colony

1739 War of Jenkins' Ear begins

1740 King George's War begins

1744 Granville District created

1744 Westward expansion begins

4

ROGUES' HARBOR

Partnership in Piracy

The two men eyed each other across the dimly-lit cabin. Searching his memory, the captain could not recall anything quite like this in all his years at sea. Mr. Bonnet, sitting opposite him, was a trim and prim little dandy. He was tricked out in smart pantaloons, a bright-colored coat, and a neat wig. He had the smooth speech of a gentleman and the confident airs of one who expected to be listened to with respect. But the captain bit his lip to hold back a roar of laughter. The little fellow kept insisting that he was a pirate! If so, then he was quite the prettiest little pirate the captain had ever met. All this would make a merry tale to carry back to the Bahamas next winter.

Stede Bonnet stared back at the figure before him. He wondered if he had not been hasty in accepting the captain's request to come aboard. Two piercing black eyes glared at him from beneath heavy black hair and bristling eyebrows.

Edward Teach, known as Blackbeard, was the most famous of the many pirates in the early eighteenth century.

There was only a hint of cheek below the eyes before the face disappeared again behind a mass of hair. Around the shoulders hung braided pigtails, each tied with a colored ribbon. Together with the captain's tall, strong body, the effect was as terrifying as anything Bonnet had ever seen in human form. Captain Blackbeard was indeed an awesome creature.

The afternoon's talk wandered over many subjects connected with the sea. But to Major Bonnet, it ended in a strange and rather uneasy agreement. The two were to join forces as partners in piracy. It was not quite clear to Bonnet whether he had any real choice in the matter. His years as an officer in the King's Guards had not prepared him for dealing with the kind of scoundrels among whom he was now to seek his fortune.

Even so, the partners made a good start. Bonnet's ten-gun sloop, the *Revenge,* was a fine ship. It was a useful ally to Blackbeard's big forty-gun *Queen Anne's Revenge.* They had been at sea only a few days that spring of 1717 when they seized the sloop *Adventure* in the Bay of Honduras. When the *Adventure's* crew offered to join the pirates, they became a fleet strong enough to challenge any naval vessel afloat. Blackbeard fretted that there were too many hands among whom to divide the booty. But he thought he knew a way to handle the problem when the time came.

The pirate fleet moved across the Gulf of Mexico and toward the Florida Keys. Blackbeard then decided to replace Bonnet as captain of the *Revenge.* He told Bonnet that to command a ship was a dirty job for so fine a gentleman as he. Blackbeard then put his own first mate in command of the sloop. He gave Bonnet a cabin on the *Queen Anne's Revenge.* Uncertain whether he was a prisoner or a guest, Bonnet kept his worry to himself. But he admired the work of the pirates as they captured one ship after another. During May, they ran

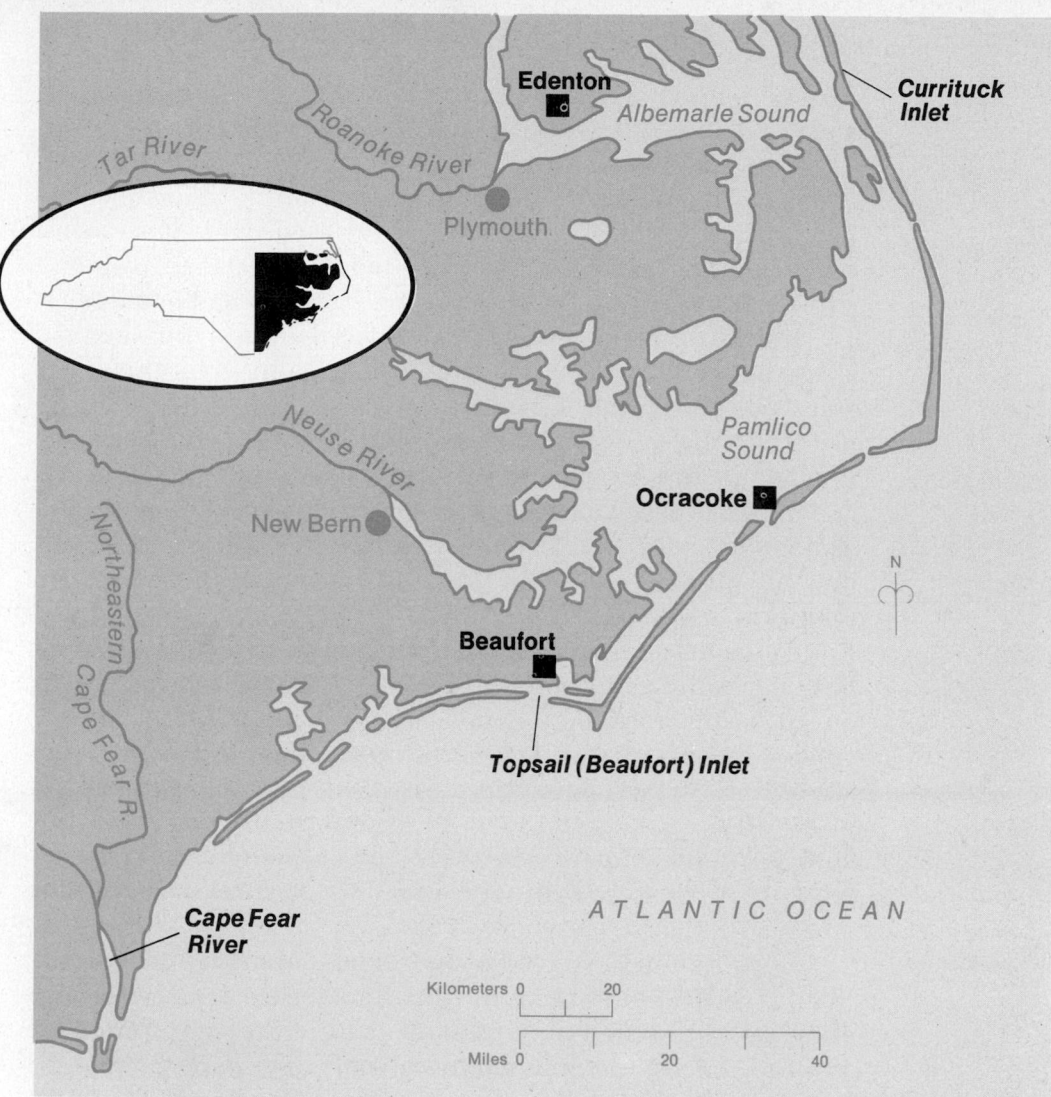

Rogues' Harbor, 1715

Brigs are two-masted sailing vessels.

Maritime means relating to the sea.

down a small ship off the coast of Jamaica, another near Cuba, and two sloops and a brig bound for Charleston. None of them offered any resistance. Bonnet wondered why he had spent so many years in the army. He could have done much better as a pirate.

In May 1718, the pirate fleet arrived outside Charleston harbor. It took control of the city's maritime commerce. Stopping every vessel entering or leaving the harbor, the pirates helped themselves to whatever they liked on each ship and sent it on its way. When they took a vessel with four of South

Carolina's leading citizens on board, Blackbeard had a bold new idea. He locked up the passengers. He sent some of his men ashore to bargain with the lives of the prisoners for drugs and medicines needed by the pirate surgeon.

The governor and council had no naval vessels to call on for aid. They rushed out a boat with supplies demanded by the pirates. The prisoners were released and Blackbeard sailed merrily away northward. Stede Bonnet had to admit that Blackbeard was the most daring pirate he had ever seen.

Blackbeard was pleased with his success. But he had saved his best trick for his fellow pirates. In June, the pirate ships entered North Carolina waters at Topsail (now Beaufort) Inlet. The crews, almost four hundred men, were eager to divide the booty from their voyage. Calling Bonnet to his cabin, Blackbeard proposed that his "partner" go to Bath Town and accept King George's recent offer. This was to pardon any pirate who turned himself in and took an oath to give up piracy.

Bonnet took the bait and hurried away in a small boat for Bath. He left the *Revenge* at the inlet. As soon as Bonnet was out of sight, Blackbeard called his best men together. He began loading his own ship with the most valuable plunder from the others. Stripping the other vessels of supplies and leaving many of the pirates stranded, he sailed rapidly out to sea. Instead of having to divide the wealth among hundreds, he would now have to split with less than 20. It was the master stroke of a master criminal.

Stede Bonnet received his pardon. He hurried back to the inlet to help divide the loot. But Blackbeard was gone! The stranded pirates, left without food or water, were storming for revenge. Angrily determined to have his fair share, Bonnet fitted out his own ship (he was lucky Blackbeard had left it!). He dashed away in pursuit of his faithless partner. But no trace of Blackbeard could be found. Bonnet, ignoring his oath to the king, had to be content with the prizes he was able to take as he searched. He had been thoroughly outwitted.

It spite of his bravery and energy, Stede Bonnet lacked the cunning and experience for life as a pirate. In late September, he made a fatal mistake. He entered Cape Fear River to make repairs on his ship. Reports of this reached Charleston, one hundred fifty miles south. There, many of the citizens still shook with fury over the treatment they had received from Blackbeard in May. An armed force of South Carolinians was sent to the Cape Fear. They found Bonnet and, after a sharp fight, took him and some of his crew prisoner. Bonnet escaped from his captors in late October but was caught near Charles-

Booty means captured goods.

George I became king of England following the death of Queen Anne in 1714.

A **prize** is a captured ship.

ton two weeks later. After a trial and conviction at Charleston, he was hanged on December 10.

In the meantime, Blackbeard had been up to more of his tricks. Having sailed to Bath, he received his pardon from Charles Eden, North Carolina's new governor. He gave his oath to give up piracy. He bought a fine house in Bath and married a local girl (said to be his fourteenth wife). He took up the pleasant life of a colonial gentleman. He threw expensive parties and gave handsome gifts of rum and sugar to his friends. He showed off valuable stolen goods, such as gold, jewelry, and clothes. Governor Eden, whose plantation lay just across the creek from Bath, is said to have conducted Blackbeard's wedding and to have become one of the pirate's best friends in North Carolina.

In spite of his oath, Blackbeard had no intention of giving up so profitable business as piracy. Instead, he made a base for his ship at nearby Plum Point. He continued to chase and

Stede Bonnet was hanged by authorities at Charleston, South Carolina, in December 1718.

rob small vessels using the Carolina sounds. Many complained to the governor and to Tobias Knight, chief judge in the colony. But their appeals were ignored. There were rumors of a tunnel from Eden's house to the shore. There, he could meet Blackbeard secretly and share in the stolen goods. The pirate, it seemed, could get away with anything in North Carolina.

By the end of his first summer at Bath, Blackbeard had tired of his new life and was restless for the sea. He told everyone that he was going on a trading voyage to the West Indies. He set sail in his ship down the Pamlico River. Not long afterward, he was back at Plum Point with a French merchantship as a prize. The ship had a cargo of sugar, cocoa, spices and other valuable wares. The governor held a court to determine whether Blackbeard could legally keep the stolen goods. No one was surprised when it was announced that he could. Some people whispered that the governor and Judge Knight shared a large amount of the stolen cargo.

An old woodcut shows Blackbeard (center) in the death struggle with Maynard during their encounter at Ocracoke in 1718.

Blackbeard was back at sea by early fall. He cruised from Philadelphia to Georgia and took frequent prizes. North Carolina ship merchants complained uselessly to Governor Eden. They said it was dangerous to go to sea with Blackbeard on the prowl. Chesapeake Bay mariners pled for help from Governor Spottswood of Virginia. They showed that as much as six weeks passed without a Virginia vessel leaving port. There were also other pirates operating off the Virginia coast and Carolina Banks. They were made more bold, perhaps, by the stories of Blackbeard's tender treatment in North Carolina.

Governor Spottswood finally concluded that something had to be done. He heard that Blackbeard's ship had just come into Ocracoke Inlet with its latest prize. The governor sent two Virginia sloops in pursuit of the pirate and his crew.

The sloops put to sea from the Virginia coast on November 17, 1718. They came within sight of Ocracoke four days later, towards evening. They remained at anchor that night. The next morning they began moving cautiously into shallow water. There, Blackbeard's ship lay in wait. One of the sloops, the *Ranger,* ran aground. The other, under the command of Lt. Robert Maynard, moved on alone. As it drew within his range, Blackbeard ran up his skull and crossbones flag. He let fly a round of cannonballs. They tore into the deck of the Virginia vessel, injuring 21 of its crew. Maynard ordered most of his men below deck to avoid being hit.

The Virginians drew within a few yards of the pirate, too close for Blackbeard to train his cannon on the sloop. He ordered his crew to begin hurling their "bombs"—bottles of gunpowder with fuses attached—onto the deck of the sloop. As the two ships came together, Maynard and his men came from below decks. They began firing muskets and pistols. Now was the moment in the fight that would decide the fates of Blackbeard and Maynard.

The pirate captain, pistol and cutlass in his hands, ordered his men to board the sloop for hand-to-hand combat. Suddenly, amid the screams of the wounded, the crack of pistols, and the smoke of bombs and guns, Maynard found himself face-to-face with the pirate. His black pigtails were swinging wildly among the smoking coils of the fuses that Blackbeard had hung from under his hat to add terror to his appearance.

At the same instant, each man fired at the other. Blackbeard missed his mark. But Maynard burned a hole through the pirate's thick body. As if untouched, Blackbeard roared forward, swinging his cutlass at Maynard. He snapped Maynard's own cutlass like a twig. He was drawing back to deliver the death blow when one of Maynard's men struck Blackbeard a sword blow in the throat. As Maynard watched in stricken awe, Blackbeard snatched another pistol from his belt, aimed, and toppled forward dead. His body was later found to have 25 wounds, including five from pistol balls.

The crew of the pirate ship, seeing their captain dead, gave up the fight. Some jumped overboard to try to swim ashore. Nine others lay dead on the sloop's bloody deck. Maynard added another measure of gore by cutting off Blackbeard's head. He tied it to his own ship's bowsprit. With the proof of victory swaying in the sea breeze, the Virginians set sail for Bath Town to report the good news.

Gore is blood.

A *bowsprit* is a beam or spar attached to the bow of a ship.

In the colony of North Carolina, shipping people received with joy the word of Blackbeard's death and the reopening of the sea lanes to peaceful trade. But Charles Eden and Tobias Knight feared for their own safety. A score of people had so far kept silent. They now saw their chance to bring to justice all those who had helped to make North Carolina the "rogues' harbor" it had been in recent years. Would a pirate's death bring down the government of the colony of North Carolina? Many people had hopes that it would.

Rogues are rascals.

A Change of Heart

After the Tuscarora War, the North Carolina colony was forced to make a fresh start from the ruins of battle. It was now independent of South Carolina and ruled by its own proprietary governor. The war had left the colony in a sad condition. Its eastern Indians were broken in body and spirit. Its white population was injured and exhausted. Plantations would have to be rebuilt, herds restored, fields replanted. The government was deeply in debt to those who had furnished help against the Indians. An epidemic of yellow fever in 1712 caused the death of Governor Hyde and other survivors of the Indian assault.

An *epidemic* is a widespread outbreak of disease.

In many respects, the years following 1713 were a time of progress in the rebuilding and renewed expansion of North Carolina. A new town, soon to be known as Edenton, was rising on the north shore of Albemarle Sound. Another, known as Beaufort, was being built on Bogue Sound, 40 miles south of New Bern. The town of New Bern, abandoned during the Indian War, was resettled by the remains of the Graffenried

An early woodcut shows Blackbeard's head swinging from the bowsprit of Maynard's sloop.

A *privateer* was a privately-owned ship (or a crewman on board one) authorized to be used for war or piracy.

A *cove* is a sheltered place along a coast.

colony and some of the more recent settlers. Bath enjoyed a good recovery. It even boasted a new law to prevent hogs from running loose in the streets. This was a welcomed improvement. An "age of peace and quietness," as some called it, was coming to North Carolina.

The colonial legislature met in 1715. It began to revise the laws of North Carolina. These would give it better government than in the past, when rebellion, war, and neglect by the Proprietors had cost so much. Harsh penalties were enacted against any who, like Cary or Culpeper in years gone by, might try again to rule the colony by force. All officials who handled public money were required to sign bonds. These guaranteed the colony against the loss of its money through personal mishandling. A new Vestry Act strengthened the Anglican Church. But Quakers and other dissenters from the Anglican creed were assured of the right to worship freely. They could hold office in the government.

Other laws of 1715 encouraged immigration to North Carolina. The laws promoted the building of roads, bridges, gristmills, sawmills, and ferries. Efforts were made to prevent further unfairness in dealings between whites and Indians. For the first time, the legal and administrative systems of England were becoming well adapted to the conditions of North Carolina.

The government of North Carolina had tried several times to discourage piracy and smuggling. For this the colony had a poor reputation. The Proprietors regarded these as the worst crimes committed. Such activities reduced the profits of the colony's owners. But the legislatures and governors in North Carolina somehow never seemed to be able to take effective action. Sothel and Eden were only two of several governors accused of tolerating piracy and even making profit from it.

The truth was that many North Carolinians disagreed with the Proprietors over the harm of smuggling. On this side of the ocean, England's strict trade laws were regarded as a bother and a nuisance. If the English could not resist being unreasonable about trade laws, the colonists thought it reasonable to find ways around the law. Many respected colonial merchants were engaged to some degree in smuggling illegal goods to and from the colonies. The English government encouraged privateering—the commissioning of private ships to seize or sink enemy vessels. It was only a short step from privateering to piracy. Besides, the pirates were a source of supplies that North Carolinians often found hard to get through legal channels. North Carolina, with its long Outer Banks and its thousand tiny creeks and coves for hiding places, was a pirate's delight.

In the end, the crippling of the pirate menace was brought about not by North Carolina's authorities, but by those of South Carolina and Virginia. In fact, the North Carolina government seemed to resent the help of nearby colonies. Besides the head of Blackbeard and other trophies, Lt. Maynard came into Bath in November 1718 with strong suspicions that North Carolina officials had aided the pirate. At Bath he learned that Chief Justice Knight had possession of the cargo Blackbeard had seized from the French ship some weeks earlier. The Virginians demanded the cargo for use as evidence in the trial of captured pirates. But Knight denied that he knew anything about it. When the goods were found in his barn, hidden under some hay, Knight made up a story. He said he thought Blackbeard was just an honest merchant, and he had only been storing merchandise for him.

Maynard took the recovered cargo and sailed with it back to Virginia. There, the trials of the pirates were held the following March. North Carolina officials protested that the Virginians had had no right to send their ships into North Carolina waters. They had no right to try the pirates in Virginia courts. But it looked as though the protests were made for fear of who might be caught in the net of criminal conspiracy.

One piece of evidence at the Virginia trials was a letter found by Maynard on Blackbeard's ship. In it, Tobias Knight had hinted a warning to "My Friend" Blackbeard about the Virginia expedition. It made reference to Governor Eden's

Blackbeard lived for a while at Bath and was probably aided in his piracy by members of the Carolina government.

friendship for the pirate. Some of the pirates on trial testified that Knight had shared in the stolen goods.

All these things were now made public. Governor Eden could not avoid calling his council together to investigate the suspicions of official wrongdoing. Knight was given a hearing. He explained that his letter to Blackbeard had been misunderstood and that, in any case, it had been sent at Eden's instructions. Others gave evidence that seemed to strengthen the case against the chief justice—if not the governor as well. But the council saw it all as a plot against "a good and faithful officer." Knight was found innocent. The case was closed before the facts could be turned against the governor himself.

Stede Bonnet and 48 other pirates were hanged in South Carolina in 1718. This, with the execution of most of the survivors of Blackbeard's crew in Virginia in 1719, all but broke up piracy on the Atlantic coast. Never again would a pirate find it safe to operate on the North Carolina coast. Danger to mariners soon disappeared. Charles Eden died in office in 1722. But the memory of him and his chief justice was forever stained by the court of public opinion. There, both were judged guilty. For pirates, as for rebels, North Carolina could no longer be considered a "rogues' harbor," at least not for those of a seafaring kind.

The end of the pirate menace to North Carolina was but one of the many ways that progress came to the colony in the years following the Tuscarora War. Within ten years or so after Blackbeard's death, a road was opened from the Neuse to the Cape Fear River frontier, a hundred miles south. Harbors were dredged, ferries established, and court houses and jails were constructed. Immigration reached the rate of a thousand families a year. New counties had to be created for the rising population. Bertie and Carteret were founded in 1722, Tyrrell and New Hanover, in 1729.

An Irish doctor, John Brickell, lived at Edenton and elsewhere along the North Carolina coast for a few years before returning to Ireland in 1731. He wrote a book about the colony. Like Lawson, whose *New Voyage to Carolina* he copied at length, Brickell was full of praise for North Carolina's soil and climate. But he also could boast of the delivery of mails to and from Virginia "in two or three Days and from some places in a few Hours." He claimed that "Provisions and Naval Stores never fail of a good Market" in North Carolina. He wrote that he had seen produced there "as good Brick as any I have met with in Europe." He had seen "plenty of Horses

The town of Edenton is named for Governor Eden, but was known before 1722 as Queen Anne's Town.

Naval stores were materials used in ship building, such as lumber and tar.

Stede Bonnet, one-time partner of Blackbeard, was captured
on the Cape Fear River in 1718.

. . . Carts and Wagons'' travelling on roads ''as good as in most
parts of the World . . . , especially the Road from Edenton to
Virginia, being broad and convenient, for all sorts of Car-
riages. . . .''

In 1728, the long-standing boundary line dispute with Virginia was finally settled in a way that pleased North Carolinians. Each colony appointed four commissioners. These, together with their work crew, met at Currituck Inlet in March
1728. Although the Carolina party broke off earlier, the Virginians stayed with the work until late October. The line ended
at the present Stokes County, North Carolina, 233 weary miles
west of its starting point. To the displeasure of the Virginians,
the line was found to run somewhat north of where they had
hoped it would. A good many settlers formerly regarded as
living in Virginia now found that they were in North Carolina.

The boundary line expedition was also notable for an excellent book. It was written by William Byrd, head of the Virginia surveying party. Byrd kept a private journal of the expedition. He made daily entries about the Indians along the
route. He noted the animal and vegetable life, the rivers, forests, mountains, and so on. For more than half the distance
covered by the surveyors, there were also frontier families,
both black and white, with whom the surveyors found lodgings whenever they could.

Progress was made by North Carolina following the Tuscarora War and the break-up of piracy. However, the colony remained to many people of refinement and sensitivity a place of sin, sickness, and savagery. The letters of the Anglican missionaries, who had been sent to convert pioneers to the Gospel, told gruesome stories of the ungodliness of the society they served. The Reverend John Urmstone wrote home to England in 1715. He said that the Lords Proprietors "ought to be ashamed" of the colony. They wanted others to do "as Lawson did write a whole volume in praise of such a worthless place: he has had his reward. . . ." Even after he had returned home in 1721, Urmstone continued to complain. He wrote that North Carolina was "inhabited by the dregs and gleanings of all the English Colonies. . . ."

Dregs and gleanings means worthless people.

What probably offended well-bred people more than anything else was the rude style of life. This went hand in hand with the hardships of the frontier. Most settlers of the early eighteenth century were people of humble background. They were almost entirely without education or refined upbringing. In such a society, even those few who had such advantages were likely to take on the character of those about them. Colonial leaders often complained to England, for example, of how the Anglican ministers among them took so readily to liquor and other vices. They soon became worthless to the Church.

Crude as they were, these pioneers were often intelligent and hard working. They made an important contribution to the progress of the colony. They were the kind of people who could clear forests, build roads, and make a life for themselves. This was often done on a piece of land 20 and more miles from their nearest neighbor. But many lived on the brink of riot and anarchy. At any moment they might break out in personal violence against one another.

The last two proprietary governors of North Carolina illustrated the peculiar mixture of good and bad qualities that were typical in these years of so many of the colonists. George Burrington was appointed to succeed Eden as governor. He arrived in the colony to begin his new duties at the beginning of 1724. But he was only able to hold onto the governor's office for a little over a year. He got into trouble with other leaders in the colony when he took the side of the popular party in the Assembly against the government party, the proprietary agents, and their sympathizers. To the latter, it was a form of treason when Burrington announced that he would allow the sale of land within 20 miles of Cape Fear River. This was in spite of the Proprietors' ruling against it.

Treason means a crime against one's country.

His enemies circulated ugly stories about Burrington.

They said he had been in jail in England, that there was "not a worse Rogue and Villain in the world." Chief Justice Christopher Gale became leader of the government party. He came into sharp conflict with the governor. Gale soon went to England where he complained to the Proprietors that Burrington had put him "in bodily fear of his life." Burrington threatened to cut off his ears, blow up his house, and put him in irons. Gale's wife added that the governor had come to her house on a Sunday morning. He began to smash windows and swear that "he would have the dogg her husband by the throat."

These tales about Burrington were probably exaggerated. The Proprietors, besides, had no doubt long since ceased to be surprised at anything they heard about the goings-on in North Carolina. There were rumors that Burrington intended to start a revolution in their colony. This led them to replace him in 1725 with Sir Richard Everard.

A ***baronet*** was a British title of distinction or honor, a nobleman.

Although he was a baronet, Everard was a disgrace to the governor's office. He caused Burrington's enemies to long for his return. A strutting, ill-tempered, dim-wit of a man, Everard was constantly involved in outrageous incidents. In the streets of Edenton in 1726, Everard witnessed a fight between John Lovick and Edmund Porter. They were two of the leading men of the province. Porter shook his fist in the governor's face. He called him worthless, dared him to draw his sword, and threatened to raise a rebellion against him. The governor later had a fist fight with Lovick. In 1729, he was called into court over his dispute with Robert Pearce. It seems that the governor had come to the window of Pearce's lodgings one night. He had broken the glass, fired several shots at Pearce, broken open a nailed door, and fired more shots. None of the bullets hit Pearce. But the gun was close enough at one point to cause powder burns on his face and hands.

George Burrington, still living at Edenton, announced that Sir Richard was "no more fitt to be Governor . . . than a Hogg in the Woods and that he . . . is a Noodle and an ape. . . ." When these compliments failed to draw any thanks from the governor, Burrington went to Sir Richard's house. As a court record told it, Burrington "called him the sayd Sr. Richard calves head" and said he would "scalp your . . . thick skull." With the governor and ex-governor acting in this way, ordinary citizens must have felt that the law of the jungle had at least as much authority here as the laws of England.

Burrington was far the more capable of the two men. But Everard and Burrington were no better or worse than many of their subjects in North Carolina. They were stormy and un-

Christopher Gale served as Chief Justice of North Carolina for several terms prior to his death in 1718.

ruly men. So was their society—a society in which the rule of law and the reign of order were still not taken for granted. Both of them were, in many respects, typical of their time and place.

The End of the Proprietary

The administration of Richard Everard helped to bring about the most far-reaching change in the government of North Carolina since the founding of the colony in 1663. During his term, the colony's government became a disgrace. Many began to hope the Proprietors might give up their charter to the king and let North Carolina be ruled directly by the Crown.

The English Crown had for many years been interested in such a change. South Carolina had already become a royal colony. The Proprietors of North Carolina had not found their ownership of the colony to be a profitable or agreeable one. In January 1728, Everard was at the height of his foolishness. Seven of the Proprietors petitioned King George II to allow them to sell their interest in North Carolina to the Crown. An Act of Parliament made the transfer of authority legal. In 1729, the King paid the seven Proprietors twenty-five hundred pounds each for their rights. John Carteret, later the Earl of

Pounds means British money.

The Granville District included all of North Carolina from the present Virginia line to a point some sixty miles south of the line. This was considered an eighth of the original proprietary grant, including both the Carolinas.

Granville, while giving up any claim to political authority in North Carolina, decided to hold onto his claim to one eighth of the land. In 1744, a large area known as the Granville District was marked off for him. North Carolinians learned with joy and celebrations that they had become a royal colony. They had good reason to cheer. North Carolina was about to experience great new progress. The year 1729 was a turning point in North Carolina's history.

The proprietary phase of North Carolina's history ended in scenes of personal violence and name-calling. However, there were signs of a social and political maturity in the colony. These were not present 50, or even 20 years earlier. The disputes that led to successful rebellion in 1679 and to unsuccessful rebellion in 1711 now amounted only to private battles. They fell short of threats to the political structure. There were serious disagreements among various factions in North Carolina. But people thought less in the 1720s of settling these disagreements by armed uprisings. It was probably not so much that the colonists had changed very much. It was the existence of means other than warfare through which many problems could be solved. The proprietary period did not bring the blessings of good government to North Carolina. But it did reflect a gradual trend for the government to be less bad. Perhaps with the king in charge of things, that trend would gain momentum. Perhaps the colony could actually begin to hope for a time when its government would be admired and respected.

Chapter Checkup

PEOPLE

Blackbeard	Stede Bonnnet	George Burrington
John Carteret	Charles Eden	Christopher Gale
Robert Maynard	Tobias Knight	Richard Everard

PLACES

Cape Fear River	Topsail (Beaufort) Inlet	Beaufort
Ocracoke Inlet	Edenton	Currituck Inlet

FACT

How was the pirate menace finally broken up on the North Carolina coast?
How did the geography of North Carolina's coast help the pirates?
What did North Carolinians think of smuggling?
Why did the Lords Proprietors think smuggling was one of the worst of crimes?

INTERPRETATION

In what ways had North Carolina experienced progress since the time of Culpeper and Durant? What were its major failings in the time of Blackbeard?

VOCABULARY

Privateer   Treason   Maritime

ACTIVITY

Make up an original code message giving directions about how to locate treasure Blackbeard might have buried on the N.C. coast. In class, exchange yours with someone else and see if you can figure out each other's message.

SUGGESTED READING

Lefler, Hugh T. and Powell, William S. *Colonial North Carolina, A History.* New York: Charles Scribner's Sons, 1973. Pages 81–86 relates piracy to general expansion and unification of the colony of North Carolina.
Rankin, Hugh F. *The Golden Age of Piracy.* New York: Holt, Rinehart and Winston, 1969. Fine account of early 18th century pirates and their activities.
Rankin, Hugh F. *The Pirates of Colonial North Carolina.* Raleigh: State Dept. of Archives, and History, 1960. Brief survey of early 18th century piracy along North Carolina coast.

1724 Burrington becomes governor

1726 Settlement of Cape Fear progresses

1729 North Carolina becomes a royal colony

1734 Gabriel Johnston becomes governor

1739 War of Jenkins' Ear begins

1740 King George's War begins

1744 Westward expansion begins

1746 Assembly limits each county to two votes

1747 Spanish Alarm

1748 Spanish ships attack Brunswick

1752 Death of Governor Johnston

1754 French and Indian War begins

5

THE GOOSE CREEK FACTION

A Cape Fear Jaunt

The Cape Fear refers to the area bordering the Cape Fear River.

The earl was going to be a hard man to please. It was bad enough trying to find pregnant opossums to ship to England—but a pair of buffaloes! This was asking a great deal, especially since buffaloes were rarely seen on the Cape Fear. Gabriel Johnston didn't mind packing plants and saplings for the Earl of Wilmington. But he hoped he would not have to stock the parks and gardens of the earl and all his friends. Serving as governor of North Carolina promised to be a big enough job as it was.

But the wishes of the earl would have to be granted. He had nominated Johnston for the governor's office. He was arranging for him to receive large grants of North Carolina lands. If he demanded, along with everything else, long letters of information about the country, Johnston would have to find time to answer the earl's questions. What the earl gave he could also take away. Buffaloes he wanted. Buffaloes he would get.

The Earl of Wilmington, *an English nobleman*

Gabriel Johnston, *Governor of North Carolina*

John Lapierre, *Cape Fear's first Anglican preacher*

Roger Moore, *a wealthy and powerful landowner*

Richard Marsden, *a preacher and tradesman*

Cornelius Harnett *(the elder), an innkeeper and landowner*

Henry McCulloh, *a London merchant*

"Botanick dress" means using botanical or scientific language.

Fortunately, a great deal of information could be gathered without much effort. Some travelers had already gone far up both branches of the Cape Fear River. They returned and told what they saw. Johnston himself had gone a good distance by boat along both branches. In the fall of 1734, an Englishman was at Brunswick Town who could tell Johnston much about the upper reaches of the northwest branch. This was beyond where Johnston's own lands were being laid out. There was also young Hugh Meredith. He was the Pennsylvanian who had written for Benjamin Franklin's newspaper about the Cape Fear and its settlements. Between these two, Johnston could answer many of the earl's questions. Johnston hoped the earl would "be so good as to excuse my [not] putting it in botanick dress, with long-sounding Greek and Roman names, which have always thrown me into convulsions."

The Englishman (nobody knows now what his name was) had delightful stories to tell about his upriver trek. He had started from Brunswick Town on the lower part of the river in mid-June. He had gone up to "Kendall" plantation, two miles beyond, for a brief stay as a guest of Roger Moore. On June 20, he left Kendall in company with Roger's brother, Nathaniel. They continued on horseback, swinging northwest at the fork and striking off into the forest that rimmed the river. There were already some great estates along the route. Ten years before, no white man had ever set foot there. One of the first places on the river above Moore's was the farm that had lately belonged to the Rev. John Lapierre.

People along the river still buzzed over the trials of Lapierre. He had come there in 1728 to serve as Cape Fear's first Anglican preacher. But he ran into trouble trying to collect his salary from his congregations. He had trouble with a

90

rascal preacher named Richard Marsden. In 1732, Marsden began offering services at his own home at no charge. This was a price the Cape Fear Anglicans were happy to pay. Lapierre was soon out of business. He struggled on for a few months by working his farm. But finally he had to sell practically everything he owned in order to feed and care for his family. Now he was gone. But his letters to his superiors still rang with bitter words against Marsden and the people of Cape Fear.

Pock-marked means scarred by smallpox or similar disease.

Richard Marsden, a tall, stoop-shouldered, pockmarked man, was a lovable scoundrel. He was an excellent preacher. But the strictest church members held it against him that he earned his living as a tradesman. This shocked some people. His background was not known in the fall of 1734. But it was later found that he had many outraged colonial and European merchants after him for unpaid debts. He was finally dismissed from the ministry in 1739, but only after Gabriel Johnston and others had embarrassed themselves by their loyalty to him. Johnston may have been speaking of Marsden when he complained to the earl. He said that, in Cape Fear, "a cheat of the first magnitude is treated with all the distinction

Magnitude means size or degree.

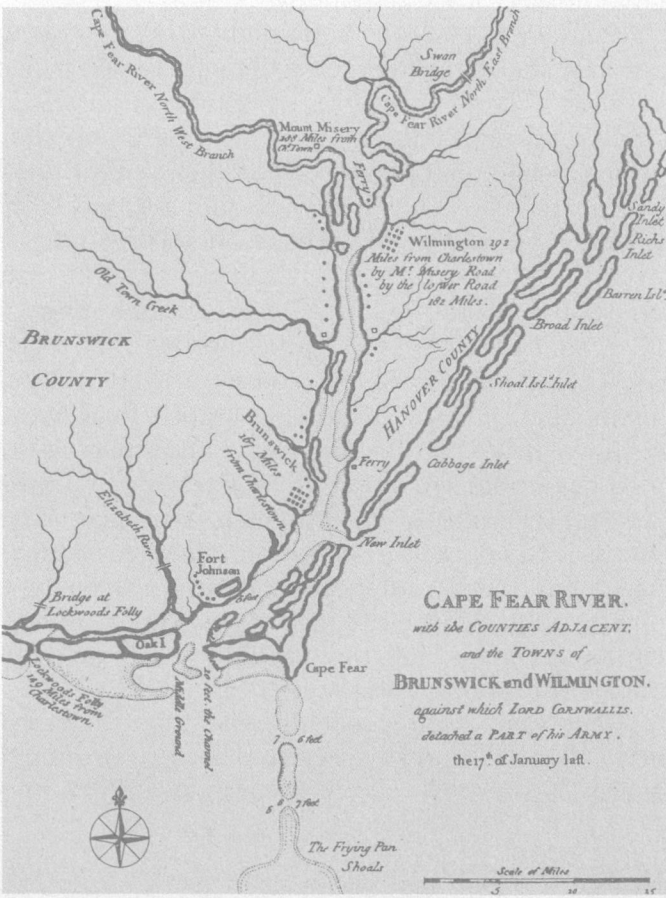

This early map shows Wilmington, Brunswick, and other sites along the two branches of the Cape Fear River.

Orton, one of the earliest homes built on the Cape Fear
River, was the home of "King Roger" Moore, head of
"The Family."

Yarns are stories.

To plague is to worry
someone.

and regard which is usually paid to men of merit . . . in other
parts of the world."

Leaving Lapierre's, Nathaniel Moore and his English companion rode on through the woods and the various plantation
clearings. They visited the handsome plantation of Captain
Gabourell, one of the greatest merchants on the river. Here
were no less than five vessels loading lumber for the West Indies, a sign of greater things to come. Beyond Gabourell's, the
travelers passed Mount Misery before coming to the lands
owned by Cornelius Harnett. Harnett was the innkeeper and
ferryman at Brunswick. He had some fine yarns to tell about
the years he had spent at Edenton. He told of tricks he and
George Burrington had played on Sir Richard Everard and on
one another. His son, also named Cornelius, was still only an
eleven-year-old. But he was destined to plague the last of the
royal governors even more than his father had the first one.

From Harnett's, the travelers had ridden on to Roger
Moore's "Blue Banks" plantation. There, the owner was thinking of building another brick mansion even more imposing
than Kendall. The bluff there was 100 or more feet high. It
overlooked a vast meadow on the other side of the river and
much of the countryside around.

The travelers, approaching the outer fringes of the settlements along the northwest branch, next day dined with John
Davis. They looked over the nearby sawmill, one of the few in

92

the province. Davis had a Dutch-style house with one front on the river. Another faced the woods behind, through which the owner had recently cut a two-mile-long avenue. By 2:00 P.M., the travelers were off again. By evening they had reached Nathaniel Moore's own estate, 40 miles above Brunswick. This was almost the last place before the Welsh and Palatine settlements 40 miles further along. A 100-ton South Carolina sloop lay there loading corn. This was the finest corn the Englishman said he had ever seen. Moore predicted that ocean-going ships would be able to go much farther once the stream was cleared of the fallen logs and trees that now blocked passage.

The Englishman's many notes on the northwest branch were matched by those of Hugh Meredith for the northeast branch. The latter arm of Cape Fear reached far up through Onslow Precinct into unsettled parts of Bath County. It passed many large plantations along its way. Far upriver lay the plantation of David Evans. He was a Delaware native who accompanied Meredith on his long canoe trip of 1731 back

The Cape Fear River Region, 1730

down the river to Brunswick. The sandy soil along this branch was widely planted in beans, potatoes, squash, and pumpkins. There was a wonderful Indian corn that grew in stalks up to 18 feet high and produced almost 100 bushels an acre.

Gabriel Johnston had to depend much on fur trappers, Indian traders, and the like for data about the upper river. He could, however, rely on his own observations to describe the lower parts of the river for the Earl of Wilmington. In the nine years since George Burrington camped here, "above a hundred miles from a Neighbor in a pathless country," there had developed fine farms and river landings, as well as two new towns. The older town was Brunswick, on the south side of the river. It had its own ferry, tavern, and 15 or 20 houses. It had an anchorage deep enough for ships of 50 or 60 tons. Quarterly sessions of court met here, but Hugh Meredith called it "a poor, hungry, unprovided Place." Most people agreed that the swamps nearby made it one of the unhealthiest spots in the colony.

A few miles upriver from Brunswick, and on the north side, was the newer town—a hamlet, really. This was known to some as New Liverpool and to others as New Town or Newton. As yet, it was only a tiny cluster of log huts. But already it was starting to lure some of the shipping business away from Brunswick. The two places were developing a frantic rivalry with each other. Some years would occur before this town, by then known as Wilmington, surpassed Brunswick.

Johnston's letters to the Earl of Wilmington spoke highly of the prospects for wealth and progress along the Cape Fear River. But he was sorry to see how little the inhabitants appreciated the promise of the region. Forty-two loaded ships had left the river in 1734 for foreign ports. But the settlers were, for the most part, "the lowest scum and rabble." They lived in "a rich and fruitfull country, where with very small labour they can build themselves sorry huts, and live in a beastly sort of plenty and all the rest of their time devoted to . . . lying, tricking and cheating; a people into whose heads no human means can beat the notion of a public interest. . . ."

Even so, Johnston had to admit that there were a few "men of integrity and candor" who might succeed in building the Cape Fear into a great market. Among those whose estates bordered the lower river were, besides Roger Moore, his neighbor Eleazer Allen at "Lilliput" plantation. Across the river lived James Wimble at "Wimble's Castle." Some were experimenting with hemp and mulberry trees (for silk). Some tried winemaking and other ways to add to the business of the

*A **hamlet** is a very small village.*

***Candor** means honesty.*

The Earl of Wilmington took a keen interest in the Cape Fear settlement and was a valued friend of Governor Gabriel Johnston.

A *faction* is a group which is part of a larger group.

river. They had armies of slaves at work clearing land, building wharves, and in other ways hacking a settlement out of the wilderness. It was, indeed, a rich man's country. The business of the Cape Fear River was under the control of a tight little group of powerful men. They were willing, if need be, to defy governments to build the kind of settlement they wanted.

The lords of Cape Fear were mostly related to one another by marriage. They were known throughout the colony as "The Family." They included Edward Moseley, Jehu Davis, Samuel Swann, and the three Moore brothers—Roger, Nathaniel, and Maurice. Among them, they owned an empire of more than eighty thousand acres of land. More than half of it belonged to Maurice and Roger Moore. So wealthy and powerful was the latter brother that he was known in the Carolinas as "King Roger." This title was soon to have more meaning because of the palace he was to build for himself near Kendall. The new place was to be known as "Orton." It would have two-feet-thick brick walls lined with loopholes. Through these, guns could be fired at attacking Indians or pirates. Orton was built to protect its owner against the storms of man and nature. It was magnificent with its giant trees hung with Spanish moss. It would be the only one of these great plantation houses to survive the centuries. However, it was much altered by later additions.

The Moores had been among the great men of South Carolina long before they began building their Cape Fear empire in the 1720s. They and others of the Cape Fear settlers were known in South Carolina as the "Goose Creek Faction," North Carolina's leading landholders. By 1734, they were so well established that Gabriel Johnston could not be certain of controlling them. The optimistic young Scotsman began his term of office with the hope that, as he told the earl, "with a little assistance from home," he would "be able to make a mighty change in the face of affairs. . . ."

Two years later, he could say to the earl that events had "cur'd me of my mistake."

The Second Colony

Up to 1724, the Cape Fear country defied every attempt by whites to make a permanent settlement. In the 1690s, the Bartram family from Pennsylvania was captured by the Indians while trying to establish a plantation. Around 1715, the family of Thomas James, also of Pennsylvania, was killed at the Cape Fear by Indians. In 1724, there were few Indians left. But the Proprietors still managed to discourage settlers. They required that all applications for Cape Fear grants come directly through themselves.

When George Burrington became governor in 1724, he chose to ignore the Proprietors. He issued Cape Fear grants on his own authority. Only in this way could North Carolina's best waterway be used to promote the growth of the colony. Burrington also made several trips to the Cape Fear. He explored the country, charted the river's channels, and began a road to connect the Cape Fear with the northern counties. He took possession of a ten-thousand-acre tract called "Stagg Park" for himself. He also began issuing large grants to those who promised to set to work at once to develop them.

Four people in particular gained from Burrington's Cape Fear policy. These were Roger Moore and Eleazer Allen, whose wives were sisters, and John Porter and Maurice Moore (Roger's brother), who had also wed sisters. It was this pattern of relations that was the foundation of The Family. It was later extended by intermarriage with other powerful people. For many years afterward they were the rulers of the Cape Fear. Because of their blood-ties, The Family was somewhat like a political party. It could stand as a united front against other groups or other sections of the colony whose loyalties were less firm.

Settlement of the Cape Fear was in full swing by the late spring of 1726. By that time Maurice Moore had settled there. He had mapped the town of Brunswick and started to sell town lots. Others followed rapidly. These were not only members of The Family, but groups of lesser South Carolinians who were unhappy with the policies of their own government. There was even talk of a third colony on the Cape Fear, which would have been independent of both the Carolinas. The talk was cut short when North Carolina became a royal colony in 1729. Richard Everard continued the Cape Fear policy of Burrington. By 1731, there were 23 persons who had acquired more than a hundred thousand acres there, besides a few with smaller grants.

The Cape Fear "honeymoon" ended for The Family with Burrington's appointment as the first royal governor in 1731. When Burrington came back to North Carolina after some months in England, he found that certain members of The Family had tried to cheat him out of his Stagg Park plantation. Burrington's inborn hatred of self-importance rose up inside him. He declared war, in effect, on the whole Cape Fear faction. He set out with all the energy he had to break the power of The Family. It was the beginning of one of early North Carolina's longest and bitterest feuds.

A *feud* is a fight or quarrel.

Burrington had a weapon to use in his struggle against The Family. It was the Crown's permission for him to reclaim for the government any grants not cultivated within a reasonable time. He charged that possession of so much land by so few people denied the right of settlement to many small farmers or others who might wish to settle along the river. Albemarle planters and businesspeople, jealous of the rapid rise of The Family, supported Burrington in his campaign.

The Family recognized Burrington's threat to its power. It was possible to cultivate only small parts of the huge tracts they claimed. The governor might take away most of the domain they had won. They argued that they had brought the first farms, ferries, and commerce to the Cape Fear. They felt they were entitled to the thanks of the government for their pioneering work.

The dispute between Burrington and The Family was more of a personal and political rivalry than a real disagreement over the best way to develop the Cape Fear. Even Burrington recognized that the river country was not suitable for small farms. It would probably have to be developed as large tracts of forest land for the naval stores industry. It was almost certain that The Family would acquire immense estates and power. The trick for Burrington and his successors was to prevent that power from taking over the whole colony. The aim of The Family was to turn Burrington and any others who stood in their way out of office.

The man who took over this state of affairs in 1734 did not seem to be well qualified to bring it to a peaceful solution. A glance at Gabriel Johnston's previous career did not show any experience that might help him steer a successful course between powerful and ruthless rivals. He had been the editor of a London literary magazine and a professor of Hebrew at a Scottish university. He studied for a master's degree in theology in Scotland and a medical degree in Holland. In this there was no evidence of a crafty politician. There were those months he had served in the municipal government of Glasgow, Scotland. But it seemed a safe bet that the young professor would be run out of class by his new pupils before the bells sounded recess.

Ruthless means without mercy.

Crafty means smart or shrewd.

Gabriel Johnston had, however, certain qualities that might have been overlooked in 1734. He had a strong and well-trained mind. He also had a gift for tact in his dealings

This sketch of an unidentified colonist was found inside the cover of an early volume of North Carolina court records.

Endurance is the ability to keep going.

Quitrents were so called because the settler was "quit" of any further obligation to the Proprietors once it was paid.

with people. This was rare in a North Carolina governor. Most importantly, he had a sense of how to play two sides against each other. Even these qualities would not save the colony from severe crises in the years ahead. But Gabriel Johnston was destined to remain in office until his death 18 years later. His record of endurance has never been equaled.

Most of the problems with which Johnston had to deal were related to the old Proprietary constitution of the 1660s and the efforts of the northern leaders to block any departures from its terms. Johnston demanded, for example, that quit-rents be paid at central points instead of at the payer's house. He required cash rather than the produce that had been used before. Five hundred people in Bertie and Edgecombe Counties "rose in arms." They threatened violence against any who came to collect.

A compromise was reached on the issue. South Carolina was persuaded to give up its claim to that part of North Carolina lying on the south side of Cape Fear River. But the issue that refused to die was that of representation. It was this issue that tore the colony apart in spite of Gabriel Johnston's best efforts.

The five oldest counties lay in the northern part of the colony. Since 1668, they had enjoyed the right to elect five representatives to each Assembly. Newer counties to the south, at first thinly populated, had only two delegates each. That figure was not raised as these counties gained population. This meant that the five older counties kept control of the legislature long after they had fewer of the citizens of the colony. But northern leaders fought attempts to change representation.

Johnston agreed with The Family and others that representation in the Assembly was unjust. But it was not easy to decide what to do about it. In 1741, the governor announced that the Assembly would meet that year at Wilmington. Meeting so far south, most of the northern members would not be able to attend. Those delegates who did come could change the law of representation to suit themselves. But enough northern delegates managed to reach Wilmington to prevent the scheme from succeeding. In 1746, the governor tried again. This time bad weather prevented all the northern delegates from reaching Wilmington. The Assembly voted to limit each county to two votes. One additional member was to be added from each of the major towns—Edenton, New Bern, Bath, and Wilmington, the so-called "borough" towns. Also, New Bern was chosen as the permanent site for the Assembly's sessions—the colonial capital.

The stage was now set for the showdown of 1747. In that year, the northern counties elected five representatives each, as they always had. These delegates demanded recognition at New Bern. They claimed that the representation act of 1746 was not valid until the Crown approved it. The governor and his supporters refused recognition. The northern delegates quit the session. For the next seven years, the northern counties boycotted the Assembly. They refused to pay any attention to its enactments. Other counties, unwilling to take upon themselves the whole tax burden of the colony, took only a limited part in the business of government. By the time Johnston died in 1752, one observer reported that "much confusion reigned" in North Carolina, especially in the older counties. Crimes went unpunished, people refused to serve on juries, jails were broken open. ". . . in short," he wrote, " 'fist law' is about all that is left."

The dispute had slowly been working its way toward the attention of the English Crown. In 1754, King George II finally decided that four of the northern counties should have five delegates each—Bertie three, and the others two each. Each borough town should have one. This might have seemed to some a victory for the northern counties. But they had lost two valuable seats. In addition, the governor could now create new counties as often as he saw fit. It meant that the northern

Valid means lawful.

Boycotted means refused to attend.

counties would grow less and less influential in the colonial Assembly. The representation was still unfair. But new issues soon drew people's attention elsewhere.

Sections and Classes

During the 1730s, the Albemarle and the lower Cape Fear remained locked in disputes. At that time, a tide of immigrants poured into the colony. It surpassed anything in previous years. Two colonies of Welsh settled far up on the Cape Fear around 1730. Waves of Highland Scots followed them into the same region. This included three hundred fifty who arrived together in 1739. The government was pleased to have these industrious settlers. Urged by its Scottish governor, it voted to relieve the newcomers of taxes for ten years. An uprising in Scotland was crushed by the English in Scotland in 1746. This led to further immigration by Scots to North Carolina.

Meanwhile, a large number of German and Scotch-Irish started moving down the "Great Wagon Road" from Pennsylvania into North Carolina. Most of them settled in the western part of the North Carolina Piedmont. This was well to the west of the deepest eastern settlements. Here they soon developed a good business in indigo, flax, and other products, which they exported through Charleston.

Many of the new colonists in the Cape Fear backcountry were helped in their immigration by a London merchant named Henry Eustace McCulloh. With his associates, he became the largest investor ever in North Carolina lands. He gambled that rising values and prices would repay him many times over. The McCulloh group acquired over a million acres of land in large tracts. These were scattered widely about the colony. The group began to sell tracts to settlers in small amounts. In 1736, they arranged for the settlement of some poor families of Protestant Irish on the northeast branch of Cape Fear. Some Swiss colonists from South Carolina settled nearby.

New counties reflected the rising population in both the west and east—Onslow, Edgecombe, and Bladen in 1734, Northampton in 1741, Granville and Johnston in 1746. The colony expanded more in 15 years than it had in the previous 75.

The colony continued to expand through the 1730s and 1740s. Some people began to notice differences between set-

Scotch-Irish were Scots who had made their homes in Ireland.

"Great Wagon Road" was a route beginning near Philadelphia and running south into western North Carolina.

Indigo is a plant used in making dyes.

Flax is a plant used in making cloth.

The dense forests along the Cape Fear produced lumber, tar, turpentine, and other materials used in ship building.

tlers in the west and those in the eastern counties. Instead of small plantations, these new settlers mostly occupied small farms of a few hundred acres. Instead of many slaves working in fields and forests, the more recent colonists owned few slaves or none. These and other differences took on political meaning. It led western delegates in the Assembly to oppose bills sponsored by the East. It became clear that this was a basic new fact in the life of the colony. The people of the Albemarle and Cape Fear began to feel that they had more in common with one another than with the western groups. This awareness of regional differences and loyalties, called sectionalism, became a permanent element in North Carolina life.

Besides the differences between sections, North Carolina had by now developed other differences. These did not depend much on where one lived. One in very four persons was a slave. But there were also free blacks and persons of mixed ancestry. Some were part Indian, part white, part black, or combinations of all three. A lower class of white people made up the hunters and trappers, the unskilled laborers, the sailors, and the poorest farmers. The middle class, the largest class in the colony, was composed mostly of people who owned large farms. These people could afford some cattle and a few good tools. If not farmers, they were tradespeople, skilled workers, or clerks. The "planter class"—people like the members of the Cape Fear Family—were the ruling group. They often split into subgroups among themselves. But they were always conscious of their wealth and position. Lawyers, great merchants, ship owners, ministers, and doctors mingled with this group. They married its daughters and took its side in class disputes.

Few people saw anything wrong with this system of class differences. However, most would gladly have traded their own status for a higher one. English and European society had given the colonists a heritage of class distinctions that the great majority took for granted. It was assumed that some people were born to rule society. But they had an obligation to behave decently toward those less fortunate. Everybody wanted all the social and political freedom they could get. However, this didn't mean that all should be equal.

And yet, much depended on the ability of the ruling class to hold the respect of the classes beneath it. If the behavior of the mighty became too arrogant and self-important, there was likelihood that resentment could rise up and boil over in the hearts of ordinary men and women. These people's ancestors had survived the Peasants' Revolt of 1381, Wat Tyler's Rebellion, and the Scottish revolts of 1715 and 1745. In the western

Heritage means tradition.

The work of slaves was hard and their food and clothing were often inadequate. Women worked alongside men in heavy labor.

settlements, grand ladies and self-important gentlemen were very few. It was not hard to stir up resentment there against great people who misbehaved.

The expansion of the Carolina colonies was one of many sources of trouble in these years between England and its old European rivals, Spain and France. To the south of the Carolinas lay Spanish Florida. To the west was a vast French territory. There, trading stations on the Mississippi River sent agents to the very fringes of the new English settlements near the Appalachians. Further expansion in either direction could become a cause for conflict.

England's rivalry with Spain in the West Indies and elsewhere led to war. This conflict was known as the War of Jenkins' Ear. A certain Jenkins, captain of a British ship, was said to have been captured by the Spaniards. His ear was cut off and he was set adrift with his crew, and war broke out in 1739. It dragged on for more than ten years, merging into the war of Austrian Succession. Spain remained England's enemy throughout the years of shifting alliances and motives.

Up to 1741, North Carolina was involved in the war only through its young men recruited for service in the West Indies and some economic aid furnished at the request of King George II. But Spanish ships menaced the coastal waters. Sometimes they captured North Carolina prizes, discouraging the colony's commerce. In 1741, the Spaniards actually built a fort on Ocracoke Island. They began harassing the colonists by land and sea. An English privateer chased them off and destroyed the fort. But Spanish ships remained a problem.

In 1747 came the "Spanish Alarm." In June, Spanish privateers sailed into Beaufort harbor and captured several English vessels. In August, they came again. They took control of the town for three days before leaving with their loot. There were landings at Ocracoke, Core Sound, and other places. The invaders carried off slaves and cattle. Clearly, North Carolina was unable to defend itself. The Spaniards prepared for still bolder operations.

On September 4, 1748, the people of Brunswick were startled to see two Spanish privateers sailing up the Cape Fear toward their town. When Spanish landing parties rushed into the streets of the town, terrified people fled into the nearby woods and swamps. They organized a counterattack two days later. But the Spaniards, returning to their ship (one had continued upriver), now began to bombard the town. They threatened to leave it in ruins. The colonists took cover. Suddenly a fire broke out on the deck of the Spanish ship. Moments later it exploded and sank. The other privateer returned downstream and, after trying to arrange an exchange of prisoners, took some prizes and left. Only colonists old enough to remember the Tuscarora War had known such panic as that of 1748. A peace treaty ended the war a month later.

A *patron* is a person of wealth who supports a person, an activity, or an institution.

Over a decade before, in 1737, Gabriel Johnston had complained to his patron, his great English friend, the Earl of Wilmington. He spoke of his disappointment that he had received so little support from his "superiors in England." Without such support, his only hope was to "do nothing, which upon a fair hearing . . . can be reasonably blamed, and leave the rest to time, and a new sett of inhabitants. . . ." These were the words of a prophet. They signaled his own actions during the next 15 years and the eventual cure of North Carolina's most serious problems.

English government failed to act promptly in many critical situations. This was the cause of much of the disorder during Johnston's term. The Crown did not provide assistance against the Spaniards in the 1740s. It had not acted to settle the seven-year representation dispute. If it had, Johnston might have enjoyed the success he deserved. In the light of the struggle launched by Burrington and helped along by grasping people in the Albemarle and Cape Fear sections, Johnston's very survival was an accomplishment. But he also proved to be a man of honor and good sense. North Carolina had not had such a governor in many years. By the time he died in 1752, that "New sett of inhabitants" he longed for in 1737 had come. They changed the character of the colony and undermined the influence of the eastern landlords.

Although Johnston died in the midst of chaos, the quarrel between factions was then dying down. The times were ripe for progress. Johnston's encouragement of rapid immigration was the best gift he could have made to North Carolina. Indeed, it was time for a new generation to make a fresh start toward the solution of the colony's problems.

Chapter Checkup

PEOPLE

Earl of Wilmington	John Lapierre	Maurice Moore
Gabriel Johnston	Richard Marsden	Henry McCulloh
Hugh Meredith	Roger Moore	

PLACES

Brunswick   The Welsh Tract   Great Wagon Road
Orton Plantation   Wilmington   Core Sound

FACT

What did Gabriel Johnston see as the main solution to the problems of North Carolina in his time?

How did settlement of the Cape Fear River differ from that of the Albemarle Sound area?

What was the difficulty between Governor Burrington and the Cape Fear family?

What was the cause of the representation controversy in the Colonial Assembly in the 1740s and 1750s?

How did the western settlers tend to be different from those of the coastal areas?

INTERPRETATION

Was it in the Albemarle or along the Cape Fear that westerners were more likely to find political allies in future years? Why?

Do you approve of the way Gov. Johnston handled the question of representation in the Assembly? Explain.

VOCABULARY

Sectionalism   Protestant
Faction   Immigration

ACTIVITY

Using an outline map to assist your presentation, show how geography played a part in the pattern of settlement in colonial North Carolina. Write a brief essay to accompany the map.

SUGGESTED READING

Lee, E. Lawrence, Jr. *The Lower Cape Fear in Colonial Days.* Chapel Hill: UNC Press, 1965. Chapters 6 and 9 contain good survey of beginnings and permanent settlement of lower Cape Fear region.

Lefler, Hugh T. and Powell, William S. *Colonial North Carolina, A History.* New York: Charles Scribner's Sons, 1973. Chapter 4 has an account of the Cape Fear settlement in relation to the rest of colonial North Carolina.

1753 First Moravians settle
in Wachovia

1754 French and Indian War begins

1756 French become allies
with the Cherokees

1763 Treaty of Paris ends the
French and Indian War

1766 Building of Salem begins

1768 Regulator Advertisement,
Number Four

1770 Regulator attack
in Hillsborough

1771 Battle of Alamance

6

TWO PATHS TO AN UNKNOWN FUTURE

Salem

Bethania is a village on Muddy Creek in western Forsyth County.

Bethabara is a village in central Forsyth County; name changed to Old Town in 1835.

January 6, 1766: "Monday, a dozen Brethren, partly from Bethania, partly from Bethabara, took a wagon and went to the new town site where . . . they cut down the trees on the place where the first house was to stand, singing . . . as they worked. . . . Our text was beautifully appropriate: 'I will defend this City.' Last night it was so piercingly cold that in our Apothecary shop certain drugs dissolved in spirits froze and burst."

The non-Moravians on the frontier had learned not to be surprised by anything these German-speaking people did. It seemed natural that they would pick the coldest day of the year to begin their new project. It was typical that they would send just 12 people to begin building a city. And it was predictable that the 12 would sing while they did it! Everything the Moravians did was wonderfully strange. No one expected that their way of building cities would be any different.

Gotthelf Rothe, *an early Moravian settler*
William Tryon, *Governor of North Carolina*

Edmund Fanning, *a government official*
Herman Husband, *a leader of the Regulators*

Eastern North Carolinians were skeptical of the Moravians in the northern Piedmont. They had known for years of how these refugee Europeans, by way of Pennsylvania, meant to build a great religious community on their hundred-thousand-acre tract. But the Carolinians were familiar enough with grand projects not to take them too seriously. There were still people around in 1766 who recalled the great plans of the Baron von Graffenried. They knew what had become of them. Let the Moravians hack away at the forests. They would soon learn by hard lessons what older settlers could have told them.

Settlers living closer to the Moravian towns were not so sure. Thirteen years ago everyone thought the first Moravians would be swallowed up by the forest. They might be scalped by the Indians or whatever happened to people who disappeared into the Piedmont wilderness. But now it looked different. The Moravians had hung on and even prospered. They had a couple of small towns and some fine farms. They got along well with the Indians. They could produce for themselves almost everything they needed. So now, if the Moravians sent 12 people to build a city, nobody laughed.

It was well they didn't. Four months passed and the brethren had only a log cabin to show for their work. The dream of a city—a place they would call Salem (meaning Peace)—might have seemed a bit foolish. But each month saw some improvement. There was new evidence that the forest would give way to Moravian axes and yield a city despite itself. Gotthelf Rothe looked foolish walking around with a crooked stick—his divining rod. He was looking for a place to dig a well. The workmen dug where he said. Thirty-nine and a half feet down they found plenty of water. Everybody seemed amazed except Gotthelf Rothe.

Melchior Rasp was a master mason. Non-Moravians noted with amusement that Salem had no kiln for making bricks. There seemed to be no work for a mason. But Rasp got

A **divining rod** is a stick thought by some to be useful in locating underground water or metal deposits.

A **kiln** is an oven in which clay is baked into brick.

along splendidly without bricks. He laid foundations for houses by setting rocks from nearby hills into bases of wet clay. The stuff dried as hard as brick. It would support a house of almost any size. Very well, but what about lumber? Salem had no sawmill and could get no boards or planks or beams. Was it, then, to be a city of wretched little log cabins daubed with mud? Not at all. Christian Triebel was a master carpenter. With trees, he could build houses that looked and served as well as any rich merchant's house at Edenton or Halifax. He did it by setting squared timbers upright in Rasp's foundations. He joined them with smaller trees, called laths, wrapped in clay and straw. Maybe the Moravians were right about God having sent them here with a promise to look after them.

Most things that could go wrong did so. But still the city grew. A few Moravians were killed by nearby Indians and workers had their share of accidents. But nothing seemed to discourage them. They thought every obstacle was put there by God to test their faith. They saw every problem as a divine call to greater effort. The non-Moravians had seen it all many times. If these 12 people said they were going to build a city, then the chartmakers might as well put it on their maps. It would soon rise up where they told it to.

Christian Reuter came with a surveying party. He started laying out streets. There was a big main street with back

Daubed means covered or coated.

This drawing of the village of Salem was made by Ludwig von Redekin, a Moravian, in 1787.

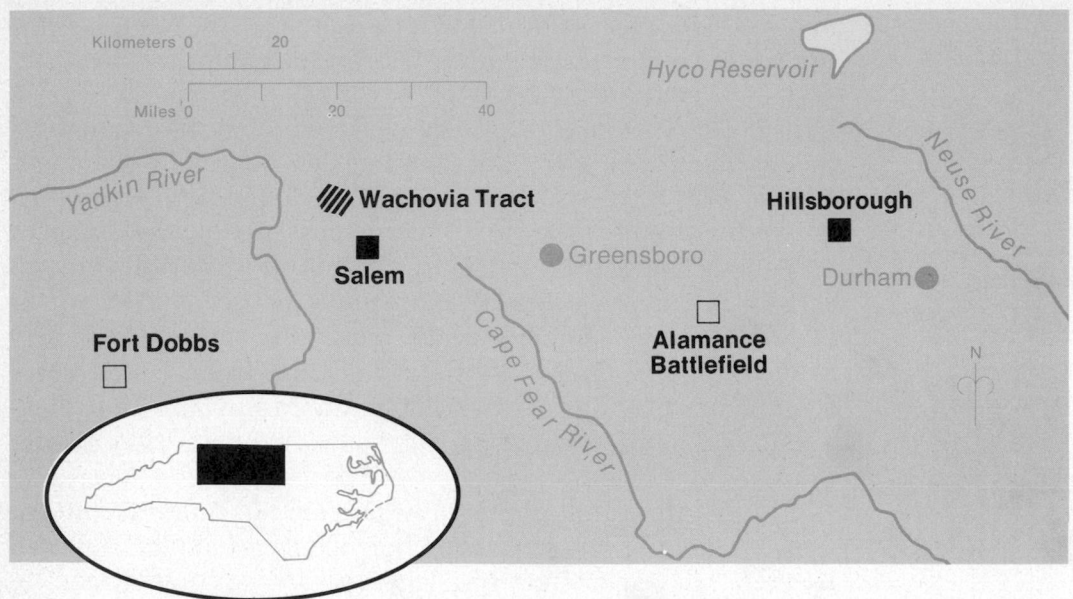

The Wachovia Tract, 1770

A *tannery* is a place for making leather from animal hides.

streets parallel to it on each side. They marked off cross streets and chose sites for houses. They looked for places for a brick kiln, tannery, warehouse, mill, tavern, pottery, apothecary shop. This was to be the best and most convenient town in the colony. It would have a school for boys and another for girls, the first in North Carolina. By 1774, Salem was a town of 125 people.

As the human body was but the temporary home of the eternal soul, so the city of clay and timber was but a physical arrangement for building the spiritual community. Salem was to be a place where love for God and one's neighbors was to be the guiding principle in all things. Its rules were designed to promote love and fellowship in all the inhabitants did. In effect, Salem was to be a loving family. The concerns of each were the concerns of all.

Eternal means everlasting.

The neighborly love sought by the Salem Moravians was felt to be the result of social discipline and harmony. All who came to live there must accept a rigid code of conduct. They must always put the needs of the community before their own. It was a rule that no one could live there unless approved by the church leaders. The way of deciding this, as in all important matters, was by lot. Each church leader put a ballot in a box. Then one ballot was taken out. The vote on this ballot was presumed to be God's will and the community

Rigid means strict.

took action accordingly. No one could worship with a Salem congregation until approved by lot.

Salem had no government except that of the various boards and conferences of church leaders. Violation of a rule did not mean jail but a warning from the Elders' Conference. Repeated violations could lead the Elders to send the violator away for a while or even permanently. The disharmony or lack of discipline of one could be a bad example for others. It could threaten the downfall of the community.

Even small matters of daily life were controlled by the Elders' Conference. A Salem resident must not wear fancy clothes; no silver buckles on the shoes or feathers at a saucy angle in the hat. Such things showed pride in personal appearance. They distracted both wearer and onlooker from God's work. Still worse, of course, were drunkenness, idleness, and the habit of getting in debt. Once a year, lots were cast that could lead to the expelling of anyone considered undesirable.

Single men and women must live in separate buildings. They had to work and relax separately. It was all right for young men and women to take a Sunday stroll provided they went in different directions. No secret meeting, let alone secret marriage or engagement, could take place between members of the opposite sexes.

All the land in Salem and for three miles beyond its limits belonged to the church. Anyone building a house there must submit plans for approval. A house, when built, could be sold only with permission of the church. Most businesses were owned in common by the residents. Workers and managers were city employees who turned over all profits to the community. Some trades operated as private businesses. But the church tried to keep control of the trades to limit competition.

Bethabara, later known as Old Town, was established by the Moravians in 1753. It declined after Salem was established.

The Moravians thought competition was harmful in any area of life. It was a threat to love and harmony. Efforts were made to control prices and keep them close to the cost of raw materials. In the words of a Moravian minister, one must look for "the supplying of bodily needs not to the profits but to the pleasing of God."

Only such a community, the Moravians believed, could make possible the living of a truly Christian life. It would enable them to do the missionary work among Indians and others. That was their design in coming to North Carolina. Salem was to be the hub of a great wheel of Christian influence that they would command in the North Carolina Piedmont and, some day, far beyond.

Salem was a kind of religious commune, practicing a sort of religious collectivism. But it was an island of collectivism in a sea of individualism. Did its many ideals and practices offer North Carolinians better ways and higher beliefs than they had brought from the British Isles? Was the Moravian ideal a desirable one? Would it work? Salem faced North Carolina with a challenge to its basic values and convictions. This challenge was to leave its mark on the generations that followed.

A *commune* is a close-knit community organized to promote some common purpose.

Collectivism is the idea that the interests of the group are more important than those of the individual member of the group.

Individualism is the idea that the interests of the individual are as important as those of the group, if not more so.

The Land Rush

The westward push of settlers in the 1740s and 1750s meant a return of trouble between whites and Indians. France used the lull in the wars with England after 1748 to strengthen its military outposts in America. Encouraged by the French, the Indians of the Appalachian Mountains resisted further trespassing on their lands. In 1754, the French and Indians became allies in a war with England. It was to last for seven years.

The North Carolina Assembly voted money for the war and raised troops for service. Two companies of militia were sent to protect the frontier from attack. Fort Dobbs, named for new governor Arthur Dobbs, was built near the Yadkin River (near what is now Statesville). Indian raids soon became frightening. Some of the settlers retreated eastward. The small pioneer population of Rowan County, the westernmost part of the colony, was reduced by half in the first three years of war.

In 1756, the French gained the help of the Cherokees and their allies. This was a new menace to the western pioneers.

Rowan County was formed in 1753.

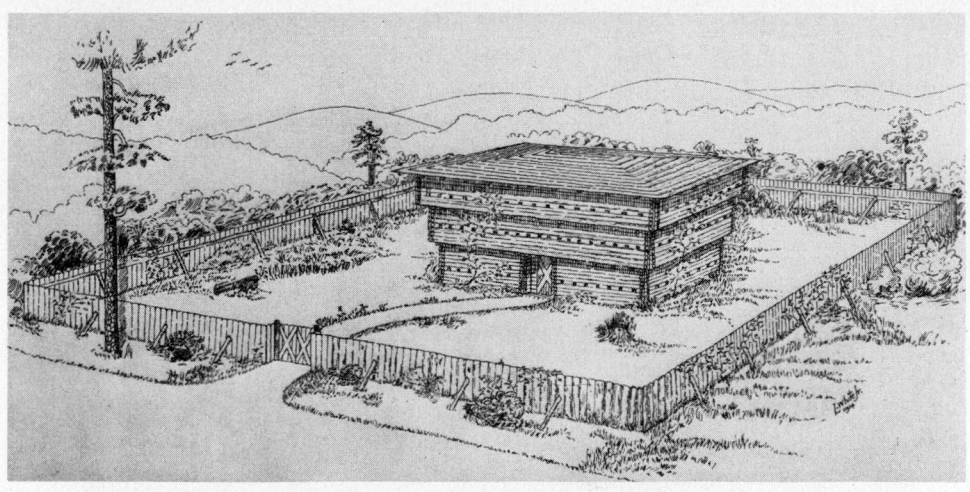

Fort Dobbs, built in 1755-1756 to protect western settlements from Indians, stood in the central part of Iredell County.

Again, Rowan was the scene of hard fighting. It included a daring Indian raid in 1760 on Fort Dobbs. Aided by troops from other colonies, the North Carolina militia dealt the Indians several serious defeats in 1761. By the end of the year, a peace treaty had been signed with the Cherokees. The frontier became uneasily quiet again. The war ended with the signing of the Treaty of Paris in 1763. This was a great victory for the English and their colonial subjects.

After the war, Governor William Tryon made agreements with the Cherokees and other tribes which allowed North Carolinians the right to settle as far west as the foothills of the Appalachians. There were already settlers up to the limits of the line agreed upon. There was good reason to expect more trouble. For the present, however, peace in Rowan and the new western counties, Mecklenburg and Tryon, meant a stampede of settlers into the frontier region.

As different as they were from one another in origin, speech, and customs, westerners had in common a resentment of the way they were treated by the North Carolina government. Most of the people of wealth and power lived near the coast. They controlled the Assembly and other branches of government. They had no intention of sharing their power with the westerners. It did not matter how much the population of the West might grow in comparison to the East.

An important difference between the sections was in religion. The Anglican Church now had considerable authority in the coastal counties but little in the backcountry. Presbyterians, Baptists, and other "dissenting" groups were strong on the frontier. The Anglican Church, like the society in which it developed, was less democratic than the dissenters. It was more respectful of authority and centralized order.

There was a lack of good roads to the east. But the "Great Wagon Road" led northward and rivers led to the southeast. Because of this, westerners did their trading with merchants in South Carolina and the northern colonies. This made for greater sectional differences within North Carolina and clashes became frequent. For a permanent capital, westerners favored Hillsborough, a town about midway between the farthest eastern and western settlements. But Albemarle and Cape Fear leaders joined in 1766 to make New Bern the capital. This was a serious inconvenience to westerners. But they had too few Assembly delegates to prevent it. Tryon got the Assembly to raise fifteen thousand pounds for a governor's palace in New Bern. The westerners complained that the price was too high for a poor colony. Eastern landlords agreed that the money should be raised by a poll tax. But westerners were quick to see that this exempted slave property from being taxed for the palace. A poor man would have to pay as much as a rich one.

By 1771, half of North Carolina's quarter-million people lived in the western counties. They were represented in the Assembly by 17 delegates. The eastern half of the population had 61 representatives. The governor, from his mansion in faraway New Bern, controlled appointments of county and local officials. As Tryon himself saw and regretted, many local officials in the West were corrupt. They cheated the settlers out of fees and taxes for their own good.

Tryon Palace (right) was the home of William Tryon while he was governor. Below is the palace as it appeared on a bill of colonial currency. The palace burned in 1798 but has been rebuilt.

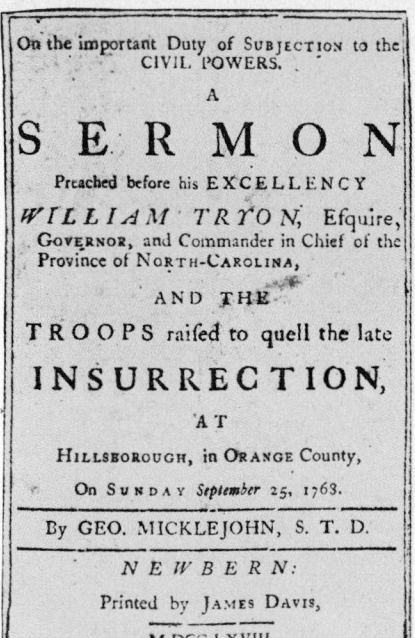

On the important Duty of SUBJECTION to the CIVIL POWERS.

A

SERMON

Preached before his EXCELLENCY

WILLIAM TRYON, Efquire, GOVERNOR, and Commander in Chief of the Province of NORTH-CAROLINA,

AND THE

TROOPS raifed to quell the late

INSURRECTION,

AT

HILLSBOROUGH, in ORANGE County,

On SUNDAY *September* 25, 1763.

By GEO. MICKLEJOHN, S. T. D.

NEWBERN:

Printed by JAMES DAVIS,

M,DCC,LXVIII.

This published sermon, preached by an Anglican minister, was in praise of Tryon's victory at Alamance in 1786.

Acquitted means found not guilty.

Tryon made efforts to halt the evil. But some officials, like Edmund Fanning of Orange County and John Frohock of Rowan, were not stopped. Both held several offices at the same time. This practice suggested they could not attend to all their duties. It was easy to think the worst about such people.

Finally, there was anger in the West, especially in the so-called "Granville District" over the behavior of land agents. They charged high prices and rents for land. There was a riot in Halifax County in 1759. It was over the unfair charges demanded by Francis Corbin, agent of the Earl of Granville. In 1765, Mecklenburg County witnessed the "war of Sugar Creek." This was a violent protest against agents of the great land dealer Henry McCulloh. Westerners issued one protest after another. The Assembly gave them little satisfaction.

It seemed clear to many westerners by 1765 that the only way to deal with a government run by easterners for their own benefit was to resist forcefully. By 1767, a resistance group known as the Regulators appeared in some of the western counties. They wanted better regulation of the government. In August, they issued the first of several appeals for united action against corrupt officials and other abuses of the government.

Though they failed to remedy any of the problems they complained about, the Regulators gained many supporters in Orange, Rowan, and other counties. One of the most impressive protests was a pamphlet, *Regulator Advertisement, Number Four*. It was drawn up by Herman Husband and other Regulators in 1768. It declared that the protestors would no longer pay public officials fees higher than those required by law. They would pay no more taxes until they could be sure the taxes were lawful. They would meet as often as possible to discuss solutions to their problems.

The town of Hillsborough was a focus of Regulator demonstrations. In April 1768, about 70 of them rode into the town and fired guns at Edmund Fanning's house. Tryon issued orders against the practices they complained of. But many of the abuses continued. Meanwhile, Fanning was arrested for taking excessive fees. Herman Husband and another Regulator named William Butler were jailed for "inciting the populace to rebellion." All three were tried at Hillsborough in September, along with several other Regulators. Tryon sent militia forces to the town. He had heard rumors that the Regulators meant to march on Hillsborough to set their friends free. The march did not take place. But it is said that there were three thousand Regulators in town when the trials began. Husband was acquitted and the other Regulators received light fines.

Edmund Fanning, a western government official, was hated by many people in the 1760s and 70s, especially the Regulators.

Routed means defeated.

Diverged means separated.

The hated Fanning, though found guilty, was fined only one penny and costs of court. The Regulators left Hillsborough in anger at the quality of justice they had seen.

Growing more bold, the Regulators marched to Hillsborough in September 1770. They invaded the court house, assaulted a lawyer, and dragged Fanning through the streets. Tryon went before the Assembly and demanded harsh laws to help him deal with those who resisted his government. The result was the Johnston Riot Act. This was a series of stiff penalties for those interfering with normal processes of government. Tryon was authorized to use force, if necessary, to put down the Regulators.

With Regulator activity spreading to Anson, Johnston, and other counties, Tryon decided to take action. In the spring of 1771, he led fifteen hundred militia on a march from New Bern to Hillsborough. On May 16, his army met a force of two thousand Regulators at Great Alamance Creek just west of Hillsborough. The Regulators asked to meet with the governor. But Tryon refused as long as they were "in arms against the government." He gave them an hour to put down their weapons and leave. When the time ran out, he attacked. In two hours the Regulators were routed, each side losing nine dead and many wounded.

Following the Battle of Alamance, Tryon arrested some of the Regulator leaders and tried 12 for treason. Six were hanged and the rest were pardoned. Those who would lay down their arms and promise to obey the government were also offered pardon. Many, possibly thousands, fled into Tennessee. Their flight meant the collapse of the Regulator movement and the return of peace to western North Carolina. For 70 or more years, the memory of these incidents delayed any serious action against these injustices of which the Regulators had complained. Perhaps their protest should not have become violent. But it was easy to see why some considered violent protest their only hope of success.

The spirit of the Regulator movement had an individualism that was not shared by all westerners. The Moravians could not be tempted to join in resistance. They seemed willing to put up with all manner of ill-treatment from the government. They had a tradition of obedience to lawful authority. But there was a great gap between these remarkable Germans and Scandanavians and their neighbors of British descent. These two groups represented two paths that North Carolina might take in its future development. As in Robert Frost's poem about two paths that "diverged in a yellow wood," it would make "all the difference" which path was taken.

St. John's Church in Williamsboro, built in 1757, is the
oldest frame church in North Carolina.

Everyday Life

Whether they lived east or west, many North Carolinians
shared a way of life. It helped draw them together in spite of
regional differences and conflicts. For example, the houses of
the poor who were the great majority in both sections, were
usually made of logs. Clay was stuffed between the logs to
hold back cold and rain. Such houses rarely had a brick chimney. Their two rooms, with maybe a loft above or lean-to attached, did not often have even a simple plank floor. A few
crude tables, chairs, and bedsteads were often the entire furnishings. Slave cabins, east and west, often lacked even these
few comforts.

Such houses contributed to the general poor health of the
North Carolina colonist. They insured enough chill air and
moisture to maintain a high rate of lung diseases in winter.
Pneumonia, influenza, whooping cough, and so on were widespread in cold seasons. But it was in summer, and especially

in the swampy Coastal Plain, that the colony became a huge sick ward. Malaria, smallpox, and yellow fever were but a few of the illnesses. These killed thousands every year.

In more remote and backward regions, the faces and postures of the people showed the effects of chronic ill-health. Up to 1740 or later, it was not unusual to meet North Carolinians whose noses and palates had been destroyed by the ulcers that came with yaws. This was a disease of people who lived in hopeless filth and poverty. They had no knowledge of sanitation, personal hygiene, or proper diet. Others were scarred by the ravages of smallpox. Some were left with a sickly complexion from going too long without milk.

Neither the few doctors nor concerned housewives could do much more than try to comfort the sick through their illnesses. There was a kind of bark that helped malaria. There were some herb remedies or chemical mixtures that could be effective in other illnesses. But colonial medicine was mostly a matter of bleeding away "ill humors." At times, some peculiar diet was forced on the patient. This probably destroyed more lives than it saved. Well-to-do families, with better nourishment and better sanitation, suffered less than the poor. But none escaped sickness.

East and west, rich and poor, North Carolina families tended to be large. This was despite the great number of infants who died in their early weeks or months. A woman dying before 40—and most did—would often have spent up to two thirds of her adult life in pregnancy. But, pregnant or not, there was always a great deal of work for women and girls. Besides housework, they often had to help with harvesting or hog killing. They made clothes, bedding, and candles. They cooked and took care of the sick. These duties left women with little time for literary education and few chances for recreation. Girls were often married at age 13 or 14.

Recreation was a public matter. It was usually enjoyed in the company of as many people as could be found to share it. A militia muster, court session, house raising, even a religious meeting, was almost always a time of fun as well as seriousness. Owners of good horses challenged each other to races. They matched one another's gamecocks, compared their brandy and applejack. There might also be a noisy bear baiting or gander pulling. Often there was a fiddler and some dancing, or even a nasty gouging match, for which North Carolinians were widely known. Local toughs kept their nails and teeth filed for such contests.

Nearly everybody in all sections made liberal use of tobacco. Clay pipes were popular with all ages and sexes.

Chronic means frequent, continual.

Palate is the roof of the mouth.

"Ill humors" meant, in early medicine, that disease was thought to occur when the bodily fluids, or humors, were out of balance.

Muster is a meeting for purposes of drill.

Bear baiting is setting dogs to fight a captive bear.

Gander pulling was a sport in which galloping riders try to pull the head off a gander suspended by its feet.

Snuff-taking was common. Poor people "pinched" snuff (ground up tobacco) by sniffing it up the nose. They might "dip" it by holding a bit between gum and cheek. Tobacco was thought to be desirable for good health as well as the pleasure it gave. A snuffbox or tobacco pouch was part of every man's attire. But few could match the mink-skin pouch of a Halifax lawyer: it had "the hair, Feet and Claws and Tail on," and resembled "a little dead black Cat."

Rustic is crude, simple.

Observers varied widely in their general views of the North Carolinians. A Scottish lady wrote that the "peasantry" seemed to spend their time "sauntering thro' the woods with a gun or sitting under a rustic shade, drinking New England rum made into grog, the most shocking liquor you can imagine." But John Lawson had found them "very laborious." The women were "often fair, and . . . as well featur'd, as any . . . , and have very brisk charming Eyes. . . ." Another found the settlers to be "a streight, tall, well-limb'd and active People, their Children being seldom or never troubled with Rickets, and many other Distempers. . . ." A lot depended on one's point of view.

Rickets is a bone disease.

By 1750, many families of Germans were settling in the North Carolina Piedmont, especially in Alamance, Guilford, and Orange counties. Others followed, gradually spreading west through Davidson, Rowan, Stanly, Iredell, Cabarrus, and

Log cabins were widely used by settlers of the middle and late eighteenth century. Later they were used as slave cabins.

other counties toward the mountains. Some were natives of Germany itself. Others were the children and grandchildren of Germans who had originally settled in Pennsylvania. Many at first spoke little or no English. The town of Salisbury had a printing press that produced almanacs and religious works for the Germans of the region.

There were already many Germans in the Piedmont when the Moravians first began arriving there in the 1750s. The Moravians belonged to a religious group that began in Bohemia and Moravia (in what is now Czechoslovakia). In the 1730s, they began sending groups of missionaries to America. They

Almanacs are books or pamphlets containing calendar, weather charts, and other information useful to farmers and others.

This Salem home (above), built in 1819, has been restored and is now a Moravian Museum. The carriage in front is in the Wachovia Museum. The Tycho Nissen house (below) was later used as a school for children.

tried to build communities in Europe and America where they could live such a life as they felt the earliest Christians had lived. Each person in a Moravian community was expected to contribute to the common effort. One would take no more than one needed. Elders of the church were responsible for the operation of each community in both religious and non-religious activities.

In 1752, a group of Pennsylvania Moravians visited North Carolina in search of land. From there, they were to take their spiritual mission into the lives of Indians and pioneers. They chose a tract and named it Wachovia, from two German words meaning meadow and stream. Here they settled 15 men in the fall of 1753. They were given orders to clear land, plant crops, and make the place ready for Moravian families. From this beginning, a large and vigorous settlement developed within about a dozen years.

Despite their missionary spirit, the Wachovia Moravians clung together. They made no great effort to convert their neighbors. They seemed to sense that they were in danger of being overwhelmed by those with other beliefs and customs. As a result they held on to much of their own religious and cultural tradition for over a century. But they remained almost isolated from the life of the colony. They offered only their example of hard work and Christian devotion, without changing the ways and beliefs of most of those about them. In fact, they sometimes angered others by refusing to fight in wartime, even during the American Revolution. Since the beginning, North Carolinians had been marked by a strong sense of individualism. It was the belief in the right of each person to fair treatment under the law—a full opportunity to find happiness and well-being. The Moravians did not deny these goals. But they felt they were best achieved in a setting where the individual was devoted to the needs of the whole community, not merely one's own needs.

What results did the Moravians achieve with their peculiar lifestyle? Let a non-Moravian easterner offer a judgment as set down in his diary in 1786:

Aspect means appearance.

The moment I touch'd the Moravian territory, I notic'd a sudden change in the aspect of the houses & farms—even the Cattle appear'd larger & in better order. Here every shoulder is pushing on the wheels of Industry ... every farm looks neat & cheerful—their houses decently furnish'd and abounding in plenty. . . . Late in the Even'g arriv'd at Myers tavern in Salem, the best public house I have met in the State in all respects. . . . Salem contains

40 houses, mostly brick . . . every house is supplied by water brought thro' conduits 1½ miles.

But the passion and inspiration died with the first generation of settlers. By the time of the Civil War, Salem and the other Moravian towns of the Piedmont were not very different from other North Carolina towns. Why did the experiment fail to achieve its goals? It may have been that the Moravians demanded more self-denial than people are ordinarily capable of. It may also be that the lack of personal freedom in Wachovia the want of opportunities for individual self-expression, was too foreign to the American frontier spirit to take strong hold. But their experience continues to have meaning for the present. Wachovia, like America, was an experiment. It was a quest for the best blend of individual and group interests. The Moravians failed to find utopia. But in some ways, at least for a while, they came a good deal closer than their neighbors.

Chapter Checkup

PEOPLE

William Tryon   Edmund Fanning   Herman Husband

PLACES

Salem   Hillsborough
Wachovia Tract   Alamance Battlefield
Fort Dobbs

FACT

Do you think the Moravians were more nearly helped or hurt by reducing competition among themselves? How so?

In what ways did Moravian ideas challenge those of other North Carolinians of the time?

Why did western settlers continue to have less voice in the colonial government even after they became a majority of the North Carolina population?

What parallels do you find between the Regulators and the patriots of the American Revolution?

Was Tryon right to crush the Regulators?

INTERPRETATION

For what purpose did the Moravians come to North Carolina?
Why did the Moravians put so much stress on conforming to community rules?
What was the cause of the Battle of Alamance? What was the result?

VOCABULARY

Collectivism	Regulators
Commune	Individualism

ACTIVITY

Make a set of rules for your town such as might have been made by a Moravian in 1765. In what important ways would the town be different if it followed these rules?

SUGGESTED READING

Fries, Adelaide L. *The Road to Salem.* Chapel Hill: UNC Press, 1944. Novel based on history of Moravian settlement in North Carolina.

Fries, Adelaide L. "The Moravian Contribution to North Carolina," *N.C. Historical Review* (Jan. 1930), pages 1–14. General survey of Moravians from early times to modern.

Hamilton, Kenneth G. "The Moravians and Wachovia," *N.C. Historical Review* (April 1967), pages 144–157. Discusses long-range effects of Moravian settlement upon the area where they were located.

PART THREE

Revolution and Statehood

Alamance Battleground—
state historic site near
Burlington

1775-1800

1765   Wilmington Stamp Act riots

1770   Russian naval forces
defeat Turkish fleet
in Agean Sea

1772   Prussia, Austria,
and Russia gain in Partition
of Poland

1774   Edenton Tea Party

1775   Second Provincial
Congress at New Bern *(April 3)*
● News of Lexington and Concord
Battles reaches Wilmington
(May 8)
 ● Mecklenberg Resolves *(May 31)*
 ● Third Provincial Congress
at Hillsborough *(Aug. 20)*
  ● Janet Schaw leaves for Scotland
(late summer)
  1776   Dr. Fallon jailed at
Wilmington *(Jan.)*
   ● Battle of Moore's Creek
Bridge *(Feb. 27)*

1775   British and Americans
clash at Lexington and Concord
(April 19)

1776   American colonies
declare their independence

7

A LADY
OF QUALITY

The Man of Mystery

The **Committees of Safety** were patriot groups set up in 1774 to enforce agreement by colonies not to trade with England.

The Wilmington Safety Committee had been jumpy all during 1775. This was particularly so since November 13. That was the day they heard from Brunswick. Another British warship, the *Scorpion,* along with a transport full of British regulars, had anchored near Fort Johnston, at the mouth of the river. Governor Martin, for five months a resident aboard the H.M.S. *Cruizer* nearby, must be ready to open his long-awaited assault on the lower Cape Fear River. The Safety Committee was struggling to organize its defenses. But there were some in the community who wondered whether royal tyranny was as much to be feared as a Committee of Safety.

The Committee had already banned all public dancing, horseracing, and billiards. But now there was the more serious question of private firearms. On November 13, they sent a party of men around town to examine the guns in every home. They had orders to take every gun over and above one

Josiah Martin, *the last royal governor*
James Fallon, *a man of mystery*
Janet Schaw, *a lady of quality*
Robert Howe, *a colonel in the militia*

William Houston, *a stampmaster*
John Rutherford, *a member of the governor's council*
Donald McDonald, *a British general*

Confiscated means seized and taken away.

from each white man in a household. They would give receipts for the confiscated weapons and turn them over to the Committee. On November 18, they decreed that "No Vessel whatever shall load any cargo to any part of the World from this Port until further Orders from this Committee. . . ." It went hard with merchants to be told they couldn't trade abroad.

The Committee went on like that into the late fall and winter of 1775. On November 20, they forbade selling food and supplies to the British ships. They ordered boats to be sunk in the channel to block the river. There was a report that day that the British intended to burn Brunswick and march on Wilmington. This led the Committee to conduct a survey of houses and other property in town. Some would have to be destroyed to insure a proper defense. All the lead in town was ordered to be bought and made into balls. All available brimstone and saltpeter was collected to make gunpowder.

The Committee seemed to suspect a Tory plot behind almost every application sent to it. Captain William Gibbs wanted to send a ship to Cape Lookout to fetch some naval stores cast ashore in a shipwreck. He produced a license from the New Bern Safety Committee to remove the cargo from Cape Lookout. But he was refused permission by the Wilmington Committee to bring it into the Cape Fear River. Captain Batchelder asked to sail an empty brig to New York. He was reminded that no vessels could leave until further orders.

On January 9, 1776, all river traffic to Brunswick except on Jacob Phelps' boat was halted. Despite the growing inconvenience of such demands, many residents accepted them as necessary precautions. They felt that the Committee had the best interests of the community at heart. Others, however, thought the Committee was acting in a high-handed manner. What was the use of defying a tyrant in London, they wondered, and then obeying a committee of tyrants at home?

On Monday, January 15, Committee Chairman John Ancrum came in with a pamphlet. He had found it tacked up at

Flora MacDonald was a Scottish heroine. She saved "Bonnie Prince Charlie" from the British in 1745 and later settled in North Carolina.

128

Untrammeled means free, not restricted.

Unanimity is unity of opinion.

Insinuating means hinting of evil.

the court house. Its title was: "To those who have a true sense of . . . Justice and untrammeled *Liberty,* residents of the borough of Wilmington." In two pages, the writer, signed "a Lawyer", attacked the Safety Committee with what the members considered "many false & scandalous reflections on the Committee tending to inflame the minds of the people; to create divisions & dissentions amongst us, by destroying that unanimity so essentially necessary to our mutual defense. . . ." The Committee obviously didn't like to be criticized.

The Committee found that the pamphlet was in the handwriting of one William Green. But Green claimed to have copied it from an original belonging to Dr. Fallon. It was the Committee's opinion that Fallon was "the author & publisher of the said paper." He should be arrested and "kept in close Custody untill he gives sufficient Security for his good behavior for . . . Six Months in the Sum of £500. . . ." The doctor announced that he would not pay security. He was promptly locked in the military guardhouse.

Within 24 hours, Fallon had become the central figure in a conflict. It was between the Committee and its critics over the proper scope of its authority. On Tuesday it became necessary to tighten security at the guardhouse. No one was allowed to see the doctor unless approved by Colonel James Moore or the officer of the guard. Fallon was permitted to have pen and ink. But all persons allowed to see him were to be carefully searched before leaving. They might smuggle out letters not examined by the duty officer.

On Wednesday, Colonel Moore notified the Committee that Fallon was "an insinuating & dangerous Person" among the guards. It would be "injuring the common cause & running the risk of the public safety, any longer [to] keep the said Fallon in the Guard House." The Committee resolved that the doctor should be sent "to the Common Jail . . . untill he makes a full confession for his offenses to the public and asks pardon of this Committee for the repeated insults which he has in person offered." Colonel Moore was ordered to place guards "near to the Jail." But he forbade conversation between the guards and Fallon except by permission of the officer of the guard. Examination of the doctor's mail would continue.

The change from guardhouse to jail did not appear to affect Fallon's campaign against the power of the Safety Committee. On Saturday, they learned that the prison doors had been open ever since Fallon was put there. They learned that anyone who wished to see him had only to walk in. They found that he was sending out letters without having them inspected. These included one to the sheriff further attacking the Committee. The Committee demanded that the only person hereafter to see Fallon should be a servant. The servant would take him "necessaries & keep his apartment clean." The jail must be kept locked and the mail examined. Fallon wrote on Monday to demand copies of the paper he was supposed to have written and the proceedings against him. But the Committee saw fit to furnish only the latter. No one was sure how to handle the man.

By January 22, there must have been many in Wilmington wondering who this Dr. Fallon was. The man had been in town only a short time. No one seemed clear just what he was doing here. The only thing certain was that he had managed to carry on—from a jail—a campaign that the Safety Committee was hard-pressed to stop. Given the momentum of unchecked power built up by the Committee in the past year, it was no small accomplishment for the stranger. Some felt that the true voice of liberty was better represented by this defiant person than by the voice of the Safety Committee.

Momentum is force of movement.

James Fallon must have remained a man of mystery as long as he stayed in Wilmington. He has remained a mystery to this day. A good deal is known of his later adventures for his name appeared often in the newspapers. He became a rather well-known figure. But his background remains obscure. His purpose at Wilmington in early 1776 has never been satisfactorily explained. Knowledge of these matters seems limited to two sources—the minutes of the Safety Committee and a memoir composed by Fallon himself some years later.

Obscure means vague.

Memoir is a written recollection.

According to his own account, James Fallon was born in Ireland in 1749. He claimed to have visited Paris around 1770. He decided to study medicine while staying there. He says that he first took a tour of the leading universities to acquaint himself with medical education in them. After touring France, Switzerland, Italy, Germany, and Holland, he settled in London as a medical student.

After several months in London, Fallon went to Scotland and enrolled at the University of Edinburgh. It was then the leading medical school in the world. He became a student of Dr. William Cullen, the great medical teacher of the age. He spent two years there before leaving for a tour of Scotland. He earned no degree but, in the informal fashion of the day, adopted for himself the title of doctor anyway.

In early 1774, Fallon took a brig for Charleston. He was shipwrecked at Cape Hatteras. But he managed, according to his account, to salvage his money and letters of introduction. Reaching Edenton in May, he found a warm reception. He visited for some months among leading families of Albemarle.

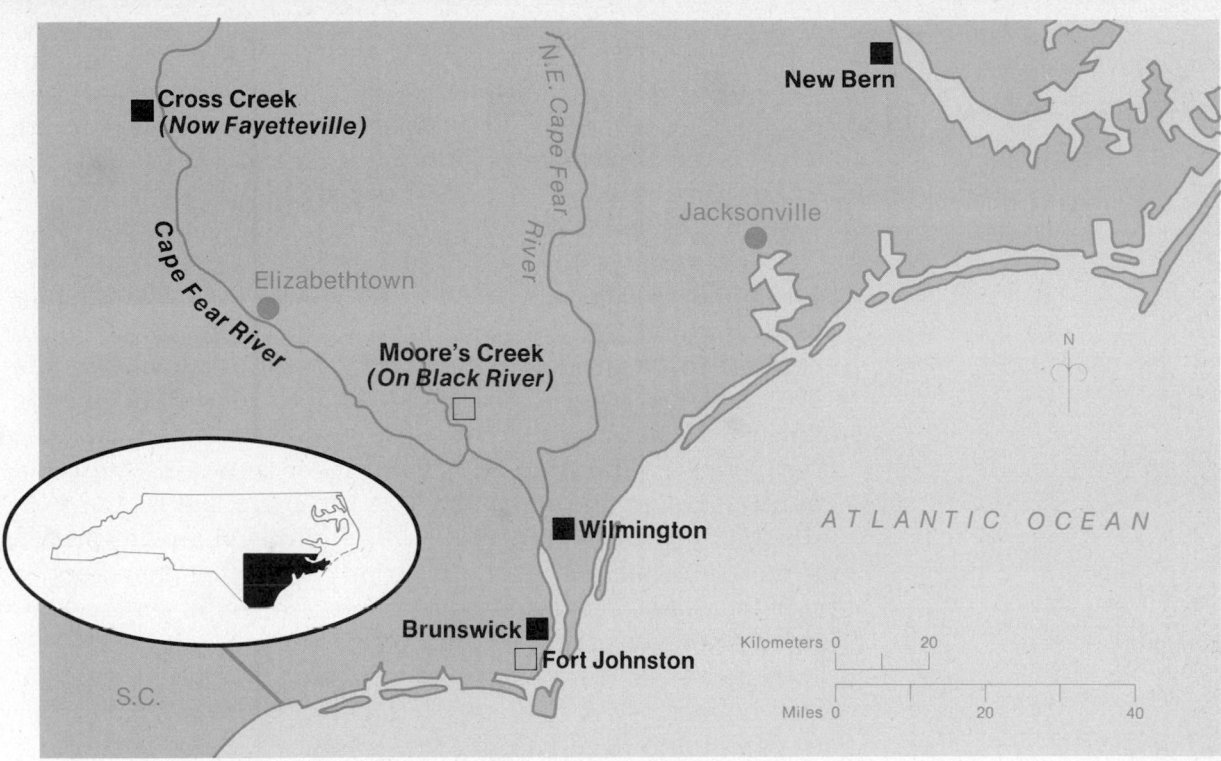

The Cape Fear River Region, 1775

He finally resumed his journey to Charleston. But when he reached Wilmington, he decided to rest for a few weeks before going on. At this point, it is necessary to follow more precisely his own version of events, written in the third person:

"While here," Fallon wrote, "the most influential families . . . requested strongly, that he would settle and practice among them. These were Martin, [the] Governor . . . , the Moores, Ashes, Howes, and James agreed. All America at this time was aroused with political spasms, . . . and James gloried in the idea; he had no sooner breathed the American air, than he perceived the stronger impulses of liberty, and the desire of humbling the ancient oppressor of his native country. These rebellious sentiments were disclosed to his friend, the Governor, who labored exceedingly to have him on his side; they fell out, on which James wrote very animatedly against him, . . . as well in verse as in prose. A Scot and he had a duel, the Scot had his pistol-arm broken; James cured him. The Governor and Council, for these writings, committed him, for three days to his own house; The County Militia, under Gen-

Animatedly means earnestly.

eral Ashe, consisting of 800 men, carried him on their heads, in an arm-chair, through the streets, and the tumult was such that the Governor was constrained to fly his Government, and to take shelter on board a King's ship then in the river—he (the Governor) never came on shore afterwards."

Described in this way, the role of Fallon in North Carolina would appear to have been crucial to the revolutionary cause. It seems that it was Fallon's imprisonment that led Josiah Martin, the last royal governor, to flee North Carolina in 1775. It is the story of a young man, well educated and widely traveled. He was boldly committing himself to the cause of liberty and risking all in its behalf. What is missing in his account, however, are his actions as the opponent of the Wilmington Safety Committee. He does not reveal how he stirred up trouble against Cornelius Harnett and other members of the Committee and refusing to apologize for it. Fallon confines his story to other incidents of his Wilmington sojourn.

For the historian, the problem here is to show the agreement between the apparently conflicting versions of Fallon's activities in the Safety Committee minutes and his memoir. Or one must find out which one is wrong. It is a ticklish question because it is not altogether certain that either is wrong. On the other hand, it is not hard to think of reasons why Fallon might falsify his own account in later years or why the Safety Committee might persecute even a good patriot who accused it of dictatorship.

It is a case where the context of the situation must be considered—the larger pattern of circumstances and events of which Fallon's experience was but a tiny part. But this larger context reveals things that show pretty clearly why there seems to be a contradiction in the sources and who was responsible for it. With a little care, a hoax can be pinned down and the rascal who started it can be exposed.

A Tory Perspective

From down here on the river, Miss Schaw was thrilled by her first sight of "Hilton" plantation. The manor house commanded a breathtaking view. It was handsomely set off by the huge lawn that swept down to the water's edge. She was sure she had never seen "a more glorious situation." Fresh from Scotland, she had already heard what a model housekeeper Mrs. Harnett was. Mrs. Harnett was the charming hostess at Hilton. It would be delightful to meet her, perhaps become a customer for the "minced pies, cheese cakes, tarts and little biskets" she sent down every day to Wilmington.

Catching herself, Janet Schaw recalled that this must never be. *Mr.* Harnett, by all accounts, was "at best a brute." He was the greatest cause of that "cruel and unjust treatment" inflicted by the rebels on the friends of the king. She could not help noticing, too, that old Harnett had neglected the grounds at Hilton. He had allowed the lower part of the yard to grow up in briars and weeds. What a pack of rogues these Carolina men had turned out to be!

Propelled along the water by the uniformed slaves in Mr. Rutherford's six-oared boat, it seemed almost no time before they reached the wharf at Wilmington. Stepping from beneath the boat's gaily-colored awning, Miss Schaw was greeted by her friends. She was taken to her rooms at Dr. Cobham's, the best house in town. It was good to get away from Schawfield for a few days. How nice it was to come up to town for the latest news and maybe a little shopping at the market.

Janet Schaw woke up the next morning with a violent headache. She recollected that she did not really like Wilmington at all. On her first visit here a few weeks before, she had been awakened early one morning by "an outcry like that of a score of hogs going ... to be slaughtered. ..." It turned out to be the cries of witnesses to a large fire in some nearby

The Cape Fear River home of Cornelius Harnett was an impressive sight for Janet Schaw in 1775.

buildings. The fire might have consumed the whole town had not some British sailors come to the rescue. The town was a fire trap, no doubt about it. But it was also unbearably hot in this late spring of 1775. And the mosquitoes were ghastly.

Mainly, Janet Schaw admitted to herself, it was the people themselves who made Wilmington so unpleasant. The Scottish merchant families included some lovely people. But most of the townsfolk were riff-raff. They were the same ruffians, no doubt, who made all that stir over the Stamp Act some years ago. Janet knew about Robert Howe and old Harnett. They marched through the streets on Halloween night, 1765. They were carrying an effigy of "Liberty" in a coffin to the graveyard. Just as the burial was about to begin, someone shouted that Liberty's pulse was returning. They all paraded around shouting defiance to Lord Bute, whom they ignorantly blamed for the Stamp Act. Janet felt that must have been a shameful spectacle!

There had been an outburst of rebelliousness here after that. In the late fall, the "Sons of Liberty," as the radicals called themselves, had forced the resignation of Dr. William Houston. He was the Stampmaster, or distributor of the hated stamps. Not long afterward, they marched to the home of Governor Tryon at Brunswick. They insulted him and forced an officer there to release two ships seized for carrying unstamped papers. All this talk of "liberty"! The colonists were simply using it to mask their refusal to help pay the costs of their own western defense line.

Scottish newspapers had followed this clamor in the colonies. All decent people were shocked by it. It was disgraceful of Parliament to have withdrawn the Stamp Act. Parliament backed down later on the Townshend duties except for that on tea. The Boston Tea Party of 1773 had been the work of rum-soaked traitors. The Edenton Tea Party of 1774 was the foolishness of bored housewives. And now, reluctant to be left out where any treason was concerned, the "ladies" of Wilmington had lately "burnt their tea in solemn procession." King George ought to send a couple of regiments. He should remind these people whose subjects they were.

Janet's cousin, John Rutherford, was a member of Governor Martin's Council. They had done all that loyal men could to stem the tide of rebellion. The Massachusetts législature called for a Continental Congress at Philadelphia in September 1774. But Martin refused to convene the North Carolina Assembly to consider it. Rebel leaders gathered at Wilmington and called for the colony's first Provincial Congress at New Bern on August 25. Deaf to all counsels of restraint, the Pro-

Ruffians are crude people.

An *effigy* is a crude figure representing someone who is disliked.

This cartoon from England of the Edenton Tea Party of 1774 seems to poke fun at King George III. His face seems to be that of the "lady" at the right holding the gavel.

To *convene* is to meet.

Provincial is of a province, or colony.

General Robert Howe was North Carolina's highest ranking soldier in the Revolution.

North Carolina was the first state to instruct delegates to vote for independence.

A *moderator* is a leader.

vincial Congress elected Joseph Hewes of Edenton, Richard Caswell of Kingston (now Kinston), and William Hooper of Wilmington to represent the North Carolina radicals at the Philadelphia convention.

Recently, John Rutherford had come home from New Bern in a rage. He described the disgusting scene there to Janet. Governor Martin, hoping to find a solution to the colony's difficulties, had summoned the Assembly to convene at New Bern on April 4, 1775. John Harvey, Speaker of the Assembly, scheduled a second Provincial Congress to meet there on April 3. The two bodies were composed of almost entirely the same men. They met in the same hall with Harvey presiding over both. Whenever an aide of the governor appeared at the door, Harvey, moderator of the illegal Congress, would change himself into Speaker Harvey. He would gravely receive the governor's message. The Governor sent the Assembly home in disgust after a few days. But not before the Congress had voted to send Hewes, Hooper, and Caswell to the second Continental Congress. The radicals appeared to think all this was terribly clever and amusing.

One day there was something called a militia review at Wilmington. Miss Schaw and her friends found perches on Dr. Cobham's balcony to watch the event. The review consisted of Bob Howe and some junior officers. They were in charge of some "soldiers, or what you please to call them," as Janet wrote in her journal. There was a great deal of grog. This did not have a very good effect on the drill they had to perform, which was practice in what was called "bush fighting." It seemed more appropriate to Indians than to white men. It was performed on a field uncleared of its scrubby oaks. It was impossible for spectators on the balcony to know "whether they performed it well or not."

At last the bush fighting was over and the men were assembled in rows on an open field. "... I must really laugh," Janet wrote, "when I recollect their figures: two thousand men in their shirts and trousers, proceded by a very ill-beat drum and a fiddler, ... who played with all his might. They made indeed a most unmartial appearance." And these were the soldiers to challenge the might of the British Empire!

After the review ended, several of the officers came to Dr. Cobham's to dine. Among them was Bob Howe himself. He was never more full of the devil than when there were pretty women around. Miss Schaw resolved to keep clear of this playboy, of whom she had heard many racy stories in her few months in North Carolina. She had already entered into her private journal the observation that he was "the worst character you ever heard thro' the whole province. . . . He is deemed a horrid animal, . . . and that no woman can withstand him." She was confident that she could get through the evening without falling prey to him. But it would be best not to get too near him.

Unmartial means unmilitary.

A courier from Boston brings news to Charlotte of the recent encounter at Lexington and Concord.

Piqued means to be offended.

Reproved means scolded.

Prodigals—the word suggests wasteful people, but Miss Schaw may have meant to say Prodigies, meaning amazing or abnormal.

Coventry is a town in England to which Shakespeare, author of the play, was referring.

Howe had not been long in the house when he slipped away from the others. He went into a room where Janet had been reading. He returned in a few minutes. He was holding the open book she had just laid aside. "I was piqued at his freedom," she wrote later, "and reproved him with a half compliment. . . . He owned his fault and with much gallantry promised to submit to whatever punishment I would inflict. You shall only, said I, read aloud a few pages which I will point out, and I am sure you will do Shakespear justice. He bowed and took the book. . . ."

Colonel Howe read only a line or two before he realized that the young lady had played him a smart trick. The passage was one from *Henry IV*. In this passage, Falstaff describes the soldiers he has recruited. Howe, "colored like Scarlet" before his amused audience, had to read that he was "ashamed of my soldiers. . . ." They were such men as would soon "hear the devil as a drum," "such indeed as were never soldiers, but discarded . . . serving men," "a hundred and fifty tatter'd prodigals lately come from swine-keeping. . . . No eye hath seen such scarecrows. I'll not march through Coventry with them. . . ."

He was not one to miss a chance of turning defeat into victory. Howe, when he had finished the passage, "recovered himself," wrote Janet, "and coming close up to me, whispered, you will certainly get yourself tarred and feathered; shall I apply to be executioner?" She knew enough of Bob Howe's previous "executions" to decline the honor.

May 1775 in Wilmington was a memorable month. On the eighth, news reached town of a battle between Redcoats and Minutemen at Concord, Massachusetts. But, in the middle of the month, Janet Schaw and the Rutherfords received an invitation from Governor Martin to come to New Bern. There they would celebrate the king's birthday on June 4. This was enough to chase away the gloom of bad news from New England. It would turn Janet's thoughts to gaiety and fashion. It would be the high point of her visit to the colonies.

They were all set to leave for New Bern when, in the last days of May, came the most astonishing news yet. A drunken mob had attacked Governor Martin's house. It was in protest over his hiding some cannon from the New Bern Safety Committee. Governor Martin was forced to take refuge on a British ship in the harbor. There would be no celebration of the royal birthday after all.

The summer was miserable for Janet Schaw. Governor Martin arrived at Fort Johnston, later seeking safety on the *Cruizer*. Alexander Schaw, Janet's brother, hurried to join the

In 1804, the legislature established a permanent "Court of Conference." In 1805, the name of the court was changed to Supreme Court.

Mock hangings of Tories were popular all along the Atlantic seaboard in the early stages of the Revolution.

Depredations are acts of injury and destruction.

governor on the ship. But Wilmington was in an uproar. Many of the Scots and others loyal to the king began packing to leave. News arrived about a set of resolves by rebels in Mecklenburg County. On May 31, they all but declared their independence from Great Britain. Rumors flew everywhere that the governor was about to attack the Cape Fear rebels and restore royal control.

By late July, Janet was ready to leave by the first boat for Scotland or any other safe place. On July 18, Howe and his "soldiers" burned Fort Johnston. On August 20 another provincial Congress met at Hillsborough. The delegates created a Provincial Council to govern the colony when the Congress was not in session. The Council put local government formally into the hands of the Safety Committees. They also authorized the recruiting of two regiments under Howe and James Moore. They made other arrangements to prepare North Carolina for war.

Governor Martin issued a call for his Council to meet with him on board the *Cruizer.* Only John Rutherford showed up. When he got back home, the Safety Committee demanded that Rutherford resign his office. Since he was unwilling to do this, he gathered Miss Schaw and his children together and slipped away to the *Cruizer.* In her journal of her North Carolina adventure, Janet wrote of her relief at being safe at last. But she also wrote of her fears for the future of the troubled colony she was leaving behind:

> . . . farewell unhappy land," she wrote, "for which my heart bleeds in pity. Little does it signify to you, who are the conquered or who the victorious; you are devoted to ruin, whoever succeeds. Many years will not make up [for] these last months of depredations.

The Bridge at Moore's Creek

Week by week, the rebel forces increased in strength and determination. Josiah Martin had been making plans to crush them and return North Carolina to obedience. In June 1775, he sent Alexander Schaw to London with a message. It was for the Secretary of State for the Colonies, Lord Dartmouth. The message outlined and sought approval for a plan. This was to use British troops and North Carolina Loyalists in an operation to recover control of all the rebellious southern colonies.

North Carolina troops in the Continental Army wore uniforms such as this—when they could get them.

Martin's plan was altered and enlarged before it was adopted. But Dartmouth agreed to send seven regiments and some artillery to the mouth of the Cape Fear River. The governor was to recruit Loyalist forces. He claimed he could raise twenty thousand, half the fighting men in the colony. If things looked promising when the regulars arrived from England, Martin was to land what forces he needed. He would send the rest on to the recovery of South Carolina. He would then join the British and Loyalist troops and subdue the North Carolina rebels.

Martin received information about approval of the revised plan in January 1776. He immediately issued a call for supporters of the king to march to Brunswick. They were to meet him there on February 15. Rebel forces had already aided in defeating British and Loyalist troops at Norfolk, Virginia and in South Carolina. They were becoming bolder daily. No time must be lost in striking back.

On February 9, news reached Wilmington that British General Donald McDonald had issued some orders. They were for Loyalists of the upper Cape Fear River to gather at Cross Creek (now Fayetteville). From there they were to march downriver and join the governor at Brunswick. Colonel James Moore set out at once with his First North Carolina Regiment. He was to try to block the route of the Tories and prevent them from reaching Brunswick. With a force of eleven hundred men, he reached Moore's Creek, 18 miles above Wilmington. They seized the bridge there, which McDonald's forces must cross. The state was set for the first battle of the Revolution in North Carolina.

One of many accounts of this battle was composed later by James Fallon. He was the person jailed at Wilmington a month before by the Safety Committee. Having been freed—by patriot forces or some other means—Fallon was ready to join in the coming battle. His story, still written in the third person, is taken up at the point where it was left off earlier in this chapter:

"The design of the [Tories]," wrote Fallon, "was [besides the reinstatement of the Governor] to seize . . . the stores . . . the people devoted to liberty had been collecting at Wilmington, for the . . . [patriot] army. . . . General [John] Ashe, in cooperation with Colonel Moore's detachment, marched from Wilmington to Cross Creek. . . . James accompanied the General as a volunteer, but 50 young gentlemen, the sons of respectable families, in and about Wilmington, who composed a troop of cavalry, soon elected [Fallon] their captain. The . . . Tories . . . were increased to near 3000 men; from desertion, the revolutionary force scarcely amounted to 700 men. Ashe and Moore were . . . constrained to retreat towards Wilmington, to cover the stores of that town. At or near Moore's Creek, they were reinforced by 300 men, under Colonel Caswell, then at a bridge which gave passage over the Creek. . . . The [Loyalist] forces attempted to force their way over the bridge, a battle ensued, and the Americans gained the day. This was the first military action James had, at this time, seen. He . . . distinguished himself . . . so much, that a Captain's Commission in the regular Army of the United States, was soon sent to him. . . ."

No two accounts of the Battle of Moore's Creek Bridge, of February 27, 1776, are just alike. Fallon's varies in certain details from others. It is generally agreed that Moore's forces had about the strength that Fallon gives them. But McDonald had barely half the three thousand claimed by the doctor. Moreover, Ashe and his men were not, as Fallon suggests, present at the battle. They had gone back to Wilmington before it began. Nor did Moore fall back in order to protect sup-

British forces looked for an easy victory at the lower Cape Fear, but were defeated by the patriots at Moore's Creek Bridge.

North Carolina troops fought in all major battles of the Revolution and shared the long winter with General Washington at Valley Forge.

plies at Wilmington. He needed to gain time while awaiting reinforcements. Finally, there is no known record to support Fallon's claim to have been present at the battle.

The faults with Fallon's account of the battle recall the questions raised earlier. These concern his experiences at Wilmington in January. One must carefully follow the description of the activities of Governor Martin in 1775 and 1776 in this chapter. Then one can see the difference between those movements and the account of them given by Fallon. It does not seem that Martin's flight from New Bern in 1775 had anything to do with Fallon being arrested. The only arrest recorded was that of January 1776 by the Safety Committee.

These conflicts leave a strong impression—not quite proof—that Fallon lied about his role at the Battle of Moore's Creek Bridge and his political adventures at Wilmington. It is known that he was in Wilmington at the start of 1776. But most of the claims he makes seem false or exaggerated. He had no friendship with the governor. He was not arrested for publishing attacks against Martin. He was not held in high regard by the people of Wilmington or freed from jail by patriot forces.

This judgment gains strength from a glance at Fallon's later career. By 1777, he had become a surgeon in the Continental Army. He seems to have served faithfully in that capacity until the war's end. But after the war he was constantly involved in various plots. He tried to negotiate with Spain to keep Spanish Florida from falling under the control of the United States. He dealt with the Indians for the creation of a new western colony separate from the United States. He tried to get himself employed as an American secret agent. And there were other schemes. None of his plots amounted to anything by the time of his death in 1793.

James Fallon, as far as one can tell, may have stood up heroically to the Wilmington Safety Committee. This was in the dark days of 1776 when individual liberty seemed threatened. But he was far more concerned for his own gain than with the success of the American republic. He may be set down as a self-interested adventurer, primarily, and a revolutionary patriot, secondarily, if at all.

Whatever the situation of Dr. Fallon at the time, the Battle of Moore's Creek Bridge was an important one to the cause of independence. Fighting against a much larger force led by officers of the British regular army, the patriots had won a smashing victory. They had lost only one man killed and one wounded. This is compared with the Loyalist loss of about 50 dead and wounded, including their commander, Colonel Alexander McLeod, killed in battle. Colonel Moore pursued the retreating Tories and captured most of their equipment, including fifteen hundred rifles. General McDonald and other officers were taken prisoner. The *Annual Register,* an English publication, noted soberly that the North Carolina troops "had encountered Europeans [who were supposed to hold them in the most sovereign contempt, both as men and soldiers] and had defeated them with an inferior force."

And three thousand miles from Wilmington, Janet Schaw sat in a comfortable apartment on St. Andrew's Square in Edinburgh. Perhaps she had had time by now to finish *Henry IV.* If so, she could reflect upon the fact that Falstaff's "tatter'd prodigals lately come from swine-keeping" had defeated their enemies in battle. Bob Howe had the last laugh after all.

Sovereign means great or profound.

Chapter Checkup

PEOPLE

James Fallon	Janet Schaw	John Rutherford
James Moore	Robert Howe	Josiah Martin
Cornelius Harnett	William Houston	Donald McDonald

PLACES

Fort Johnston   Moore's Creek Bridge   Cross Creek

FACT

What accounts for the support Fallon received from some people at Wilmington?

What objection did Wilmington patriots have to the Stamp Act?

How did the patriots frustrate the Assembly called by Martin in April 1775?

What was Martin's plan to reconquer North Carolina?

INTERPRETATION

How much of Fallon's statement on pages 139-140 is doubtful? Why?

Why do you suppose the militia was drilled in "Bush fighting" instead of the regular formations of the British Army?

James Fallon and Janet Schaw were from different parts of the British Isles. Do you suppose this helps account for their political views? Explain.

How much evidence do you find in this chapter that differences in wealth and status separated Whigs from Tories?

Notice that doctors played important roles on both sides between 1765 and 1776. Today, doctors seem to have more wealth and status but less political influence. What do you think may account for this?

VOCABULARY

Committee of Safety   Perspective
Confiscated   Provincial
Memoir   Convene
Sojourn

ACTIVITIES

Compose an attack on the Safety Committee such as you think Dr. Fallon may have written in Jan. 1776.

Prepare a time line of major events from 1763 to 1776 in North Carolina and the other colonies. Does the sequence suggest that North Carolina was leading other colonies or being led by them? (Use at least ten events from North Carolina and ten from elsewhere in the colonies.)

SUGGESTED READING

Andrew, Evangeline and Charles H. (eds.). *The Journal of a Lady of Quality.* New Haven: Yale University Press, 1923. Janet Schaw's journal of her experiences in and around Wilmington in 1775.

Butler, Lindley S. *North Carolina and the Coming of the Revolution, 1763–1776.* Raleigh: Division of Archives and History, 1976. Good brief survey of main events in the background of the Revolution.

Parramore, T. C. and Barbara M. *North Carolina in the Revolutionary Era.* Raleigh: State Dept. of Public Instruction, 1974. Curriculum guide to study of the period 1763 to 1789.

1776 Fourth Provincial
Congress at Halifax *(April)*
● Fifth Provincial Congress
at Halifax *(Dec.)*

1776 American colonies
declare their independence

1777 France recognizes
American independence *(Dec.)*

1780 Cornwallis invades North
Carolina; defeated at King's
Mountain *(Sept.)*

1781 Battle of Guilford Court
House *(March 15)*
● Governor Burke captured
by Fanning *(Sept. 12)*
● Battle of Lindley's Mill
(Sept. 13)
● Surrender of Cornwallis
at Yorktown *(Oct. 19)*

1782 Fanning leaves North
Carolina *(spring)*

1782 Peace talks begin
in Paris *(April)*

8

DAVID FANNING'S WAR

The Tory Colonel

The early morning fog hung very thick over the village of Hillsborough in this fall of 1781. The town guard, squinting into the gloom, could not make out the hands of the clock in the Anglican church tower. The intersection of King and Churton Streets would be noisily alive in an hour. But just now it was still peacefully quiet. No step could be heard in the vicinity of the great, barn-like court house. It was quiet around Johnston and Thackston's store across the street. Courtney's tavern and the market house seemed strangely still for places usually so full of activity. The private residences along Tryon and Wake and Queen Streets still slept into the early dawn.

A single figure, wearing a buckskin jacket and carrying a hunting rifle, slipped silently along the edge of Margaret Lane. His reddened eyes stabbed nervously into the fog ahead of him. Another edged his way past the stocks and toward the jail behind the court house. Still another crept through the

Stocks were a device for punishing criminals, with holes for ankles and, sometimes, wrists as well.

145

cemetery toward King Street. A sleepy guard paid no attention to two men coming up the hill from the direction of the Eno River. There were still a few more seconds of autumn calm. And then the first cries went up from startled sentinels. The first reports of muskets rang along the streets.

Irritated people turned restlessly in their beds. They muttered curses at the guards for their ill-timed sport. The colonel would hear from them about this. If he couldn't control his men, then he should be relieved of command and replaced by an officer who knew something about discipline.

The outcries of the black servants alerted the citizens. This was not just a drunken target practice. The sound of shooting could be heard now in every direction. The hoarse bark of commands proved to the last skeptics that the town was under attack. In 40 houses, frightened parents began ordering children into cellars and attics. They began throwing silver spoons and gold watches behind loose bricks, snatching muskets and swords from their racks. It had to be Tory cutthroats who were attacking. Lord Cornwallis had already taken up his winter quarters in Virginia.

The noise of the shooting gained intensity toward the eastern part of town. Robert Mebane's mind groped for the meaning of the invaders' objective. Eastward lay the governor's quarters. Very likely they meant to burn the house in revenge for some injury. Another moment passed before Mebane got hold of his thoughts. The raiders must be trying to kill or capture the governor himself. North Carolina was about to lose its governor!

Governor Thomas Burke had been blasting away with his pistols from an upstairs window since the first ghostly

Skeptics are doubters.

A *Tory* was a person who supported continued allegiance to Great Britain.

146

An ***aide-de-camp*** is an assistant.

An ***orderly*** is a soldier assigned as attendant or assistant.

shadow darted across the lawn. Captain Read, Burke's aide-de-camp, the faithful secretary, Mr. Huske, and an orderly, had taken up stations in other parts of the house. This was to cover all outside doors. There was no chance of escape—the governor could see that. Powder-blasts now came from behind almost every tree or shrub in the yard. The only thing left was to shoot it out to the death. They would make the vandals pay dearly for their victory. There need be no thought of surrender. These were outlaw Tories who would hang a prisoner as quickly as they would bayonet an enemy!

The unequal exchange of fire went on for quite some time. Suddenly, out of the shrubbery, a white flag appeared. One of the attackers walked with it slowly toward the house. Governor Burke and his defenders held their fire. They watched the approaching figure, now clearly an officer dressed in a British uniform. When he came within hearing, the officer identified himself as a British Highlander. He told the governor that he must surrender. But he could expect to be treated as a prisoner of war and not a common thief. The invaders were mostly loyalists, but there were Scottish regulars among them. They would insure that the rules of civilized war be followed. Burke discussed the matter briefly with Read

A ***Highlander*** is a native of the mountainous region of Scotland.

As a boy of 13, Andrew Jackson was struck by a British officer when he refused to clean the officer's boots.

and Huske. He measured once more the alternatives he had. Finally, he told the officer he would surrender. Within a few minutes, North Carolina had lost its central government.

It was late in the morning before David Fanning could pause a few moments and take stock of his success at Hillsborough. Two years ago, he had been a hunted fugitive with a pair of bullet holes in his back. He had nothing to call his own but the clothes he wore. Now, September 12, 1781, he had suddenly become the decisive influence in the affairs of North Carolina. The governor was his prisoner. Several members of the governor's council, some Continental colonels, and 71 Continental regulars were also his captives. Fifteen rebels lay dead in the streets, with 20 others wounded. All this had been accomplished at the cost of one man injured among Fanning's forces. It had to be one of the most thrilling feats of arms so far in the war. And all the credit belonged to this Johnston County farmboy, who had planned and executed it.

Even Thomas Burke, the one-eyed and pock-marked governor, was shaken by his first glimpse of the famous Tory leader. He knew that Fanning's silk cap was never removed in the presence of others. It covered hideous bald scars left from a boyhood case of tetters, or ring-worm, that went too long untreated. He also knew something of Fanning's background. There was the death of his father when he was a child and his

Continental means in the service of the Continental Congress.

Hillsborough-Halifax, 1785

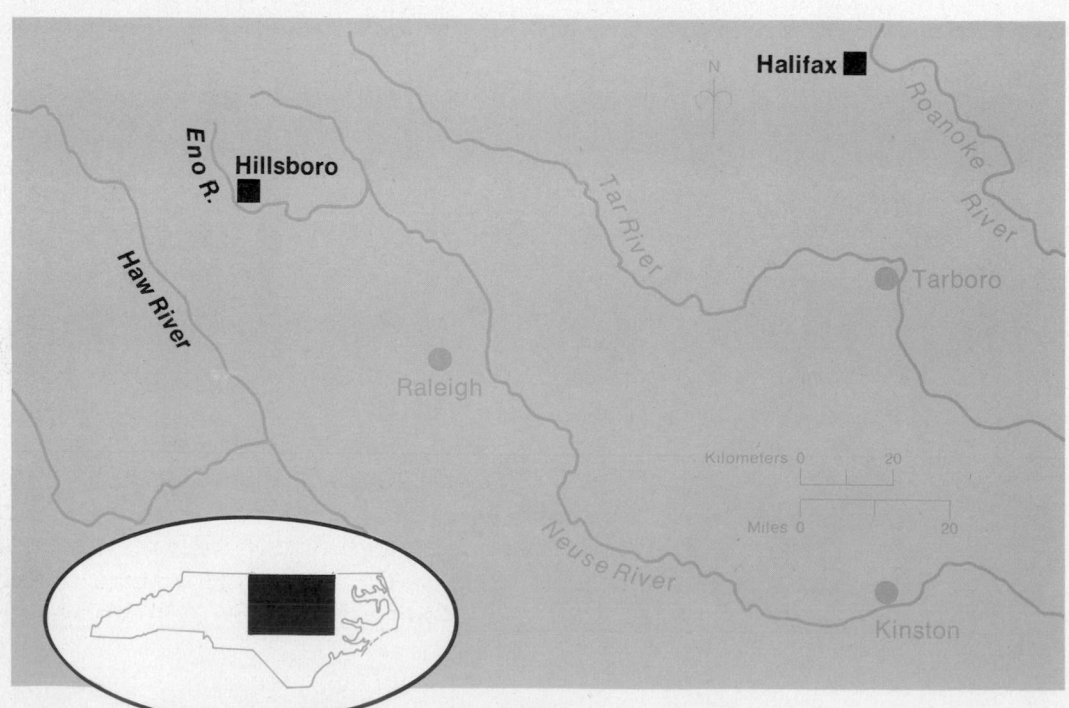

apprenticeship to a cruel master in Johnston County. He knew of his escape to South Carolina, and his employment there as an Indian trader before the war. But now, at 25 years of age, this unschooled orphan runaway had done something that the bravest Redcoat officers scarcely dreamed of doing.

Burke had heard of Fanning's early experience as a Tory guerrilla in South Carolina. Fanning had been captured at least 12 times by South Carolina rebels. Sometimes he was chained naked to the floors of rebel jails and brutally treated. But each time he had found some way out—either by a hair-raising escape or a promise of good behavior. Before the ordeal was over, he became, in his own words, "a rack of nothing but skin and bones, . . . my wounds had not been dressed, my clothes all bloody. My misery was beyond explanation, and no friend in the world that I could depend on. . . ."

He had also become something else. He was a daring and artful guerrilla fighter, an expert horseman, and a crack pistol shot. He asked no mercy from his enemies and gave none. In late 1780, he found that the South Carolina backcountry was hopelessly overrun with rebels. He moved into the Deep River country of the Piedmont section of North Carolina. Here, in Randolph County, the old love of King George lived on in the hearts of hundreds of settlers. David Fanning hoped for a chance to take revenge for the injuries he had received.

The army of Cornwallis arrived in North Carolina in early 1781. This revived the hopes of Tories that they might yet see the province recovered. Not since the last weeks before the Battle of Moore's Creek Bridge had there been such high hopes of a British victory. New Tory units sprang up in a score of places. They responded to Cornwallis' call for help. In Randolph and Chatham Counties, the Tories elected David Fanning as their leader. They began attacking the Whigs. During the spring and early summer of 1781, Fanning led one bold raid after another. He surprised Whigs at their camps and fell upon wagon-trains of Whig supplies. He destroyed the houses and property of leading patriots. Within six months, Fanning became the most feared and respected Tory leader of the war in North Carolina. North Carolina patriots were too hard-pressed by Cornwallis to give proper attention to guerrilla bands. They tried to defeat the Redcoat army—at King's Mountain, at Cowan's Ford, at Guilford Court House.

Meanwhile, Fanning went to Wilmington, occupied by the British in early 1781. There, he obtained a commission as a colonel of loyalist militia. He was promised British support for his campaign in the Piedmont. He also discussed an idea with Colonel James Craig, British commander at Wilmington.

Guerrillas are independent soldier bands who attack an enemy's supply and communications lines by surprise raids.

He had a plan for capturing the rebel governor and turning him over to the British.

In early September 1781, Fanning gathered together almost a thousand Tories. He furnished them with guns and supplies from Wilmington. He had been joined by Highland regiments from Cumberland and Bladen Counties. He then learned that Governor Burke was at Hillsborough with only a small detachment to guard him. Setting out on September 11, Fanning let his men believe that he meant to attack a Whig force west of Hillsborough under General Butler. They proceeded about half-way to the announced destination. Fanning then ordered a change of course and revealed the real plan. After marching all night, the Tories surrounded Hillsborough before sunrise on September 12. Before noon that day, he had performed what has been called "without doubt the most brilliant exploit of any group of Loyalists in any state throughout the Revolution."

It was one thing to capture the governor, however daringly it was done. It was quite another thing to deliver him and some two hundred prisoners across one hundred fifty miles of country to Wilmington. Whig war parties were still close by. The patriots would run any risk to rescue the governor. Fanning must expect desperate fighting along the entire route. In fact, unknown to the Tory colonel, a force of Whigs had started in pursuit of him almost before he left Hillsborough on the twelfth.

During the morning, Robert Mebane managed to slip through the Tory dragnet at Hillsborough. He borrowed a horse from a farmer and galloped off in search of General Butler. He rode into Butler's camp, not long after Fanning tore the last of his men away from the rum kegs and the division of spoils. Fanning set out for Wilmington but camped overnight a little south of Hillsborough. He crossed Haw River the next morning. Butler, by now, had his men in position at Lindley's Mill, directly in the line of Fanning's march.

The Tory column stretched for perhaps a mile along the narrow road leading to Lindley's Mill. The prisoners were near the rear of the column. Fanning had failed to make certain that scouts were sent out ahead. He had no warning of the ambush that awaited him. The front of the column was wading across Stafford Branch, a small arm of Cane Creek. Around 10 A.M., a hail of fire suddenly came pouring down from the plateau above—on the far side of the branch. Tory soldiers began dropping all around. At the same moment, a Whig force attacked the rear of the column. The Whigs attempted either to free the prisoners or create such confusion that they could escape on their own.

A **dragnet** is an organized force of searchers.

Spoils are property taken by force.

A **plateau** is level land which rises above adjacent lands.

Now the self-confidence and quick wit of David Fanning came out. Although surprised and shaken, he was able to recover from the first assaults. He positioned his men for defense and counterattack without losing control of the prisoners. He got the governor and other captives into Spring Meeting House, a Quaker church. He sent a detachment around behind the plateau at Staffords Branch to strike at the Whigs from the rear. The battle raged on for about four hours. Neither side was able to gain a clear advantage over the other. But at last the Whigs withdrew far enough from their first position to allow Fanning's force to pass. As the firing faded, Fanning was hit in the arm by a rebel bullet. He spent the next several weeks recovering at the home of a Tory.

The Battle of Lindley's Mill was one of the bloodiest actions of the war in North Carolina. It cost the lives of 27 Tories and at least 24 Whigs. But Fanning had preserved his captive governor, who was taken to Wilmington. With the other prisoners, the governor was turned over to the British. For Thomas Burke, the long march was an ordeal of "hunger, thirst, and fatigue," as he later wrote, "and . . . frequent dangers" along "vast pathless tracts of intermingled Sand and Swamp very thinly inhabited and which ought not to be inhabited at all."

For North Carolina, the loss of the governor was the last in a painful series of blows. These left the state at the point of collapse. Most of its army had been captured by the British at Charleston in 1780. The militia was poorly equipped. It was unable to defend the state against guerrillas, let alone the army of Cornwallis. The treasury was bankrupt. The destruction of more than six years of fighting had drained the patriots of much of their strength and spirit. The fight for liberty had become a struggle for survival. The dreams of 1775 seemed all to have been betrayed. Liberty seemed to be a snare, democracy a delusion. What had gone wrong? Why had the great enterprise failed?

The Battered Alliance

The ink was not yet dry on the Declaration of Independence when North Carolina patriots, firmly united in what they were against, began disputing over what they were for. Tories, of course, had no part in shaping the new state government. But Whigs split politically into two broad types as to the means by which democracy and liberty would be sought. Perhaps the root of the difference was a sort of moral attitude about the limits and capacities of human nature. Whatever it was, the difference was to become a permanent part of the political life of North Carolina and of the new union of the states.

The Whig leaders were soon identified as either radicals or conservatives. To be a radical was to favor rule by a majority of citizens. This would be achieved through a strong legislature representing all classes equally. The government, in turn, would be controlled by the legislature. Thus North Carolina would have rule by the people.

Conservatives doubted the wisdom of such a scheme. The mass of the people, they felt, needed a strong governor. Only such an officer could hold the people's loyalty and obedience. The people were not ready for self-rule. They might never be. They needed a leader who was free to shape state policy without a lot of legislative meddling. They needed the guidance of those of good birth and training who were the natural leaders of society.

This difference did not emerge immediately, but it was evident soon after the war began. When the Fourth Provincial Congress met at Halifax in April 1776, there was only one great subject. It was independence, and everybody there was for it. The delegates instructed their representatives at the Second Continental Congress to vote for independence, "reserving to this Colony the sole and exclusive right of forming a Constitution and laws" for itself. There was much celebration on August 1, 1776. This was after Cornelius Harnett read the Declaration of Independence for the first time in public.

For the next several months, North Carolina was ruled by a single, statewide Council of Safety. It replaced the district safety committees of the past. Harnett, as council president, was, in effect, governor of the state. But in October there were elections for another provincial congress that would draw up a state constitution. It was at this point that the Radicals parted company with the Conservatives. Samuel Johnston of Edenton was the leading Conservative. Willie (pronounced Wiley) Jones of Halifax was the foremost Radical.

The Fifth—and last—Provincial Congress held its sessions at Halifax in November and December 1776. The constitution they agreed upon gave North Carolina a legislature of two houses, a senate, and a house of commons. A governor and governor's council were to be elected annually by the two houses. To vote for a member of the house of commons, a person must be a taxpayer. But a person could vote for a senator only if at least 50 acres of land was owned. To serve in the house required ownership of one hundred or more acres, in the senate, not less than three hundred. Other high officials, including judges of the supreme court and delegates to the Continental Congress, would be elected by the General Assembly.

Radicals rejoiced that the governor would have no veto. He would have no power to summon or dismiss the legislature. But Conservatives felt that the constitution protected the position and influence of people of property and education from too much meddling by the masses. The fact was that representation in both houses was based not on population count but on counties. This seemed to be another feature that would curb the power of the masses. The constitution insured that North Carolina, for the next 60 years, would be a democracy in theory only. It was, in fact, an oligarchy, a state ruled by the privileged minority.

Both parties had won "victories" that were to serve North Carolina ill. Samuel Johnston's Conservatives had a dim view of the common people. They may have seen that the majority were not ready for intelligent self-rule. But it would have been wise to demand that the constitution promote the speediest overcoming of the people's lack of education. This would hasten the time when they could direct their own affairs. Instead, the constitution had only a vague clause calling for "a School or Schools . . . for the convenient Instruction of youth, . . . and one or more Universities." Not surprisingly, North Carolina would remain backward in educational facilities for a long time to come.

If the injury inflicted by the Conservatives was long-range in effect, that done by the Radicals was more immediate. The first governor, Richard Caswell, was appointed by the last provincial congress. He was elected in the following spring by the General Assembly. But Caswell had a title that carried little real power or freedom of action. The hero of Moore's Creek Bridge had the respect and admiration of the legislature. But he did not have the authority needed to wage war on a strong enemy or to cope with a civil war at home.

Two issues particularly plagued Caswell and the new government as they struggled to mount some kind of effective war effort. The first was the old problem of unfair representation. The second was the new problem of virtual bankruptcy.

The representation issue went back to the 1730s. It had to do with the continuing over-representation of the eastern counties in the General Assembly. With less than half the white population of the state, the East had 37 delegates to the West's 21. It was not as bad as it had been, but bad enough.

The *masses*—The majority of the people.

An *oligarchy* is a form of government ruled by a few persons.

Westerners found this more and more of an aggravation during the war years and the peace that followed.

There was nothing the governor could do about representation. There was not much he could do about finances. The state was born with empty pockets. It had little foreign trade and few manufactures. Its need for money exceeded anything in its previous history. Enough paper money was printed to raise prices by some eight hundred percent as the war dragged on. But soldiers could still not get guns and uniforms. Many were enticed into the army by promises of land if the Whigs won. Many became discouraged at the lack of progress toward victory. Desertion was high. Caswell, pressed by Harnett in 1777 to help recruit more soldiers, had to point out that the constitution did not give him this authority.

Like Dr. Frankenstein, the Fifth Provincial Congress had created a powerful body with a weak head. North Carolina had great physical and human resources. But it lacked the leadership needed to harness and direct those resources toward productive ends. A poor situation in a time of peace, this was a disaster in time of war.

For patriots in the eastern part of the state, the Revolutionary War was mainly a maritime struggle. American merchants were denied access to their normal markets in Great Britain or its colonies. They tried to open new routes of trade—to France and Spain, the Mediterranean, the French and Dutch West Indies. But the Royal Navy seemed to be everywhere. North Carolina traders were heavy losers to British warships. Many North Carolina sailors spent long periods in British prisons. Some were even persuaded to work for the English.

Prices rose so rapidly that the risk of going to sea was still worth it. North Carolinians built many ships during the war. Some of these the state managed to arm as privateers. Now and then the privateers were able to capture British vessels. This prevented the sea war from being so one-sided. The state also built two row galleys on the Blackwater River. They were sent to the defense of the sounds.

There were many tales similar to that of the schooner *Polly*. Few, however, ended as happily for the Whigs. The *Polly* was built in Currituck County in 1779. It was sent early in 1780 with a cargo of pork, peas, and beans for the French West Indies. But it was hardly out of sight of land when it was run down by a British privateer. Its three-man crew was imprisoned below deck by a British boarding party.

The prize crew turned the *Polly* toward British-occupied New York. Two white men of her American crew were

Enticed means lured.

Dr. Frankenstein is a fictitious doctor who created the Frankenstein Monster.

Row galleys are ships equipped with oars for movement in shallow water or at greater speed.

The schooner *Mary* was typical of thousands of New England ships that visited North Carolina in the early nineteenth century.

A *marlin spike* is a pointed iron tool used to separate strands of rope in splicing.

chained in a small room below. Ja⎯, a black slave who belonged to the *Polly*'s owner, was l⎯hed down to the main deck in freezing weather. Waves we⎯ constantly breaking over him. After 24 hours, the British found that Jack was frostbitten. But he had worked partially free of his bonds. They put him below with his fellow crewmen.

The captives agreed that Jack should try to pass himself off as a Tory. He might get free and find a way to release the others. The prize crew, needing help in stormy seas, accepted Jack's pledges of love for the king. He was put to work despite his frostbitten feet. After a few hours, Jack was able to help free his comrades. With a marlin spike, he helped overcome the prize crew. The Americans sailed the *Polly* to Annapolis. There, Jack received the thanks of Congress and an appeal to his master to set him free. The master refused, but Jack was later able to buy his freedom. The state, at his request, passed a law giving him the name John Jasper White. His middle and last names honored crewmen on the *Polly*.

In 1775, the Continental Congress asked North Carolina to raise some six thousand men for the Continental Army. But the state never had as much as a third of that number in Continental service. With over ten percent of the population of the country, North Carolina provided about two percent of the regular army. Weak as they were, however, North Carolina regiments saw service in some of the bloodiest actions of the war. These were at Brandywine and Germantown in 1777, Monmouth in 1778, and Stony Point in 1779. Some of them endured the long winter of 1777–1778 with General Washington at Valley Forge. But North Carolina made no significant contribution to the war effort before 1780.

For three years, the main fighting of the Revolution took place in New England and the Middle Atlantic states. In 1779, in the hope of using strong Tory support to help split off the

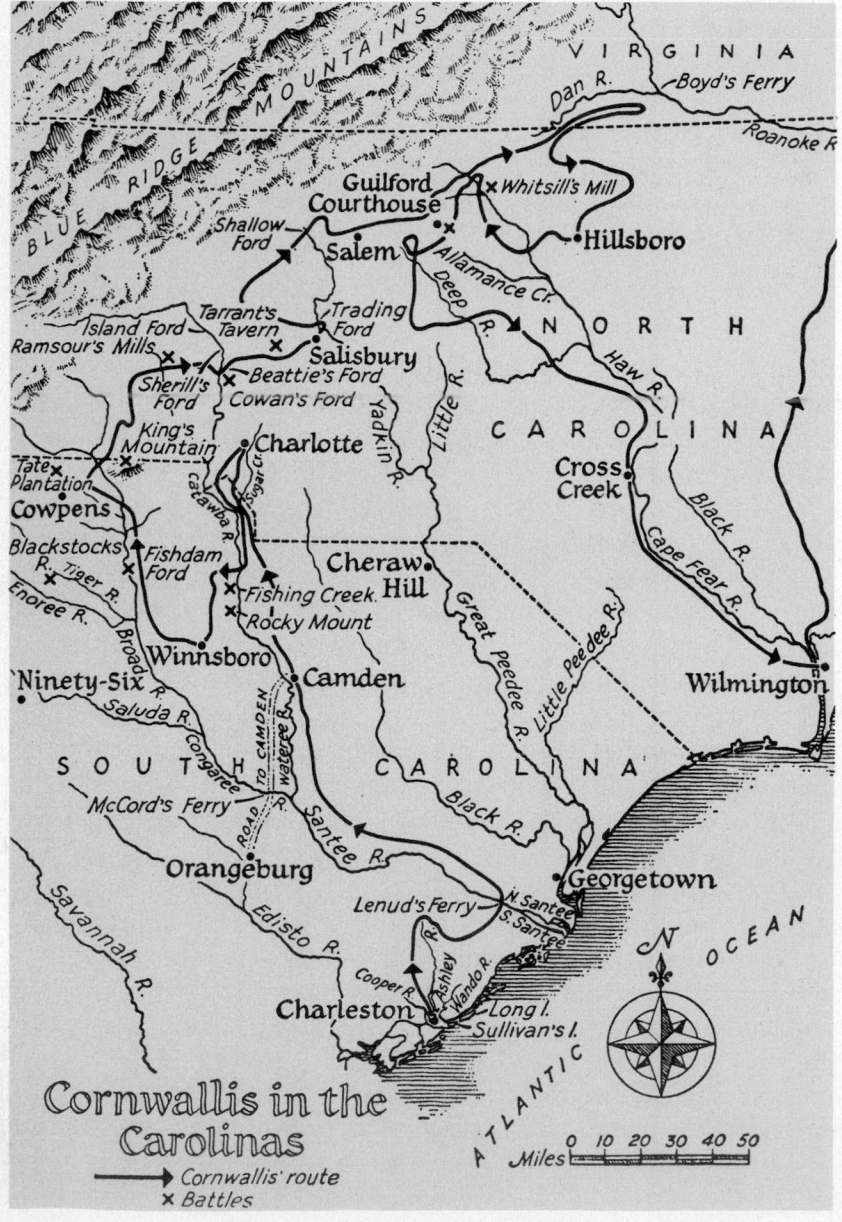

Cornwallis in the Carolinas

→ Cornwallis' route
✕ Battles

This map shows the route of the British Army under Cornwallis as it marched through North Carolina in 1780 and 1781.

southern states, the British shifted their attention to the South. The occupation of Savannah at the end of the year cleared the way to the return of Georgia to royal rule. This was followed by a British siege of Charleston in 1780. The city fell in May. With it, more than fourteen hundred North Carolina troops were lost. It was the bulk of the state's forces. A North Carolina loyalist regiment had a hand in the British successes. The regiment was under Colonel John Hamilton, formerly a great Halifax merchant.

Lord Cornwallis was now placed in charge of the British Army at Charleston. He was directed to proceed with the conquest, first, of South Carolina, and then North Carolina and Virginia. No doubt a quick strike at North Carolina would, indeed, have cost General Washington the support of this state. But Cornwallis was never in a hurry to do anything. He let himself get bogged down in a difficult guerrilla war against South Carolina partisans, especially Francis Marion, "the Swamp Fox." Tory forces in North Carolina attempted to help clear a path for the approach of Cornwallis. But they found similar difficulty with guerrillas led by Colonel William R. Davie and other skillful Whig warriors.

Partisans are bands engaged in fighting against an occupying army.

Abruptly, the British and Tory forces found themselves once again in a position to stamp out Whig resistance in the South. On August 16, 1780, Cornwallis won a brilliant victory over the Continentals at Camden, South Carolina. Some four hundred North Carolina patriots were killed in this action. Others were captured, again leaving the state with almost no army. Abner Nash, succeeding Caswell as governor, could not even get his discouraged council to attend its meetings. The General Assembly, at the urging of Nash, created a Board of War. It had emergency power to direct preparations against invasion. The board struck that power down when Nash complained that his own power was now less than ever. A "Council Extraordinary" replaced the Board of War.

Cornwallis, dawdling along into North Carolina in September, had a grand plan for the conquest of the state following his splendid victory at Camden. One army would occupy Wilmington to give him a convenient base of supplies. Another would veer westward to defeat a rebel force called "the overmountain men." They were known to be gathering in the Appalachian foothills. The main body of troops, led by his lordship, would march on to Hillsborough. There, Tories were to collect supplies and enable Cornwallis to rest before starting the conquest of Virginia.

Cornwallis had scarcely reached Charlotte when he realized that he had been misled about Tory sentiment in North

Carolina. The people of Charlotte and Mecklenburg were viciously anti-British, "more hostile to England," the British thought, "than any others in America." But it was the "overmountain men" who thoroughly spoiled the reception of Cornwallis in North Carolina. At the Battle of King's Mountain (a mile and a half inside South Carolina), a scruffy band of patriot mountaineers crushed the British. The patriots killed and captured almost eight hundred British. They lost only 28 of their own. Cornwallis drew back into South Carolina in shock and dismay. He puzzled over what to do next.

There followed another defeat at Cowpens, South Carolina, in early 1781. Cornwallis, his reason perhaps clouded by his setbacks, resolved to launch a full-scale offensive. He marched again into North Carolina. He was lured into a tiring cat-and-mouse chase by the new Continental Commander in the South, General Nathanael Greene. A showdown finally came at Guilford Court House on March 15. Cornwallis, technically speaking, won a victory that day over the Americans. But it was so costly in deaths and injuries that his army was no longer the great machine it was before. He now turned east for a pause at Wilmington. Then he marched on into Virginia where he was destined to surrender at Yorktown on October 19. It was not yet the end of the war, but it sealed the fate of the American Revolution.

An important victory for patriot forces occurred at King's Mountain, South Carolina, on October 7, 1780.

This dramatic moment occurred in the Guilford Court House Battle, March 15, 1781, a battle costly to the British.

The One-Man War

David Fanning's magnificent exploit at Hillsborough preceded the surrender of the British at Yorktown by only 34 days. At the peak of his strength and fame, he suddenly saw his work of over six years thrown away by a sorry general. To make matters worse, Governor Burke was paroled by the British. On his word of honor he was to take no more part in the war. But he broke parole by escaping and was soon back in power.

It was a maddening end to the great struggle, one that Fanning found he could not accept. He made up his mind that he would continue the war somehow. He hoped that some miracle of salvation might yet justify his suffering, revenge his wounds. It was a faint hope, but it was all he had left. He had to be lifted onto his horse after more than three weeks in bed from his wound at Lindley's Mill. But within the next hour he had won another victory over the Whig militia.

Even the news that the British had abandoned Wilmington, his base of supplies, did not discourage Fanning. It did not hinder his ability to inspire the Piedmont Tories. The war in this section became, during the winter of 1781–1782, more savage than ever before. Fanning's own account of the period relates the most shocking deeds by himself and his enemies. He tells of many chilling incidents: ". . . this party took one of my men, . . . David Jackson, and hung him up without ceremony," "fell in with one of [Capt. Colson's] men who had been assisting the rebels, I killed him," "fell in, with a man who had been very anxious for to have some of my men executed . . . but I shot him," "three of their people followed Capt. Linley; and cut him to pieces with their swords . . . I took two of them and hung them . . . both on the limb of the same tree," "I . . . delivered him up to some of my men, who he had treated ill when prisoners; and they immediately hung him."

But even David Fanning at last saw the uselessness of the fight. In the spring of 1782, he left the state for good. Fanning died in 1825 in peaceful old age in Nova Scotia. He had become a legend in his own time—the symbol for the cause of all the sufferings experienced by North Carolina patriots during the war.

Nova Scotia is a province of eastern Canada.

More appropriately, however, Fanning was a symbol of another kind. His career owed something to the determined individualism of those who had framed North Carolina's constitution in 1776. They had created a government that could interfere but little in the individual liberties of those it called citizens. The government was bound to respect individual liberty. But it was not capable of defending it. The problem was how to keep the government obedient enough to leave individuals alone, but strong enough to defend them. It might be said that the North Carolina constitution granted too much individual liberty. One result was that the state government was too weak to rescue itself from David Fanning.

Where was the proper balance of conflicting aims here? Where were the law-makers wise enough to give it force? The problem was not that of North Carolina alone. It haunted the new union of states and the creation of a common constitution for them all.

Chapter Checkup

PEOPLE

Thomas Burke	Willie Jones	Abner Nash
David Fanning	Richard Caswell	Lord Cornwallis
Samuel Johnston	John Jasper White	

PLACES

Lindley's Mill Battlefield   Charlotte
King's Mountain Battlefield   Guilford Court House

FACT

How did Fanning gain the confidence of the British and the Carolina loyalists?

What were the major weaknesses of North Carolina's patriots in October 1781?

What flaws in the state constitution contributed to this state of weakness?

What ideas distinguished Radicals from Conservatives?

INTERPRETATION

Do you feel that North Carolina made an important contribution to the patriot victory in the war? Explain.

In what respects can it be said that the North Carolina Constitution of 1776 gave too much scope to individual liberty? How did this happen? Was there a connection between North Carolina's role in the new Continental government and its traditional individualism?

ACTIVITY

Draw up terms of a brief constitution for North Carolina that would have avoided the drawbacks of the one actually written.

SUGGESTED READING

Crow, Jeffrey J. *A Chronicle of North Carolina During the American Revolution*. Raleigh: Division of Archives and History, 1976. Brief descriptions of events which highlighted each year from 1763 to 1789.

Mathews, Alice E. *Society in Revolutionary North Carolina*. Raleigh: Division of Archives and History, 1976. General survey of life in the colony and state in the troubled era.

Troxler, Carole W. *The Loyalist Experience in North Carolina*. Raleigh: Division of Archives and History, 1976. Brief survey includes career of David Fanning and many other loyalists.

1777 France recognizes American independence *(Dec.)*

1778 Articles of Confederation adopted

1781 Congress names peace commission

1782 Peace talks begin in Paris *(April)*

1787 North Carolina delegation sent to Philadelphia convention
- General Assembly calls for constitutional convention in North Carolina for July 1788 *(Dec.)*

1788 Elections held for constitutional convention *(March)*
- Convention rejects federal Constitution *(July)*

1789 North Carolina ratifies federal Constitution *(Nov. 16)*

1789 French Revolution begins
- Washington inaugurated President *(April 30)*

9

THE FIRST SECESSION

The Ten-Mile Square

The 1788 *State Gazette* at New Bern devoted over half its October 4 issue to the text of the proposed federal Constitution. The idle thoughts of recent months promptly broke into the Great Debate. New Bern's other paper, the *North Carolina Gazette*, came out with an essay. It proved to all but the very stupid that such a constitution must "submit us to an unlimited slavery, like ancient Rome." The *State Gazette* printed some Chowan County resolutions of November 8. These showed that if the new Constitution were not adopted independence would "pass away like a shadow." Baffled North Carolinians wondered why they were being asked to choose between America's freedom and its independence. They had hoped, somehow, to keep both.

Abraham Hodge of the *State Gazette* and Francis X. Martin of the *North Carolina Gazette* both seemed to think they held the fate of civilization in their ink-stained hands. Hodge

Hugh Williamson, *an author of the Constitution*
Elkanah Watson, *a Federalist*
Lemuel Burkitt, *a Baptist preacher*

Archibald MacLaine, *a Federalist Wilmington attorney*
James Tate, *a schoolmaster*
Willie Jones, *an anti-Federalist*

At a stand means halted, or stopped.

Heralded means reported.

published the Edenton District Grand Jury's declaration of November 12. It said that the country had been "a union in nothing but name" for a decade. North Carolina's trade was "at the very verge of ruin, and all private industry at a stand. . . ." Martin's paper replied that the new Constitution would let Congress force "strange new courts" on the states, "abolishing trial by jury." It would impose a standing army. This was always regarded by Americans as "an insult and dangerous to the liberty of the people. . . ." But many readers remained unclear why either commerce or trial by jury had to be sacrificed.

Every boat from north or south brought new swings of the political pendulum. They brought more gloom or cheer for the worried New Bern editors. In his issue of November 29, Hodge heralded the news that six states had already called for

Francois X. Martin became famous as a printer, historian, and public figure. He edited a New Bern newspaper during the 1789 debate over the federal Constitution.

164

Elkanah Watson, a
Massachusetts native, was a
strong Federalist during his
sojourn in North Carolina,
1787-1788.

Gilded means gold-colored.

conventions. These were to consider adopting the federal
Constitution. On December 19, Martin proclaimed that the
people of New York regarded the document as "a *gilded
trap*." The governor of that state had refused to call the legislature even to consider a convention.

The *State Gazette* pointed out that Benjamin Franklin,
George Washington, and North Carolina's own Dr. Hugh Williamson had helped to write the Constitution. The *North
Carolina Gazette* declared that John Jay, also an author of the
Constitution, now thought it was "as deep and wicked a conspiracy as has been ever invented . . . against the liberties of a
free people." Even the voice of patriotic wisdom, alas, spoke
with a forkéd tongue!

North Carolina's General Assembly met at Tarboro in December. It decided to call for a constitutional convention to
assemble on July 21, 1788, at Hillsborough. Elections for delegates would take place on March 20 and 21. The new year,
therefore, opened on a still more frantic note of debate. At
Warrenton, an anti-Federalist named William Faulkner announced that he would be a candidate for the convention.
Robert Leming, a Federalist merchant at Edenton, circulated a
rumor that Faulkner was a man of low character and a British
spy as well. Faulkner indignantly denied both charges.

Anti-Federalists were
opposed to the federal form
of government as creating a
too-powerful central
government.

Elkanah Watson, a Federalist in Hertford County, published a letter in the Edenton *Intelligencer* of February 27. He

openly attacked and ridiculed Faulkner's background. Barely escaping an attempt to tar and feather him at Edenton, Faulkner replied through the *North Carolina Gazette* of March 5 that the charge was a lie. Even if it were true, he added, "the incoherence [of the author] ... proves him inadequate to judge my abilities and incompetent to the task he has undertaken." There were many signs that the constitutional debate was getting out of hand.

As election time approached, nearly every county was in an uproar. There were debates over whether to elect candidates favorable to the Articles or the new constitution. The election itself brought outbreaks of violence. In Dobbs County, Federalists put up an outstanding group of candidates. These included former governor Richard Caswell and Secretary of State James Glasgow. The anti-Federalist candidates were obscure men of little political experience. The ballot-counting, conducted at Kinston, began while voting was still in progress. Each hour saw the Federalists slip farther behind. One angry Federalist was making threatening remarks to an election official. Another knocked a candle from the official's hand. The anti-Federalists bolted out through doors and windows as the rest of the candles were put out. A brawl began. Somebody in the darkened building knocked the sheriff down and ran off with the ballot box.

The next day, the ballot box was found empty near the jail. The votes were scattered on the ground. The sheriff ordered a new election, but only 85 votes were cast. The anti-Federalists refused to honor what they felt was an illegal second election. The Federalists won, but the Convention in July threw out both elections. It declined to seat anybody from Dobbs County.

In Hertford County, the strongest anti-Federalist was a Baptist preacher named Lemuel Burkitt. A few days before the election, Burkitt held an assembly at his church to "explain" the new Constitution. Elkanah Watson and two other Federalists showed up at the packed meeting. They took front-row seats. Burkitt began by calling attention to the proposed new capital city, known so far only as "the ten-mile square." "This, my friends," said Burkitt, "... will be wall'd in like unto the Walls of China. Here 50 perhaps 100 thousand regulars will be finally embodied, sally forth and enslave the people, who will be gradually disarmed."

Dr. Patrick Garvey, one of Watson's companions, stood up at this point. He held a copy of the Constitution from which he intended to read. An outbreak of shouts and curses, however, put the Federalist trio to flight from the building.

Incoherence means mixed-up, jabbering.

The Articles of Confederation was the first constitution of the original 13 states, adopted in 1781. It was replaced by the present Constitution in 1789.

The *"ten-mile-square"* was the term used for the then-unnamed city of Washington, D.C.

Embodied means collected.

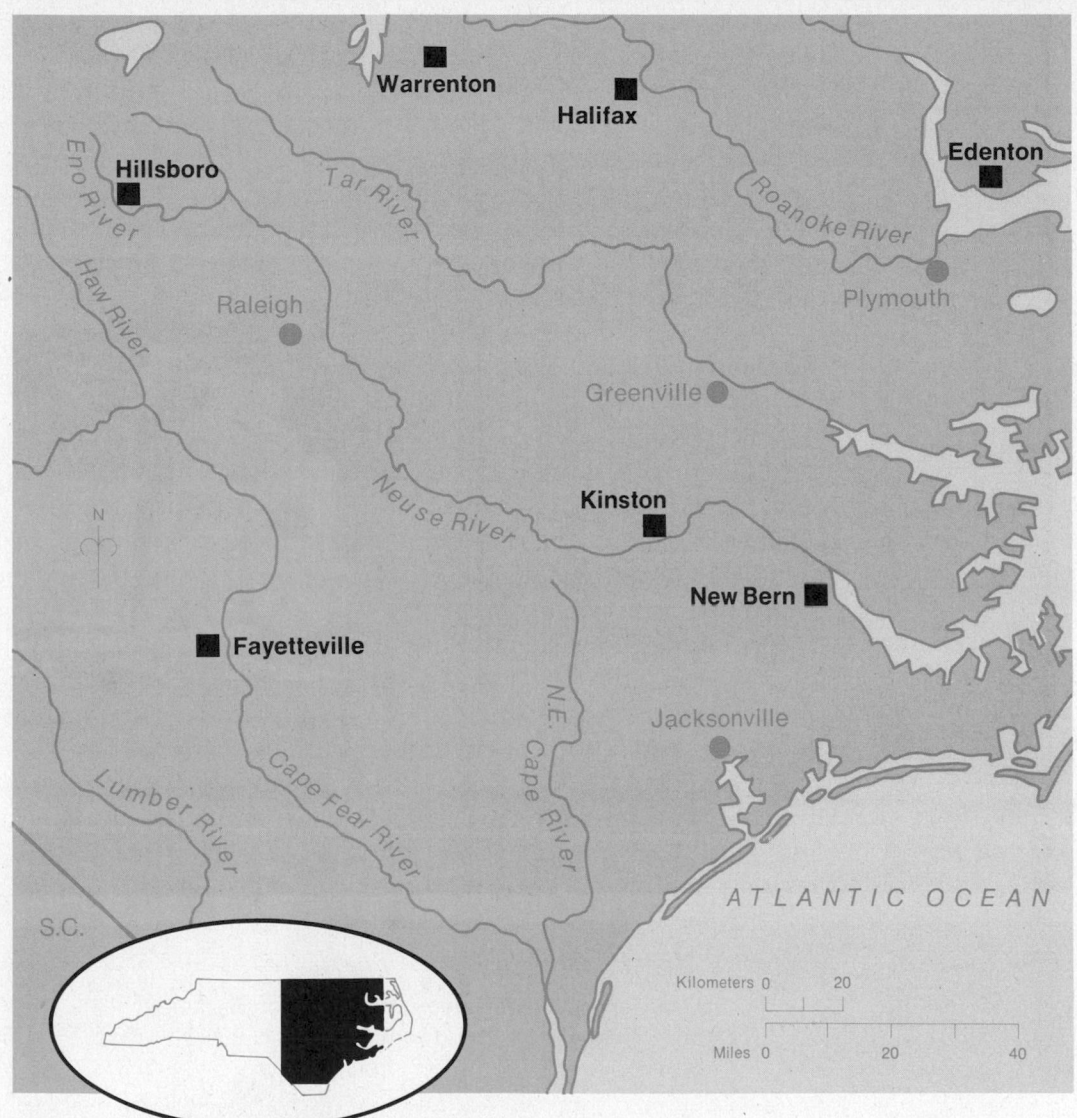

Eastern North Carolina, 1790

Avail means purpose.

Safely back home, Garvey and Watson drew a cartoon showing Burkitt in the pulpit braying like a jackass. They put it up at the court house, hiring some men to guard it. The Federalists were delighted on election morning when some of Burkitt's friends tried to pull the cartoon down. A riot broke out. It was all to no avail; Burkitt was elected anyhow.

Anti-Federalist delegates outnumbered their opponents. But the Federalist press still had four months in which to try to win the minds and hearts of the people. On March 27, Archibald Maclaine, a Federalist Wilmington attorney, took up the whole front page of the *State Gazette* with a defense of the proposed Constitution. Six states had already adopted it and others were expected soon to do so. It seemed important to Maclaine to raise a question: "What will become of North Carolina if we refuse our assent? . . . Can we repel a powerful enemy?" He also had an answer—that ". . . we shall be the most contemptible state on the face of the earth—despised and ridiculed by all the nations. . . ."

It was wrong to imagine, Maclaine argued, that the new President of the United States, as created by the Federalist Constitution, "is only another name for King, so that we shall be subject to all the evils of monarchical government." There could be no such danger from an executive who could be removed after four years. The executive was also subject to impeachment at any time. The same would be true, he added, in the case of the other elected officials. They would remain in office only at the will of the people.

Anti-Federalists struck back with an address, apparently by schoolmaster James Tate, in the Wilmington *Centinel and General Advertiser* of June 18. The people were being asked, he felt, to grant "too much power to their chosen leaders." Massachusetts, New Jersey, and Maryland had agreed to adopt the plan only with reservations. Rhode Island and New Hampshire had not yet agreed to it at all. Many hoped the President would have only a one-year term instead of four.

Impeachment occurs when formal charges are brought against a public official for misconduct in office.

A cartoon by Watson and Garvey shows Parson Burkett in his pulpit. The label says, "And lo he brayeth."

James Iredell fought hard for the 1789 constitution with his pamphlets and speeches. He later became a justice of the U.S. Supreme Court.

An *infidel* is one who does not believe in God.

They hoped there would be no toleration act. They did not want it so "every Jew or Infidel could come into office." But there were other powers suggested for the government that were even more dangerous:

> The army, navy, and a general mint, wrote the critic, are the three greatest and most powerful objects which will enforce obedience against all resistance. Troops when once in pay and service, make no distinction, if employed against a foreign enemy or their own relations, . . . though kept up by our taxes. We have no neighbours who can make war upon us without our being informed in time, and . . . our militia is strong enough to oppose them, when properly trained and officered. . . .

Eton College is in England.

Though few in numbers at the Hillsborough Convention, the Federalists commanded great respect. Governor Samuel Johnston was a Federalist delegate, as was his gifted brother-in-law, James Iredell. Archibald Maclaine was also there. Leading anti-Federalists included Willie Jones, the Eton College man from Halifax, and Thomas Person of Granville. The latter had called Washington "a damned rascal and traitor" for signing the Constitution.

Governor Johnston was chosen president of the Convention. But Willie Jones rattled the Federalists by calling almost at once for a vote. He thought everybody's mind was already made up. Federalists grasped for time in which to unmake some minds. They demanded and got a decision to review the Constitution clause by clause. This process took more than a week. It gained the Federalists nothing. Their opponents refused to see North Carolina "swallowed up," as one of them put it, "by the great mass of powers given to Congress." They would not hear of a Congress with authority to decide for itself when, where, and how national elections would take place. They could not be tempted to believe that the central government would fail to abuse any power granted to it to levy taxes. The office of President still looked to them much like a throne.

After the last clause of the Constitution had been considered, Willie Jones made a motion. It was that they refuse to ratify unless certain amendments were added to further limit the power of the central government. The motion passed by a vote of 184 to 93. North Carolina, in effect, had seceded from the United States.

To *ratify* is to agree to or adopt.

The Confederation

By the Articles of Confederation of 1778, the 13 original states came together almost like passengers on a city bus. They all shared the same living space. But each passenger had a destination and was free to get off whenever the moment was right. Every state recognized its dependence upon the others in a time of war. But each was determined to decide for itself all major matters concerning its welfare. During the war, they behaved in the fashion of 13 different countries formed into a voluntary alliance. In North Carolina, with its strong tradition of individualism, such notions of independent status were almost a mania.

Voluntary means by choice.

Mania means madness or unusual excitement.

Sovereignty means power to govern without external control.

Thomas Burke, representing North Carolina at the Constitutional Congress in 1777, demanded that the Articles of Confederation recognize the full sovereignty of each state. Mainly at his insistence, an article was inserted. It gave to individual states all powers not specifically granted to Congress by the document. Not all the delegates agreed with this. But the final draft guaranteed to each state full "sovereignty, freedom, and independence" within the Confederation. A common struggle against Great Britain would hold them together for the time being. However, no one could predict what would happen at the coming of peace.

Most North Carolinians appear to have been well pleased with the first national constitution and government. Their individualism had rebelled against a powerful executive authority in England. Now, outside the state itself, there was no executive authority at all. The colonists had complained about a legislature, like the English Parliament, with authority to regulate commerce and taxes, maintain a standing army and navy, and conduct courts. The new legislature, Congress, would not be able to do any of these things. It had a few carefully limited constitutional powers. But even the use of these powers depended upon voluntary cooperation by the states. No individual had reason to fear that the power of the new government would interfere with hard-earned liberties.

Radicals and conservatives in North Carolina and other states felt about the Articles of Confederation much as they did about the constitutions of the states. North Carolina radicals were generally western, agricultural, Protestant, rural, and poor. They were inclined to mistrust government and to agree that the less there was of it the better. Conservatives were mostly eastern, commercial, Episcopalian, urban, and well-to-do. They favored strong central authority. The Confederation, in their view, could do little to revive a commerce destroyed by war. It could not even maintain a military force strong enough to protect the nation's borders and sea lanes.

Somehow, to the surprise of its critics, the Confederation had some successes. It gained allies for America. It enjoyed enough popular support to win the war and gain a peace treaty with England. It devised sound policies for the sale of public lands to help pay its debts. It planned well for the admission of new states to the union. Most important for many North Carolinians, it left them alone as the meddling royal

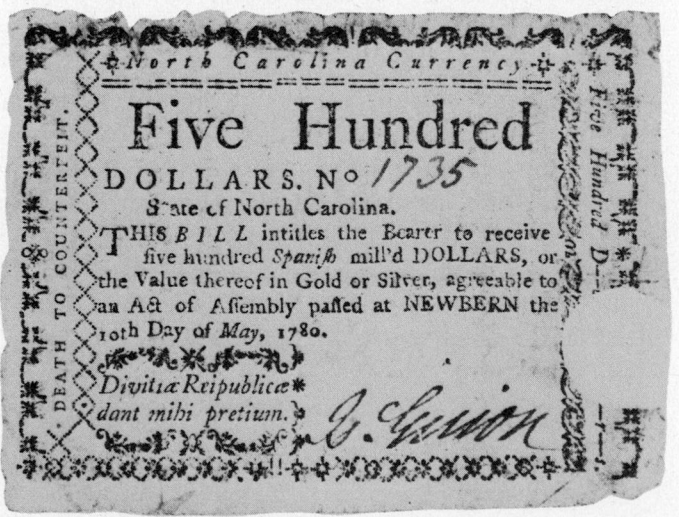

Wartime currency printed by the new state of North Carolina fell drastically in value as the war progressed.

government had never done. Life seemed sweeter without demands by the central government to do this or hand over that. North Carolinians wanted only relief from official requirements—and they got it.

The mid-1780s offered a kind of vacation from some ordinary duties of citizenship. But vacations are not forever. By 1786, most Americans probably sensed that theirs was about to end. North Carolina Conservatives had the advantage of the best writers and speakers. They chipped away month by month at the illusion that all was well with the Confederation. With Conservatives elsewhere, they raised a demand that the Articles of Confederation be amended to give the central government control of commerce and other powers. There must be a Congress, they insisted. It must be powerful enough to settle conflicts among states, make commercial treaties with foreign states, and provide security from invasion.

The main problem was that the Articles of Confederation could not be amended in any way without the approval of all 13 states. Approval might require years to achieve. It might not be possible at all. However, there was one way around the difficulty. If the states would agree to a constitutional convention, an overhaul of the Articles might be possible. Such a convention, recommending certain alterations and additions, might accomplish quickly what could not be done through the plodding amendment procedure required in the Articles.

North Carolina's legislature agreed in 1787 to send a delegation to such a convention at Philadelphia. The delegates were William Blount, Hugh Williamson, Alexander Martin, William R. Davie, and Richard Dobbs Spaight. All were prominent and well-to-do citizens. All but Martin were from the eastern part of the state. They were ready—more than most North Carolinians—to consider basic changes in the character of the national government.

The North Carolina delegation joined the others in agreeing that the Philadelphia Convention should rewrite the Constitution. It should provide for a national executive, judicial, and legislative authority. Although North Carolina was the fourth largest state, it sided with the smaller states in the "Great Compromise." This gave each state equal representation in the national Senate. The North Carolina group approved of the measure by which slaves were to be counted. Each slave was counted as three fifths of a person. This affected the number of representatives in the House of Representatives and the state's share of direct taxes. But they opposed the idea of a president independent of Congress. All

Conservatives were those who favored a federal Constitution.

Plodding means slow, difficult.

voted for the final draft of the Constitution, however, except for Davie, who was absent at the time.

The chance that North Carolinians would ratify the Constitution was not great. But leading Federalists set out with missionary zeal to convert them. They had a frustrating time ahead, for the mass of the people of their state could see no great reason for drastic changes in their form of government.

Zeal means enthusiasm.

E pluribus unum is a Latin motto of the United States. It means one out of many.

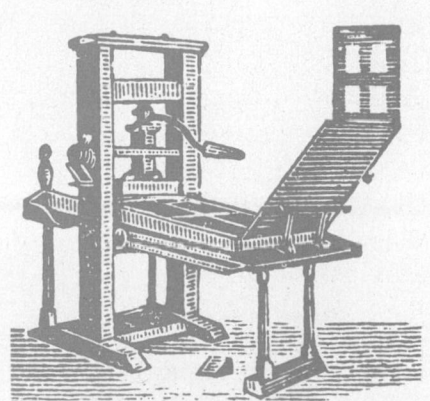

Hand-operated printing presses were slow, but they played a major role in the constitutional debates of 1788-1789.

Interludes are spaces of time between events.

Prevalent means widely or frequently practiced.

E Pluribus Unum

North Carolina's 16-month history as an independent nation brought no more joy to anti-Federalists than to their opponents. Eleven states had adopted the federal Constitution. The Articles of Confederation had been replaced as the nation's basic law. Federal economic policies dealt with North Carolina and Rhode Island, the two states failing to ratify, as foreign countries. The southern states, aware of the need for a stronger southern voice in Congress, pressed North Carolina to reconsider. The other states were fearful of attack by the British or by Indians or other possible enemies. They reminded North Carolinians of the mutual need all states had for protection.

North Carolinians were sensitive about their peculiar status and the attitude of citizens of other states toward them. This was especially true after publication of Jedediah Morse's *American Geography* in 1789. Morse was a Massachusetts clergyman. In his book, he described each state according to the features that, in his view, set it apart from others. These comments were often flattering. Page 418 dealt with North Carolina. But the description left North Carolinians gasping:

> The citizens of North Carolina who are not better employed spend their time in drinking, or gaming at cards or dice, in cock-fighting or horse-racing. Many of the interludes are filled up with a boxing-match; and these frequently become memorable by feats of *gouging*.
>
> In a country that pretends to any degree of civilization, one would hardly expect to find a prevailing custom of putting out the eyes of each other. Yet this more than barbarous custom is prevalent in both the Carolinas, and in Georgia, among the lower class of people.

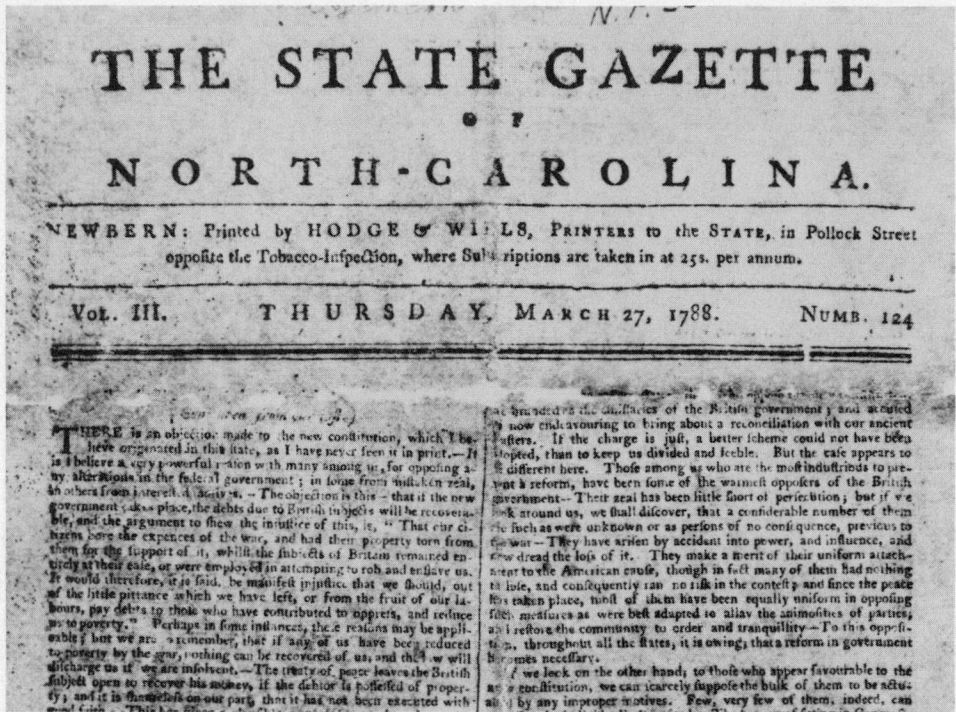

A portion of the front page, March 27, 1788, contains a strong article endorsing the proposed federal Constitution.

Literate means able to read.

Literate North Carolinians were appalled at the image of their state thus presented for all the world to see. It did not help matters when attorney William Barry Grove of Fayetteville spoke out. He said if he ever met Morse he would gouge his eyes out.

A later edition of the *American Geography* softened the harsh picture of North Carolina. But there was no denying that the author's remarks had merit. The frontier code of behavior still prevailed in much of the state, whether in an upper-class pistol duel or a lower-class gouging match. It was a result of the idea that each person's fate, one's reputation among other people, rested on the individual's strength and daring. One must prove courage and self-reliance by a willingness to fight for one's honor. A person must not take refuge either in the process of the law or behind the shield of religion. Richard Dobbs Spaight, following his terms as governor of the state, was one of those to pay with his life for his belief in this primitive code. Fighting was not the only way that the tradition of individualism expressed itself in North Carolina. But it was one of the best known.

The same attitude had permitted North Carolinians to imagine that they could stand alone, without the help and aid of other states. What one person should be willing to do, one state could do as well or better. Self-respecting North Carolinians should not concern themselves particularly with what other states did. North Carolina would keep its own private counsels and go its own way.

Some Federalist leaders recognized that they must strike at this level of emotional response. North Carolinians had to be persuaded to cooperate with citizens of other states and with one another. In September 1788, a writer in the *State Gazette,* probably James Iredell, faced the issue squarely in an essay addressed "to the people of the Edenton District." North Carolina, the writer slyly admitted, was now free to "form alliances at our pleasure with Great Britain, France, Spain, Turkey, the Bey of Algiers, or Rhode Island. . . . While the United States are fettered with the necessity of pursuing a common interest, there is no check upon our separate wisdom, or the free course of our own noble exertions."

Fettered means chained or tied up.

Exertions means efforts.

But the delegates at the Constitutional Convention of 1787 had been more concerned with the whole group of states than with any one in particular. They had found it necessary to sacrifice local interests "to the general good," to serve a "patriotism and wisdom . . . to which narrow souls could never reach. . . ." No constitution could have been written without "the mutual aid of a number of sensible men. . . ." The leading principle of the new Constitution was "that in all cases where the peace and interest of the union at large are concerned we should, as a people united in a common object, be governed by common counsels. . . ."

The *State Gazette* writer reminded fellow citizens of examples when European states had come near destruction. This was because of the "extreme jealousy" of one or more cities or provinces toward the rest. In recent years, Rhode Island had behaved the same way toward the Confederation, "inducing other states to adopt a separate and selfish policy. . . ." By peacefully changing the government, the Convention had brought a new principle into political practice: "In every other country revolutions of government can only be expected to take place by means of civil war." The new means of amending the federal Constitution would prevent future violence. It showed the progress of civilization that "the contemptible vanity of self-perfection gives way" to a willingness to show restraint in the interest of cooperation. Never again would "one or two wicked members in the union . . . defeat the real interest of the whole."

Vanity means self-pride.

The *State Gazette* essay probably changed few minds in North Carolina. But it was only a pellet in a shotgun blast of pamphlets and speeches. Federalist propaganda, the shame of Morse's unsparing judgment, the practical need for union, and other sorts of pressures all combined to defeat North Carolina's resistance. Before the end of 1788 the General Assembly narrowly passed a motion to reconsider the federal Constitution.

On November 16, 1789, North Carolina's delegates met in convention at Fayetteville. By a vote of 195 to 77, they agreed to ratify the federal Constitution. It was, very likely, a grudging vote. It stemmed from practical necessity more than real commitment. But the struggle over the Constitution challenged North Carolina's individualism. An unspoken meaning of the challenge was that it was not necessary to be selfish to win dignity as an individual. It seemed to show that it is not good for any state to insist on full satisfaction of its own interests. Not all at once, but in time, North Carolinians would need to learn the lesson the Constitution taught.

Chapter Checkup

PEOPLE

Abraham Hodge	Elkanah Watson	Archibald Maclaine
Francis X. Martin	Lemuel Burkitt	Willie Jones
Hugh Williamson	James Tate	James Iredell

PLACES

Warrenton	Salisbury	Halifax
New Garden	Fayetteville	

FACT

Why did the anti-Federalists in North Carolina oppose the federal Constitution?

What were the social and economic differences between Federalists and anti-Federalists?

What were the problems presented by the Articles of Confederation following the Revolution?

INTERPRETATION

How do you account for North Carolina being so slow to adopt the federal Constitution—slower than any other southern state?

What do you suppose accounts for the extreme language used by both sides and the frequent use of violence?

Do you agree with James Iredell that North Carolina was guilty of a "selfish policy" in refusing to adopt the constitution in 1788? Explain.

Do you think that the anti-Federalists would think they had been wrong if they could see the federal government today? Explain.

VOCABULARY

Federalists	Ratify	Individualism
Anti-Federalists	Sovereignty	

ACTIVITY

Write a letter to a North Carolina newspaper in early 1788 setting forth why you hope either for the adoption or the rejection of the federal Constitution in this state. Call attention in the letter to at least three people whose views are discussed in the chapter.

SUGGESTED READING

Parramore, T. C. "A Year in Hertford County With Elkanah Watson," *N.C. Historical Review* (Autumn 1964), pages 448–463. Deals with Watson's role in the Federalist campaign in 1787–1788.

Trenholme, Louise Irby. *North Carolina and the Ratification of the Federal Constitution.* New York: Columbia University Press, 1932. Scholarly but readable account of the fight to adopt the constitution.

PART FOUR

The State Asleep and Awake

A scene in Smoky Mountain National Park

1775 Rumors of slave plot
in Pitt and Beaufort
1776 Free blacks permitted
to vote

1778 Fifty-eight black
soldiers with Washington's army

1776 American colonies
declare their independence
1777 France recognizes
American independence *(Dec.)*

1781 Congress names peace
commission
1782 Peace talks begin
in Paris *(April)*

1784 United States begins
trade with China *(Aug.)*

1789 Washington inaugurated
President *(April 30)*
● French Revolution begins

1791 Beginning of Toussaint's
revolt on Hispaniola

1794 Plot rumored among slaves
in Hertford County

1796 John Adams elected
President *(Dec.)*

1798 Plot rumored among slaves
in Bertie County

1801 Plots reported
in Virginia *(Dec.)*
1802 Colerain letter found
(June 2)

1801 Jefferson elected
President

10

A RATTLING
OF THE CHAINS

The Conspiracy of 1802

They stood there, the hot sun glaring down on Judy Raynor as she told her story. A couple of the white men watched intently. They prided themselves on their ability to spot a lying slave. They watched the flicker of the young woman's eyelids, the creases at the corners of her mouth. They asked her all kinds of sharp questions and tried to catch her in any cock-and-bull story made up to save her own skin. A couple of the men sternly reminded Judy of what could happen if she told anything less than the whole truth. But Judy got through the ordeal without a break in her voice or a slip-up in her account. The white men decided she could be trusted.

A grease-spotted note had been found. It was in the cotton barrel in Judy's kitchen on that June 1802 afternoon. There was going to be trouble for the slaves of Bertie and Hertford Counties. It was a barely legible scrawl, but everybody agreed

181

A reproduction of the
Colerain letter and the
author's interpretation
will be found on page
193.

on its meaning. After several false starts, the version they accepted was this:

> Frank Sumner Capt. will command Mereca Sumner, Ned Sumner, Cornwell Sumner and Harry, Bob Moore, Ned Moore, Jink Wateridge, Tom Simons, David Fitt, Peter Harrell, Buck Scul, Simon Hunter, Denis Hunter, Ganse Lurry and we will rise at tent of June. Men Wont Join us we will kill them and all make to Coleraine and get together and kill all, this is the line let you no Capt King Brown as you may get men in order, my guns is hid.

The slaves named on the list lived on eight or nine farms in northeastern Bertie and southeastern Hertford. They were all within eight miles or so of the village of Colerain. The message was clearly from one slave to another. It showed that a revolt was planned for the night of June 10—eight days away. Very likely there were many more slaves involved than the 16 named in the note. Members of the search party at Miles Raynor's plantation believed that they had proof of a terrible plot against the whites.

As Judy Raynor told it, the note in the cotton barrel was brought to her house by Fed Fitt. That was the previous week—the last week in May. Fed told her to hide it. He promised to come for it on the night of June 2. He had told her it was given to him by Frank Sumner, whose name was first on the note. But the first Judy had heard of the business, she said, had been in early May. Dave Murfree had come to her house one night "after the white people had gone to bed." Dave had started talking, Judy recalled, about his "Hell fire news." He told how "we Black are going to rise against the white ones," and all the rest. If the note left any doubt, Judy's story cleared it up. She had probably condemned to death many people she had known all her life.

The next 48 hours seemed critical to the whites. The plotters must be caught before word spread that the patrols had learned of the uprising. Neighboring counties must be alerted in case the plot were more than local. Special courts had to be summoned. Many people had to be questioned so the full scope of the plot could be known. Unless all this were handled quickly and efficiently, the uprising might break out anyhow. The whole region—maybe the whole South—would suffer the worst blood bath in its history.

The roundup of suspected plotters and informants took two days. By June 4, all whose names appeared on the Colerain letter had been arrested. They were taken to jails at Winton and Windsor, the county seats. Courts were scheduled at both towns for June 10. Messages were sent to authorities in other counties. Patrols were out and every well-known gathering place for blacks was being watched.

But county authorities, clamping down on the blacks, had not made preparations for handling the whites. Rumors ran wild from farm to farm. Each day saw a deepening of the panic among the whites. The sight of slaves being searched, bullied, and led off to jail only seemed to increase the problem. On June 9, an angry Bertie planter wrote to a newspaper that an "insurrection mania" had "broken out . . . in the most violent degree." People had gone "stark Mad," he said. His own farm was visited twice a day by "Twenty armed madmen," who could barely be restrained from "shooting . . . people in their huts." It was enough, he feared, "to make the poor blacks desperate." It seemed as though hysterical whites might bring about the revolt they wanted to prevent.

At midnight on the evening of June 9, a Mr. Browning at Nixonton received an express rider. The rider reported that the blacks had risen in Windsor "and committed great havoc." They had marched from there to Chowan River. He was told they were forming at the ferry. Two hours later, Benjamin Overman at Gum Bridge, a border town in Virginia, was told by John Shaw that the blacks in Hertford County had also risen "and are under arms." There were reports of more blacks "in large companies, armed" in the Dismal Swamp.

The panic may have eased in the next day or two in Bertie and Hertford as the whites realized someone was spreading false reports. But rumors were still flying everywhere. A hundred blacks were in makeshift jails at Windsor. The militia in Martin had arrested "all the negro men in the county." A hundred more blacks were in jail in Warren. The citizens of Halifax were "under arms every night" to prevent the rumored plot to burn their town. Black suspects in Edgecombe confessed their plan to have marched in columns, "one by the Cokey road and the other by the River and that when all the white men were killed the black were to take their places . . . ,

---

The **county seat** is the town in which the courthouse and other public county buildings are located.

Patrols of armed whites made regular rides through slave counties to search for runaways or evidence of plots.

An **insurrection** is an uprising.

Mania means excessive excitement.

Hysterical means uncontrollably emotional.

Havoc means destruction.

State laws offered little protection to slaves who were unfortunate enough to have cruel masters.

&c., &c." Seven blacks were said to have been shot trying to escape from a group being marched to jail in Washington County. Pitt and Northampton were in an uproar.

What started as an apparent plot to kill white people around Colerain gathered gory details with each passing day. "Their primary aim," one report declared,

> was to . . . declare themselves independent of their masters, to proclaim generally to their fellow servants . . . a general manumission, and then proceed to desolate the country with fire and sword, to murder all the male whites, and to take the females such as were handsome for their wives, and murder indiscriminately the rest, en masse.

Former governor Richard Dobbs Spaight was sure the alarm was caused by "the Quakers and the Abolition societies." He also suspected others who "would be gratified at an insurrection of the slaves in the southern states." Some blamed the French or other foreigners who might have ignited the alarm. The full scope of the plot revealed by the confession of prisoners was terrifying:

> . . . in the night of the tenth, they were to form . . . companies of seven or eight, go to each man's house, set fire to it, kill the men and boys over 6 or 7 years of age; the women over a certain age, both black and white were to share the same fate; the young and handsome of the whites they were to keep for themselves, and the younger ones of their own colour were to be spared for waiters. . . . Some were offered money . . . to go to Virginia to help the blacks fight the whites.

Sanity finally returned at the end of June. The death toll among blacks surpassed anything of the kind ever seen in North Carolina—before or since. Eleven slaves were hanged in Bertie, two in Martin, one each in Hertford, Halifax and Perquimans, two in Currituck, four in Camden, and possibly, one in Edgecombe. Seven were said to have been shot in Washington County. Many received lesser punishments. These ranged from 39 lashes laid on each of six Bertie suspects to the branding, whipping, and cutting off of the ears of another in Hertford. Others were deported from the state.

But was there really a plot at all by the slaves in 1802? What does the incident of 1802 reveal about relations between slaves and masters? How did things get to be this way? No one can say how many slaves felt ill treated. How many were

Manumission means a freeing of slaves.

To desolate means to destroy or ravage.

En masse means entirely, altogether.

Abolition societies were groups whose goal it was to see the slaves freed.

The French, because their Revolution of 1789 emphasized "liberty, equality, and fraternity," were considered strong opponents of slavery.

Deported means carried or sent away.

Black slave labor was used for many kinds of work on land and on the sea.

Bondsmen were partly free people who were required to work for certain periods of time before becoming entirely free.

driven to acts of violence or bent into helpless despair by slavery? It is not clear whether the masters gained more than they lost from the system. The incident of 1802 and its background can, however, throw some light on these problems.

The "Peculiar Institution"

Blacks first appeared in North Carolina in company with the first whites. A Spanish colony that settled briefly on Lower Cape Fear in 1525 included four black slaves. They were probably the first of their race to live in what became English America. Other blacks were brought to Roanoke Island by Francis Drake in 1586. They were probably left there when he took Raleigh's first colony home to England. Nothing is known of their fate. Their wanderings may have given rise to some of the theories about the fate of the Lost Colony. There were also slaves, and maybe a few free blacks, among the settlers from Virginia who came to Albemarle in the 1650s and 1660s.

Long before North Carolina was permanently settled, white planters in Virginia had shown there was a good profit in tobacco. This was true provided that plenty of cheap labor could be found. There had been black servants at Jamestown since 1619. But it is not clear from Virginia records whether they were at first treated differently from white apprentices or bondsmen. The earliest sign of a slave system comes only around 1640. At that time, there is evidence of blacks being required to serve their masters for life. By the time North Carolina was settled, Virginia law had a crude code of slave laws.

Despite slavery's slow development, it had gone far enough by 1669 to be endorsed in North Carolina's Proprietary Charter. Here freemen of the colony were guaranteed "absolute powers and authority" over their slaves. There were few blacks in seventeenth century North Carolina. But they seem to have participated alongside whites in the major events of the early colonial period. Black pirates roamed coastal waters in the days of Blackbeard. Two slaves accompanied Lawson and Graffenried when they were captured by Indians in 1711.

In a book he wrote about North Carolina in 1709, Lawson ignored blacks almost completely. This was a sign that they still formed only a tiny fraction of the population. Twenty years later, William Byrd led his dividing line surveyors west-

North Carolina's pine forests produced many products used in shipbuilding. Most of the work was done by slaves.

Mulattoes are light-skinned blacks.

Stocks means farm animals, such as cattle and sheep.

To submit means to accept or yield.

Treacherous means unfaithful or rebellious.

ward from Currituck. He met "a Family of Mulattoes" living in a cottage on the edge of Dismal Swamp. He noted that "many Slaves" hid themselves in such places. There, local whites used them "to raise stocks for a mean . . . Share, well knowing their Condition makes it necessary for them to Submit to any Terms."

A not always reliable source of information about blacks in the early colony is John Brickell's *Natural History of North Carolina,* published in 1737. Brickell spent about two years around Edenton and Bath. He was an Irishman and knew a good deal about slave life. But he wrote of blacks much as he did about curious kinds of animals. There was little awareness that they were human beings like himself.

Brickell found that most slaves came from the Guinea Coast of Africa. They were considered "the greatest Riches in these Parts." Those born in the colonies had not the "stubborn Natures," he thought, of the African-born. The former were "more industrious, honest and better Slaves" than the Africans. The Africans were used "to War and Hardship all their lives." He had seen Africans "frequently . . . whipped to that degree, that large pieces of their Skin have been hanging down their Backs; yet I never observed one of them to shed a Tear. . . ."

Since slaves sometimes rebelled, "and do a great deal of Mischief, being both treacherous and cruel," the law was harsh. Any slave who shed his master's blood, said Brickell, must be hanged by a fellow slave in the presence of other slaves. This would discourage them from following the example. He had known a master to make every effort to win pardon for one of his slaves after such an incident, "but to no purpose, for the Country insisted on having the Law put in execution. . . ."

Slaves who reported the misdeeds or plots of others might be "rewarded with their Freedom for their good Services." The laws were "strictly put in execution," lest the blacks "overcome the Christians in this and other Provinces. . . ." Owners of slaves executed for a crime were paid "full value" by the government. It was illegal for a slave to be a witness in any case except that of another black.

A slave marriage could be performed simply by the man giving the woman "a Brass Ring or some other Toy." Divorce occurred if and when she gave the token back. If a slave woman had no children by her husband in a year or two, she might have to take another mate. It seemed odd to Brickell that they were "Jealously inclined, and fight most desperately amongst themselves when they rival each other. . . ."

The author reported that many planters provided their slaves with "convenient houses." They let them plant a little tobacco of their own. Money could be earned from sale of the tobacco or from the snakeroot they were allowed to gather on Sundays. It could be used to "buy Hats, . . . Linnins, Bracelets, Ribbon, and . . . Toys for their Wives. . . ." Some learned to read and write, or became tradespeople and even "good Artists." But most worked in the corn, rice, and tobacco fields or the naval stores industry. This, he claimed, was because blacks were "better able to undergo fatigues . . . of the hot Weather than . . . Europeans." A planter could free a slave. However, any slaves so freed must leave the colony quickly or they became the property of the first white to claim them.

Snakeroot was a plant regarded as a remedy for snakebite.

Brickell was pleased with the treatment of the slaves. However, many of his comments told another story. Thus, "old-wives" were a kind of bird eaten only by blacks and Indians, "their Flesh being black, hard of digestion, and tastes Fishy." Blacks also ate water-hens, these "being very hard of Digestion and ill tasted." Blacks suffered much from yaws, whooping cough, convulsions, and other illnesses. Slaves who worked too slowly in the tobacco fields were sometimes made to eat tobacco worms as punishment. Black children generally wore no clothing except in winter. Young men and women wore only a piece of Cloth "to cover their Nakedness." Blacks, then, were "not very expensive to the Planters for . . . Cloathing."

Slaves might become free in several ways. But freedom probably meant improvement for only a few. Now and then a slave could save enough money to buy freedom. The white father of children by a slave woman sometimes freed both mother and child in his will if not earlier. Runaway slaves were sometimes lucky enough to find places where their new identity would not be questioned. By the end of the colonial period, North Carolina's black population included about seventy-five thousand slaves and perhaps three thousand free. In contrast, there were some two hundred thousand whites.

One of the first public alarms of a slave uprising occurred in 1775, the first summer of the Revolutionary War. Slaves of Pitt, Beaufort, and adjacent counties were thought to be planning a revolt. Many were arrested and some, perhaps through torture, gave evidence that a British ship captain had inspired the plot. It was claimed that the slaves of each household were to rise on the night of July 8. They would attack their white families and march together into the western backcountry. There, agents of the Crown would furnish them with free land and weapons as a reward. Many blacks were whipped on suspicion of involvement. Some had their ears cut off. Whether there was a plot is impossible to determine.

Despite harsh treatment, many blacks fought as patriots during the Revolutionary War. Some also fought as Tories. Free blacks fought as members of some militia companies. There were 58 North Carolina blacks with General Washington's Continentals in 1778. Some slaves accompanied their masters to war and served as musicians, orderlies, and so on.

Slaves usually lived in crude, uncomfortable cabins and were given the cheapest of clothes to wear.

Sometimes, a white man, when called into service, would pay a black to take his place. William Kitchin of Edgecombe hired Edward Griffin to do this in 1781. Some, like Isaac Carter, a free black of Halifax County, gave their lives in defense of American liberty.

North Carolina blacks produced their share of heroes, such as John Jasper White, during the war. Austin Dabney, a native of Surry County, won fame in Georgia at the Battle of Kettle Creek. He saw other actions before being crippled for life by a bullet in his thigh. One of the last North Carolina veterans of the Revolution to die was Jonathan Overton. He had been with Washington at Yorktown. He died at Edenton in 1849 at the age of 101. Two years later, Jeremiah Smith, a black veteran in Johnston County, applied for a government pension. But no one was still alive who could vouch for his service. He got nothing.

The talk of liberty and equality during the Revolutionary era did not help to lighten the burden of slavery. The growing number of slaves on larger eastern plantations led to more severe restrictions against them. Charles W. Janson was an English merchant who lived at Edenton for a while in the 1790s. He witnessed a type of slavery that had not grown easier since Brickell's day. Janson wrote a book of his impressions. He often used the worst examples he could find. A system that allowed the slave conditions he described, whether typical or not, was condemned in the eyes of most civilized nations.

Janson visited a camp in a Tyrrell County swamp. There, a Mr. Blount had charge of some 60 slaves who were digging a canal. Each Saturday, the slaves got an allowance of "salt herrings, of an inferior quality, and a peck of Indian corn in the cob, to each. . . ." The rest of the day was spent grinding the corn. This was the diet for every day of the week. They had had no pork or beef for months. But none complained, "so accustomed were they to . . . this miserable existence. . . ." When someone stole some chickens, Blount asked the slaves to tell him the thief's name. When no name was given, he ordered them all beaten, taking a full day in the process. The camp included a large number of children who had been sent there because there was no chance of running away. They could be fed at little expense and they might be allowed "to run wild and entirely naked."

In the slave region, Janson observed, the first week of the year was the time for a "public auction" of blacks or for hiring their services. Infants brought not more than 40 dollars a head. But male field hands might bring up to four hundred

A *pension* is money paid to a person following retirement from work or service.

Wench is an uncomplimentary term for a girl or young woman.

dollars and a "field wench" perhaps a hundred. Many slave owners tried to keep black families together. But Janson knew of instances when husbands had been sold away from their wives, mothers from their children, and sisters from their brothers. He had witnessed brutal punishments of slaves at public whipping posts, "or tied up to the limb of a tree," or "fastened to a barrel, the hands and feet nearly meeting. . . ."

By a law going back to 1715, blacks, whether slave or free, were prevented from marrying whites. Ebenezer Hazard toured North Carolina in 1778. He reported that a Brunswick County white man was married to a mulatto woman. He knew of a Trent River white girl who bore a mulatto child. There was even weaker enforcement of a law of 1741. It required that any slave set free by a master must leave the state within six months. Beginning in the 1760s, there was a noticeable tendency for the law to give better treatment to free blacks. The state Constitution of 1776 gave them back the right to vote. (It had been denied since 1715.) In other ways, the law recognized them as ordinary citizens.

The legal situation of free blacks improved in the late eighteenth century. It was probably due to the influence of the Quakers, Moravians, and Methodists, all of whom opposed slavery. The ideas of the Revolution, with their stress on freedom, probably added to this also. Many whites did not concern themselves about the conflict between Revolutionary doctrines and the existence of slavery. But some could not ignore it. In 1778, Ebenezer Hazard wrote that the General Assembly had passed a law to arrest and sell some blacks. They had recently been freed by Quaker masters. The Quakers were unable to guarantee that "the Negroes shall not become Burthensome to the State."

Doctrines means principles or teachings.

The Call to Arms

The year 1791 was a crucial one in the history of American slavery. In that year, a slave revolt began on the island of Hispaniola in the West Indies. It was started by a former slave named Toussaint l'Ouverture. There had been slave revolts before. There had been many panics among the whites, like that of 1775 in North Carolina. But the revolt led by Toussaint was different from the others. This one was successful. Overcoming European troops and many hardships, the blacks of

Omar ibn Said, a slave in Bladen County, was educated in
Moslem schools. At right is his Bible, in Arabic.

The nation was founded on
Hispaniola. It is now part of
modern Haiti.

The *Gabriel Plot* was an
uprising led by a slave,
Gabriel Prosser.

Anxiety means distress
caused by fear.

Hispaniola fought their way into control of the island. They
created a new nation. American slave-owners were frightened
by the event. They wondered how long it would be before this
example of black victory might make itself felt among their
own slaves.

From 1791 on, the slave states felt increasing alarm over
slave plots. Among the alarms in the following years was one
in Hertford County in 1794. There was another in Bertie in
1798. But the Gabriel Plot in Virginia in 1800 created panic
throughout the slave territory. Gabriel was driven back only
by heavy rains that flooded rivers and destroyed bridges. His
army failed in its plan to attack Richmond and seize the arsenal there. Many slaves were hanged or sold away from Virginia as a result of the Gabriel Plot. White anxiety remained
high after it was over. North Carolina slave holders, among
others, thought they saw a dangerous new mood among their
slaves.

For over a year after the Gabriel Plot, there were no further discoveries of slave conspiracies. But in November 1801,
Virginia newspapers began to talk vaguely of some kind of
"unrest" among the slaves. In late December, a plot was reported in Nottoway County, Virginia. Several ringleaders
were arrested and two were quickly hanged. But a few days
later there were fresh reports from Powhatan County. Reports
came from York, Accomac, Brunswick, Nelson, and other
counties. By the end of February 1802, nearly all of Virginia

was caught up in the panic. Before it died down at the end of April, Virginia courts had sentenced at least a dozen blacks to death. Many others had been punished or sold out of the state.

The last of the conspiracy trials in Virginia was followed almost at once by a report of a plot in Currituck County in northeastern North Carolina. Two slaves were hanged there. But the excitement quickly spread to Camden, Pasquotank, and Perquimans. There, five more were executed. The panic seemed to ease for a few days at the end of May. But then, on June 2, a Bertie County patrol discovered a note in Judy Raynor's kitchen. It was the strongest evidence found anywhere so far. Several previous notes shown at various courts in the spring of 1802 looked as though they had been forged. The one in Bertie seemed very genuine.

As seen earlier, the 1802 panic brought its worst results in Bertie. There, almost half the North Carolina executions of supposed plotters occurred. But only two of the eleven slaves hanged in Bertie were among those named in the Colerain letter. The rest were slaves who were mentioned in the testimony of other blacks concerning an alleged plot at Windsor. It was not until after the discovery of the Colerain letter that information about the Windsor plot was found.

The plot revealed in the Colerain letter was an exception. All other supposed plots in North Carolina in May and June were probably based only on white hysteria. The only evidence of these other plots was testimony brought out either

Hertford County-Bertie County, 1800

Discovery of the Colerain letter led to the execution of at least 16 blacks. Below is the author's interpretation.

frank sumler Cap tain will Cum
mand marickCa sumlar ned sumlar and harry and
bob moar ned moar gink watrig tom simans
david fit danis fit petar harrl buk scul siman hutr
danis huter and gans lurra and we wil (ris at?)
tanit and if Benes min wont gine we wil kil them
and al make to Colran and git to gether and kil all
this is the line let you no Captn king Broun as you ma get min
in ordar my guns is hid

through torture, threats of torture, or promises of good treatment. Thus, court records of Washington County show that "Harris' Harry sayed nothing untill being whiped, then sayed Mrs. Brinkley's negro man said they were going to rise in Bertie. Being whipped a second time, sayed Dick & Arthur was engaged in the plot, whiped a third time, sayed Col. Blounts Guernsey said boys, suppose you all rise & murder all the whites." No doubt the authorities, proceeding in this way, could have found cause to suspect every black in the county.

The conscience of an Edenton attorney, Joseph B. Skinner, led him to cry out in the midst of the frenzy. He said all of this was "persecution under the mask of justice." He felt that

Swamps such as the Great Dismal provided some slaves
with temporary hideouts from the hardships of slavery.

Persuasion means belief.

"the judges and juries were under the popular persuasion that
it was better 99 innocent be punished than one guilty escape."
He thought that "much more ought to be apprehended from
the rank unparalleled conduct of the whites than from an insurrection of the Negroes."

The Colerain letter is the only real evidence that 16 or
so blacks in Bertie and Hertford Counties actually planned a
revolt. A close examination of the original letter, still in existence, shows that words understood by the whites as "tent of
June men wont rise" should have been read "tanit [tonight?]
and if Bens men wont rise." The words "we will all make to
Coleraine and get together and kill all," sound as if a revolt
was planned. It seems to be the only evidence turned up in
Virginia or North Carolina that is really worth taking seriously. Of the 40 or more executed, probably not more than
three were guilty.

Why did the conspiracy panic occur in 1802, rather than
before or after? Why were particular areas affected? For answers, it is worth while to look at other features of that
society. A glance will suggest the possible influence that a major religious movement may have had on the panic. The year
1802 saw the "Great Revival" in northeastern North Carolina,
the most dramatic religious event in the region's history.

Kindling means rapid growth.

At the close of the eighteenth century, North Carolina did not have a strong religious organization. Nor did it have a sizeable group interested in promoting one. There had been a brief kindling of religion, mostly in the backcountry, during the "Great Awakening" of the 1750s and 1760s. But the movement began to fade before the Revolution. It was only a memory at the war's end. Such earnest religious activity as existed in North Carolina was the work of little Quaker and Moravian communities. The majority of citizens simply took no interest in religion. Preachers and churches were few.

In 1801, Lemuel Burkitt, the anti-Federalist Baptist preacher in Hertford County, went into Tennessee and Kentucky. There, the "Great Revival" was in progress. He had heard the stories of the wonderful spiritual awakening there. He wondered if he might not be God's instrument in bringing it to eastern North Carolina. When he returned in the fall, Burkitt began organizing outdoor camp meetings. These were the kind that had been so successful in the West. They opened with a singing of gospel songs, during which people were asked to shake each other's hands. The minister might walk through the congregation during the singing and join in the handshaking. Following an emotional sermon, members of the congregation would be asked to come forward. They would "be prayed over" and confess their sins publicly. The results were like nothing seen before in the region.

Burkitt gives his own account of his work in the "Great Revival." He tells mainly of four churches he visited regularly in the counties of Northampton, Hertford, and Bertie. He describes "congregations which would draw up in such crowds as they would tread one on another," audiences "in a flood of tears, and some almost convulsed," people "so greatly affected [they] could hardly stand." The meetings drew as many as four thousand people. They would brave driving thunderstorms to stand in the open and hear the gospel message. During 1802 and 1803, some six hundred were baptized in these four churches alone.

Convulsed means shaken violently with emotion.

Slaves were apparently as caught up by the mighty new movement as masters. Burkitt mentions "the children and servants at every house." They would sing gospel songs learned at the camp meetings and other services. Testimony at the slave trials had evidence of other religious activity. Such was the "quarterly meeting at Wiccacon" church in Bertie where King Brown said he had last seen Frank Sumner.

It is possible that the greatest conspiracy panic and the mightiest revival in North Carolina's history were not related. Perhaps their happening at the same time was only a coincidence. But there are reasons why one might suspect a connection. For example, a Pasquotank court found defendant Joe George not guilty of plotting. But it warned him not to "hold any meeting, congregation, or other Assembly of slaves or other people of colour upon . . . any pretence of Preaching praying or exhorting. . . ." In Perquimans, witness Moses claimed that a plotter told him "that their different [religious] meetings was only to fix on the plot. . . ." In Bertie, witness Violet Bass swore that she had seen some accused blacks "at preaching." They were "talking two & two during the sermon." Others stated that rebels who meant to burn Windsor were to gather at a night service. Elder Aaron Spivey had arranged the service.

The evidence suggests that whites were alarmed about the revival. It gave blacks chances to talk with each other. Meetings were often held at night and under very emotional circumstances. Testimony in Bertie and Hertford showed that the "Colerain Plot" was to have begun on a Thursday. This was the same day as the Union Meeting (of five congregations) at Wiccacon Chapel, a Baptist church four miles west of Colerain. The plotters were said to have planned to march from Colerain to the chapel. There, "dreadful carnage was to begin." The revival, therefore, was to furnish the occasion for the revolt and the means for its success.

Carnage means killing.

It is not hard to imagine this as a time of high emotions. Burkitt describes it as a moment when devils and evil spirits seemed closer and more real than in normal times. It was a great irony that Burkitt and his people may have played a part in bringing about the horror of 1802.

Chapter Checkup

PEOPLE

Judy Raynor   Toussaint
Lemuel Burkitt   Austin Dabney

PLACES

Colerain   Winton   Windsor

FACT

Why did the Bertie planter complain in 1802 that whites might actually bring about the revolt they feared?

Were blacks involved in the earliest explorations and settlements in North Carolina? If so, how?

Does Brickell's book indicate that slaves were well treated or not?

What key events led up to the trouble in 1802?

INTERPRETATION

Do you trust the statements made to the whites in 1802? Explain.

How much real danger do you think there was to whites in 1802? Explain.

Why do you suppose uprisings by slaves were not more frequent than they were?

Does it seem to you that the whites misread the Colerain letter? If so, does the misreading affect the guilt or innocence of persons named in the letter?

How would you explain the fact that some slaves confessed that June 10 was the day planned for the uprising even though the whites apparently misread the note to give that date?

VOCABULARY

Insurrection	Abolition
Conspiracy	Manumission
Bondsmen	

ACTIVITY

Determine on a map of the state the limits of the panic of 1802 and its geographical relationship to Nat Turner's Revolt in 1831. See if you can find out through research why this area might have been more likely to have uprisings than most slave areas.

SUGGESTED READING

Bassett, John S. *Slavery and Servitude in the Colony of North Carolina.* Baltimore: The Johns Hopkins Press, 1896. Somewhat dated but still the most useful summary in print.

Franklin, John Hope. *The Free Negro in North Carolina, 1790–1860.* Chapel Hill: UNC Press, 1943. A fine survey and the only one on its subject.

Taylor, Rosser H. "Slave Conspiracies in North Carolina," *N.C. Historical Review* (Jan. 1928), pages 20–34. Not thoroughly reliable but the best summary available.

1815 General Assembly
resolves to purchase
Washington statue

1812 War with England

1814 Peace signed with England

1820 Missouri Compromise
(March)

1821 Washington statue
brought to Raleigh

1823 Monroe Doctrine *(Dec.)*

1824 Republicans defeated
in North Carolina elections
1825 Lafayette visits
North Carolina
● Literary Fund created
to begin public school system

1828 North Carolina supports
Jackson for President
● James Capps strikes gold
in Mecklenburg

1829 Jackson inaugurated
President *(March)*
● Walker's *Appeal*
published in Boston

1831 Washington statue
and State House destroyed
by fire *(June 21)*

1831 Nat Turner's Revolt

1834 Whig party organized
in North Carolina
1835 Constitutional Convention
in North Carolina
1836 Whig victory in North
Carolina

1836 Siege of the Alamo
(March)

11

VIDERI QUAM ESSE

"To Seem, Rather Than to Be"

In Which Too Much Is Not Enough

Resolution means agreement.

It was too bad for North Carolina that legislator Thomas Spencer of Hyde County had so little to say during the 1815 term. His one contribution was a resolution for a statue of George Washington to be placed in the State House. The proposal very sensibly avoided any mention of money. Nobody need feel guilty—yet—about what it might cost.

Governor William Miller found that the legislature had given him a puzzling assignment. So he asked Congressman Nathaniel Macon to gather a list of people who were said to know about statues and how to get them. Letters of inquiry were sent. Within a couple of weeks a letter of great authority came from none other than ex-President Thomas Jefferson. He wrote from Monticello that the only man fit for the project was "old Canova of Rome." Canova, he said, had been Europe's foremost sculptor for 30 years. The work would probably take about two years. But North Carolina ought not to

A **sculptor** is an artist who carves in stone.

199

William Miller, *Governor of North Carolina*

Antonio Canova, *an Italian sculptor*

Thomas Appleton, *American Counsul in Italy*

Archibald D. Murphey, *a political leader and state senator*

John Chavis, *a Presbyterian preacher*

David Walker, *a writer living in Boston*

Nat Turner, *a rebel leader*

Marquis de Lafayette, *a general in the Revolutionary War*

A native of Virginia, William Miller served as Governor of North Carolina from 1814 to 1817.

Revellers are merrimakers, noisy cut-ups.

expect, warned Jefferson, to pay less than eight thousand dollars for so fine an artist. Another letter from Joseph Hopkinson of Philadelphia said that Canova was known to have "a desire . . . to send some specimen of his powers to this country." That settled the question. Governor Miller would offer the project to Canova.

The General Assembly directed the governor to see that the work was completed for not more than ten thousand dollars. Contact was made with Thomas Appleton, an American Consul in Italy who had done business with Canova. In the fall of 1816, Appleton reported that Canova would do the sculpture at North Carolina's price. The figure would be carved from pure white Carrara marble at Canova's studio in Rome. A likeness of the world's greatest man by the world's most famous sculptor could only bring great credit upon North Carolina and its people.

Canova had scarcely begun to work before the legislators began to worry about the place in which the statue would stand. The State House was a dingy, red brick, barn-like structure "as plain as a gigantic dog-kennel." It would make a sorry resting place for a great work of art. Somebody suggested that they could put the statue outside on the lawn. Others warned of the danger of damage from bands of "midnight revellers." It might be struck by "a random stone from the hand of a schoolboy." The only solution seemed to be to remodel the State House.

Captain William Nichols was hired for the new position of state architect. He was assigned to enlarge and decorate the building. He could spend up to 25,000 dollars for the purpose. To hide the ugly brick walls, Nichols added imitation granite all around the outside. He put a dome over the center of the

Nathaniel Macon, a Warren County planter, rose in politics to become a major figure in Congress.

Bankrupt means broke, unable to pay debts.

The *pedestal* is the base on which a statue rests.

roof. He added columned porches in front of each door. After some interior decorating, people agreed that "the Father of the Nation" could now stand with dignity inside the State House.

Others, however, had begun to worry. Since the 1790s, the General Assembly had gained a reputation as one of the most tight-fisted legislatures in the country. Over the years it had rejected all sorts of worthwhile projects for building canals, dredging rivers, deepening inlets, and promoting education. Now, suddenly, the stingy lawmakers were voting huge amounts of money for a marble statue and a remodeled State House.

Meanwhile, Architect Nichols had come back to the legislature several times. He needed additional funds to complete the work assigned to him. Everything seemed to cost much more than anyone had figured. And this was becoming alarmingly true also of the statue by Canova. Governor Miller and his successor, Governor Branch, both ran into trouble sending funds to Appleton to keep the statue on schedule. Two agents went bankrupt while handling the money. This cost North Carolina eight thousand dollars in money it could not get back from them. Appleton himself went over his budget by paying more than seven thousand dollars to Canova for the statue. More than four thousand went to one of Canova's students for a carved pedestal. There were also charges of close to a thousand dollars for Appleton's own services and for the cost of transporting the two pieces from

Burke County-Mecklenburg County, 1820

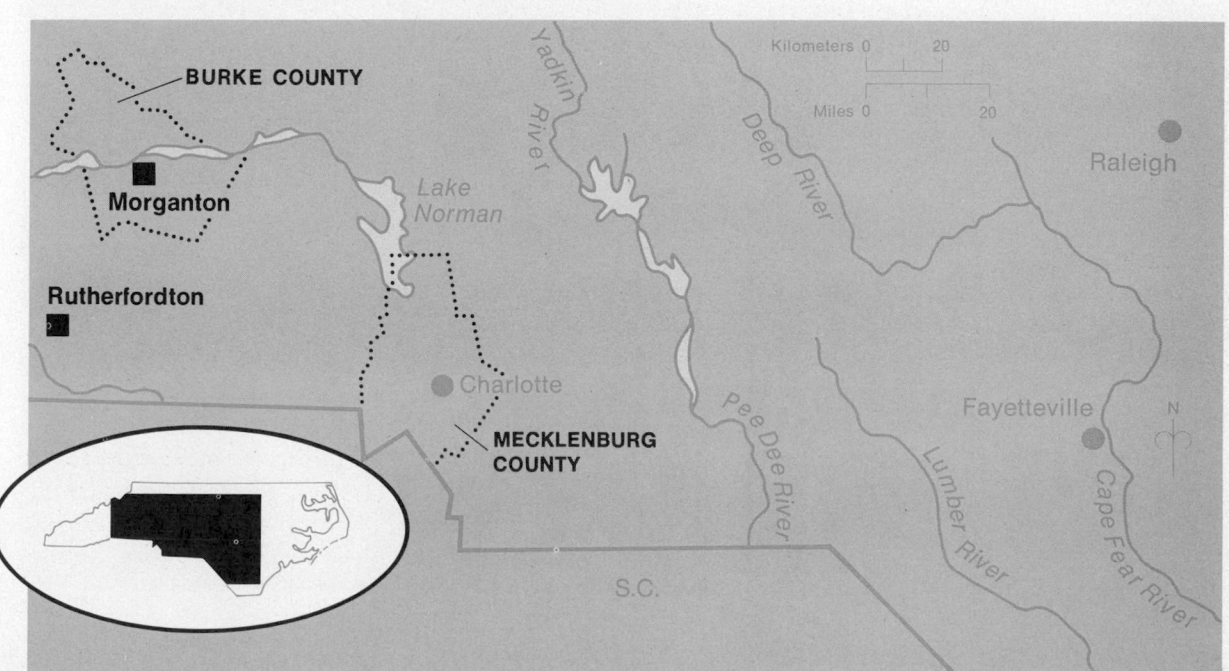

Rome to the seaport of Civitavecchia. By the beginning of 1821, North Carolina had paid out some fifty thousand dollars. And the statue was still in Italy!

A fine drama arose over the style and posture of the statue. It was agreed that the statue was to be larger than life-size. When Canova learned that the State House ceiling was only 16 feet high, he insisted that the figure must be sitting down. Otherwise, when mounted on its pedestal, it would almost touch the ceiling. The governor yielded on the point. Then the question arose as to how the general should be dressed. Common sense suggested that he should be wearing his general's uniform. But people who were said to be authorities persisted in making fine distinctions between common sense and artistic taste. Dr. Hugh Williamson advised the governor of the "uncouth appearance" of "a statue dressed in a modern coat." He proposed instead "the antient dress of a Roman." Even Jefferson seemed to feel that "the Roman" would be better, since "our boots and regimentals have a very puny effect." The general, then, would wear a toga and some sandals.

Uncouth means crude, undignified.

Antient is an old style of spelling ancient.

Regimentals means military dress.

A *toga* is robe worn by a Roman officeholder.

At left is a duplicate of the Washington statue. An artist who had not seen the statue sketched Lafayette examining it in Raleigh in 1825 (right).

The statue and pedestal left Italy in the spring of 1821 aboard the U.S.S. *Columbus.* They reached Boston Harbor in July. They were transferred to a steamboat in October and again, at Wilmington, to a Cape Fear river steamer. A specially-constructed wagon, drawn by 16 oxen, received the eight tons of marble at a wharf near Fayetteville in early November. After a slow trip over bad roads, the statue and pedestal reached Raleigh on Monday, December 23.

After six years and fifty thousand dollars, North Carolina was entitled to a celebration over the safe arrival of the statue. There was a parade from the edge of town to the capitol grounds. It was led by a band and included the chief officers of state, many citizens, and some Revolutionary War veterans. One of the veterans, Colonel Thomas Polk, made a speech. The militia fired a 24-gun salute. Within a week, the statue was in position in the new rotunda of the State House. It stood directly under Mr. Nichols' dome. The Raleigh *Register* informed its readers that the statue was said "by Connoisseurs in the fine arts, to be finished with a boldness of outline, and delicacy of taste, which rank . . . with the choicest specimens of antiquity."

Well, maybe so. But some people thought that the general looked ridiculous in his Roman "soldier suit." Others complained that the face and figure looked like a hundred other people. Some said it looked more like Julius Caesar. But such critics were modest compared to one who told a Chapel Hill audience it was "a useless piece of marble." The legislature, he said, was famous for its penny-pinching ways. It had now "unwisely and unaccountably gone to the opposite extreme. . . ." Could not so much money have been better used for education and internal improvements? "Does the magnificence of the statue," he asked, ". . . a fragment of ancient ostentation, at all correspond with the . . . plainness and simplicity of North Carolina?" It was a late hour to ask such questions.

The General Assembly soon returned to its tradition of tight spending. Once more it began to guard the public's dollars with fanatical caution. Alfred Moore of Brunswick County suggested spending a few hundred dollars more to mount the statue on rollers so it could be moved to safety incase of fire. He found no backers for his idea. Viewers might have thought they saw a shadow of dismay pass across the face of the stone man in the rotunda.

Could fifty thousand dollars worth of stone and imitation granite buy North Carolina the respect lost by years of neglect of its educational and commercial resources? Many people seemed to feel it could.

A **rotunda** is a circular hall or room with a dome.

Connoisseurs are those capable of passing judgement on matters of art and taste.

Antiquity means ancient times.

Ostentation means show, display intended to impress others.

Dismay means discouragement.

The statue did, indeed, bring North Carolina some degree of the respect it craved from other states. A Boston tourist, passing through Raleigh in May 1824, gave this impression of his visit:

> The statue . . . is well worth a visit, . . . on purpose to see it . . . the likeness is very bad but the execution most beautiful . . . the hero is . . . clothed in the Roman costume however improper & inappropriate this may be it has given the artist great scope. . . . the drapery is exquisitely done . . . The Pedestal is also of beautiful proportions. . . . The manner in which N Carolina the least wealthy, & enterprising of us obtained this exquisite work is singular Some member of the house [of Commons] voted for a Plaister bust. . . . this was amended by another member for a whole length figure & by another as an equestrian but still in plaister finally the discussion became warm & a proposal for a Marble Statue to cost 10,000$ was unanimously carried & the statue ordered but when nearly finished the merchant who gave the order & had the funds failed & a new appropriation of 10,000$ was necessary so that in stead of a plaister bust costing 10$ the cost of the statue was upwards of 20,000$ besides this the state house cost originally 12,000$ had laid out upon it 60,000$ in alterations and additions consequent on placing the Statue in it which cost the State directly & indirectly upwards of 80,000$ all arising from a proposal for the expenditure of 10$.

Plaister is an old way of spelling plaster.

An *equestrian* is a horseback rider.

In Which "Rip Van Winkle" Begins to Stir

Jefferson's Republican party used the opening years of the nineteenth century to try to bring the United States under a one-party system of government. The party skillfully handed out offices to those it favored or whose favor it sought. Republicans thus hacked away at the basis of the Federalist party's support and helped destroy it. In North Carolina, a politician's public commitment to federalism was almost a suicide note. North Carolinians showed little interest in national affairs. They devoted themselves to internal and strictly private concerns. This viewpoint was perfectly suited to republican government.

The early years of the nineteenth century were an age of

Republican means favoring a relatively weak central government.

Federalism means favoring a relatively strong central government.

economy in government. The Republicans cut public spending to the bone. The state budget for 1801 was only 35,000 dollars. The governor received 1,600 of that for his salary. Governor Benjamin Smith complained that the governor's residence was not fit to live in. The 1804 General Assembly considered moving its sessions to Fayetteville. This was to avoid the high rents of Raleigh's boarding houses. Funds for the state university, considered to be a hotbed of federalism, were severely reduced. This threatened the school's existence and forced it to beg for private contributions across the state. Nathaniel Macon from Warren County was the speaker of the House of Representatives from 1801 to 1807. He saw to it that North Carolina's economical ways were also those of the federal Union.

Commercial revival in the United States after the War of 1812 affected North Carolina very little. Each year saw the state slip further behind other Southern states. By now it was common for outsiders to refer to North Carolina as the "Rip Van Winkle State."

Forebears means ancestors.

The largest towns, New Bern and Fayetteville, had populations of only about thirty-five hundred. The huge majority of the people lived on farms. These they worked by the same methods brought from Europe by their forebears of a century and more before. The exhausted land produced little surplus for export. Certain small regions, including the Roanoke and Cape Fear River valleys, enjoyed a fair prosperity. But most North Carolinians lived either in poverty or not far from it. What export trade there was fell mainly into the hands of New England merchants and profited the state little. Efforts to promote steamboat navigation on the eastern rivers and sounds had little success. As in colonial times, roads remained few and poor.

Poverty is a condition of having little or no money or property.

In other respects as well, North Carolina was probably the most backward state in the Union. In 1815, the state industry was made up of one small cotton mill, a few iron works, some paper mills, and a few firms making hats. There were some whiskey and turpentine distilleries, and corn and flour mills. All the banking in the state was handled by the little state bank at Raleigh. There were private banks at New Bern and Wilmington.

Those connected with the state government seemed to believe that taxation and republican philosophy did not go well together. Land was taxed at the low rate of six cents for every 100 dollars of value. There was a poll tax of 20 cents a year on each white male inhabitant. Even these tiny amounts were resented by the citizens. No one in the legislature dared propose

Dividends means money paid to shareholders out of earnings.

any increase. These two taxes, with a little income from the sale of public lands and dividends from state-owned bank stocks, had to pay the entire state budget.

Along with taxation, people's ability to read and write was another thing that did not agree with republicanism as it was understood in North Carolina. Even among the whites, nearly half the people (including most women) could not recognize their names in print or form the letters that spelled them. Not many saw this as in any way harmful to a democratic society. However, the Federalist minority insisted it was so. The idea of a tax on all for the benefit of some—those to be educated—seemed foreign and unwelcome. A letter in the Raleigh *Register* in 1829 expressed alarm over proposals to establish public schools. It was well known, according to the writer, that this would lead straight to a new privileged class. It might well lead, in addition, to an increase of one percent in taxes. Other states might boast of their superior schools, the writer declared. But North Carolinians could still reply with pride that "our taxes are lighter than theirs."

North Carolina remained a slow-moving, sleepy, "Rip Van Winkle" state for many years. But not everyone was content with the state's poor roads. Not everyone was content to see North Carolina citizens—both black and white—suffer from lack of education. One citizen who was impatient for progress was a white lawyer, Archibald D. Murphey. Another important reformer was a black minister and school teacher, John Chavis. Both Chavis and Murphey did what they could to make the state wake up to its public responsibilities.

John Chavis was one of Raleigh's most remarkable citizens. He was a free black who had fought in the Revolutionary War. At the beginning of the nineteenth century, he came to North Carolina to teach school and to run a Presbyterian church. His school in Raleigh was recognized as the finest in the area. Leading families sent their children to him for instruction. Chavis taught white children in the daytime and blacks at night. His students are said to have included several who later won national fame, among them the governors of two states.

Meanwhile, the white reformer, Archibald Murphey, was also concerned about schools—as well as every other public need of North Carolina. As a senator from Orange County from 1812 to 1818, Murphey wrote several reports about the state's problems. His reports concluded that only a strong, positive government effort could awaken North Carolina from its slumbers. Murphey used every available method to arouse interest in a program of reform. His program concentrated on

Archibald D. Murphey's foresight and public spirit helped prepare North Carolina for its progressive movement in the 1840s and 1850s.

three areas: transportation, education, and the state constitution.

First of all, Murphey said there should be a special state agency to improve the state's primitive system of transportation. This new agency, he said, should have the power to cut a long-needed inlet through the Outer Banks. The new inlet would then connect the Albemarle Sound region with the ocean. Other inlets should be deepened, said Murphey. Canals should be dug. Swamps should be drained. Obstacles should be removed from the channels of the western rivers. A new system of roads should link the mountain regions with rivers leading to the North Carolina coast. Such a program, said Murphey, would free the state from dependence on South Carolina and Virginia. It would stimulate agriculture, commerce, and industry alike. It would unite the sections of the state.

A second state agency, said Murphey, should administer a state-wide system of schools—for white boys. The schools should provide basic instruction for young children as well as university training for older students. According to Murphey's plan, each county should have at least two primary schools. There should be ten regional academies across the state. There should be a school for the deaf and dumb and stronger support for the University of North Carolina. Poor children should have three years of free schooling. The most promising students should be financed all the way to their degrees.

The third important part of Murphey's program was constitutional reform. Murphey wanted to break the hold of the East over the General Assembly. He suggested that a convention meet to overhaul the old state constitution of 1776. He said all free men of the state—westerners as well as easterners—should vote on whether to have a convention. In this way, Murphey hoped to make state government more responsive to the will of the majority of people.

What finally happened to the dreams of the black teacher, John Chavis, and the white reformer, Archibald Murphey? Both men were bitterly disappointed.

Chavis's life—and the life of all blacks in North Carolina—was upset by a little pamphlet that angrily attacked slavery. David Walker, a free black from Wilmington, North Carolina, wrote the pamphlet in 1829 after moving to Boston. Walker's essay on slavery was entitled *An Appeal to the Coloured Citizens of the World*. It called the victims of American slavery "the most degraded, wretched, and abject set of beings that ever lived since the world began." The pamphlet asked white Americans if their own suffering under the British was "one

Abject means hopeless.

hundredth part as cruel and tyrannical as you have rendered ours under you?" It was perhaps the most forceful attack yet made on slavery in America. It was to send shock waves through the South for years to come.

White North Carolinians learned to their horror that copies of Walker's pamphlet were circulating among the blacks in the state. Governor John Owen feared the pamphlet might touch off a race war. He asked the state legislature to give him special power to fight the danger. Armed patrols roamed the countryside. Many blacks were arrested and harassed. But no eivdence of a conspiracy was found. For a while, public excitement declined and the patrols went home.

But then, one August morning in 1831, a hysterical young man rushed into the streets of Murfreesboro, a town near the Virginia border. He was screaming about a revolt of the slaves in neighboring Southampton, Virginia. News spread fast about the bloodiest slave revolt in American History—Nat Turner's Insurrection.

A slave named Nat Turner and his little band of rebels had taken the lives of more than 50 whites. Finally, militia companies from North Carolina and Virginia put down the revolt. The white community reacted with fury. Angry white leaders searched for a cause for the revolt. They found not one cause, but a hundred. In particular, they blamed David Walker and the northern abolitionists. But they also thought free blacks were the secret agents of rebellion. New laws poured forth from legislatures in North Carolina and other slave states. Free blacks lost their rights as citizens. They were told they could no longer vote, teach, preach, or bear firearms.

The white backlash was costly to North Carolina. The state lost the contributions of some of its most gifted citizens. Louis Sheridan, a well-known black businessman, was forced to sell his land and property. He liberated his 19 slaves and moved with them to a new home in Liberia, West Africa. At the same time, the new laws of North Carolina, forced John Chavis to retire. He was no longer allowed to teach or preach. He could no longer help to overcome the state's problem of illiteracy. Chavis lived out his years in poverty.

Liberia was a colony created in Africa as a home for freed slaves and other blacks.

Meanwhile, what had become of Archibald Murphey's program of reform? At first, the program excited considerable interest—especially his ideas for improved transportation. A state engineer was hired to make surveys of rivers, inlets, and proposed canals. Some roads were started in the West. State money was invested in navigation. But these small steps produced little of lasting value.

Still less came from Murphey's ideas about education. After much resistance, the legislature set up a literary Fund and

Gold discoveries on their land were one reason the
Cherokees were forced to leave their North Carolina home.
During the Great Migration to Oklahoma, many died of
hardship.

a Literary Board in 1825. They were supposed to build a public school system. Instead, the revenue set aside was too small and no schools were built.

Murphey was keenly disappointed. Most of his ideas had been defeated by Eastern legislators who feared their section of the state would have to pay higher taxes. The Easterners argued that most of the taxes would help the West, not the East. The Easterners also defeated Murphey's proposal for a constitutional convention. They had little sympathy for a convention aimed at breaking their own power in the Assembly.

Murphey had spent his own money trying to improve the state's transportation system. He finally went bankrupt. Because he could not pay his debts, he was thrown in jail.

But Murphey's efforts at reform were not completely in vain. Largely because of him, the Republican Party's iron grip on politics in the state ended in 1824. In that year, the Republican candidate for President, William H. Crawford, was defeated in North Carolina. He was beaten by the popular war hero, Andrew Jackson. (Another candidate, however, John Quincy Adams, was finally elected President.) The Republican defeat in North Carolina was a victory for the small farmer West over the large planter East. It was also a victory for Archibald Murphey.

In the 1820s, more was needed to wake up the Rip Van Winkle state than the efforts of a single reformer. What was

Miners ascended and descended the mine shaft to the tunnels which reached out in many directions following the gold veins.

needed was something that could shake the state with the force of an earthquake—something like the discovery of gold. In 1828, a poor dirt farmer named James Capps found gold on his farm in Mecklenburg County. The news touched off a great rush of people into the western counties. Everyone, it seemed, wanted to dig for gold and strike it rich. Hundreds of people came flocking into North Carolina. They came from neighboring states and even from foreign countries. They swung their picks at the soil of Mecklenburg County and panned the rushing mountain streams of Burke.

The year 1829 was only the beginning of the great gold rush. The year 1830 was better in the gold fields and 1831 better than that. Someone stumbled onto a gold deposit near Charlotte in 1831. It contained one hundred twenty pounds of gold in one place in pieces of up to eight pounds each. By now there were single mines employing up to a thousand workers.

Much of the gold mined in North Carolina was sent to Philadelphia. There, the United States mint converted it into coins—nine million dollars worth by 1860. But the first gold coin ever minted in the United States was made in North Carolina itself. It was made by Christopher Bechtler, a German immigrant who founded a private mint at Rutherfordton in 1831.

Mills with heavy pestles, or stamps, crushed the gold-bearing ore into fine particles.

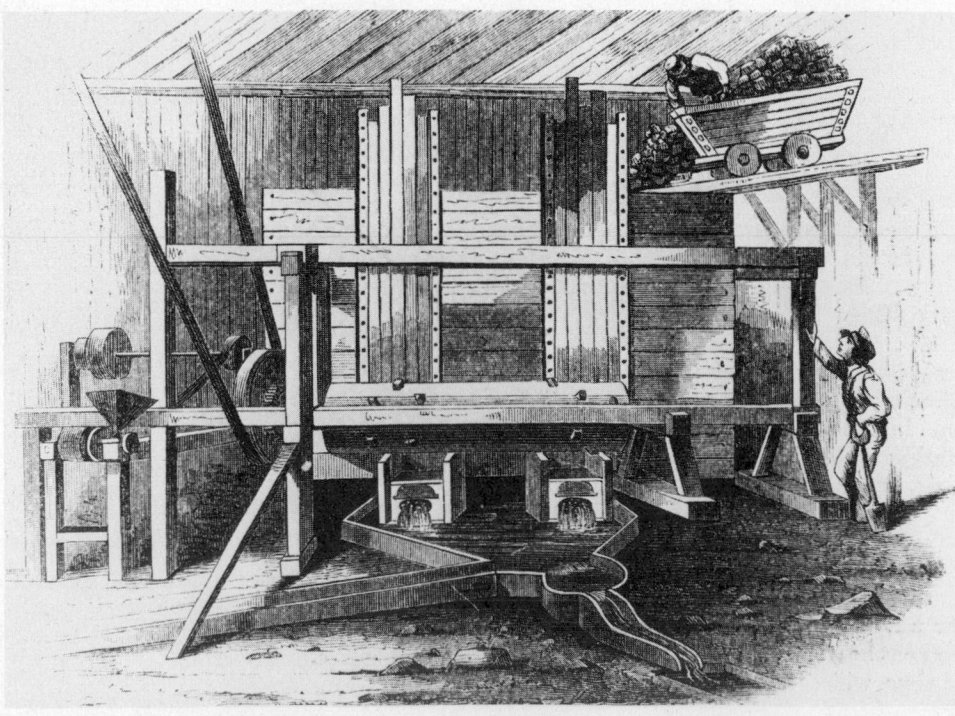

The first gold coins minted in this country were made at Rutherfordton in 1831 from North Carolina gold.

Could all of this new wealth help to wake up the Rip Van Winkle state at last? Could at least some of the precious yellow ore be used to give a new birth to North Carolina commerce? Yes, the gold rush in the western counties did make an important difference. It helped to create a new mood of self-confidence and optimism across the state. At last, the time had arrived to do many of the things that Archibald Murphey had urged for so long.

The General Assembly and the voters of the state called for a constitutional convention to meet at Raleigh. In 1835, the convention met to review and change the state's basic laws. It was the first such convention in almost 60 years. It was to be a new beginning for North Carolina and its people.

The convention, like the legislature, was dominated by easterners. But the new grouping of westerners, which now included delegates from Albemarle and Pamlico Sound, held out strongly for reform. Despite the objections of Eastern planters, some important changes were made in the state's constitution. First of all, borough representation was abolished. The sessions of the General Assembly were reduced from one a year to one in two years. From now on, the governor would be elected every second year by all adult white male taxpayers. Most important of all, county representation in the House of Commons was changed. The larger a county's population the more delegates it might elect.

At the same time, the Senate was allowed to remain an undemocratic body. Its 50 members would be chosen from ten senatorial districts, whose people paid equal amounts of state taxes. In other words, the wealthier Eastern counties would be better represented in the Senate. The Western counties would be better represented in the House.

Unfortunately, some citizens were discriminated against in the changed constitution. The word Christian was substituted for Protestant in the qualifications for office-holding. This helped the state's Roman Catholics—but not the Jews. Despite some strong speeches in their behalf, free blacks were denied the vote.

None of these changes in the constitution could become law until approved by the voters. The proposed changes were generally unpopular in the plantation East. But the state-wide vote was 27,000 to 22,000 in favor of the change. By this small margin, the citizens of North Carolina made their most important decision in the entire period between 1789 and 1861. The reformed state constitution would permit real progress in North Carolina in the next two decades.

A new political party, the Whigs, was responsible for much of this progress. This party came into existence to op-

The Raleigh and Gaston Railroad line was completed in 1840. Railroad President Vass stands atop an engine in 1850.

Edward B. Dudley was the Whig governor (1836-1841) when North Carolina began to awake from its "Rip Van Winkle" slumbers.

pose the policies of a powerful American President, Andrew Jackson. In 1828, the people of North Carolina had helped to elect Jackson. But as President, Jackson disappointed many of his supporters in the western counties. The Whig Party was then formed for two reasons—to oppose Jackson and to shape a constructive program of government.

In 1834, the Whigs in North Carolina came out strongly for constitutional reform. They fought for reform and won. In 1836, they elected a Whig candidate to be governor of the state. Whigs held the governor's office for the next 14 years. Their opponents, now known as the Democratic party, would return to power later. But first, the Democrats would have to adopt a more progressive political platform.

One great achievement of the Whig era was the building of a railroad system in North Carolina. The construction of a railroad in the state had been discussed as early as 1827. At that time, however, the General Assembly was not prepared to act on such a strange new venture.

The first railroads in North Carolina were built by private firms in the 1830s. A notable one was the Wilmington and Weldon. When completed in 1840, this 161½-mile line was the longest railroad in the world! Its first president, Edward B. Dudley, became the first Whig governor in 1836. The Whig government then took an active role in securing loans for the Wilmington and Weldon project. Another railroad, the Raleigh and Gaston line, also received help from the Whigs.

212

Meanwhile, westerners too demanded a railroad to overcome the transportation problems that had troubled them for a century. Finally, in 1849, they won the approval of the General Assembly for a railroad from Goldsboro through Raleigh to Charlotte. This was the most ambitious venture the state had ever made in internal improvement. It called for two million dollars for a state-owned rail line 223 miles long. The crescent course of the railroad ran through Hillsborough, Salisbury, and Concord. Completed in 1856, this route was to become the most prosperous and well-developed portion of North Carolina.

North Carolina in 1850 was not the same state that it was 30 years earlier. Railroads, a constitutional convention, and a gold rush had all helped to develop the western part of the state. Even the costly stone statue of George Washington had changed during these years. What had happened to it? The next section of this chapter completes the strange and sad story of the unfortunate statue.

Crescent means shaped like the moon in its third quarter.

In Which Lafayette Sees Himself

The most celebrated event in the history of North Carolina occurred in the first half of the nineteenth century. It was the visit in 1825 by the Marquis de Lafayette. The 68-year-old general had come to the United States in the summer of 1824 as the official "Guest of the Nation." He was cheered and honored throughout the northern states during the fall. On a visit to Yorktown and other Revolutionary battlegrounds in Virginia in October, he was urged by representatives from North Carolina and other southern states to extend his visit farther southward. In late February 1825, Lafayette left Washington determined to visit every state before returning to France.

Raleigh was in a frenzy of excitement and celebration. The *Register* proposed that Lafayette might wish to visit the town if only to view "the Statue of the immortal Washington; in which the general would recognize his venerated companion and friend." The editor of the *Register*, therefore, was pleased to report of the visit that Lafayette beheld the statue and said that "the likeness was much better than he expected to see." Later, Lafayette told friends that Canova, in "the most

Frenzy means wild enthusiasm.

Immortal means unforgettable, undying.

Venerated means highly praised or worshipped.

inexcusable action of his life," had made the work "as much *like me* as the great Washington."

The Raleigh visit was mostly speeches, dances, and banquets. But there were incidents that broke the tension of the moment. This included one preserved among the traditions of the Polk family:

> At the conclusion of Col. [William] Polk's address, from the steps of the Capitol, Lafayette turned to him and before the old soldier knew what he was about, threw his arms around his neck and tried to kiss him on the cheek. Col. Polk straightened himself up to his full height of six feet four, instinctively throwing his head back to escape the osculatory act, but Lafayette, being a dapper little fellow, tiptoed and hung on to the grim giant, while a shout of laughter burst from the spectators and was with some difficulty turned into a cheer.

The humorless Raleigh *Star* reported that the two old veterans embraced one another, both weeping. In the next breath, the *Star* proclaimed that Lafayette was "much pleased" with the Canova statue. He had "pronounced it to be a good likeness of the Father of our country." (Did he mean himself?)

From Raleigh, Lafayette, accompanied by his son George Washington Lafayette, with the governor and a large escort, traveled on through Averasboro and Cumberland County. He reached Fayetteville, his namesake town, next day. There, he was lavishly entertained by its citizens in spite of bad weather. Following a night there, the general was escorted to the South Carolina line. He was then turned over to a delegation from that state. His route took him southeast to the lower Mississippi and north in the spring. He returned to France later in the year. Many North Carolina towns bore the news of his death in 1834 with the same grief as Fayetteville. There, it was decreed that citizens should wear crepe armbands for 30 days. But, as the following account shows, the general outlived the monument to his old friend.

Around nine o'clock on the morning of June 21, 1831, alarm bells sounded for a fire. Downtown Raleigh residents were shocked to see smoke pouring from the ventilators under the roof of the capitol building. Those who first rushed to the scene found old Colonel Polk and others wrestling with the four-ton statue. They were trying to move it from the burning building. Ten minutes of frantic efforts with a beam and handspikes failed to budge the great statue so much as a fraction of an inch. Someone in the crowd urged that it be broken

Osculatory means kissing.

Crepe is a silk fabric sometimes worn as mourning.

Ventilators are openings for admitting fresh air.

Lafayette was a hero of both the American and French revolutions. Greatly admired throughout the world, he visited North Carolina in 1825.

Ignite means to set fire to.

An *epitaph* is an inscription on a tombstone.

into three or four pieces. From these pieces it might be rebuilt, but this was shouted down.

The fire, descended slowly from the roof where it had been set by a careless workman. It finally reached the statue itself. It was hot enough to ignite the marble. The statue, "white hot and crumbling, among the forked tongues of flame," gradually shattered into fragments before the horrified onlookers. David L. Swain was a witness to the "sheet of blinding, hissing flame." Long years afterward, he recalled having heard a little boy, standing in the midst of the "breathless silence of the stupified multitude," provide a fitting epitaph: ". . . poor State House," he whispered, "poor Statue, I so sorry."

In the stunned aftermath of the fire, English sculptor Ball Hughes proposed to restore the statue from charred fragments. (Canova had died in 1822.) Hughes was contracted for five thousand dollars and received part of the fee in advance. But he gave one excuse after another for delaying the work. It was abandoned after several years. Further proposals for replacing the statue were made from time to time in the years that followed. Canova's own plaster of Paris model remained in a museum in Florence, Italy. Early in the twentieth century, the Italian government presented North Carolina with a cast made from it. Renewed efforts resulted in the carving of a duplicate of the original. It arrived in Raleigh in 1970 and stands, at this writing, in the State Capitol.

The Canova statue and the alterations to the capitol had been the largest public expense in the history of the state. Even without the fire, it had been a badly planned venture for so poor a state with so many other vital and pressing needs. Few people, if any, were willing to overlook North Carolina's social and economic backwardness provided only that a handsome statue stood in the State House. Auguste Levasseur, secretary to General Lafayette, praised the statue warmly in writing of the visit of 1825. But he closed his remarks with the observation that North Carolina "appeared to me the most backward [state] . . . I had seen as yet." The main cause, he thought, was slavery. But he also felt that North Carolina was to blame in its "long neglect of the measures to extend primary instruction." No marble statue, however handsome, could blind outsiders to reality.

Chapter Checkup

PEOPLE

William Miller	Antonio Canova	Archibald D. Murphey
Nathaniel Macon	William Polk	John Chavis

PLACES

Portsmouth	Jackson
Weldon	Rutherfordton
Murfreesboro	

FACT

Why did the Washington statue end up costing so much?
Why did North Carolina want the statue?
How did North Carolina avoid invasion during the War of 1812?
What was the danger some people feared from the gold discoveries?
What factors led to the rise of the Whig party in North Carolina?

INTERPRETATION

What accounts for the strong republicanism in North Carolina in the early 19th century?

What do you suppose accounts for the willingness of legislators to spend as much on the statue and State House at just this time in the state's history?

What indirect benefits do you think North Carolina realized from the gold discoveries? Explain.

VOCABULARY

Republican   Virtuous
Federalism   Venerated
Bankrupt

ACTIVITY

Trace Lafayette's 1825 route through North Carolina. Try to find out through research all the places he spent a night in North Carolina and, using a modern highway map, mark off a "Lafayette Highway" that would commemorate the route on today's highways as near as possible.

SUGGESTED READING

Johnson, Guion G. *Antebellum North Carolina, A Social History*. Chapel Hill: UNC Press, 1937. A work of huge research and good reliability. See especially chapters V and VI on towns and town-life.

Lemmon, Sarah M. *Frustrated Patriots: North Carolina in the War of 1812*. Chapel Hill: UNC Press, 1973. An interesting survey of personalities and issues of the war period.

Turner, Herbert S. *The Dreamer, Archibald DeBow Murphey, 1777–1832*. Verona, Va.: McClure Press, 1971. An admiring biography.

1829 Mecklenburg Declaration debates begin
1830 Report of panel upholding Mecklenburg Declaration

1829 Jackson inaugurated President *(March)*

1834 Publication of J. S. Jones's *Defense*

1836 Siege of the Alamo *(March)*

1839 Passage of public school law
1840 First public school opened in Rockingham

1841 William Henry Harrison inaugurated President *(March)*

1845 George Moses Horton *Poetical Works* published

1846 War declared on Mexico

1847 Publication of Wiley's *Alamance*

1847 Liberia established as first independent black republic of Africa

1851 Publication of Wiley's *Reader* and Wheeler's *Sketches*

12

AN INTELLECTUAL AWAKENING

The "Fizzle-Winkle" Papers

It was a little like praying for a breeze and getting a cyclone. Sensitive North Carolinians had long wished for a history of their state by a native author. They wanted a book that would examine North Carolina's problems and achievements fairly but sympathetically. The earlier histories, written by an Englishman, an Irishman, a Frenchman, and a Pennsylvanian, were all either too old, too dull, or both. National histories, mainly for this reason, generally ignored North Carolina's role in the growth of the country. But now, in the fall of 1851, came two histories at once by native North Carolinians. Now, the gap in history was suddenly filled. It appeared as though North Carolina literature, up to then a barren wasteland, was at last bursting into full bloom. It was easy to forgive the excitement of those who never thought such a thing could happen.

John Hill Wheeler, *author of Historical Sketches of North Carolina*

Calvin H. Wiley, *author of North Carolina Reader*

Joseph Seawell Jones, *a writer and an attorney*

Mary Bayard Clarke, *a writer*

Momentous means very significant or important.

Patronage means financial support by those who buy the books.

A **travelogue** is a lecture describing travels.

Acclaimed means applauded, praised.

The unlikely authors of this momentous event were John Hill Wheeler of Hertford County and Calvin H. Wiley of Guilford. Neither was previously known to the field of historical studies. Wiley, the younger of the two, had published two modestly successful novels about early North Carolina. He was otherwise known as a lawyer and newspaper editor at Oxford. Wheeler, former superintendant of the Charlotte mint and state treasurer, was unknown as a writer. But each now found himself pushed into the rank of a foremost authority in his field. It might have seemed too sudden a promotion for either one. But it was perfectly reasonable to say that the state's *only* historians were therefore its *best* historians.

Those who worried about the reactions of critics were quickly relieved of their fears. Wiley's *North Carolina Reader* was intended mainly for school children. It was judged by the Raleigh *Register* to have lived up fully "to the high expectations we had . . . , and every way recommends itself to the patronage of the people of the State. . . ." It was a travelogue and a collection of choice essays by native authors, as well as a history. The *Reader* was acclaimed by another reviewer for being "as entertaining to us as a novel, . . . the outpouring of an ardent and patriotic heart. . . ."

Wheeler's *Historical Sketches of North Carolina* was a more formal history. It received its share of flattering reviews. Everyone seemed pleased with the mass of details the author had compiled in his tireless survey of every county. George Bancroft of Massachusetts was America's leading historian. He wrote Wheeler that he had "expected a good deal" of him but that Wheeler had "gone far beyond my expectations." Former Congressman Romulus M. Saunders of Caswell County called it "a work of great value and places us all under great obligations" to the author. Responses like this, said Wheeler, "amply repay me for years of toil, and nights of painful research."

Wheeler's history was published at Philadelphia. The

220

earliest review of it appeared in northern journals. These were faithfully reprinted by North Carolina papers. But several weeks passed before the *Sketches* reached some North Carolina reviewers. Whig editors no sooner began to look through the book when they began to utter groans of dismay and indignation. Wheeler's Democratic bias seemed evident to them on almost every page. The longest and most flattering biographies were those of leading Democrats, both living and dead. Whig leaders were often faintly praised or even ignored. There were seven closely-written pages on Nathaniel Macon, a hero of the Democrats. But there were only 14 lines on John Motley Morehead, the dynamic Whig governor of the 1840s. The difference in tone between the two was almost as great as the difference in length.

Closer examination by both Whig and Democratic critics revealed an even more serious shortcoming: the book was full of mistakes! Wilmington's annual lumber exports were slashed by Wheeler from almost half a million dollars a year to fourteen thousand. New Hanover's annual fish catch was put at 109 barrels. This figure was often surpassed by a single haul. The author had scarcely got Richmond Pearson of Rowan born in 1770 before commissioning him a lieutenant in the Revolutionary Army in 1775. But even the case of the five-year-old lieutenant was surpassed by that of Judge William H. Battle of Forsyth. His distinction was to have been born three years after the death of his father! After this blunder, it seemed petty to complain about Yadkin's county seat being named for the wrong man or for the error of 13 years in the settlement of Fayetteville. The lines Wheeler devoted to his own grandfather's service "in the Revolutionary War" did not mention that he was a Tory officer.

The harshest critics were those who got after Wheeler about his blunders with the English language. In a single sentence, the author claimed that Nathaniel Macon looked upon a seat in Congress as both "the goal" and "the penultimate" of his political ambitions. A Whig editor asked sourly how the seat could have been both the last and next-to-last of Macon's aims. Subject constantly battled against verb in Wheeler's involved sentences. "The General Assembly," he wrote, "... is conscious that no acts ... can express their veneration. ..." The legislature appeared to be either singularly plural or plurally singular. Author Wheeler was uncertain which to call it. "To the student," proclaimed Wheeler's preface, "[the book] ... will afford a data to more extended inquiry. ..." But if data was singular, what was datum? Some reviewers complained of the author's unfortunate efforts to translate an oc-

Dynamic means vigorous, forceful.

John H. Wheeler, first superintendent of the Charlotte mint, became the first native North Carolinian to write a history of the state.

Data means facts, information.

Calvin H. Wiley, first superintendent of schools in North Carolina, was an attorney, a novelist, and a journalist.

Proverbial means having become commonly noted or referred to.

Probity means truthfulness.

Unassuming means modest.

The "Mecklenburg Declaration of Independence," like the fight for independence at Alamance, was a yarn from folklore and not a fact from history.

Oppression means exercising cruel or unjust power.

Conceit means exaggerated opinions of one's own abilities.

Yaupon is an evergreen holly. Its leaves can be used as a substitute for tea.

casional Latin motto. Every week brought exposure of some new horror by the author of the *Historical Sketches.*

Calvin Wiley's *North Carolina Reader,* meanwhile, had enjoyed a somewhat more favorable reception. This was true among Democratic editors, although the author was a strong Whig. As a schoolbook, however, it had not been so carefully analyzed as the *Historical Sketches.* Wiley, therefore, was well pleased with the critical response—until the morning of December 20, 1851. On that day, the Raleigh *Register* published a jolting attack on both books at once.

The letter to the *Register* editor came from a critic signed "Fitz Van Winkle." The writer called attention to what Wiley had described as "the North Carolina character." As often as that character had been misrepresented, Wiley had written, it was still

> unequalled by any in the world. Take it in the valley of the Mississippi and in the far west, and it is proverbial for honesty, probity and honor; and to it does the great South West owe much, if not most, of its real greatness. There is no other people *so honest and so reliable;* and while they are among the most unassuming, the least ambitious and the least ostentatious of all the races of the world, they are undoubtedly among the bravest.

It was asking a lot to accept this evaluation. It implied, as one critic wrote, "that there never has been a native born North Carolina *rascal* from 1584 down." But John Hill Wheeler had also erred on the side of exaggeration. He claimed that in North Carolina "the blood of the colonists first flowed for liberty (at Alamance, May 1771). . . ." Wheeler also boasted that "no doubt now exists" that North Carolinians "at Charlotte in May 1775, were the first to throw off the yoke of English oppression."

To "Fitz Van Winkle," such boasts as those of Wiley and Wheeler were but "vain conceits." North Carolina, so long "doomed . . . to silent contempt or broad ridicule, seems now fairly in the way of being crushed . . . under the weight of the burdensome donations thrown upon her." But "airs of importance," he concluded, were alien to the state's spirit and the people could never be "caught like flies with such *molasses and water* as this."

A main theme for Wiley was the need for North Carolina to become economically independent of other states. This also drew the wrath of the mocking "Fitz." It appeared to the critic foolish to produce all the state's needs at home or drink only yaupon tea because the soil would not produce coffee. Such efforts, he said, must end in making everything "clumsier" and more costly "than what we can get from our neighbors."

It required only a few days for Wiley's defenders to rush to his rescue. This brought the literary debate to a crisis. "Fitz Van Fizzle," a Wiley admirer, accused "Van Winkle" of condemning North Carolina to permanent servitude to its more fortunate neighbors. Tongue-in-cheek, "Van Fizzle" proposed that the best interests of all might be served if North Carolina were simply broken up and divided between South Carolina and Virginia. "Pax Vobiscum" complained to the *Register* that Wiley's words and sentences were entirely too long for school children. At this, Wiley went on the attack in his own *Southern Weekly Post*. The larger Whig papers followed the debate throughout January 1852.

The casual witness to the literary battle of 1851–1852 might have thought that the writers in North Carolina were like the Christians in the Colosseum. But to pass such a judgment would be missing the point. What was important was that some North Carolinians were publicly debating the standards of good literature. They were discussing historical scholarship. It did not matter that they were doing it crudely. The remarkable thing was that they were doing it at all. It was a novel event in the state's history. What was done in a clumsy way this time would perhaps be done better next time—by both authors and critics.

Servitude means slavery or bondage.

Tongue-in-cheek means not seriously meant.

The **Colosseum** is the ancient amphitheatre in Rome.

Peace Institute, a Presbyterian school for girls at Raleigh, was a pioneer in women's education. It opened in 1857.

There was another point that the casual observer might have overlooked. The 10,000-copy first edition of Wheeler's *Sketches* was sold out within three months of its publication. No North Carolina book had ever before come close to that sales record. Wiley's *Reader* was also widely used in the state's school system. It found some favor with the general public as well. A reading public, no doubt small and uncertain as yet, had been found.

What had brought this about? Surely it was not the questionable merits of the two books. The state had not recently come into unexpected new wealth. It had not been invaded by book-hungry immigrants from Rhode Island and Massachusetts. Something deeper and less obvious was taking place. There was an underlying current that was changing North Carolina from its cultural backwardness. In part, it was a longing for something to be proud of. But there was also something else. For this, Wiley deserved chief credit.

Charlotte-Oxford, 1850

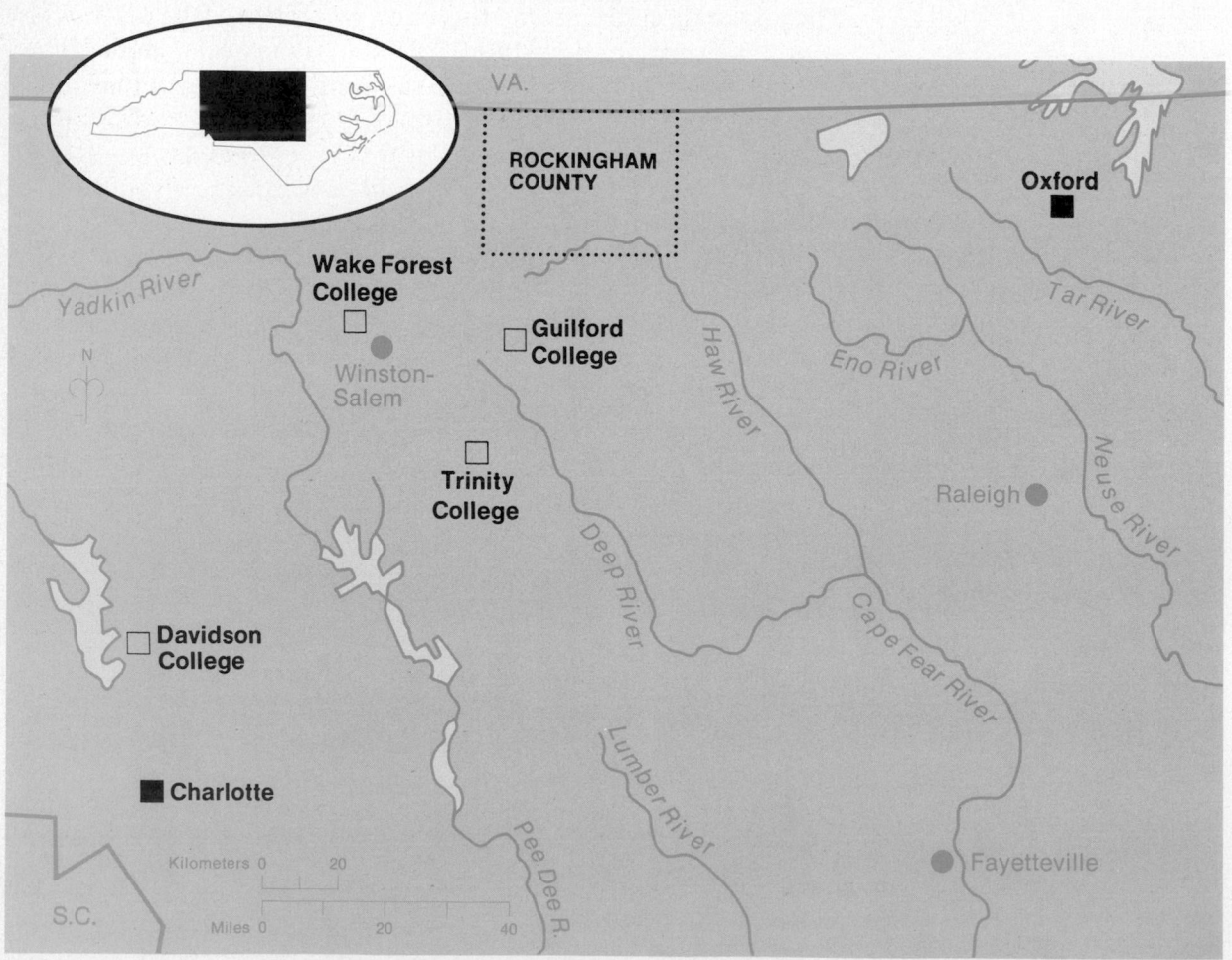

Edgeworth Seminary was opened at Greensboro in 1842 by
John M. Morehead. The building burned in 1872.

A Little Literature

A great achievement of the Whigs in North Carolina was the
passage of a public school law in 1839. It was passed over
many protests as to the need, cost, and philosophy of such legislation. The act called for each county to vote on whether it
wished to have public schools or not. Each county voting to
adopt such schools was then to divide itself into school districts. It was to select a school committee for each district.
Any district also voting a certain amount of taxes for its
schools qualified to receive additional help from the Literary
Fund to hire teachers and provide equipment. In the sub-
sequent election on this question, 61 of the state's 68 counties
agreed to start such a school system. The others joined later.
On January 30, 1840, Rockingham became the first county in
North Carolina to open a public school. By 1850, the state
would have more than twenty-six hundred public schools.

The new public schools were free. But there had been private schools in North Carolina since the early eighteenth century. For these, students paid tuition. "Old field schools" were
started by a teacher or parent. They operated during the winter months in small communities. They had been the typical
schools up to the 1840s. On a little higher plane were private
academies, chartered by the state. These had boards of
trustees and usually enjoyed some regular support in their
communities. Every sizeable town had one or more of these.
Some were first-rate schools. They were mostly for white

boys, but a few were for girls and some were coeducational. In many cases, these academies were taught by Yankee schoolmasters. Some teachers were graduates of the University of North Carolina or other southern institutions. On the eve of the Civil War, North Carolina had over four hundred academies scattered across the state.

Not many of North Carolina's children of school age were served by these schools. Many families could not afford the cost. Others did not particularly approve of the idea. Almost a third of the whites were still illiterate in 1840. This was also true of all but a fortunate few free blacks and slaves. An education at a good academy stressed Latin, Greek, mathematics, astronomy, rhetoric, logic, and moral and natural philosophy. This was the key to university admission. Outstanding lawyers, and sometimes doctors, ran their own schools of law and medicine. However, most doctors were educated in Pennsylvania. There were also experiments with military schools or other specialized institutions. But the outstanding students of the state's educational system tended to be those few who graduated from the University of North Carolina or one of North Carolina's struggling private colleges.

In 1840, there were four private colleges operating in the state. One was Wake Forest, opened by the Baptists in Wake County in 1834. Three others were church-related schools, all of which opened in 1837. Davidson was established in that year by the Presbyterians, North Carolina's educational pioneers. Trinity was founded by the Methodists in Randolph County, and New Garden (later Guilford College) was located in Guilford County. New Garden was the only one of these to admit girls as well as boys.

The education of women still had not become a popular or widespread idea. Most parents were willing to see their daughters trained in household arts, drawing, painting, music, and other "polite" attainments. But few wished the business to proceed any farther. Salem Female Academy was a good Moravian institution which accepted girls of other faiths. The town of Warrenton had a Female Seminary run by Jacob Mordecai. There was also Greensboro Female College, opened with Methodist support in 1838. But few other schools existed in which a girl might receive anything more than a restricted training in ladylikeness.

Literature and the arts suffered from the inability of so many North Carolinians to read. Few people read seriously. Camden Congressman Lemuel Sawyer wrote two silly plays, *Blackbeard* and *The Wreck of Honor*, both written in the 1820s. These plays formed the entire library of native North

Illiterate means unable to read or write.

Rhetoric means the study of the effective use of language.

Natural philosophy is the study of science.

The University of North Carolina was established at Chapel Hill in 1793 under the leadership of William R. Davie.

Attainments means achievements.

Carolina drama. *Eoneguski* is a tale of the Cherokee Indians by Robert Strange. It was the sole novel by a North Carolinian prior to 1847. George Moses Horton, the slave-poet, remained the only North Carolinian to have produced a volume of poetry. His second book, *Poetical Works,* appeared in 1845. None of these authors saw more than the most limited sales. Few of their fellow citizens had ever heard of them.

Compared with past generations, the last 14 years before the Civil War saw an amazing literary growth in North Carolina. Several new volumes of poetry appeared in this brief period. One was Mary Bayard Clarke's *Wood-Notes,* containing the works of some 40 North Carolina poets. Hinton Rowan Helper's *The Impending Crisis* was an attack on slavery. It won national recognition for the Davie County native. It was condemned, however, in his home state. Francis Lister Hawks' *History of North Carolina* (1857–1858) and Griffith J. McRee's *Life and Correspondence of James Iredell* were outstanding works of their kind. A large number of works of lesser note were also coming off the state's presses. A generation of North Carolinians tested abilities they had never before tried to use. Still far behind most of her neighboring states, North Carolina's intellectual life had begun to awaken.

Probably the best pieces by North Carolina writers were in folk humor. A pioneer in that field was Charles Napoleon Bonaparte Evans. He was the editor of the Milton *Chronicle.* He was the creator of a popular character of fiction known as "Jesse Holmes," also called "the Fool-Killer." Evans' paper often carried letters supposedly written to him by "the Fool-Killer," whose only mission in life was to rid the world of its many different kinds of fools. For this purpose, he carried a huge club. With this he felled whatever fools crossed his path in his rambles across the North Carolina Piedmont.

In a typical episode, "the Fool-Killer" leaves Leesburg, in Caswell County, and sets out for Raleigh:

> . . . I encountered a chap, *en route,* who seems to have heard enough about me to know me at sight, and taking me one side he said that he supposed I knew everything, and as he was courting a girl who had a wealthy aunt, and who, report said, intended giving her all of her property when she (the aunt) died, he would like to know of me if he could rely on the report as being true.
>
> "Why do you wish to know?" I enquired.
>
> "Because," he replied, "if it is true I'll marry that girl before Saturday night, as her old aunt can't live long—and if it is not true, I don't want her—as her daddy has but little plunder.

Impending means approaching.

Robert Strange was North Carolina's first novelist. In 1839 he published the Cherokee Indian tale *Eoneguski.*

The Fool Killer was a fictitious
creation of C. N. B. Evans.

"See here, . . . " said I, are you flying around that girl
and pretending to be in love with her?"

"I am," was the reply.

"And are you making 'plunder' the consideration of
your marriage?"

Perceiving me warm up and glance my eye at my
faithful club, he lifted his hat and began to scratch his
head as if embarrassed for a reply, when I walked up to
him and putting my hand in his collar I told him that I
was about the last man that he had any business with—
that he would probably fare better to thrust his head in
the angry lion's mouth. . . . You are, said I, pretending to
be monstrously in love with a young lady, but it seems
that you love her aunt's property more, and thereupon I
pitched into him with the savageness of skinning skunks,
and mauld him about right.

Hamilton C. Jones was better known in the South and nationally than Evans. He created "Cousin Sally Dillard," whose
wit and wisdom was regularly featured in many periodicals.
While Jones was attending a theatre in Baltimore, word
passed around that "Cousin Sally's" author was in the audience. The crowd "laughed, cried, roared, screamed, [and]
beat the benches . . ." before Jones finally gave in and allowed
himself to be introduced on stage. Still more widely celebrated was Johnson Jones Hooper of Wilmington. His "Captain Simon Suggs" became known from coast to coast.

Fictitious means imagined.

Calvin H. Wiley embodied the spirit of the age in North
Carolina. He was partially responsible for creating that spirit.
Born in Guilford County in 1819, he attended Caldwell Institute, a well-known academy at Greensboro. He then enrolled at the University of North Carolina. After he graduated
in 1840, Wiley studied law for a year. He was admitted to
practice, settling at Oxford, in Granville County. He became
editor of the Oxford *Mercury* and sometimes contributed to
his own paper the "memoirs" of a fictitious homespun character known as "Demi-John." They were, it seems, his earliest
attempt at fictional writing. But neither his law practice nor
his newspaper earned him more than a bare living.

In 1843, Wiley gave up his newspaper and soon quit his
law practice. He went home to Guilford to help his family. He
wanted to complete a novel he had been working on for some
time. It was entitled *Alamance*. It dealt with the lives of various characters, more or less fictitious, in the Piedmont section
of North Carolina during the American Revolution. In spite of
some colorful descriptions and personalities, the book did not

have very much of a plot. It earned little praise for its author and even less income. Following a trip to various historic towns and sites in the Coastal Plain, Wiley published a second novel in 1848. It was called *Roanoke*. It was less successful than the first. It dealt with early colonial North Carolina and tried to blend a variety of topics into a regional panorama. The book started an intense little controversy. Readers found that one of Wiley's characters was a fugitive slave named "Wild Bill." He was allowed to make several speeches attacking slavery. But controversy did little or nothing for sales of the book. Wiley then decided to find a more rewarding craft than fiction. In 1851, the year his *Reader* appeared, he became editor of Raleigh's *Southern Weekly Post*.

The newspaper business was none too promising at this time in North Carolina. However, the prospects were probably improving. The Raleigh *Register* had become the state's first daily newspaper in 1850. It was joined in 1851 by the Wilmington *Daily Journal*. But most papers were still little four-page weeklies. They were not very different in style and content from the earliest papers published at New Bern a hundred years before. One of the more interesting enterprises up to this time was the Raleigh *Microcosm*. This was started in 1838 by Leonidas Brock Lemay, a nine-year-old boy. The son of the editor of the Raleigh *Star*, Lemay used his father's press to print a weekly. It featured news items and essays, jokes, and poetry including at least one poem by George Moses Horton. Lemay also printed letters-to-the-editor. One he received from a young female subscriber offered an intriguing proposal: ". . . I thought I should like to see you setting the types, and I am sure if you look as neat and pretty as your paper, a body might afford to help you set types if they knew how." The *Microcosm* continued its appearance until 1843. Lemay, now a ripe veteran of 13, went in search of other fields to conquer. His bright prospects were cut short by his death in Texas. He died of cholera in 1860.

From the beginning of his writing career, Calvin Wiley was a man with a mission—overcoming the poverty and backwardness of his native state. Wiley tried to awaken a spirit of pride among his fellow citizens through his books and newspapers. Like his earlier writings, the *Reader* talked of North Carolina's heritage in terms of great achievements and noble deeds. He wanted readers to feel a sense of healthy rivalry with other states. He wanted them to think of how much better the future could be than the present or past. But neither through books nor newspapers could he find that he was making much impression on North Carolinians.

A *panorama* means a wide survey.

This Quaker church at New Garden, sketched by
John Collins in 1869, drew hundreds of worshippers
to the Yearly Meeting.

Heathen means not religious
or not enlightened.

At some point in his thinking, maybe around 1849, Wiley
seems to have decided that little could be done to change the
older generation. What then of the younger? His *Reader* was
written to mold the minds of North Carolina youth before
taunts and jibes robbed them of pride and ambition. When
the General Assembly approved the office of superintendent
of public schools, no one doubted that Wiley should take the
job. From January 1, 1853 and for the next 13 years, he held
the office. In the course of this time he would make a lasting
contribution to the development of the state he loved so well.

Wiley was like a missionary carrying the Word to the
heathen. He threw himself into the work with almost fanatical
passion. He traveled all over the state to make addresses and
gather information about the difficulties that faced him. He
searched constantly for able teachers. He insisted on rules for
certifying teachers before they were permitted to enter the
classrooms. He encouraged districts to build more and better
schools. And he fought to overcome hostility to the public
school movement. Gradually, he wore down his opponents
through sheer persistence. He built respect for the school system and a belief in the promise it held for the future.

Some of Wiley's proudest gains included the establishment of the *North Carolina Journal of Education,* which he edited. He gave help to schools in getting libraries and equipment. He succeeded in raising the quality of textbooks used in the classrooms. And he improved his own *Reader* in later editions. He started the Educational Association of North Carolina. He required regular reports from schools on their activities and established county institutes for the training of teachers. In short, he completely changed the educational system in the state. He helped reduce illiteracy to less than 23 percent by the opening of the Civil War. By 1860, North Carolina, to the wonderment of many, had the best public school system in the South. Few North Carolinians ever served their state so successfully as Calvin Wiley.

Backward Glance and Forward Leap

The ***Mecklenburg Declaration,*** supposedly passed on May 20, 1775, declared that county's independence from Great Britain.

Public interest in the history of North Carolina had been slowly building since the 1820s and the beginning of the controversy over the "Mecklenburg Declaration of Independence." Many North Carolinians accepted the tradition that citizens of Mecklenburg County had gathered at Charlotte on May 20, 1775. There, they supposedly approved a document declaring their independence from England. Some writings of Jefferson's, published in 1829, contained a letter from Jefferson to John Adams. In it, Jefferson raised questions about the truth of the tradition. The General Assembly hoped to prove that the North Carolina declaration preceded that of Jefferson by more than a year. The Assembly appointed a "blue ribbon" panel to get the facts. The panel was composed of distinguished men but lacked anyone trained in history. In 1830, the panel issued a report which upheld the validity of the Mecklenburg Declaration.

Defiant means rebellious or opposed.

Later discoveries showed that those who recalled such a declaration at Charlotte were actually remembering some defiant resolutions of May 31, 1775. The resolutions denounced certain acts of the English government. But they were short of an outright call for independence. In the meantime, Joseph Seawell Jones, a Warren County attorney, had published two volumes in defense of the Mecklenburg Declaration. These were his *Defense of the Revolutionary History of North Carolina from the Aspersions of Mr. Jefferson,* in

1834, and his *Memorials of North Carolina*, in 1838. Both volumes blazed with patriotic fire in behalf of North Carolina. But neither one shed much light on the issue in question.

Jones's books showed the interest stimulated in North Carolina history by the Mecklenburg controversy. One of Archibald D. Murphey's projects had been that of writing a history of the state. He collected some documents and urged an interest in preserving North Carolina history. But Murphey's personal troubles wrecked this plan as it had most of his others. An appeal in Raleigh newspapers in 1833 for the formation of a state historical association came to nothing. But the Raleigh *Harbinger* kept the issue alive for several years thereafter. Finally, in 1844, David L. Swain, then president of the University of North Carolina, managed to form the North Carolina Historical Society. It began collecting books and documents on the state's past.

A firm in Washington, N.C. advertised this cotton press as "having no equal" for simplicity, being cheap and efficient.

This sketch from the cover of an 1856 North Carolina farm journal includes the state capital and farm scenes.

Moldering means crumbling, decaying.

Meanwhile, in 1843, the state legislature had arranged for the publication of an *Index of Colonial Documents Relative to North Carolina.* This was largely through the efforts of State Treasurer John Hill Wheeler. Five years later, the General Assembly authorized the governor to spend a thousand dollars to have copies made of documents in England relating to the history of North Carolina. Some people undoubtedly believed that proof of the Mecklenburg Declaration lay moldering in the British Public Record Office. A thousand dollars would be a small price to give North Carolina a chance to proclaim a patriotism greater than that of Virginia. Many North Carolinians had come to resent Virginia's leadership over them. But matters moved slowly. The work was just getting under way when the Civil War cut it short. Not until 1886 were the main British records available in North Carolina.

It would not be hard to find a certain amount of childish nonsense in all this hoopla over history. The motives of most of its sponsors were doubtless a mixture of serious inquiry, envy, pride, and pure malice. But one can also see that it was, in general, a healthy and beneficial movement. Out of it was to come a clearer and more truthful understanding of North Carolina's role in the history of the nation. That role, when revealed, was not so deep as the most ardent "professional North Carolinians" hoped. Nor was it so unworthy as many outsiders had always said. But the fact that such an inquiry was beginning in the 1830s and 1840s showed a new depth and maturity among large numbers of North Carolina citizens.

Rigmarole means confused or foolish talk.

The new historical interest, at least in these early years, was more nearly a result than a cause of the growing mood of self-respect in North Carolina. Calvin H. Wiley's historical accounts had played a key role in bringing it about; so had John Hill Wheeler's slip-shod rigmarole of myths and statistics. Johnson Jones Hooper, C. N. B. Evans, and "Ham" Jones also played important parts. But there was still far to go as John Hill Wheeler wrote Calvin Wiley in late 1851: "The evidences of a new vitality are awakening around us." He was not only right, for a change. He even got his verb to agree with his subject. That was progress.

Chapter Checkup

PEOPLE

John Hill Wheeler	Robert Strange	Hamilton C. Jones
Calvin Henderson Wiley	Mary Bayard Clarke	Leonidas Brock Lemay
Lemuel Sawyer	C. N. B. Evans	Joseph Seawell Jones

PLACES

Oxford   Milton   Davidson College

FACT

What did the "Mecklenburg Declaration" have to do with the interest of North Carolinians in historical scholarship?

What was Wiley's reason for publishing his *Reader*?

What accounts for the popularity of the books published by Wiley and Wheeler in 1851?

What political bias affected Wheeler's book?

INTERPRETATION

Do you think that the "patriotic" bias of Wheeler and Wiley's books was more of a strength or weakness? Explain.

Is it significant that the "intellectual awakening" of North Carolina came while the Whigs were in office? Explain.

Do you see a parallel between North Carolina's interest in these books and black interest in the volume and film called *Roots*? Explain.

VOCABULARY

Patronage	Probity	Impending
Data	Illiterate	Panorama

ACTIVITY

Look up in Wheeler's *Sketches* the section on your county and, using recent sources, check it for accuracy.

SUGGESTED READING

Johnson, Guion G. *Antebellum North Carolina, A Social History.* Chapel Hill, UNC Press, 1937. See especially chapters XXV and XXVI on the intellectual awakening.

Walser, Richard. ''Letters of a Young Novelist: Calvin Henderson Wiley,'' *N.C. Historical Review* (July, 1954), pages 180–201. Letters written by Wiley while he was writing and publishing his early novels.

PART FIVE

The Civil War and Reconstruction

Chatham County Courthouse
at Pittsboro

1860-1877

1848 Gold discovered
in California *(Jan)*
● War with Mexico ends *(Feb.)*

1850 Democrats return
to power in North Carolina

1854 Rayner's address
at State Fair

1855 Democrats support
internal improvements

1853 Gadsden Purchase

1854 Republican party formed
(July)

1857 Property qualifications
for voting ended

1857 The Dred Scott Decision
(March)

1859 Whigs reorganize
● Ellis reelected

1861 Foster returns
to Murfreesboro *(May 9)*
● Foster seeks audience
with Lincoln *(June)*
● Foster elected at Hatteras
(Nov.)
1863 Foster rejoined by wife
and daughter

1861 Lincoln inaugurated
President *(March)*
● The Civil War Begins *(April)*

13

GROUNDS
FOR DIVORCE

The Son-in-Law

A *hack* was a hired carriage.

It was May 3 when Foster left Washington, D.C. on the hack for Alexandria. There he would take the train for Richmond. Virginia had not yet seceded. But the passengers were closely watched as they arrived at the Mansion House hotel and registered for the night. Lincoln's spies were known to be roaming the seceded states. Any hack from Washington might contain more spies, southward bound on their hateful missions.

Foster stayed the night at Alexandria before taking the Richmond train next day. He reached Richmond too late to make connections for Petersburg, so he put up at the Spottswood Hotel. He had time next day to visit a Confederate camp. He shared some rations with friends and caught the cars in the afternoon for Petersburg. At Petersburg, there was another hackride to the Seaboard and Roanoke station. Foster was surprised to share the hack with Congressman Kenneth Rayner. Rayner was on his way home after taking his daugh-

Charles Henry Foster, *a political figure*
Sue Carter Foster, *Charles Foster's wife*

Kenneth Rayner, *a congressman from North Carolina*

A *seamstress* is a woman whose occupation is sewing.

Fatigue shirts are military work shirts.

Charles Henry Foster's curious career during the Civil War was typical of many whose loyalties were divided over the conflict.

ter out of a northern school. He mentioned that he was a candidate for the upcoming convention to decide whether North Carolina should secede. He hoped Foster would vote for him. The next day Foster went on to Boykins Depot in the same cars with a Georgia regiment. By noon, he was back in Murfreesboro and the Carter home—"Rose Bower."

Charles Henry Foster had been away for over two months. When he left Murfreesboro in February, his daughter Caroline was only a week old. Now she was fat and noisy, the center of attention for her family and the servants. But the family also had other things on its mind. The place looked just like a seamstress shop. The Carter girls, Foster's sisters-in-law, were busy making fatigue shirts for the soldiers at the camp grounds. They had also made a Confederate flag and flown it over Rose Bower on May Day.

Only Sue, Foster's wife, was happy to see him. For Perry Carter and his family, Sue's husband was an embarrassment and even a danger. Everyone in Murfreesboro knew about the things Foster had done in Washington. Dr. Campbell, the dentist, had passed an issue of *The New York Times* around town. It showed Foster as a member of the "Clay Guards," organized to protect Washington from threatened attack by rebels. They had heard about his signing an oath of loyalty to the Union. And now he had returned—in the midst of a frenzy of antiunion feeling. The most violent rebels were sure to take him for a spy. No one could tell what outrage might occur.

A group of men knocked at the door around 9 P.M. They told Foster to come to the Masonic Hall where a meeting of citizens was taking place. When he arrived, Foster found a group of about two hundred men. A spokesman informed him that the purpose of the meeting was to hear and consider an explanation for his conduct and his return to Murfreesboro. Foster admitted he had joined the Clay Guards. He did so only to defend the women and children of the capital. He had taken an oath, but only because all government employees had to. He was in Murfreesboro, he said, to visit his family. He would soon return to Washington. A motion was made

240

that he be ordered to leave town at once. This was amended to allow him 48 hours. Foster was dismissed.

The next day was awful for Foster and his kin. Rumors reached them all day that certain persons were plotting to do him harm. One was said to be trying to gather 20 men to tar and feather Foster and then to ride him out of town on a rail. Others had sworn to shoot him if he appeared in the streets. Another was supposed to have said that, if Foster left home with his wife and child, they "should *all three be cut into inch pieces!*" It was no time to play the role of die-hard Unionist. Foster was risking the lives of the whole family. He must either leave at once or convince the Vigilance Committee of a sudden change of heart and politics. The latter seemed the safer course.

At his own request, Foster appeared again before the vigilantes on the night of May 7. He announced that he was giving up his position with the federal government. He was ready to take an oath of loyalty to the South. He would do whatever might be asked of him by the state. He reminded them that, though he was a native of Maine, his prewar Murfreesboro newspaper had been a strong pro-Southern journal. He spoke of his service to the Democratic party as a delegate to last year's Baltimore Convention. Might he not remain safely under these circumstances? Despite some objections, the Vigilance Committee revoked its order of the night before. They agreed to seek the governor's advice before acting further. For the moment, Foster and the Carters seemed safe.

On May 9, Foster wrote to Governor Ellis, repeating his pledge of Southern loyalty. He said he belonged to the Knights of the Golden Circle. He was bound to an oath never to take up arms against the South. If the governor did not act, he feared violence against himself and the Carters. As an added precaution, he wrote the governor of Virginia the same day, requesting a pass through the state in case he must leave.

Ellis replied that he trusted the judgment of the citizens and would take no action. Tensions eased a bit when the volunteer company was moved to a hotel across the street from Rose Bower. But, on May 20, the convention in Raleigh voted North Carolina out of the Union. It was the last state to secede. More rumors of violence against Foster arose and Rebel enthusiasm reached a noisy peak. It was time for Foster to get out if he could.

Before dawn on May 30, Foster kissed his wife and child and drove off with a friend in a carriage. They headed out of town on a main road and doubled back on a little-used side road. They came out on the route to Belfield, Virginia on the

Vigilance committees were citizens groups organized to watch for and seize abolitionists.

Revoked means taken back or withdrawn.

John Ellis was the governor at the start of the Civil War. He died in the summer of 1861.

Congressman Kenneth Rayner did not take kindly to Foster's remarks about him in the northern press.

Richmond and Weldon railroad. It was only a few miles to the Virginia border. Early in the afternoon they reached Belfield. There, Foster got a train to Richmond. Two days later he was safely in Washington.

A few days afterward, Kenneth Rayner heard that a Washington, D.C. newspaper had quoted a speech he made at Murfreesboro on May 9. "Our informant," said the paper, "himself heard Kenneth Rayner say in a speech that it was the intention of the abolitionists . . . to kill everybody in the South, . . . and then divide up the lands among the poor, by whom the North is overrun." Outraged, Rayner sent a denial to the Raleigh *Standard.* He identified Foster as the "informant." He explained that he had appeared in Murfreesboro on May 8 to find that "there was a strong disposition . . . to take Foster and *lynch* him. . . ." Rayner reminded the people that theirs was a "Christian and civilized" society. He visited Foster and warned him not to leave the house until the excitement passed. For that reason, Foster had not attended the speech by Rayner. His account of it in Washington was a lie.

During the summer of 1861, Murfreesboro heard often of Foster. It learned of his efforts to win a seat in Congress. He would represent North Carolina's Unionists. He meant to raise a regiment of North Carolina troops to "liberate" the state from Confederates. Those who had tried to protect him from violence now seemed foolish.

On July 29, Sue Foster sat at a table in Rose Bower. She poured her anguish into a letter to the editor of a nearby newspaper:

Anguish means acute distress or suffering.

> As a woman true to the South . . . I am prompted to write the following lines, however embarrassing and unpleasant it may be. . . .
>
> All persons know who have been acquainted with Mr. Foster . . ., that he left this place in . . . February . . . for a desk in the Post Office Department in Washington . . . and remained there until the 3d of May last, when he returned to this place. . . . He was accused of being untrue to the South . . . and some went so far as to believe him a spy. . . . To *all* of these accusations he pled *not guilty* and went so far as to say to me, that he intended to return to Washington and prove himself a Southern man.
>
> Mr. Foster . . . did return, and to my surprise, I have found that the man upon whom I had centered my whole affection . . . has proved himself . . . false . . . and indifferent to the life or death of his own wife and child. . . . I conclude . . . by saying, that as painful as a separation would be under other circumstances, it is with firmness and determination that I now declare every tie *severed*

Severed means broken or cut.

which has . . . bound me to Charles H. Foster. . . . I shall no longer bear his name, and will take advantage of the earliest opportunity . . . of having it legally change to . . .
Sue A. Carter.

But it wasn't going to be so simple. "Sue A. Carter" was to have her political views challenged in the months ahead by thoughts which had not occurred to her in 1861. The question of who was "a Southern man" and who was not did not always depend, she would find, on one's residence or politics.

Sue Carter Foster, Charles Foster's wife, found "grounds for divorce" in the double dealing of her husband.

Trial Separation

From 1854 to 1861, the slave question dominated North Carolina politics as it did those of the nation. Many whites believed that slavery offered blacks their best chance of survival in a cruel world. Others feared that blacks would be more of a menace to society as free men than as slaves. Some opposed slavery. But these people were heard from less and less during the 1850s.

For most whites in North Carolina, slavery was less a matter for moralizing than a fact to be accepted. The property of many was invested in slaves. They would not hear of setting the slaves free at a huge loss. Slavery, to them was not good or bad—it existed. No one could suggest a painless way to end it. Therefore, it should continue.

For the slave, the system was cruel and degrading. Probably not many were treated in cruel ways. Indeed, there were instances of genuine love and respect between slaves and masters. But to be a slave meant never to aspire to anything better, never to vote, or to hold office. One could not enjoy the benefits of education or provide for a better life for one's children. It meant hard work without the rewards that whites were accustomed to. It meant the restriction of travel to little errands for one's master. Finally, it meant to be degraded before whites day in and day out for the whole of one's life.

After the 1830s, there was little to gain from buying one's freedom, even when it was possible. Free blacks had little more in the way of security and comfort than slaves and sometimes less. The only real hope of a better life lay in escape. But flight to safety across hundreds of miles of unfriendly country was dangerous. However, many did flee, and some were able to build better lives for themselves in other parts of America.

In 1854, a Bostonian named Benjamin Drew crossed southern Canada. This was a region where thousands of refugee blacks had found new homes. He wrote a book based on his talks with scores of the refugees. Several he met were from North Carolina. They sketched for him a terrible picture of slavery for its millions of victims.

Refugees means those who flee for safety.

Mrs. Coleman Freeman of Windsor, Ontario, was from Halifax County. Her father had fought for seven years in the Revolution. He had received a small pension, but only late in life, three years before he died. She told Drew that the slaves sometimes held religious meetings "in the groves." Whites would seize them as they came out and examine them for passes. Those without passes would "break and run like cattle with hornets after them" to avoid the whips of the whites.

But this was before Nat Turner's Revolt in 1831. It happened near where Mrs. Freeman's family lived. "The white people that had no slaves," she said, "would have killed the colored" during the revolt, "but their masters put them in jail to protect them from the white people. . . ." Patrollers came to the house of Mrs. Freeman's family and searched for guns. "We were as ignorant of the rebellion," she said, "as they. . . . I made up my mind not to remain in that country."

Rows of poorly furnished shacks were the typical slave quarters of the Civil War period.

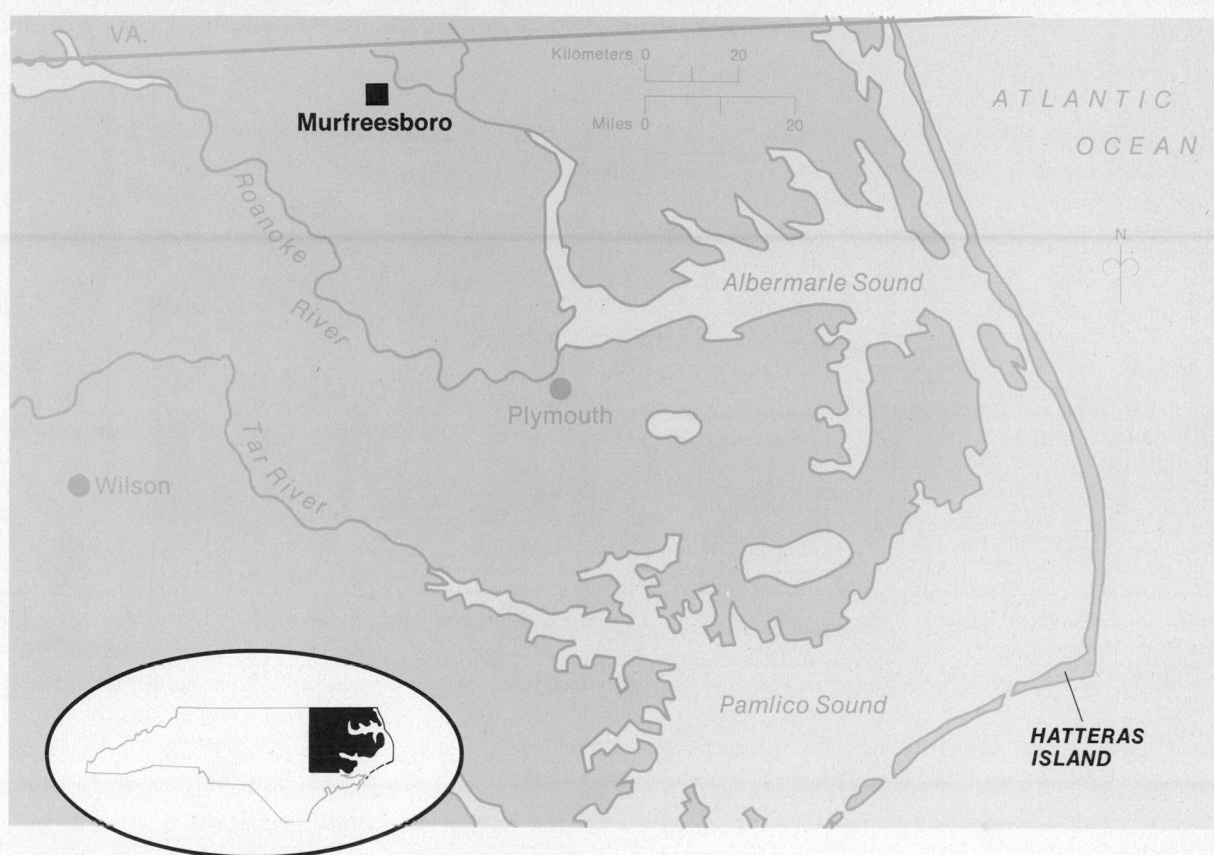

Northeastern North Carolina, 1860

Thomas Hedgebeth of Chatham, Ontario, was another refugee free black from Halifax. "A free-born man in North Carolina," he told Drew, "is as much oppressed, in one sense, as a slave: I was not allowed to go to school." He was not allowed to visit among slaves, But sometimes he worked alongside them. He recalled them saying "that they worked hard, and got no benefit, that the masters got it all. . . . they often grumbled about food and clothing, that they had not enough. . . . They were generally religious, they believed in a just God, and thought the owners wrong in punishing them in the way they were punished."

Hedgebeth said that he had seen slaves "nearly starved out, and yet stripped and whipped; blood cut out of them. . . . After a whipping they would often leave and take to the woods for a month or two, and live by taking what they could find." There were places where slaves had no meat given them. They had to get along on three pints of corn meal a day.

A Yankee photographer took this picture of some New Bern ladies in 1864. The house stood on Broad Street.

James K. Polk was a native of Mecklenburg County. He served as the 11th President of the United States, 1845-1849.

John Little of Queen's Bush was from Murfreesboro. He told Drew that he had never been to school and was not allowed, as a slave, to attend religious worship. He remembered being sold at auction in Murfreesboro when he was a boy. His master "abused me like a dog—worse than a dog, not because I did any thing wrong, but because I was a 'nigger.' My blood boils to think about him. . . ." Little finally escaped and made his way to Canada. Drew found him with one of the best farms in the region, "much respected, wherever he is known. . . ."

When he spoke at the second State Fair in 1854, Congressman Rayner addressed perhaps the largest group ever assembled in North Carolina—eight thousand people. His theme was that North Carolina was favored among the states of the nation. Situated midway "between the chilling frosts of the North and the scorching heat of the South," it was "free of the disadvantages of either but able to enjoy what is most profitable in both."

The speaker had some eyeopening statistics. North Carolina had a little over half the population of Virginia. But it produced 25 times more cotton. Though one fifth larger than South Carolina, it grew 15 times more tobacco. It raised double the wheat of South Carolina and five million pounds of rice a year to Virginia's none. Total North Carolina produce, both farm and manufactures, greatly surpassed either state. It was the same for "intellectual and moral culture." North Carolina's 1,800 churches were far more numerous for its size than Virginia's 2,400 or South Carolina's 1,200. The 100,000 children in North Carolina schools represented a far higher proportion of its people than Virginia's 110,000 or South Carolina's 40,000. It was time that "witlings and upstarts" from those two states stopped jeering at "our poverty and ignorance," for "a brighter day is dawning upon us."

A few months before, Frederick Law Olmsted, a New York landscape architect, passed through North Carolina. He wrote about conditions there. He thought the State House in Raleigh, built to replace the one burned in 1831, was "in every way, a noble building." The hotel where he stayed was "not only well supplied, but . . . excellent well kept. . . ." At Mrs. Barclay's stagecoach inn on the way to Fayetteville he had "the best entertainment that could be asked for." He admired the all-weather plank road from Fayetteville to the Piedmont. It was the world's longest of its kind. But Olmsted was still influenced in part by what he called the state's "proverbial reputation for the ignorance . . . of her people; being, in this respect at the head of the Slave States."

There was more he might have praised. At the urging of Dorothea L. Dix of Massachusetts, the General Assembly had authorized construction of an asylum for the mentally ill, which opened in 1856. A school for the deaf opened with state support in 1845. It was soon providing training for the blind as well. Progress had been made in reforming the penal code. The legal status of women was improved. Changes in tax laws doubled annual tax income between 1835 and 1850.

Most of the improvement could be credited to the Whig leadership of the 1840s. But the Democrats, back in power in 1850, were equally earnest in promoting reform. A movement to end the 50-acre requirement in voting for the state legislature was gaining ground. It would become part of the state constitution in 1857. Pressed by public opinion, the Democrats would pledge state money in 1855 toward building railroads between Goldsboro and Beaufort, between Salisbury and the Tennessee line, and between Wilmington and Rutherfordton. The latest President of the United States (1844–1848) had been James K. Polk, a native North Carolinian.

Better than Frederick Law Olmsted, Kenneth Rayner

Witlings are people who try unsuccessfully to be amusing.

An **asylum** is an institution for the care of handicapped persons or others needing help.

could speak in behalf of the energy and spirit of North Carolinians in the 1850s. They recognized that "Rip Van Winkle" was finally awake from his long sleep. The state, in fact, seemed to be finding a new image of itself in relation to the rest of the country. As Calvin H. Wiley had put it in 1851: "It is a land between extremes, . . . exempt . . . from the gloomy fanaticism and chilling selfishness of the North, and from the bloody scenes and blazing passions of the South." A writer in the Raleigh *Standard* in early 1861 reminded fellow citizens of their self-appointed mission. The time was approaching, he thought,

A ***mediator*** is a person who tries to bring agreement between disagreeing persons or groups.

Conciliating means overcoming hatred or distrust.

> when a mediator, a moderator, in other words, an adviser and friend, may be needed in balancing and conciliating between the border and Cotton States. North Carolina, occupying a sort of Middle and, therefore, temperate ground between them, may be well qualified for this office, as in morals, truth and safety are to be sought for in the centre of two extremes.

If this was North Carolina's role, it was about to be put to a severe test.

Sapping means draining.

Both the Whig and Democratic parties of North Carolina upheld slavery. The latter did so more earnestly, slowly sapping Whig strength. Democrats, along with some Whigs, agreed that Congress had no right to meddle with slavery in any state. The so-called State's rights wing of the Whigs drifted away from the Federal Whigs. They held that Congress had the power but ought not to use it. State s rights Whigs, after the Wilmot Proviso of 1846, began converting to the Democrats, especially in the eastern counties, where there were more slaves. Whigs seemed unpatriotic when they opposed the war with Mexico in 1847. At the same time, a prominent Democrat, Louis D. Wilson, was leading almost a thousand North Carolinians off to war. The result was that Democrats would take control of the state in the 1850s and hold it until after the Civil War.

The ***Wilmot Proviso*** declared that slavery should be forbidden in any territory that the United States gained from the Mexican War, 1846–1848.

The Democrats continued the Whig program of supporting internal improvement and the reform of human rights. Their party became more conservative in the 1850s. Eastern and Piedmont slave owners took control of the party. They backed a program of State's rights, Southern interests, and slavery. In 1858, the more progressive western Democrats wanted Raleigh editor William W. Holden for governor. But slave owners managed to win the nomination for John W. Ellis, who was elected. It was not hard to foretell the coming breakdown of the alliance between western and eastern, slaveholding and nonslaveholding Democrats.

A result of control of the party by slave owners was that rising costs of government could not be met by taxes on slaves. Slaves were one of the state's most valuable forms of property. Slave owners successfully demanded that taxes be raised from incomes, land, savings—in short, from anything but slaves. So the nonslaveholder bore the burden of taxes. The slave owner, in this respect, escaped it. On the eve of the Civil War, North Carolina seemed more class conscious than at any time since before the Revolution.

The Kansas-Nebraska Act of 1854 extended slavery into a region where it had not existed. This led to the rise of the new antislavery Republican party. Some Whigs joined yet another new party, the American. It did not succeed widely or for long. Meanwhile, the boasted even temper and moderation of North Carolinians was dissolving in anger and confusion.

The Republicans ran John C. Fremont for president in 1856. Some leading North Carolina Democrats openly talked of secession if he were elected. Benjamin S. Hedrick, a professor at the University of North Carolina, was dismissed and run out of the state for supporting Fremont. The Rev. Daniel Worth, an aged Guilford County Wesleyan Methodist, was arrested for distributing copies of Helper's *Impending Crisis*, an antislavery work. Following John Brown's Raid on Harper's Ferry in 1859, North Carolina whites seemed to think of little else but slavery and how to defend it. Neither freedom of the press nor of speech any longer existed on this issue.

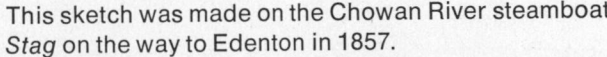

This sketch was made on the Chowan River steamboat *Stag* on the way to Edenton in 1857.

Eastern North Carolina had many such mills for producing turpentine from its teeming pine forests.

The **platform** of a party is a statement of its principles and objectives.

Driven by fear that the Union might be destroyed, North Carolina Whigs reorganized in 1859. They nominated John Pool for governor. Their platform called for a constitutional amendment to permit taxing slave property. The Democrats charged that the Whigs were attacking slavery and aiding abolitionists. In a climate of high emotion, Ellis was reelected

This Civil War photograph shows two Rockingham County entertainers in the midst of their act.

by a reduced majority. But the Whigs were again an effective opposition. Planter domination seemed doomed.

In the campaign of 1860, both the Republicans and Democrats split into factions. They nominated separate candidates. Southern Democrats supported John C. Breckinridge. Northern Democrats backed Stephen A. Douglas. The Republicans divided between Abraham Lincoln and John Bell. With Lincoln's election, the long-threatened disruption of the Union began. Within a few weeks, South Carolina seceded and other states prepared to follow. North Carolina wavered for five more months. Then it joined the Confederacy and seceded for the second time in 74 years.

The Reunion

Charles Henry Foster barely reached Washington in June 1861 before he was writing to President Lincoln. He asked for an interview to discuss ways to protect North Carolina Unionists from rebel tyranny. He also wrote *The New York Times* and informed it that North Carolina Unionists were "frequently found dead by their friends." He said that the rebels insured the good conduct of Unionists by holding their wives and mothers as hostages. Many of the larger northern papers carried his charges. But Lincoln made no response to his letter.

A few days later, Foster had a printer run off handbills. They announced that he was a candidate for the Special Session of Congress that would meet on July 4. The handbills were addressed to the voters of North Carolina's First Congressional District. Presumably they were to be distributed there even though mail service with the South had been cut off. When the Special Session met, Foster was on hand with 21 ballots—"certified by a magistrate"—which he said had been cast for him in a secret First District election on June 12. Congress rejected his application. But it passed no judgment on his argument that North Carolina Unionists were entitled to representation and federal protection.

No doubt the result did not surprise Foster. He was already at work on another scheme to insure that he would be seated when the Regular Session of Congress met in December. In July, he mysteriously disappeared from Washington. He left hints that he was on his way to North Carolina. His intention was to campaign in a state-wide Unionist election in

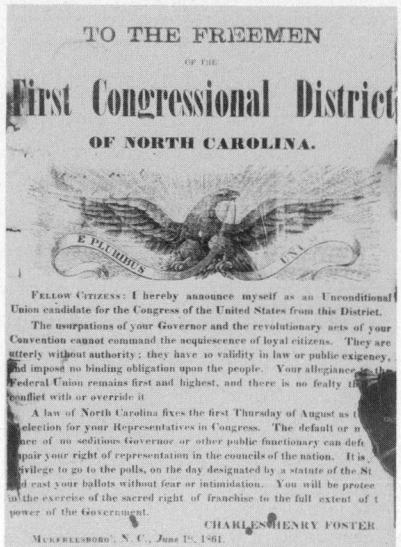 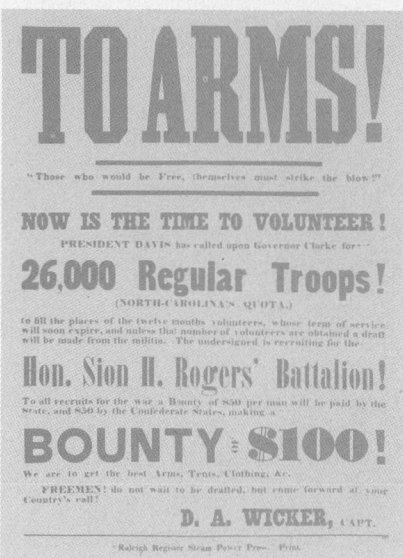

Foster's handbill tried to prove he was running for
Congress (left). Patriotism ran high early in the war (right).

August. It was not clear how Unionists were to vote under the
very noses of the rebels, But *The New York Times* and other
papers wished him success.

During the six weeks that he was absent, northern papers
printed a series of letters from a "special correspondent" in
North Carolina. The writer, who was not identified, wrote of
the tide of Union feeling sweeping the state. The writer told
what was seen and heard at Salisbury, Raleigh, Edenton
(where he told of seeing Charles Henry Foster), and other
towns. He spoke of the coming Unionist election and of the
delegation that was to be sent to Washington. There was also
news of a brigade of North Carolina troops under the command of "Colonel Foster." They were seeking arms from the
federal government. The letters created excitement in the
northern press and some angry answers in Confederate journals. The impression left by the letters was that North Carolina was about to rid itself of rebellion and return voluntarily
to the Union.

On September 3, Foster turned up again in Washington.
He had escaped, as he claimed, rebel scouts who lay in wait
for him in Virginia. He had documents and ballots showing
that he had been elected to Congress by a big majority of
Unionist voters. He spoke of Union brigades in North Carolina that were ready to join the Union Army. He said that his
"certificates of election" bore "the signature of the Governor."

(John Ellis had died in July and was replaced by Henry T. Clark.) On September 11, Foster spoke with the President about the brigades awaiting orders from the federal government.

Skeptics raised doubts about his election. But Foster was looking into another way of assuring his seat in the next Congress. In late August, a Union force invaded and captured Hatteras Island on the North Carolina coast. If Foster could get there, he could hold an election in full public view. He could return with a claim that no one could dispute. By September 20, he was on a military steamboat bound for Hatteras.

Provisional means serving temporarily.

During the fall, Foster held an election on Hatteras, which he won unopposed. He also created a "provisional government" for the state. With the help of several islanders, he talked the Methodist minister there, Marble Nash Taylor, into acting as governor in the new administration. The "governor" then issued an official call for an election. He certified Foster's victory. Foster hurried to Washington in time for the opening of Congress on December 4. He laid the evidence before the Election Committee. He showed that he had been elected in the First District in August and the Second in November. After a careful investigation, the Committee rejected both applications. Foster made other efforts later, but he was never granted a seat in Congress.

Foster returned to Hatteras and devoted much of his time to recruiting North Carolinians for the Union Army. He raised most of two regiments, one of which he commanded briefly.

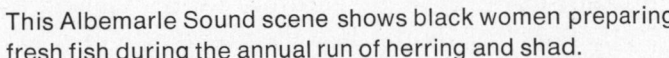
This Albemarle Sound scene shows black women preparing fresh fish during the annual run of herring and shad.

In 1863, he was reunited with his wife and daughter. They came through the lines to join him. After the war he returned to Murfreesboro. There, he supported his family as a journalist and merchant. In 1878, he moved with them to Philadelphia. There, he was a writer for the Philadelphia *Record* when he died in 1882.

For the historian, the career of Charles Henry Foster raises puzzling questions. There is no doubt that he tried to lie his way into Congress. He wrote the "special correspondent" letters, probably while hiding in Lexington, Kentucky. The letters were full of falsehoods. The first two elections he claimed to have won were fictitious. His methods turned many against him. He emerged from the war with a reputation as a self-seeking opportunist. But his efforts during the war are not so easily labeled.

Congress seated some delegates from seceded states during the war, even though the districts they represented were partly under rebel control. This policy was adopted in the hope of encouraging Southern Unionists and shortening the war. Foster's wife rejoined him in spite of her earlier rejection. His daughter wrote of him at his death that he "detested sham, and had no sympathy with affectation of any kind." And it must be recalled that the lies he told came in the midst of death, destruction and disunion.

If false claims could shorten the war by a year or even an hour, are they still to be condemned? Foster's lies had no such effect. But had North Carolina Unionists, encouraged by false reports, struck a united blow at the Confederates, might North Carolina not have seceded? Possibly so. If that had happened in 1861, there is little doubt that the war would not have lasted another six months. The possibility may be unrealistic. But it is Foster's judgment that stands condemned and not his motives. The questions remain in doubt, and history's jury has not yet delivered its verdict.

A **verdict** is a judgment or final decision.

Chapter Checkup

PEOPLE

Charles Henry Foster	John Little	James K. Polk
Kenneth Rayner	John W. Ellis	Benjamin S. Hedrick
Sue Carter Foster	Dorothea L. Dix	

PLACES

Murfreesboro   Hatteras Island

FACT

Why did the Murfreesboro Vigilance Committee suspect that Foster might be a spy?

Why did he leave Washington in the summer of 1861?

What did some regard as the vital role that North Carolina might play in the crisis of 1860–1861?

How were the Whigs able to threaten Democratic political control of the state in 1859?

INTERPRETATION

Do you feel that Foster "proved himself a Southern man" as he promised his wife he would do? Explain.

Why do you think North Carolina was so slow to leave the Union in 1861?

What do you suppose made Sue Foster change her mind about divorce and rejoin her husband?

Do you think North Carolina would have joined the Confederacy if the Whigs had won the 1859 election? Explain.

VOCABULARY

Revoked   Conciliating
Asylum   Humanitarian
Mediator

ACTIVITY

Debate in class the issue of whether or not Charles Henry Foster proved himself to be "a Southern man."

SUGGESTED READING

Barrett, John G. *The Civil War in North Carolina.* Chapel Hill: UNC Press, 1963. Scholarly account of battles and problems of war for the people of the state.

Barrett, John G. *North Carolina as a Civil War Battleground.* Raleigh: Department of Archives and History, 1964. The Civil War as fought in North Carolina.

Roske, R. J. and Van Doren, Charles. *Lincoln's Commando: The Biography of Commander W. B. Cushing, U.S.N.* New York: Harper and Brothers, 1957. Well-written and fast-paced account of Cushing's life and hair-raising exploits.

1861 Occupation of Hatteras
Island *(Aug. 28)*

1861 The Civil War begins
(April 12)

1862 Battle of Roanoke
Island *(Feb. 8)*
- Fall of New Bern *(March)*

1863 Work begun on *Albemarle*
- Vance elected governor

1863 Lincoln's Emancipation
Proclamation *(Jan. 1)*

1864 Attack on Plymouth
- *Albemarle's* first fight
- Flusser's death *(April 19)*

1864 Lincoln reelected
President *(Nov. 8)*

1865 Fall of Fort Fisher
(Jan. 15)

1865 Lee surrenders
at Appomattox *(April 9)*

14

CUSHING'S REVENGE

A Secret Weapon

Nearly every day in late 1863, people gathered on the North-ampton shore to watch the builders at work. They'd stand around and ask the same questions day after day: "How can you get it to float if it's made of iron?" "If it's a steamboat, where's the paddle wheel?" "How can you tell which is the front end and which is the back?" Patiently, workers on the construction crew would try to answer. Somehow they never seemed convincing. Old men walked away shaking their heads. Laughing boys kept asking when the sinking was to take place. James Cooke smiled and kept on working.

Sometimes the boat would sit there for weeks in the middle of Smith's cornfield. Its bulky silhouette did not change and no progress could be seen. Then a flatboat of junk iron would tie up at the wharf. For a couple of weeks the place would swarm with workers. The boat would grow a few feet longer or higher. But every added pound seemed to make

A **silhouette** is an outline or general shape of something.

257

James Cooke, *a Confederate naval commander*
Charles Flusser, *a Union naval commander*
Robert F. Hoke, *a Confederate general*

William B. Cushing, *a Union naval officer*
Zebulon B. Vance, *Governor of North Carolina*

it that much less likely to float. The thing finally sprawled out for 152 feet in length. It measured nine feet from deck to keel. Somebody said that it was not really a boat at all. Maybe it was to be sunk in the river to keep the Yankees away from the railroad bridge at Weldon.

A *ram* is a warship built especially for ramming other ships.

The mission of the boat, a Confederate ram, was to win back the sounds and rivers of eastern North Carolina from the Yankee fleet. For two years now, since the fall of Roanoke Island, Albemarle and Pamlico Sounds had been Yankee lakes. The Federals had occupied nearly every community within a hundred miles of Roanoke Island. They had sunk or seized every rebel ship in these waters. But the embattled Confederacy was preparing to counterattack with its superboat. This vessel could outfight any ship in the Federal fleet. The fate of North Carolina seemed to some to depend on the success or failure of the Roanoke River ram.

The idea to build the ram at Edwards' Ferry had come from William J. Smith. He owned a nearby farm. There was a gentle slope from the construction site to the river. The place was far enough up the Roanoke River to make Yankee attack almost impossible. But in almost all other respects, it was an awful place for building a boat. Commander Cooke had been sent from Richmond to supervise the work. He was to command the ram when it was finished. He felt that no ship "was ever constructed under more adverse circumstances." With the help of Smith and his sons, Cooke scoured the countryside for equipment. A portable sawmill was found and moved to Edwards' Ferry. A blacksmith's forge was set up. Local farmers cut oak and yellow pine and carted timber to the sawmill.

A *forge* is a furnace or hearth for heating metal for shaping.

Cooke ransacked the Roanoke Valley for iron in any form, from bolts and nuts to railroad spikes. They had a blueprint and a parts list from John L. Porter, the ram's designer and chief constructor for the Confederate Navy, but little else to guide them. The ram's two 200-horsepower engines were a collection of odds and ends, cleverly stuck together. The ar-

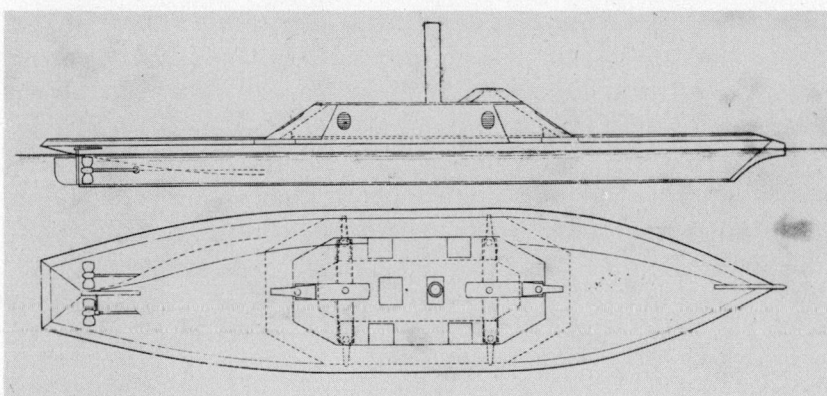

The *Albemarle* (above) had to be built far up the Roanoke River so Union raiders could not destroy it before it was launched. This sketch (below) gives details of the construction of the Confederate ram.

A *bluff* is a steep hill or cliff.

mor plating on the sides was two inches thick. The work of putting the iron plate on was held up for weeks. They had no way to drill holes in it. But Peter Evans Smith, son of William J. Smith, worked in the blacksmith's shop. He invented a twist drill that would bite through the iron in four minutes.

In the early weeks of 1864, the ram was far enough along to be launched. There was a bad moment at the launching when it hung briefly on the low bluff at the bank. But the boat was finally jerked free. To the wonder of many of the onlookers, the thing stayed afloat. But much work remained to be done. For this, the ram was towed to Halifax. Even later when the craft steamed down the river, work crews remained on board doing final work. The *Albemarle,* as it was named, spent a few days at the town of Hamilton. There Cooke was visited on April 16 by Robert F. Hoke, 27-year-old boy-general of the Confederacy. Hoke informed Cooke that the vessel must be ready by April 19. On that day, his division would attack Plymouth at the mouth of the river, a place that had been in Union hands since December. Cooke protested that more time was needed. But with a promise of more workers, he finally agreed that the ram would go into battle on April 19, ready or not.

Cooke now drove his work crews ruthlessly toward the deadline. Forges were set up on deck. Men with sledgehammers battered away at the heavy spikes joining wood and

Captain James W. Cooke commanded the *Albemarle* when it challenged Union naval supremacy in 1864.

Robert F. Hoke, a youthful Confederate general, cooperated with Cooke and the *Albemarle* in the recapture of Plymouth.

metal. The two junior officers who would serve under Cooke reached Hamilton on April 17, barely in time for a brief target practice next day. It was near nightfall on April 18 that Cooke finally released his workers and unloaded their equipment. The *Albemarle* was ready for war at last.

To challenge the Union fleet and several enemy forts on the lower Roanoke River, Cooke had a total of two cannons. These were mounted on pivots and could be rolled to any of the six portholes in the ram's turtle-like turret. The Yankees had tried to close the river's channel above Plymouth. They sunk ships in it and strung explosives across it. But on the evening of April 18, a scouting party from the *Albemarle* discovered that the high water resulting from recent heavy rains would make it possible for the ram to pass safely over the obstructions. Around midnight, Cooke cast off from Hamilton, and started downriver. The *Albemarle* faced its first test of battle.

At dawn of April 19, the ram steamed past the two Yankee forts. Their cannon balls bounced harmlessly off the sloping turret like "pebbles thrown against an empty barrel." But Cooke, peering downriver into the morning haze saw two Union gunboats approaching. They were lashed together with spars and chains. The Yankees, it seemed, had been giving a good deal of thought to ways of stopping the ram.

Charles Williamson Flusser was the commander of the gunboat *Miami.* He had planned for this moment for the past 12 months. Spies had kept him informed of the ram almost from the day its keel was laid the previous spring. As early as June, he had known details of the size and armament of the boat. He had begged the councils of the Union Navy for a raid on Edwards' Ferry to destroy the ram before it did any damage. His scouts had tracked the *Albemarle* from bend to bend down the Roanoke River. When the ram put out from Hamilton on the evening of April 18, a message went to Flusser to be prepared.

Flusser realized there was not a ship in the Union Navy in these waters capable of stopping the new Confederate iron monster. With other officers, he had worked out a plan. This was to try to snag the ram between his own gunboat and the *Southfield.* After that, all three craft would be blown to pieces. Flusser had earned the title "lionhearted" which was ironic because of his secret knowledge that he was dying from incurable heart disease. The man was afraid of nothing.

James Cooke, taken by surprise by Flusser's tactics, was equal to the challenge. He turned the ram quickly toward the

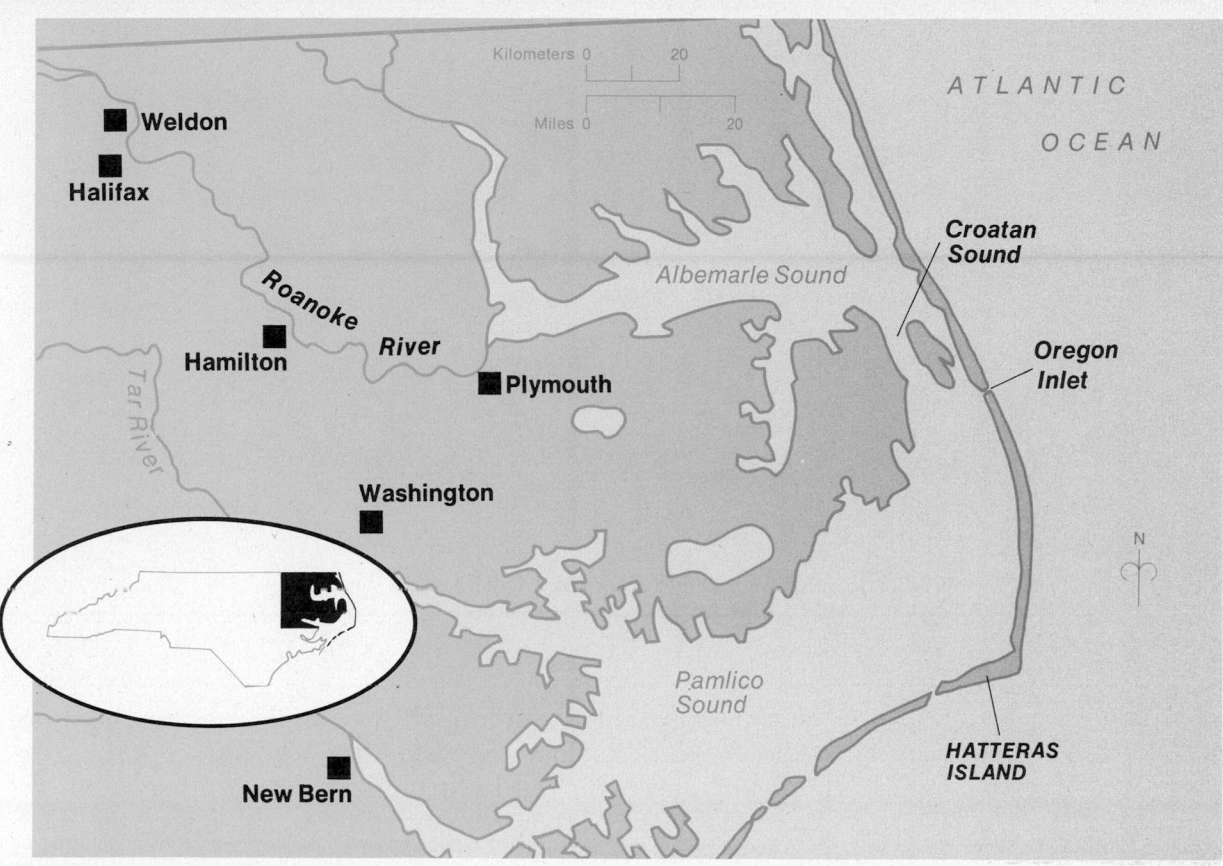

Pamlico Sound-Albemarle Sound, 1865

A **turret** is a low, revolving deck structure in which guns are mounted.

north bank of the river to avoid running between the gunboats. Then he suddenly cut back, opened full throttle, and drove the ram headlong into the side of the *Southfield*. The wooden hull of the Union vessel ripped like cardboard. The gunboat began to sink at once. Cooke threw his engines into reverse but found that his bow was caught in the side of the sinking *Southfield*. The ram was being pulled down with it! With a mighty last effort, the *Albemarle* jerked backward and wrenched loose from the doomed gunboat. By this time, the *Miami* with its guns blazing at point-blank range, had come alongside the ram.

Cooke and his crew squinted from the iron turret through the smoke at the enemy gunboat a few yards away. They saw a sight that froze the blood of the most hardened veteran. Flusser, with the firing cord of a cannon in his hand, stood on the near deck. He was fully exposed and stared straight down into the guns of the ram, daring death to take him. At almost

The Union gunboat *Sassacus* tried to sink the *Albemarle* by ramming. The *Sassacus* succeeded only in damaging itself.

the same moment, a cannonball was fired from the mouth of Flusser's gun. It slammed into the *Albemarle*'s turret, rebounded, and exploded in the gallant officer's face. With the mangled corpse of its commander sprawled across the deck, the *Miami* retreated hastily down the river. The *Albemarle* had won its first victory.

Meanwhile, Hoke's army was closing the noose around the Union defenders inside Plymouth. Finding the ram free to assist him, Hoke sent orders that Cooke should bombard enemy gun positions on shore. One by one the Federal positions were overrun. The next day, the last Union forces surrendered. The rebels had twenty-five hundred Yankee prisoners and warehouses full of captured equipment. More important, Plymouth was recovered and the Roanoke River belonged to the Confederacy again. A few days later the Federals also abandoned the town of Washington. They stripped its citizens of their valuables as they left. If New Bern could also be recovered, the Union forces south of Albemarle Sound would have only their Outer Banks sand spits left to them in North Carolina. Hoke, the hero of the hour, was promoted to major general. But much of the credit belonged to the ram.

Within a few days of the fall of Plymouth, Hoke presented Cooke with his plan for taking New Bern. It would involve the *Albemarle* crossing Albemarle, Croatan, and Pamlico Sounds. It would then sail up the Neuse River to New Bern through a beehive of Federal warships. Cooke recognized the danger, but agreed to try it so as to assist Hoke as much as he could. On the afternoon of May 5, the *Albemarle* set forth on its hazardous journey. It was accompanied by two small Confederate vessels. But seven gunboats waited at the head of Albemarle Sound to stop the ram from getting to other waters.

It was almost 5 p.m. when Cooke came upon the Union squadron, including the *Miami*. It carried a net to foul the ram's propellers. There was a torpedo under the bow to be rammed into the *Albemarle*'s hull. The first shots by the ram damaged one of the gunboats. Heavy shelling from the *Sassacus* had no effect on the ram's armor plating. But Commander Roe of the *Sassacus* now backed off a few hundred yards. He ran straight in on the *Albemarle* in the hope of crashing into it. Cooke was unable to avoid the onrushing gunboat and the *Sassacus* thundered straight into the ram's side. The collision opened a great hole in the bow of the Union vessel. With its engines dead, the dismayed crew of the *Sassacus* watched the ram move slowly away downstream. The shooting went on until nightfall. Cooke found his steering mechanism and smokestack damaged. He retreated to Plymouth for repairs. It would not do to send the ram to New Bern without the aid of strong support vessels. On orders from Richmond, Hoke called off the attack on New Bern.

Gloom-and-doom-sayers in North Carolina were jolted into great hope by the action of the *Albemarle*. A boat that could hold its own against Union fleets, whose hull turned cannon balls aside as if they were walnuts, might turn the war around in North Carolina. Also, the state had several more such vessels planned and under construction. Three years of fighting had brought one setback after another on the North Carolina coast. Now, suddenly, things had changed. A ripple of excitement passed through North Carolina from the seacoast to the mountains. Maybe the sink-proof superboat would save the Confederacy yet.

Inglorious means dishonorable.

Inglorious Encounter

Not often in history had a people headed more joyfully toward disaster than white North Carolinians in the summer of 1861. Nearly all the signs seemed hopeful to them, every new development welcome. There were Confederate victories in Virginia that summer, in which North Carolina units participated effectively. These seemed to show that the Southern boys were the better warriors. The seizure of the Federal arsenal at Fayetteville provided thirty-seven thousand muskets and rifles and the machinery for producing countless more. Nearly all steamboats on the eastern sounds and rivers were bought by the state. They were armed and assembled into a flotilla for coastal defense. Volunteers came forward by the thousands to swell the new regiments.

A **flotilla** is a group of small naval vessels.

As long as people ignored the unprotected seacoast, North Carolina seemed prepared for war. Maybe a few thrashings of Old Abe's armies, the seizure of the Federal capital, or the entry of England into the war on the side of the rebels would bring a quick victory—and peace. Meanwhile, forts of mud and dirt were built at Hatteras, Ocracoke, and Oregon Inlets. Seven hundred green soldiers were sent to defend them against the United States.

On the morning of August 28, a Federal fleet began shelling the forts at Hatteras. By noon the next day, the forts were lost. Forts at the other inlets were simply deserted. Although they had captured over seven hundred rebels and killed others, the invaders had not lost a man! So much for the coastal defenses of North Carolina.

As the war's major fighting grew in Virginia and on the lower Mississippi, a small Federal force was left to hold Hatteras and Ocracoke. By this means, the Confederacy lost its best hiding place for raiders against Federal shipping. Also, the Union gained a base for future campaigns in eastern North Carolina. But the psychological results were perhaps even more important. It was the first major Federal victory of the war. It had weakened the confidence of North Carolinians in their ability to defend themselves. The first thrill of victory had worn itself out in three months. What remained was to be more than three and a half years of futile bloodshed.

With the loss of the approaches to the sea, North Carolina was forced to find ways of preventing the invaders from storming onto the mainland. Planners on both sides agreed that Roanoke Island was the key to the state's interior defenses. Situated between Albemarle and Pamlico Sounds, it was a base from which both sounds and their river systems could be controlled. But the Union seemed in no hurry to take advantage of its Hatteras victory. This gave the Confederates five months to plan for the expected assault on Roanoke. Heavy winter storms along the "graveyard of the Atlantic" delayed the attack further. But on February 8, 1862, the seven converted steamboats of North Carolina's defense squadron were called upon to defend the island against a Union fleet of some 50 warships.

While General Ambrose E. Burnside was landing ten thousand Federal troops on Roanoke Island, the little Confederate flotilla was quickly chased away. Within three days, all but one of the rebel boats were destroyed or captured. The sounds and rivers were at the mercy of Union forces. In seizing Roanoke Island, Burnside lost about 40 men, the price for capturing twenty-five hundred at the rebel garrison in less than 24 hours. Northern and Southern observers alike were shocked at the speed and ease of the operation. Whatever feats Lee and Jackson might perform in Virginia, they had a weakness in North Carolina that was bound to drain their strength. It would cost them dearly in the months ahead.

In early 1862, the Burnside Expedition followed up its Roanoke Island success. New Bern was seized in early March. Fort Macon, the key to control of Beaufort Harbor, fell in late April. The town of Washington fell in early May. The state government called home thousands of troops sent to Virginia earlier. This slowed the Union advance but could not stop it. Federal troops occupied Norfolk in late spring. After this, the Confederacy lost interest in trying to defend that part of the state lying east of the Chowan River. The counties of Chowan, Gates, Pasquotank, Perquimans, Currituck, and Camden be-

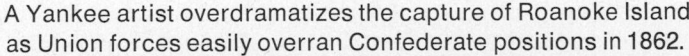

A Yankee artist overdramatizes the capture of Roanoke Island as Union forces easily overran Confederate positions in 1862.

This scene by a Union artist shows Wilmington's occupation by Federal forces in early 1862.

A **blockade** is the closing of a port or harbor by enemy ships or troops.

came, for all practical purposes, Federal territory. Thousands of slaves from the surrounding country had fled. They sought refuge at Norfolk or Roanoke Island. The port of Wilmington came under a tight blockade.

At the same time, the Lincoln administration was taking steps to start a new government in the occupied areas of eastern North Carolina. Charles Henry Foster's comic opera regime was brushed away. But Edward Stanly, a prominent Whig from New Bern, was named governor of the Union-occupied areas. The problems Stanly faced were enormous, including what to do about the masses of escaped slaves now camped within Federal lines. Many were put to work building fortifications. Some were even formed into all-black infantry and cavalry units. But feeding and housing them put a strain on both military and civilian resources. Emancipation had not yet been proclaimed, and no one was certain what the future status of the former slaves was to be.

The war in eastern North Carolina entered a new phase in July 1862. Burnside took some of his forces to rescue hard-pressed Federals in Virginia. Union strength in North Carolina was reduced by seven thousand. This left the Federal garrison on the defensive and anxious to save what they had already won. During the rest of 1862 and 1863, the fighting consisted mainly of raids by one side or the other. There was not much change in battle lines. The outcome of the war was being determined elsewhere. North Carolina would have to bleed slowly until the issue was settled.

In the western mountains, the Confederacy maintained a light guard and loose control until early 1864. Then, Union raiders from Tennessee began attacking Confederate positions. A small force of Confederate whites and Cherokees was attacked at Qualla Town. They "fought nobly . . . until their ammunition failed" and they retreated. Satisfied that the rebel defenses in the Appalachians were weak, Union forces stepped up their raids and broke the resistance.

Federal invaders were often guided by the fabled "Keith" Blaylock of Grandfather Mountain. Blaylock and his wife Malinda, or "Sam," had joined the rebel army early in the war as privates. Later they tricked rebel officers into discharging them. They spent most of the war recruiting and scouting for the Union Army. By mid-1864, Federal pressure and the growing Union sentiments of the mountain people made the Appalachians as uncontrollable to the rebels as the seacoast. But by this time, even large areas of the Piedmont were at the mercy of outlaw bands. The Confederacy was breaking up.

The Lost Cause

The death of Charles Flusser in his daring attack on the ram *Albemarle* was a severe loss to many officers in the Union Navy. He had been widely admired for his acts of valor. No one admired him as much as the reckless young man who had been his junior officer on the *Commodore Perry* earlier in the war. This was William B. Cushing, a 21-year-old officer. In 1861, he became the youngest lieutenant in the history of the Navy. When he was told of Flusser's fate, Cushing remarked: "I shall never rest until I have avenged his death."

In early July 1864, Cushing was called before Admiral Samuel P. Lee. He was asked to propose a plan for destroying the rebel ram. The *Albemarle,* since its fight with the *Sassacus* and other ships in April, had been tied up at Plymouth. It was awaiting the construction of support vessels it would need in future engagements. There would probably be no better opportunity to destroy it than while it was there. But the rebels, alerted by an unsuccessful attempt to blow up the ram in the late spring, were expecting more attacks. Cushing, however, had been studying the problem for weeks. He thought he could solve it.

A *launch* is a heavy, open boat propelled by oars or engine.

With the Navy's approval, Cushing got a 30-foot steam launch from the Brooklyn Navy Yard. He equipped it with a small cannon. Engineers attached a long boom, or spar, to its bow. On the end of the boom, a torpedo could be mounted. A man in the launch could lower the torpedo into the water. By pulling two cords, he could set the fuse and release it. Just

Zebulon B. Vance was a Confederate officer in the early part of the war. He was elected Governor of North Carolina in 1862.

William B. Cushing's valor was well known on both sides well before the war's end. Sinking the *Albemarle* was only one of his heroic endeavors.

how an open launch was supposed to get close enough to the *Albemarle* to do that was not clear. But Cushing was convinced that it was possible.

The torpedo was only an emergency weapon. What Cushing really expected to do was land a crew of men near the ram. He would attack and capture it, and make off down the river with it. Only if that plan failed would he have use for the torpedo. Returning to North Carolina in mid-October, he selected a crew of talented sailors. He began training them for the mission he had in mind. Finally, on the evening of October 26, Cushing felt that he was ready for the attempt.

A little before midnight, the launch pulled away from the gunboat *Shamrock*. It was part of a Federal squadron blockading the mouth of Roanoke River. Behind the launch a cutter was drawn. It was carrying about a dozen more men who would take part in the effort to capture the ram. Plymouth lay eight miles upriver, most of which was patrolled by rebel sentries. The launch's steam engine had to be muffled with canvas and the men ordered to make no sound whatever. A little past 2 A.M., the dark outline of the great rebel vessel came into view alongside Plymouth wharf.

The wharf itself was now visible. Cushing, standing at the wheel of the launch, silently turned toward it. He intended to land his men there. But just as he was about to reach the wharf, a barking dog alerted Confederate sentinels. Shouts of "Who's there?" told Cushing that it was useless to try to get his men on shore. Changing course, he headed straight for the ram itself. He would attempt to sink it with the torpedo. The distance closed to 50 yards—40—30. Rebel guards poured rifle balls at the dim shape of the boat. But they could not see it well enough to hit it. Suddenly, the sky blazed with the light of a great bonfire the rebels had ready for such an emergency. Cushing and his men were now in full view, outlined against the black waters of the Roanoke.

With bullets striking the boat and the water around it, Cushing now had the launch within 20 yards of the ram. At the waterline of the *Albemarle,* the attackers saw that the rebels had placed floating logs to protect the ram from a torpedo attack. The launch, which had slowed down for the wharf, was not moving fast enough to ride over the logs. Cushing spun his wheel and turned toward the middle of the river. A blast of buckshot tore the back out of his jacket and ripped his shirt. But still no one in the launch had been injured. Near mid-stream, Cushing came around in a wide circle. Shouting for full speed amid the hail of fire, he again raced toward the ram. Again the distance closed until, with a jolting crunch, the

Lieutenant Cushing pilots a launch (above) toward the *Albemarle* in one of the war's most daring exploits. The explosion of the torpedo (below) lights the night sky at Plymouth.

bow of the launch rested on top of the logs. Ten feet before him, the mouth of a rebel cannon stared into Cushing's face. He could hear the defenders scrambling to load and fire it.

He knew that it would take about 20 seconds to load and fire the *Albemarle*'s cannon. Cushing lowered the torpedo boom carefully into the water. It was a ticklish operation, for any jerking motion might break the firing pin. He counted slowly to five to give the torpedo time to rise under the hull of the ram. From the deck of the rebel boat, riflemen continued to fire a rain of bullets. One of them punctured Cushing's collar. Another ripped through his sleeve and two more pierced his clothing. Still he had not been hit.

As Cushing triggered the torpedo, the ram's cannon fired a charge directly over the launch and into the water behind it. The air pressure of the blast pushed the launch under water. It bobbed up only to be filled again by a wall of water from the exploding torpedo. Cushing shouted for his men to save themselves. Tearing off his shoes, he dove into the river.

Dodging a torch-lit boat sent to take prisoners, he swam off downstream. At one point he had an arm around a wounded member of his crew. But the exhausted officer's grip weakened and the man slipped away and drowned. Dazed with his actions, Cushing was able, later that night, to drag himself on shore. In another day, he was safely within Union lines.

At Plymouth wharf, the ram *Albemarle* lay in eight feet of water. Its bottom was blown out and only its turret was above the waterline. Within four days, Plymouth itself had been retaken by the Federals. Some of Cushing's crewmen had died in the river and others were captured. But the last great hope of saving North Carolina was gone. Afterward, even the captain of the *Albemarle* said of Cushing's feat that "a more gallant thing was not done during the war." "Lionhearted" Charles Flusser had been avenged. When Cushing himself died some years later, his body was buried a few paces from that of Flusser.

The sinking of the *Albemarle* came in time to help assure the re-election of Lincoln a few days later. It also lifted the war-weary spirits of the North. The strong Confederate position at Fort Fisher was guarding Wilmington and the mouth of the Cape Fear River. It finally fell to a combined land and sea attack on January 15, 1865. Wilmington and the Wilmington and Weldon railroad were crucial to the supply of Lee's army. They were captured in February. The army of General Sherman was marching northward to link up with General Grant after the destruction of both Georgia and South Carolina. Reaching North Carolina in early March, it destroyed the

In a raid from Norfolk in 1863, General Wild recruited blacks for an 1800-man regiment of black Union troops.

Fayetteville arsenal and defeated General Joseph E. Johnston's rebels at Bentonville. When Sherman reached Raleigh on April 12, Lee had surrendered at Appomattox three days earlier. Johnston's army gave up two weeks later at the Bennett House, near Durham.

In the closing days of the war, a Federal Army from Tennessee, led by General George Stoneman, crossed the mountains and marched into the Piedmont. It captured Salisbury, breaking up the Confederate prison there. It seized Wilkesboro, Greensboro, Shelby, Morganton, Asheville, Waynesville, and other towns. North Carolina was now fully subdued and defeated. On April 29, it was placed under the command of General John M. Schofield. The experiment in secession was over.

During the last three years of the war, North Carolina had been controlled politically by the "Conservative" party. Zebulon B. Vance was the governor. In the election of 1862, the "Confederate" party was strongly loyal to the government of Jefferson Davis. It wanted the State's rights philosophy to be abandoned so that no support would be denied to insure a Southern victory. The Conservatives were less closely attached to the Confederacy. They put the interests of North Carolina before those of the Davis government. They also upheld civil liberties and personal freedom. The Confederate party seemed willing to create a dictatorship if it would promote military victory. Vance was elected by a margin of almost three to one. This was an indication that North Carolinians, though hoping to win the war, also hoped to keep the Davis government at arm's length. As governor, Vance was often in disputes with Davis over how far North Carolina should go to support the Confederacy. There was even a threat by Vance at one point to "take North Carolina out of the Confederacy" if Davis did not back away from his demands.

Confederates of both parties became very much alarmed in 1863 over a peace movement that became popular in many parts of the state. People held peace meetings and urged a statewide peace convention. They wanted the Davis government to settle the national issue peacefully. These meetings were held in half the counties. Vance viewed the movement as a threat to the war effort. But in 1864, peace advocates nominated William W. Holden, editor of the Raleigh *Standard,* for governor. Denouncing both Vance and the Confederacy, the "peace party" ran poorly and Vance was re-elected. The Conservative governor was a warm and winning man with great talent as a speaker. He had a genuine concern for his people. He was becoming one of the most beloved leaders in the history of his state.

A ***dictatorship*** means a government of absolute power.

The Civil War had cost North Carolina over forty thousand soldiers. More than half that number died of disease. Many others were seriously injured. Slaves valued at two hundred million dollars were freed. There were great losses in wrecked railroads, bridges, and buildings. The state's banks, school system, and university faced bankruptcy as did many private institutions. Farms not properly tended in four years lay in ruins. Most of the gains of the prosperous prewar years were wiped out. Governor Vance was in a Union prison. Most who served the rebel cause had lost their rights as citizens.

Even so, there were signs of hope. One hopeful sign was that the state had lost less in the war than other rebel states. A still more hopeful sign was the destruction of slavery. The end of slavery opened the door to a healthier and more varied economy. There would also be more humane social relations. For the blacks, freedom meant more chances to contribute to society and to improve their lives. In some respects, the Civil War was like a painful operation on a diseased body. Although weak and exhausted at first, the patient would be better off during recovery than before. It would, however, be a slow recovery.

Had North Carolina learned a lesson about the Union it had joined so hesitantly in 1789? Perhaps so. Thoughtful people agreed it was important that there be legal safeguards against the abuse of political minorities by the majority. It had been known since the eighteenth century that one state—or a minority of states—had a right to a fair hearing. This was so even when the minority ideas did not agree with the majority. But the Union also had a right to defend itself. The nation could not tolerate a minority seeking to defend a position—on slavery or anything else—to the point of secession. Perhaps, in North Carolina and the South, this verdict of history would now be accepted.

Chapter Checkup

PEOPLE

James Cooke
Charles Flusser
Robert F. Hoke

William B. Cushing
Zebulon B. Vance
Edward Stanly

PLACES

Edwards' Ferry	Oregon Inlet	Fort Fisher
Plymouth	Fort Macon	Bentonville
Hamilton	Washington	Bennett House
Croatan Sound	Grandfather Mountain	

FACT

In what respects was the *Albemarle* superior to ordinary naval vessels?

What was the mission of the *Albemarle?*

How was the secession of the Confederacy like the secession of the colonies from Great Britain?

What problems were encountered in building the *Albemarle?*

Why did North Carolina sometimes have trouble cooperating with the Confederacy?

INTERPRETATION

In what respects was the secession of 1861 like the "first secession" of 1788? Explain.

What does the difficulty of constructing the *Albemarle* suggest about the shortcomings of North Carolina industry at the time?

Are there indications that North Carolina's role in the Confederacy was less than enthusiastic? Explain.

VOCABULARY

Flotilla	Emancipation
Martial	Commando
Strategists	Barricade
Blockade	

ACTIVITY

Build a scale model of the *Albemarle.*

SUGGESTED READING

Barrett, John G. *North Carolina as a Civil War Battleground.* Raleigh: State Dept. of Archives and History, 1960. A 98-page general survey of the war in North Carolina.

Barrett, John G. *The Civil War in North Carolina.* Chapel Hill: UNC Press, 1963. See especially Ch. X "The Confederate Goliath," dealing with the ram *Albemarle.*

1865 Henry Berry Lowry declared an outlaw

1867 Republicans win election
● Black code adopted

1868 Constitutional Convention held
● State returns to the Union

1869 Ku Klux Klan activity begins

1871 Holden impeached

1872 Battle of Wire Grass Landing *(July)*

1875 Conservatives dominate Constitutional Convention

1876 Vance elected governor

1877 Federal troops withdrawn from the South

1885 Lumbees received state recognition as a tribe

1865 Lee surrenders at Appomattox *(April 9)*
● Johnson sworn in as President following Lincoln's assassination *(April 15)*

1869 Suez Canal opened

1881 President Garfield assassinated *(Sept.)*

1884 Grover Cleveland elected President *(Nov.)*

15

THE LOWRY GANG

The Battle of Wire Grass Landing

It had been a long, hot July day in 1872 for Captain McRae and his militia detachment. So the shade of Wire Grass Landing offered a pleasant setting. Surely there could be no harm in pausing for a few minutes rest in the ongoing war between the militia and the Lowry Gang.

Frogs and crickets were announcing the approach of night. And from somewhere upriver the echo of voices could be heard among the soft sounds of twilight. The scene was peaceful but Captain McRae did not relax. He heard another sound—the splash of a paddle striking the water. What was that? Taking no chances in this unfriendly country, he ordered his men to hide in the woods along the river bank.

Out of the stillness above the river bend, they heard another noise. It sounded like someone wading ashore from a boat. Then, gliding quietly around the bend, a dugout canoe paddled by a single figure appeared. Alert, Captain McRae

Henry Berry Lowry, *an Indian guerrilla fighter*
Captain McRae, *a militia officer*
Jonathan Worth, *Governor of North Carolina*
William W. Holden, *Governor of North Carolina*
Tod R. Caldwell, *Governor of North Carolina*

Parker D. Robbins, *a state official and inventor*
James H. Harris, *member of the General Assembly*
Edward H. Sutton, *a state official and inventor*

caught his breath in astonishment! It was the Indian, Henry Berry Lowry himself! Without knowing it, McRae had laid a trap for the most wanted outlaw in North Carolina. His pulse raced as he realized what the next few moments could mean for him.

The 18 militiamen were hidden behind the wooded bank. They knew better than to fire too quickly. The wily Indian had escaped from too many traps in the past. He might even elude this one if shots were fired before he was within easy range. But now, the boat came almost abreast of the landing. The time had come to strike! Without warning, a volley of rifle fire rang out toward the dark canoe.

Henry Berry Lowry wins a battle against a party of ambushers in the Scuffletown woods.

The bullets had scarcely covered the distance between shore and boat before the paddler disappeared over the far side and into the water. The militia watched to see if the boatman had been killed. Suddenly, the near side of the boat tilted upward, stayed for a moment, and then came down. At that moment, the crack of a rifle sent a bullet screeching among the militia. Before they could return a volley, the near side of the canoe had gone up again, forming a shield that protected the boatman. Bullets flayed the water and the hull of the boat. But they did no harm to the man in the river. The canoe, meanwhile, had begun to slip toward the landing itself. The rifleman behind it was nudging the boat toward the militia!

In the twilight, Captain McRae kept his men firing at the slowly approaching canoe. Now and then, the near side would dip and another bullet would whip toward the bank. Private McCormick was struck by a rifle bullet. Private Smith also fell wounded. McRae's men had used up nearly all their ammunition. The menacing canoe was now almost upon them. It seemed useless to try to hit the ghostly figure in the Lumber River. With the shade of night falling around him, McRae ordered his men to abandon the site. Carrying their wounded, the militia made their escape. The Battle of Wire Grass Landing had been won by Henry Berry Lowry. The Scuffletonians, when they heard about it, were not surprised.

The Lumber River Indians were a crossbreed people of uncertain origin. No one knew how they came to live in Robeson County. No one knew who they had been before they arrived. South Carolina Indians of the eighteenth century had raided the region. It was probably their blood that flowed through the veins of the Scuffletonians, as they were called. There was Tuscarora and Catawba blood among them, too, and maybe other tribes as well. There was also a mixture of families of other races who had been living here longer than anyone knew. Some suspected that Scuffletonian blood even included that of the Lost Colony from Roanoke Island. Whoever they were, no one could deny that their lives in Scuffletown included terrible poverty and hardship.

Lacking any tribal identity, the Scuffletonians were recognized by the state merely as "free persons of color." They were treated in the same way as free blacks. Under the Constitution of 1835, they could not vote or bear arms. They could not do many other things that whites took for granted.

Scuffletonians had it hard even in the best of times. But the Civil War almost destroyed them. From the earliest stages of the war, they were drafted into the labor battalions of the Confederacy. They were marched off to work with slaves to

Henry Berry Lowry, leader of the Lowry Gang, was a hero to the oppressed people in the Reconstruction in North Carolina.

This sketch tried to rouse white anger at stories of white people being apprenticed to blacks in North Carolina.

The Constitutional Convention of 1868 in North Carolina was dominated by the new Republican party. Nonwhites voted for the first time in the convention election. Fifteen blacks were included among its delegates. Several classes of former Confederates, not yet given full citizenship, were not allowed to vote or serve in the convention. The Republican delegates represented a group of small white farmers, Unionists, nonwhites, and carpetbaggers. The latter were recent immigrants from the North, including some who hoped to gain political power by controlling the nonwhite vote.

The chief results of the Convention included the adoption of manhood suffrage. This was the right of all adult males to vote, regardless of race. It had also removed property and reli-

The last part of the war and the postwar period saw many free blacks and former slaves fleeing to find a better life.

This group of Cherokee Indians was photographed at a gathering of North Carolina Cherokee Indian Confederate veterans.

Atheists are those who do not believe in God.

An **auditor** is a person appointed to examine accounts and financial records for correctness.

Arson is the crime of deliberately setting fire to someone's property.

gious qualifications (except for atheists) for office-holding. State and county officials would be popularly elected. The Council of State would be made up of holders of certain high offices. The term of the governor was increased from two to four years. The elective offices of lieutenant governor, state auditor, superintendent of public instruction, and superintendent of public works were created. Finally, the House of Commons became the House of Representatives. The number of capital crimes was reduced to four—murder, rape, arson, and burglary. It was hoped that these changes would make the state both more democratic and more efficient.

In the next state election, Holden again became governor and another slate of Unionists was elected to Congress. When the Congressional delegation was seated on July 20, 1868, North Carolina was, after seven years, a part of the Union once again.

In the latter part of the Civil War, the Lincoln administration set up agencies for the relief of refugee blacks in eastern North Carolina and elsewhere in the South. In 1865, the Freedmen's Bureau was created to extend aid to the newly-freed slaves who now needed it. During the three and a half years that it was active in North Carolina, the Freedmen's Bureau worked to help blacks find jobs, set up schools, buy land, and resist the problems of poverty. But such agencies were resented by whites. Their existence was one of North Carolina's most serious problems of the postwar period.

As the Confederates weakened in the closing months of the war, large areas of North Carolina were turned into lawless tracts. Bands of deserters from both armies, fugitive conscripts, and escaped slaves formed criminal groups. They raided farms and plantations. Order was not restored with the war's end. Instead, many outlaw bands remained. In such a climate, the fears of ordinary citizens gave rise to protective organizations outside the law. Several of these, known collectively as the Ku Klux Klan, directed their efforts mainly at the freed blacks. These people were scapegoats for the anarchy of the period. The Freedmen's Bureau and the Union League, a politically-oriented organization, were the focus of much white agitation.

The Ku Klux Klan first appeared in Tennessee in 1866. It quickly spread until it was active in almost every Southern state. It used mumbo-jumbo, secret signs, and outlandish costumes which were supposed to strike terror into the hearts of black people. Its officers were called Grand Wizard, Grand Dragon, and Grand Cyclops. They liked to wear starched and ironed gowns and hoods that would "glitter and rattle" in the

A **scapegoat** is one who is made to bear the blame for the deeds of others.

Anarchy means without order or government.

This sketch shows Moore County Ku Klux Klan members about to hang a Republican opponent. They were captured moments later.

This scene in Asheville in 1867 shows blacks registering to vote for the first time in their lives.

moonlight. The Klan was most active in Piedmont and western counties. There, whites outnumbered blacks by three or four to one. It was scarcely known in the eastern counties with large black populations. The Klan, in other words, had its greatest strength where the supposed threat of blacks was least serious.

In spite of its nonsense of codes and secret handshakes, the Ku Klux Klan was a menace to life and property in some parts of the state. At its height in 1869 and 1870, it was deemed responsible for five killings in Alamance County, five in Orange, three each in Caswell and Jones, and others. However, its activity was limited mainly to floggings and threats against blacks and carpetbaggers. There were 98 reported Ku Klux floggings in Alamance and Catawba counties alone in the worst period. The white members were outraged by blacks in positions of authority. They found an outlet for their anger in the Klan. Governor Holden had the options of calling in federal troops or black militia from the East to restore order. But he let the situation get out of hand.

As the 1870 elections approached and violence increased, Holden sent armed forces into Alamance and Caswell. A federal judge ordered the transfer of whites arrested there by the military to civilian courts. President Grant supported the order. Holden, deserted by the President, had other problems as well. Conservatives pointed to the great amount of spending by his administration. The state had issued bonds to repair worn out and damaged railroads. Investors were losing confidence in state bonds. They feared the administration could not pay its debts. Many examples of corruption were exposed in the passage of the railroad bonds. The Conservatives campaigned to "clean up the mess in Raleigh" and, supported by the Klan, won a big victory at the polls. Five of the new congressmen were Conservatives as were two thirds of the members of the new state senate.

The senate victory was significant. Governor Holden's term was to end in 1872 but Conservative leaders had long been calling for his impeachment. A resolution to that effect was passed in the senate in December 1870. The governor was charged with ordering illegal arrests in Alamance and Caswell, illegally recruiting soldiers, refusing writs of courts, and other unlawful acts. In a trial extending over most of February and March 1871, Holden was convicted of six of the eight charges. He became the first governor of the state to lose office through impeachment. He was succeeded in office by Lieutenant Governor Tod R. Caldwell.

By a series of acts passed in 1870 and 1871, Congress bore down on the Ku Klux Klan and other secret societies in the South. The Fifteenth Amendment forbade states from denying the right to vote to any citizen on account of race or previous condition of servitude. More United States troops were sent south to restore order. Almost a thousand Klansmen were indicted by a federal grand jury in Raleigh in 1871. Of that number, 37 were convicted, only one of whom served as long as two years in jail. But the restoration of Conservative control of the state government meant the return of white supremacy in North Carolina. The Klan now quickly disappeared.

Repeated calls for revision in the 1868 Constitution, a Republican document, led to a new convention in 1875. Republicans elected as many delegates to it as Conservatives. But the strength of the latter was enough to insure important amendments. The Convention outlawed secret political societies. It decreed the separation of schools for blacks and whites. It forbade racial intermarriage and removed county government from local to legislative control. The latter change insured that local government would be under Conservative (meaning white) influence. The revisions were ratified by statewide vote.

With the Democratic victory in national elections in 1874, North Carolina's Conservative party adopted the name Democratic. This was to promote cooperation between state and national organizations. In 1876, the Democrats nominated the popular Zebulon B. Vance for governor. They managed to defeat the Republicans. Not only white supremacy at home, but acceptance of that situation by the national government was

Impeachment occurs when a legislature formally charges and criminally tries a public official.

Writs are formal orders forbidding someone to perform a certain act or acts.

Ku Klux Klan members tried to spread terror among the blacks by violence and frightful costumes.

Supremacy is the power exercised by those of highest authority.

now assured. The missionary spirit of the North died with the assurance that slavery was permanently outlawed. Federal troops were withdrawn from the Southern states in 1877, ending the era of Reconstruction. A long, bleak night now closed around the black population of North Carolina.

The Underdogs

Edward H. Sutton was an author, an inventor, and a member of the North Carolina legislature during the Reconstruction.

For a period of four years, from 1868 to 1872, the poor people of North Carolina, primarily the state's former slaves, enjoyed a brief dignity. There was the promise of better days ahead. To some extent, however, the opportunity was lost. This was because of their inexperience of the workings of state government and the greed of certain individuals. Also, whites were determined to regain power. Some of the blacks elected to positions of authority had been people of small ability. They were easily misled by both Northern and Southern associates. But others had proven themselves worthy of roles of public trust. Brief as their era of real freedom proved to be, some made outstanding contributions to their state and nation.

Parker David Robbins was one of these. A native of Bertie County, of black and Chowan Indian ancestry, he was a carpenter who had served with the Union Army in 1864 and 1865 as a sergeant-major in a cavalry regiment. He was elected to the Constitutional Convention of 1867. In the following year, he was elected to the House of Representatives. In 1873 and 1877 he patented two inventions—a cotton cultivator and a saw sharpener. Later, while living in Duplin County, he built and operated his own steamboat.

Harde Spears was a black of Snow Hill who invented an infantry shield in 1870. E. H. Sutton of Edenton invented a cotton cultivator in 1874. Sutton, like Robbins, was a member of the General Assembly for a time. He was also a strong advocate of the rights of black people.

James H. Harris of Wake County was an important political leader. He was elected to the state House of Repesentatives in 1868. After he ran unsuccessfully for Congress in 1870, he later returned to the General Assembly for a long and distinguished career. Harris was a native of Granville, where he was an apprentice in the upholstery business before the war. While a resident of Ohio during the Civil War, he traveled through Canada, and also visited West Africa. He recruited

Lowry's wife was arrested by whites in an attempt to get at the outlaw leader. When the attempt failed, she was freed.

and led the 28th Colored Troops in the latter part of the war. He returned to North Carolina, it is said, after turning down President Johnson's offer of the ministry to Haiti. Active in the work of the Freedmen's Bureau, he became deeply interested in the cause of education. He initiated the Colored Educational Association of North Carolina. He was also a Raleigh alderman and a major figure in the Union League.

Through Robbins, Harris, and others, the nonwhites proved, if further proof was needed, that they could function well in a free society. But it would be a long time, after the 1870s, before they would have another chance to make contributions to North Carolina and to America.

Gilding lilies means to exaggerate or embellish facts.

Rhoda Lowry, the wife of Henry Berry Lowry, was a fine-looking woman. The New York *Herald* reporters sometimes engaged in gilding lilies. But they probably told it straight when it was reported that Rhoda had "large dark, mournful looking eyes, with long lashes," and a fine figure. Henry Berry had not forgotten how, on his wedding day, the militia came to snatch him away from his bride and wedding feast and throw him in jail. His honeymoon was delayed until he could saw through the bars, knock down a wall, and leave with handcuffs still on his wrists. And now, six years later, they needn't think they were going to get at him by taking Rhoda captive. They put her in the Lumberton jail, but she wasn't going to stay there long.

On the morning of July 14, 1871, Henry Berry and three other Indians went to the plantation of John McNair. They stated the matter as plainly as they could. "Mr. McNair," said the outlaw leader, "I want you to . . . go to Lumberton, where they have put my wife in jail for no crime but because she is my wife. . . . You people won't let me work to get my living, and I have got to take it from you." When he got to the jail, McNair was to deliver a message: ". . . tell the Sheriff and County Commissioners that if they don't let her out of that jail, I'll retaliate on the white women. . . . Some of them shall come to the swamp with me if she is kept in jail. . . ." There was a lot of huffing and blowing at Lumberton when they got the message. There was much talk of the things they were going to do to Henry Berry Lowry. But, four days later, Rhoda was back home in Scuffletown.

To **retaliate** means to strike back.

Law and order, Conservative-style, had settled over most of North Carolina. But the Lowry Gang still helped itself regularly to the plantation provisions of several counties in North and South Carolina. The Ku Klux Klan was all but gone and the lawlessness of the end of the Civil War was over. But Henry Berry Lowry seemed more determined than ever. His exploits became still more daring as the months passed. His most successful raid was one in which his men carried off an iron safe containing twenty-two thousand dollars and a wagonload of provisions. This was done in February 1872. The Conservative police and militia chased him hard. Some of them probably worried about what they would do if they caught him.

But the days of the Lowry Gang were now numbered. The first signs of its collapse were already visible. Zach McLauchlin, a white member of the gang, escaped from jail twice before he was shot to death. It happened one night in late 1870 as he slept by his campfire. Henderson Oxendine was captured not long after that and hanged at Wilmington. One by one, the rest followed, not to the gallows, but gunned down by bounty hunters and other pursuers.

They never did get Henry Berry. For another 60 years and more you could still find Scuffletonians who insisted that he was not dead. There were several reports in the late winter of 1872 that he *was* dead, although they varied in details. The common agreement in the stories was that he had died by a shot accidentally fired from his own rifle. Perhaps so, but his spirit lived on in the memories of generations of Scuffletonians.

W. McKee Evans, a biographer of Henry Berry Lowry, says that the Lowry legend has had a deep impact on the history of the Lumber River Indians. At the end of the Reconstruction period, there was reason to expect that the Scuffletonians would be reduced to the same semifree status as

A New York artist pictured Lumbee gang members this way for the cover of an 1872 book.

hundreds of thousands of other nonwhite North Carolinians. But they were proud, defiant, and self-conscious. In 1885, they demanded and received official recognition as Indians rather than merely free persons of color. The ruling Democratic party gave them a status midway between black and white. They managed to hold onto that status through the darkest days of Jim Crow legislation. This meant that the Lumber River people could gain full citizenship easier than other non-whites. It was a small victory but a significant one. The change from a community of wretched poor people to a recognized Indian tribe might never have taken place had it not been for Henry Berry Lowry.

But Evans also makes a more important point. He points out the difficulties that face such a minority when they confront the American two-party system of government. In North Carolina, both the Conservative and Republican parties would have ignored the Scuffletonians. But the Lowry Gang made it impossible. The Republicans had brought about a revolution. They freed the slaves and destroyed the Black Code. But most Republicans were concerned only with a political revolution. They did not wish to think about the social results of their actions. The white majority had lifted its foot from the victims' necks, but it did not offer to help them up.

Conservatives, here, were those opposing major changes from pre-Civil War conditions.

These dark-skinned people had rarely known any of the advantages of education. They were without experience in political matters. They could not, all at once, make up for these shortcomings. Even with the willing support of white people, it would have taken generations to overcome the poverty created by more than two hundred years of repression. They were faced with what often amounted to bitter opposition by those in power. Nonwhites faced the post-Reconstruction era without hope. Most dark-skinned people were passive and law-abiding in their relations with the white majority. They were rewarded with the loss of some of their most cherished gains from the Civil War. Were blacks to suffer more political and social repression? Did the times call for another black-skinned Henry Berry Lowry to lead his own race out of repression?

Repression means holding or being held under control.

The Civil War and Reconstruction imposed distasteful new ideas on Southern whites. Their hate of the means used against them would last a long time. In the long run, their feelings would cool and they would accept blacks and Indians in civic life. In the meantime, progress for the dispossessed would be measured in the decline of violence each year. But, for 80 years following the Reconstruction, the rest of the nation turned away from the plight of the South.

Chapter Checkup

PEOPLE

Henry Berry Lowry   William W. Holden
Jonathan Worth   Tod R. Caldwell

PLACES

Lumberton   Lumber River   Scuffletown

FACT

Why did the Lumbees have difficulty gaining official recognition as a tribe?
Why did many go to the swamps to live in the last years of the Civil War?
Why did the Republicans hesitate to clamp down on the Lowry Gang?
What were the Black Codes?
What brought about the decline of the Ku Klux Klan?

INTERPRETATION

Why do you think the Ku Klux Klan was more active in the Piedmont than in
the Coastal Plain?
In what respect can Henry Berry Lowry be called the founder of the Lum-
bee tribe? Explain.
Was there any sound reason for Ku Klux Klan activity after the Civil War?
Explain.

VOCABULARY

Prosecute   Anarchy   Repression
Proclamation   Impeachment   Dispossessed
Ordinance

ACTIVITY

Research the question of whether the Lumbee Indians may be considered
descendants of the Lost Colony.

SUGGESTED READING

Evans, W. McKee. *To Die Game: The Story of the Lowry Band, Indian Guerrillas of Reconstruction.* Baton Rouge: LSU Press, 1971. A com-
prehensive but readable and reliable account of the Lumbees and the
Lowry Gang.
Zuber, Richard L. *North Carolina During Reconstruction.* Raleigh: State
Dept. of Archives and History, 1969. Brief survey (67 pages) of main issues and themes, 1865–1872.

PART SIX

Setting
New Priorities

1875-1915

1865 Civil War soldiers discover Durham tobacco

1875 Buck Duke becomes his father's partner

1884 Knights of Labor organize in Raleigh-Durham area

1884 Grover Cleveland elected President *(Nov.)*

1889 Buck Duke organizes American Tobacco Company

1898 Spanish-American War begins *(Apr. 20)*

1904 Theodore Roosevelt elected President *(Nov.)*

1908 U.S. Supreme Court antitrust action against American Tobacco Company

1911 American Tobacco Company ordered to reorganize

1917 United States declares war on Germany *(Apr.)*

1918 Armistice signed *(Nov. 11)*

1924 Duke Endowment created

16

RISING FROM THE ASHES

The Tycoon

To **prime** tobacco is to remove the leaves from the stalk.

To **sucker** tobacco is to remove excess growth from the stalk.

The Bright Belt is that area in the Southeast where Bright Leaf tobacco is grown.

"Smokes" is a former name for various forms of smoking tobacco.

Old Washington Duke never made a better deal than when he took in his youngest boy, Buck, as a partner in 1875. Buck was a gangly, pigeon-toed redhead and a school dropout. But, at 18, he already knew the tobacco business from seeds to ashes. As a farmer's son, he had planted and primed and suckered since his permanent teeth came. He had killed more tobacco worms than the czar had peasants. He had tied more tobacco sticks than the peasants had freckles. He knew everything about curing leaves, stripping stalks, and making tobacco.

As partner to his father, Buck was a buyer and sales manager. During market season, he was on the warehouse floor every morning. There he was learning how to squeeze favorable terms out of the slickest veterans of the Bright Belt. In the afternoon he would be in the factory grinding tobacco leaves into smoking form. At night he would work out new schemes for selling "smokes." As soon as buying season was over,

Washington Duke, *senior member of the Duke family*

James B. Duke, *son of Washington Duke*

Edward Featherstone Small, *salesman for Duke's products*

Leonidas L. Polk, *a Raleigh newspaper editor*

Josephus Daniels, *a Raleigh newspaper editor*

Double-entry bookkeeping means entering each transaction in the ledger twice—as a debt in one account and a credit in another.

Buck would hit the road. He visited customers throughout the South and West. He would sleep on freight trains to save the cost of hotel rooms. Every penny he saved was put back into the business. In short, he was an ideal partner.

Buck Duke was soon the sharpest tobacco man anywhere. He made a trip to New York for some business school courses. He was soon back in Durham providing "W. Duke and Sons" with the blessings of double-entry bookkeeping. Up North he had noticed the growing popularity of the little smokes called cigarettes. Some people liked them better than pipes or chewing tobacco or cigars. It didn't look like much of a smoke, but Buck decided there was money in it. So he hired some Russian Jews who could roll twenty-five hundred cigarettes a day and brought them to Durham.

The southern and western customers were not impressed. They would not take orders for the little smokes. Buck decided to try a different sales pitch. He hired a high-toned eastern man named Edward Featherstone Small. Mr. Small dressed well, slicked his hair, and knew a meat fork from a salad fork. Small went to Atlanta. He talked a beautiful French actress into posing for a poster ad with a box of cigarettes in her hand. People were shocked at the sight of a woman doing that kind of thing. But orders came in like nothing Buck Duke had ever seen. Small went to St. Louis and hired a good-looking saleslady. She was the first in the tobacco business. She broke down the resistance of midwesterners who thought cigarettes were peculiar looking and funny tasting. Small also gave prizes to customers ordering the most cigarettes. He soon had a market for all the smokes the Duke factory could roll.

Down the street from the Duke firm was the Bull Durham Company. It was the largest of the North Carolina producers of tobacco. That big sheet iron bull on the front of the Bull Durham factory was a constant reminder to the Dukes of how

Washington Duke's tobacco empire had its beginning in this Durham County barn.

Buck Duke's father, Washington, was a wily businessman. He was the founder of the Duke tobacco enterprise.

far they had to go. There was a steam whistle attached to the bull. It gave off a bellow you could hear 13 miles from Durham. What Wash Duke and his three sons needed—if they were ever going to muffle the bellow of that bull—was a lot of money all at once. Even the best deals didn't bring that kind of profit. In 1878, however, they sold a fifth of the business to a Maryland businessman named Gerald Watts. He wanted a position in the firm for his son, George. The new firm of W. Duke Sons and Company started out with seventy thousand dollars in capital. Their goal was to overtake Bull Durham.

The Dukes heard about a small town in Virginia where a young man had a machine that made cigarettes. It was a flimsy contraption with tubes and rollers and cutters. But it was capable of making cigarettes at the rate of more than two hundred a minute or one hundred thousand a day. This was equal to the work of about forty expert rollers. The Dukes gambled and got two of the machines for their Durham factory. It took a few weeks to iron out some kinks. But the machines finally did exactly what their inventor said they would do. Turning out nearly a quarter of a million cigarettes a day, the Duke firm was able to push costs down from 80 cents a thousand to 30. This meant they could reduce the price of their smokes and still make higher profits. But even Edward Featherstone Small and his ladies couldn't sell a quarter million a day. Buck began giving the matter serious thought.

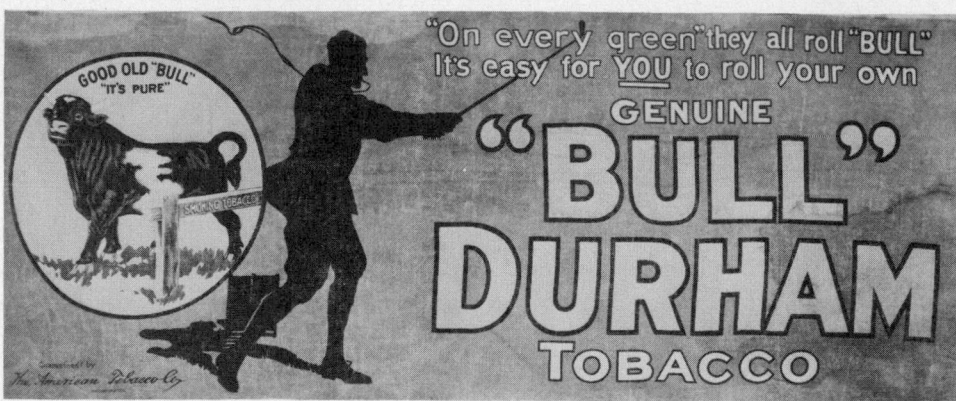

The Blackwell Company's bull was an internationally known trademark. It was taken over by the Duke company.

The Orient refers to Asia, especially the Far East.

As Buck saw it, there were still several things wrong with the cigarette market. Cigarette boxes were flimsy, crushed easily and weren't very attractive. Then there was the market itself. While manufacturers waited patiently for the American market to grow, smokers around the world were paying five cents apiece for hand-rolled cigarettes. These were no better than those the Dukes produced. It would be necessary to break down the smokers' prejudice against machine-made cigarettes to get a grip on this larger market. Buck decided that neither problem was beyond solution.

Buck invented a new kind of sliding box that looked good and didn't crush easily. He had some machines designed that could stamp them out as fast as the cigarettes poured from the machines. He sent an agent to tour Europe and the Orient for 19 months looking for new customers. The idea was to show people that the Duke brands were as good as any they were used to smoking. And they could be bought for much less. The agent visited London, Antwerp, Brussels, Rotterdam, Paris, Berlin, Stockholm, and Copenhagen. He toured Asia, Africa, Australia, and New Guinea. He came home with orders that laid the basis for a huge new market for the Duke company.

But the major breakthrough came in 1883. In the spring of that year, Congress voted to lower the tax on cigarettes. Smokers looked forward to a reduction of a cent or two in the cost of a ten-cent box. Other companies pondered whether to take off one cent or two. The Dukes suddenly slashed the price of a box to five cents. Orders rained down on the Dukes from all over the world. The old factory was soon abandoned in favor of a new forty-thousand-square-foot building. The

Dukes sold thirty million cigarettes in the first nine months after the price drop. It was scarcely the beginning. Buck Duke and his firm had laid the basis for an industrial giant such as the tobacco industry had never known.

The Dukes were seated around the dinner table after church one Sunday when Buck made his big announcement. The Big Four tobacco companies of the American market had offices and agents in New York, close to the big money. He was going there himself to try to get established. If things worked out, New York would become his permanent headquarters. The family was dumbfounded—everybody, at least, except the old man. Mr. Wash let the rest of them wave their arms at Buck. They told him what a fool he was and how those sharpies in New York would take him apart. But Washington Duke had seen his youngest son in action for quite a while. If Buck said he was ready for New York, then it would be a mistake to try to keep him in Durham. Buck headed for the big city.

For months he ate at cheap restaurants on the Bowery. At first he used a little loft in Harlem for his office. He got some orders and opened a small factory on Rivington Street. He tried to sell cigarettes by putting pictures of famous athletes and actresses in each pack. To some people it looked like a dumb idea. But picture collecting became the rage. Many people bought the Duke brands for the pictures as much as for the smokes. Buck spent all day in the factory supervising the work. He spent the evenings meeting dealers and taking orders. He got to know everyone involved in the New York tobacco trade. He found what would sell smokes and what would not. By the end of his second year, he began to show a profit. Now Buck was on his way, pushing aside the bigger manufacturers and snatching business for himself.

Any dealer who bought a five-hundred-box carton from Buck got a coupon that could be redeemed for 50 cents. Those who turned in the most empty cigarette boxes got a reward of 50 dollars. When his factory hands got to work in the morning, they would always find Buck there ahead of them. He was likely to pop up at any moment beside a workbench to check on how things were going. He would take random boxes out of a carton and pick his way through them. This was to see that each cigarette was properly made, each label properly pasted. He saved every nickel he could on production and put it into advertising. The city bloomed with Duke posters.

While Buck was taking charge of New York, Edward

The Bowery is a part of New York noted as a hangout for drunks and beggars.

Harlem is a section of New York City.

James Buchanan (Buck) Duke was a remarkable salesman, business leader, and philanthropist. He built the Duke tobacco firm into the world's largest tobacco producer.

Featherstone Small was winning the West. In Cincinnati, he put together a roller-skating team called the Cross Cuts, named for a Duke brand. He advertized them as champions of the South and called on all competitors to skate against them. Everybody that came to a match got a free box of Cross Cuts or photos of lovely actresses. Small took his team on a midwestern tour. He built them up as the finest club "in the ENTIRE United States!!!" Skating was a craze at the time and the rinks overflowed with spectators. Each one was a potential customer for Duke's cigarettes. Small hired people to go from store to store asking for his brands. They were terribly upset when the smokes weren't available. He would put people in front of tobacco shops to hand a box of Cross Cuts to every customer who came by. Between 1883 and 1885, Duke profits tripled.

The Big Four of the tobacco industry finally had its attention attracted by the annoying newcomer from the backwoods. They geared up for a fight to chase the intruder off. It was too late. In 1889, when Americans smoked 2.1 billion cigarettes, almost half of them were made by W. Duke Sons and Company. In 1889, James Buchanan "Buck" Duke organized the American Tobacco Company. He absorbed all his main competitors. He took charge of the national trade as Sherman had taken charge of Georgia. Buck Duke had created an international monopoly—and a tarnished reputation.

Tarnished means stained.

Postwar Recovery

The Civil War ruined most of North Carolina's industry—what little there was of it. It left most manufacturers too broke to rebuild quickly. Before the war, industry consisted mainly of many little turpentine distilleries. There, two thirds of the supply for the whole nation was produced. There were also hundreds of little water-powered flour and gristmills. There were some sawmills, a few cotton mills and tobacco factories, and an assortment of minor enterprises. Except for turpentine and lumber, everything manufactured in North Carolina was for local use. Nothing was exported. For a long time after the war, the state remained mainly agricultural.

Some people had a clear vision of the situation of North Carolina at the end of the war. These included some of the newspaper editors, who knew what must be done. The econ-

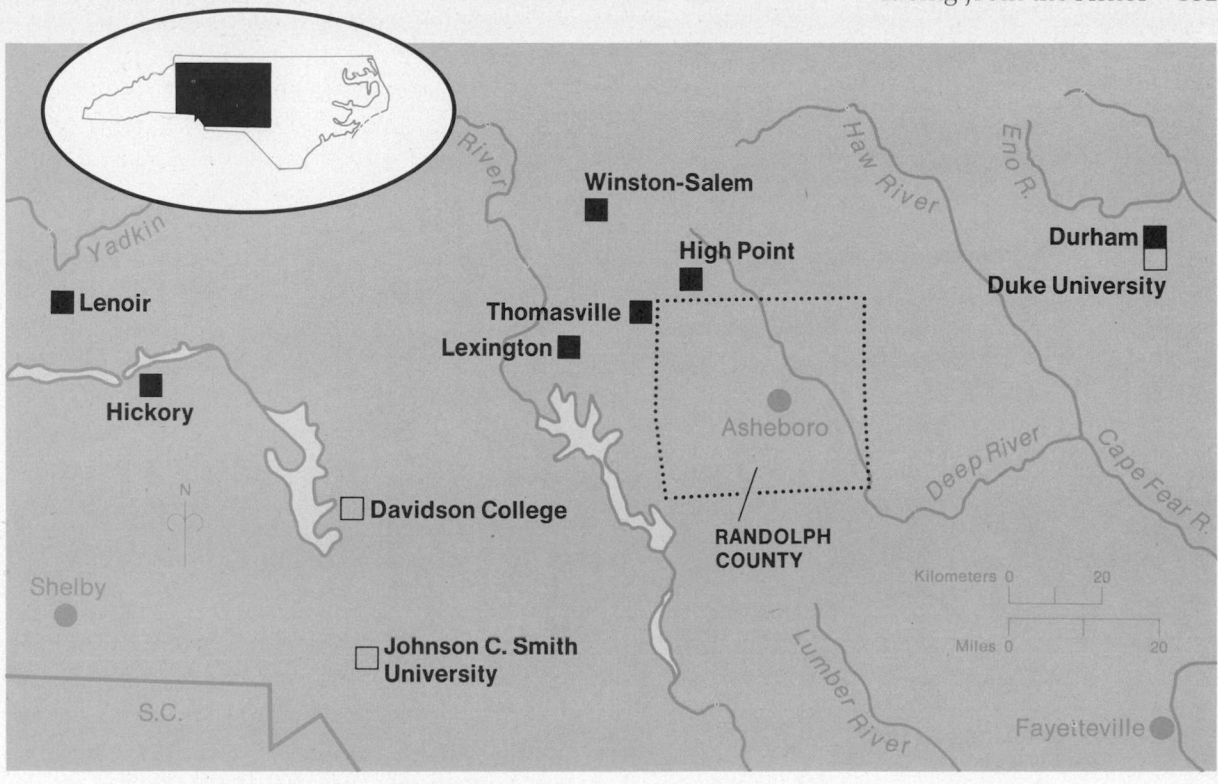

Central North Carolina, 1880

omy of the past could not be rebuilt. North Carolinians must learn to make their living in ways they had never tried before. The industrial might of the North was clearly seen during the war. It showed Southerners what a source of power and wealth they were missing. But it would take huge amounts of money to copy the northern example. Money on such a scale was not to be had. Those who had not lost vast amounts in slaves saw their hopes die with the refusal of the state government at federal insistence to honor its war debts.

One of the few encouraging signs at the war's close was the North's craving for cotton. The northeastern textile industry had known great hardship during the four years when it was denied its normal sources for cotton. Now that the war was over, demand was high and so were prices. Some Southerners in the cotton business rebuilt their fortunes rapidly. This boom lasted until 1869. After that, demand and prices began to fall to normal levels. This new wealth, together with the law governing the cotton tax, made it possible for many North Carolinians to build cotton mills during the 1870s. What

The leaves of tobacco had to be strung on sticks for drying before they could be used by tobacco companies.

The tobacco leaves were placed on sleds to be taken to barns for stringing.

the law did, in effect, was to exempt from taxes any cotton manufactured in the district where it was grown. This gave struggling new mills in the Cotton States a competitive edge against the old mills of the Northeast. It paved the way toward economic recovery in the South.

Leading newspapers devoted many columns to the success of new cotton mills and the revival of old ones. The postwar recovery of mills—such as those of Edwin M. Holt of Alamance and William S. Battle of Edgecombe—was especially encouraging. One advantage of the new mills was the chance to install machinery of the latest design. They would operate more efficiently than older rivals. Wilmington, Charlotte, and

Duke money helped build the Erwin Cotton Mills at Durham as textiles gained importance in North Carolina economy.

other towns created corporations and stock companies to spur the development of new mills. These towns raised the money to finance them.

Centered in the Piedmont, the textile industry by 1880 was producing material worth more than double the value of the best prewar year. But the greatest and most rapid growth was to occur in the last 20 years of the nineteenth century. During those last decades, North Carolina became a leading textile state. (It was outproduced in the South only by South Carolina.) By the end of the century, some northern mills were beginning to move south. This was to save money in labor and transportation costs. The North Carolina textile industry was now important in the national economy.

During the decade of the 1880s, other industries were also taking root in North Carolina soil. The furniture industry, following in the footsteps of Tom Day of antebellum Milton, began a period of rapid growth. The High Point Furniture Company opened the state's first furniture factory in 1888. There were more than a hundred others by 1902. Like the textile industry, the manufacture of furniture was confined mainly to the Piedmont. There, High Point, Thomasville, Lexington, Lenoir, Hickory, and Winston-Salem would become the chief centers of production. Despite its late start, furniture-making was soon the state's third most important industry.

Neither furniture nor textiles, however, could match the thundering boom in the tobacco industry. The business of turning tobacco leaves into various useable forms was well known in antebellum North Carolina. But it took the visits of Confederate and Union armies to the Piedmont region during the Civil War to popularize the North Carolina products.

Probably the best thing that ever happened to Durham, then a crossroads hamlet, was the decision of General Joseph

Antebellum means before the Civil War.

Milton, a town in Martin County, is now known as Hamilton.

E. Johnston to surrender his army to Sherman near there in April 1865. For nine days, details of the surrender were being worked out. At that time, soldiers from the two armies roamed the countryside. Among the places looted by the idle soldiers was John Green's little tobacco factory at Durham. The looters found Green's "bright tobacco" the mildest and best they had ever tried. It was made from a light-colored leaf and produced by curing the tobacco over smokeless charcoal instead of wood fires. After the war, the soldiers began writing back to Durham for more "bright leaf" products. The industry quickly shed its local character and began its rise to major importance. The Dukes were among the first to take advantage of the new business.

North Carolina slowly changed from an agricultural and rural state to an industrial and urban one. However, the advantages of the change were clearer than the disadvantages. A great deal of new wealth was caused by the change. This led, in turn, to a rise in industries, the construction of railroads, and many other improvements. By the 1870s, there was enough private money available to allow the state to pull out of the railroad business. It left that development to private means. State-owned rail lines were sold or leased. Democratic administrations provided various incentives to private companies. The railroad men gave out free passes and other special favors to people in government. This helped railroads toward rapid growth and prosperity.

Incentives means encouragements.

The new major rail systems were owned by groups outside the state. But North Carolina had almost four thousand miles of rail lines at the beginning of the twentieth century. A major flaw in the system was that main lines ran north and south. North Carolina still had no great east-west line to serve its major ports. This drawback, against which antebellum leaders had pled, still remained uncorrected. Another flaw was the single-minded concentration on iron rails. This kept back the development of highways and canals. Except for a few plank roads, the roads of the state were practically useless in winter. The block to communication, however, was being offset somewhat by the expansion of telegraph lines and, beginning in 1879, telephones as well.

Another major benefit of the industrial revolution was in the growth of towns. In 1820, New Bern was North Carolina's metropolis. It had a population of less than thirty-seven hundred. By 1900, the state had six towns with over ten thousand inhabitants each. These were Raleigh, Greensboro, Winston,

Agrarian means agricultural.

Charlotte, Asheville, and Wilmington. Although North Carolina remained heavily rural and agrarian, towns were important. Towns meant the rise of new social and cultural customs. They meant a new concentration of money and talent. Towns made it necessary to find solutions to some of the state's chief problems.

The evils of the industrial system in North Carolina, as elsewhere, included long hours of work, low pay, and child labor. Conditions were bad in the factories. They employed almost exclusively white labor. But it was worse on farms, where most laborers were black. A national depression, beginning in 1883, made matters worse than usual. This brought financial crisis to many North Carolina laboring families. It also led briefly to outright revolt of the poor against the system that used them.

A *depression* is a time when business drops off in a wide area.

In the year 1884 several chapters of a national organization, the Knights of Labor, were organized in the Raleigh-Durham area. Successful strikes were held in other parts of the country. Along with worsening economic conditions, the strikes brought on a rush of laborers to form new chapters of the Knights of Labor. Before the end of 1886, the new order was open to black workers as well as white, females as well as males. It had spread to Wilmington, Asheville, and many places in between. Not only field hands and mill workers were taken in, but merchants and clerical, or white collar, workers as well. John Nichols and J. Melville Broughton, both Raleigh printers, were the leaders of the state organization. It was formed in 1886.

Although nonpolitical in origin, the Knights quickly turned to politics as a means of solving the problems of labor. Nichols ran for Congress from the state's Fourth District in 1886. His platform was based on shorter working hours, outlawing child labor, and federal regulation of railroads and currency. He denounced both parties. To the shock of Democrats and Republicans alike, he won the election. In the following year, he led a drive to get the General Assembly to adopt labor legislation. But he was not to succeed.

The decline of the Knights of Labor was to be almost as sudden as its rise. The Knights wanted a Department of Labor and an industrial college. Farmers were led by Leonidas L. Polk, editor of the *Progressive Farmer,* a Raleigh newspaper. They had been developing a separate political and legislative program different from the Knights. The farmers wanted a state Department of Agriculture and an agricultural college. The North Carolina Farmers' Alliance was a good means to further such ideas. The 1887 General Assembly agreed to es-

A *land grant college* was one started on land given by the government.

Josephus Daniels, newspaper editor, was sometimes a sharp critic of the Duke firm and its business dealings.

Prestige means reputation arising from success.

tablish a Department of Agriculture with a Bureau of Labor Statistics. The Assembly chartered the State Agricultural and Mechanical College. But the rest of the labor program failed to pass. The new college (now North Carolina State University) opened in 1889. It had been the dream of Polk and others since soon after the Civil War. Funds for that purpose had been set aside under the Land Grant College Act.

There were other obstacles to the labor movement. There was growing ill will between white and black members of the Knights of Labor. Encouraged by the Democrats, this feeling further weakened the Knights. Many North Carolinians, true to their background, still feared the dangers of united groups. They clung to their spirit of individualism rather than lend support to organized labor. John Nichols was defeated by a Democrat in the 1888 election. The Knights of Labor soon had no influence in North Carolina.

Except for the Bureau of Labor Statistics, the Knights had little to show for their brief career in this state. But blacks were inspired by experience with the Knights. They formed the Negro Alliance to promote their own well-being. Moreover, the labor movement of the 1880s foretold a more serious movement among North Carolina's poorer classes. This was the creation of the Populist party in later years. There were too few urban workers. They did not identify their interests enough with those rural laborers for their movement to succeed in the 1880s. But the Knights of Labor had given North Carolina its first experience of what might become the most sweeping demand for change in the state's history.

Toward the close of the nineteenth century, the number of North Carolina farmers greatly exceeded that of mill workers. As big farms broke up with the end of slavery, small farms became the typical farming units. Some were operated by tenants. Most were owned by the families who worked them. Smaller farms meant less efficient farms and declining soil fertility. They meant a continuing low standard of living for both tenants and owners. As in the rest of the nation, North Carolina farmers saw a long era of falling prices and income. As the size of an average farm fell from three hundred sixteen acres in 1860 to one hundred one acres in 1900, the prestige of farming fell accordingly. Most bitterly affected were the tenant sharecroppers. These people paid their rents in shares of what they grew. Many sharecroppers, white and black, found the system a rat's maze. Each year they went deeper into debt to those for whom they worked. To the insecurity in sharecropping was added the unsympathetic attitude of the courts toward the plight of such families. Neither the Granger Movement of the 1870s nor the Farmers' Alliance of later years was able to break the link that joined the Democratic party to the railroad and manufacturing groups.

The Philanthropist

A *trust* is an unlawful business combination aimed at creating a monopoly.

On July 18, 1906, Josephus Daniels wrote an editorial for his Raleigh *News and Observer*. It was entitled "What the Trust Has Done to the Tobacco Growers." In 1875, said Daniels, Buck Duke was still a schoolboy. North Carolina farmers got an average of $20.45 for every hundred pounds of tobacco they sold. Ten years later, the Duke firm was one of the giants of the field. The price had dropped to $13.54 a hundred. Now, in 1906, with the American Tobacco Company commanding the world market, the price was $7.79. The manufacturers had never been in better shape—or the farmers worse off.

A week later, Daniels fired his other barrel. Under the heading "Trust Dodges Taxes," he observed that the American Tobacco Company had paid four million dollars for the Bull Durham Company. It was listed on Durham County tax books as being worth $680,385. It was possible, for the very naive, to believe that Buck Duke had been robbed blind in the purchase of Bull Durham. It was also possible to believe that the Duke firm was putting one over on Durham County and North Carolina. Neither the farmers nor the tax-paying public seemed to be getting anything from Duke's success. Both seemed to be the victims rather than the beneficiaries of Buck's magic.

Naive means easily fooled or misled.

Beneficiaries are those who profit from something.

The Dukes could be very angry about this kind of criticism. They were providing jobs for thousands who might otherwise be without work. The Dukes had been very generous to the Methodist Church. Hundreds of North Carolina merchants went home every evening a little richer for the Duke products they sold. In many respects, North Carolina was better off for having the Duke firm within its borders. It might be argued that unfair advantage was being taken of farmers and taxpayers. But where was the toreador fearless enough to do battle with Buck Duke and his bellowing bull?

A *toreador* is a bullfighter.

In 1908, the United States Supreme Court stepped into the ring, waving a red flag in the bull's face. A lawsuit was brought under the Sherman Antitrust Act. It charged that the American Tobacco Company was a "conspiracy in restraint

A *monopoly* means exclusive control of a product or service.

Dominion means power or control.

Ingredients means contents.

of trade," an illegal monopoly. The company, an octopus with 85 corporate arms, controlled four fifths of every kind of tobacco manufacturing except cigars. Almost the whole industry was "under absolute dominion of the supreme central authority." The company controlled everything "directly or indirectly connected with the manufacture and sale of tobacco products, including the ingredients, the packages, the bags, and boxes. . . ." Moreover, many smaller firms had been forced to join in unfair practices or downright threats.

The chief witness for the defense was Buck Duke himself. He denied that he had done anything to lessen competition. He had kept his ownership of many firms secret, he said. This was only because the former owners, staying on as managers, asked him to. He had never personally threatened a competitor who refused to sell out. However, he couldn't be accountable for what "anybody else said about it. . . ." The decline of leaf prices was caused by the law of supply and demand. Nobody was forced to raise or sell tobacco. He was strangely unaware of dummy companies set up by the Trust to ruin competitors. He knew nothing of corporate spies, secret accounts, and so on.

The case dragged on and on. But in May 1911, the Supreme Court issued its decision. The Trust, it said, had been "from the beginning" an effort "to acquire dominion and

The Duke firm made wide use of pictures of pretty girls to sell its brands and interest the public in cigarettes.

Buck Duke (right) and his brother, B. N. Duke, enjoyed the boardwalk at Atlantic City, New Jersey, about 1920.

control of the tobacco trade . . . by methods devised . . . to monopolize the trade by driving competition out of business. . . ." This, the court said, "was ruthlessly carried out upon the assumption that to work upon the fears or play upon the cupidity of competitors would make success possible." The American Tobacco Company must be dissolved in such a way that free trade would return to the tobacco business.

Cupidity means greed.

The plan of dissolution and reorganization was the work of Buck Duke himself. He was the only man who really understood the inner workings of the Trust. The company was split into four main organizations. These were the American Tobacco, Liggett and Myers, P. Lorillard, and R. J. Reynolds. None was to have as much as 38 percent of the total business. When the news broke that Duke himself was the author of the scheme, the *News and Observer* insisted that it was a case of a hand dividing itself into fingers. A monopoly had been converted into an oligopoly. It did not seem that Duke and his associates had lost any power by the new arrangement. Experience was to show, however, that competition among these four companies was to be intense. Even so, all four companies were to make unimaginable profits in the years ahead. The trust-busting administration of Teddy Roosevelt left office while the case was pending. The new Taft administration chose not to prosecute Duke on criminal charges.

An *oligopoly* is the market condition that exists when there are few sellers of a product.

In his late years, Buck Duke devoted much of his energy, time, and money to philanthropic and other purposes. In 1904, he organized the Southern (later Duke) Power Company. It was destined to become the largest electric utility company in

Philanthropic means charitable.

309

An *endowment* is the permanent funds or source of income of an institution.

North Carolina. He also took a keen interest in Trinity College, a little Methodist school. In 1892, it was moved from Randolph County to Durham under the sponsorship of Washington Duke and industrialist Julian S. Carr. In 1924, Buck Duke created the Duke Endowment of forty million dollars. It was to give aid to hospitals, orphanages, and educational institutions. At his death in the following year, the endowment had more than doubled. A large part of the fund was assigned to Trinity College, which changed its name to Duke University. Davidson, Furman, and Johnson C. Smith University for blacks were others who received income from the Duke endowment. It was the most generous endowment ever made in the South for any purpose.

A *tycoon* is a businessperson of great wealth and power.

Buck Duke's individualism, along with his talent and hard work, made him one of the great industrial tycoons of American history. But his success was achieved by ruthless means. This champion of free enterprise became one of the chief threats to its existence. For a time, America and North Carolina encouraged his tactics. But the day came when those tactics threatened capitalism itself. Many rivals, less talented or less fortunate, had been cruelly trampled in Buck Duke's frantic scramble to the top.

Did Duke's success justify his means? Did his good deeds pay society for his misdeeds? These questions are more nearly ethical and moral ones than historical. The age of the robber barons brought much ruthless enterprise to America. It made possible the Ford and Rockefeller Foundations, the Carnegie and Duke Endowments, and a host of private philanthropies and gifts to the American public. It also helped develop America into a corporate and industrial giant. It would lead the world before the twentieth century had reached midpoint. It is possible that America would not have reached this position without the work of the robber barons. But the moral question still remains.

Chapter Checkup

PEOPLE

James B. Duke
Washington Duke
Edward Featherstone Small
John Green

Leonidas L. Polk
John Nichols
Josephus Daniels

PLACES

Durham   Asheville
High Point   Randolph County

FACT

In what ways did Buck Duke help his father in the Durham tobacco business?
How did Edward F. Small aid the growth of the firm?
How did Buck Duke become so successful in New York?
What were North Carolina's main industries of the Civil War period?
How did the textile industry become a major one in North Carolina?

INTERPRETATION

How do the sales techniques of the Duke firm reflect the changing moral values and interests of the American people in the late 19th century?
In what ways did the Civil War actually serve to help North Carolina industry?
Do you feel that Buck Duke's philanthropy justified his illegal or unethical methods?
Did North Carolina's (and America's) belief in individualism help Buck Duke attain his millions? Explain.

VOCABULARY

Incentives   Beneficiaries   Endowment
Agrarian   Oligopoly   Tycoon
Prestige

ACTIVITY

Hold a debate in class on the ethical questions involved in the Duke story.

SUGGESTED READING

Durden, Robert F. "The Origins of the Duke Endowment and the Launching of Duke University," *N.C. Historical Review* (Spring, 1975), pages 130–146. A scholarly review based on the Duke Family papers.
Jenkins, John W. *James B. Duke, Master Builder.* New York: George H. Doran Co., 1927. An admiring biography of Buck Duke.

1888 Bill to regulate
railroads defeated

1888 Grover Cleveland
reelected President *(Nov.)*

1898 Spanish-American War
begins *(Apr. 20)*

1890 Farmers' Alliance wins
seats in General Assembly

1892 Populists active
in elections

1894 Fusion of Republicans
and Populists

1895 Fusion legislature
begins reforms

1898 Democrats exclude blacks
from party activity
- George H. White reelected
to Congress
- Wilmington race riot *(Nov. 10)*

1900 White defeated by Claude
Kitchin

1900 Boxer revolt
in China

1901 White's farewell speech
in Congress *(Jan.)*

17

THE "RED SHIRT" CAMPAIGN

The Election of 1898

There were less than three weeks left before the 1898 election. The Wilson *Advance* tried to simplify the issue for any who were still confused:

> The only issue before the people of this State [declared the editor] . . . is the question as to how we shall rule ourselves. It is not a question of free trade or protection, nor yet of silver and gold, but it is of vitally more importance to you. It is the question of *Local Self Government,* of the *Supremacy of the White Race,* or its *Subjugation by Designing White Men and an Inferior Race.*

Subjugation means under the control of a master or conqueror.

A week later, the Scotland Neck *Commonwealth* made the issue even clearer: "It is a choice between white supremacy and negro rule. Which choice will you make on the eighth of November?"

313

William H. Kitchin, *political leader and former congressman*
George Henry White, *a congressman*
Charles B. Aycock, *Governor of North Carolina*
James H. Young, *a colonel in the Spanish-American War*

William W. Kitchin, *Governor of North Carolina*
Claude Kitchin, *majority leader, House of Representatives*

But it was a rare voter who had not made up his mind months before. As far back as July, the *Commonwealth* pointed out that the voter had, in the first place, a duty to his God: "There is one eternal law," said the editor, "made by nature itself, against the social equality of the negro and white races. . . . God has made the distinction. . . ." In the second place, added the *Advance,* there was a duty to one's country: "It is the question for which our fathers fought England in 1776 and for which we will now fight the world if necessary." In addition, as a speaker at Wilson put it, there was the duty

This political cartoon sought to discredit a white candidate by linking him with Congressman White.

George H. White, a black leader, was the last of his race to serve in Congress in the Reconstruction era.

Oblivion means total disappearance.

Unmolested means not attacked.

that every man must feel toward his mother, wife, sisters, and daughters. If these were not sufficient reasons, there were plenty of others.

There was, for example, the issue of good government versus bad government. It was not claimed, "even by his white leaders," said a Populist candidate for governor, "that the negro is capable of administering a government." Yet, there were counties where blacks served as postal officials, school committeemembers, town commissioners, even police and deputy sheriffs. As a result, "Business has been paralyzed and property rendered less valuable. The . . . law has been disregarded and lawlessness encouraged." White people had ruled the earth for six thousand years, said a speaker at Tarboro. Were "Edgecomb County and North Carolina to be the first to show the world that they could not govern?"

Rumors spread about blacks and whites buying rifles and other weapons. Leading people in all three parties advised nonviolence. The *Commonwealth* condemned the lynching of black Joe Williams at Scotland Neck in July, calling it unnecessary. A Wilson editor was critical of nightriders who put a bomb in the yard of black leader George Bryant in October. Bryant and his cohorts, after all, had been "stopped in their mad careers and they will be buried," said the paper, "in silent, eloquent oblivion, as cesspools of demagoguery, at the sight of which good men will hold their noses. . . ." White people, said a Wilson speaker, "have contemplated no violence" and "it is not our purpose to do the negro any harm."

In fact, white Democrats often went to great lengths to prevent violence. Black leader John C. Dancy arrived at Wilson for a speech on November 2. He was visited by "a committee of the very best Democrats" in town. They "politely informed him," said the *Advance,* "that he must not speak, and if he did they would not be responsible." Dancy, in "a very quiet way, . . . told the gentlemen he would not speak if they said so." The committee made a similar appeal to a Mr. Butler. He was scheduled to speak on the following Saturday. Wilson, then, was able to avoid not only violence, but anti-Democratic speeches as well.

The Scotland Neck *Commonwealth* dealt with the "White Men's Club" in that town. Having learned that a white was to speak to blacks there on October 22, the club voted against it. The "colored people," said the members, "might speak among themselves unmolested, but no white man should come here, and incense the negroes by stirring them up. . . ." Club members lined up at the depot to meet the train on the morning of the scheduled talk. They announced "that if any white man got off the train to speak to the negroes he must get back and go on." The speaker reached town later in the day by carriage. He was greeted by the club, told to leave, and promptly did so. The matter had been resolved without resort to violence.

One of the more important white leaders in the Second District was William H. Kitchin of Scotland Neck. He was known as Cap'n Buck. He had one son in Congress and another about to be elected. Kitchin, a former congressman himself, was a district kingpin. At a rugged six-feet-four, he was sometimes called "the Halifax giant." He had a speaking style as impressive as his physique. He claimed to be the author of the so-called "color line" in North Carolina. Because of this, the Democratic party had become almost entirely the party of the whites.

In later years, Kitchin was remembered by Josephus Daniels as a fire-eater. "When nobody else could . . . stir the people," Daniels recalled, "he could bring them to white heat, and the burden of his speech, from the early seventies until his death, was white supremacy." He felt "that a white man in Eastern North Carolina who wasn't a Democrat was a traitor to his race. . . ." On some subjects, Cap'n Buck was a wise and progressive man. But on the race issue, he was a vulgar rabble-rouser. Long after the 1898 campaign, many still remembered a vicious speech made at Ahoskie in October. In this speech, Kitchin "pointed to some negroes present and said: 'Negroes, God Almighty has ordained you for a purpose (hewers of wood and drawers of water).' " He continued by making insulting remarks about their physical appearance. He concluded his attack by claiming that God would never have given straight hair and long noses to whites unless He wanted them to be "rulers of the universe."

Another thing Josephus Daniels remembered was Cap'n Buck's belief that "suppression of the vote of the Negroes was doing the Lord's own business and that means should not be inquired into too carefully." In October, B. B. Steptoe, a black leader in Halifax County, went to Raleigh. He got a justice of the State Supreme Court to make out a warrant against Kitchin, his son Claude, and other white men. The warrant alleged that these men had come to Steptoe's home in the night. They came with guns, broke in, and forced him to resign as voter registrar of Halifax County. When Cap'n Buck learned of the warrant, he stormed down to Raleigh and denied the whole thing. It was only Steptoe's word against Kitchin's and others named in the warrant. So the justice dismissed the case. The Democrats did not seem very curious to find out just what made Steptoe resign.

A **kingpin** is a person of high authority or importance.

Physique means bodily structure.

Ordained means enacted.

Hewers are cutters.

A **warrant** is an order for a search or an arrest.

This political cartoon shows Claude Kitchin promising that he will "bring home the bacon."

Riled means upset.

A **bugaboo** is an imaginary or groundless worry.

Tenor means meaning or intention.

Black journalists added a fair share to the tensions of the final weeks before the election. They created an uproar among whites in the eastern counties. But ways could always be found to deal with county registrars and small-time black journalists. However, the defenders of white supremacy in the Second District could not seem to find a way to handle their black congressman, George H. White. The man was a political magician. Not even "the Halifax giant" was big enough to scare him.

In 1898, George Henry White was the last black man left in the Congress of the United States. A native of Rosindale, in Bladen County, he graduated from Howard University and later obtained a law license. He served in both houses of the North Carolina legislature. He served also as state solicitor for the Second District. In 1896, he won election to Congress. Now, after almost 20 years in politics, he knew how to avoid the traps laid for him by his enemies without giving up his basic principles.

White had the irritating habit of dealing only in the flat truth and refusing to be riled by anything. One time, reporters in Washington asked him about the threat of black domination in North Carolina. It was a chance to make a bitter attack on his opponents. What he said was this:

The cry of negro domination is a bugaboo. There has never been negro domination in any county in the State. I have just attended a Republican convention in a county where negroes outnumber the whites two to one. There are thirteen county offices. Of this number the negro is given three insignificant offices. He freely gives up all others. This was done, too, by a county convention in which there were only two white men as delegates.

The Goldsboro *Argus* sent a reporter to cover White's speech in that town on September 22. The reporter described the speech as "moderate in tenor" and "respectable and decent in tone; every word of it could be given in type without reservation." A few days earlier, the Tarboro *Southerner,* as racist as any paper in the district, had said: "In White we recognize a man far above the average of his race and by long odds superior to the whites who took part in the [Edgecombe County] convention." The quest for political ammunition led Democrats to check White's every public statement, but it was useless. A man who talked only facts and kept calm at the height of the frenzy was of little interest to the newspapers.

They finally nailed him. On October 14, the *Southerner* reported how White went to a circus in Tarboro with some

This political cartoon attempts to show what will happen if a certain amendment on voting is adopted.

Evicted means thrown out.

black women and children. He took seats in the area reserved for whites. "He was asked," said the paper, "to move, but refused. A policeman was . . . asked to have him put out, but he still refused." They sent for a squad of police. This time they evicted White from the tent. The Scotland Neck editor recalled an incident the previous fall. White had taken some blacks into a Tarboro railroad station. They sat down in the area marked for white people. Their presence had alarmed several white ladies to the point that they "exposed themselves to the weather." But it was left to the Goldsboro *Argus* to spell out the moral:

> No one knows better than he [White] that the privilege he undertook to forcibly exercise is not permitted in the South, and arrangements are made—equal accommodations provided—for his race, accordingly.
> It is but an illustration of the living truth, that the negro not only aspires to a contact with the white race that destroys all distinctions. . . . When an educated negro, a graduate of a college of some standing, one who has attained a position of importance, must be forced by a policeman to keep within the bounds set for his race . . . , what may we not expect from the ignorant and more vicious of the race?

No matter how they were warned against doing so, blacks would turn out and vote for Congressman White. When the vote was counted after the voting on November 8, White had swept the district again. He outpolled the Democratic and Populist candidates combined. The Democrats carried most of the Second District and the state. But White's victory prevented the new regime from enjoying absolute control. Was there any way they could defeat the man?

A promising suggestion had been made earlier in the fall. The Wilmington *Messenger* unwisely called it "the most stupid lie of the campaign." It was a proposal that the black people be disqualified as a race from voting. The *Messenger* pointed out quite correctly that the state had "no power under heaven to abridge the political rights and to deprive of the privilege of voting the negroes any more than the whites." The voting franchise was guaranteed by the Constitution of the United States. But, now that the Democrats had won so handsomely, the idea didn't seem so stupid any more. Was it actually possible to disfranchise a whole race of citizens?

Abridged means reduced, shortened.

To **disfranchise** is to disqualify from voting.

The Farmers' Revolt

The depressed farming community, briefly allied with mill laborers in the 1880s, went its own way after 1887. It sought to win the support of the Democratic party. The ends the Farm-

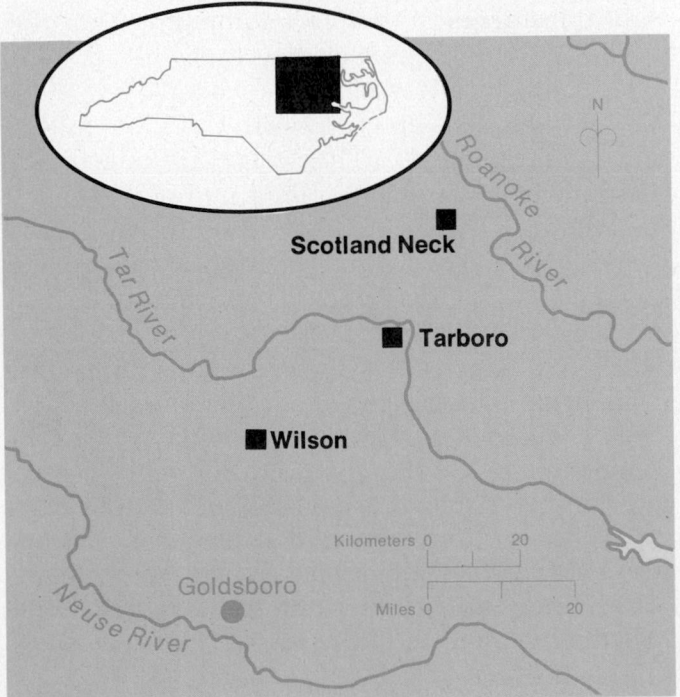

Wilson-Scotland Neck, 1890

Roanoke River

Tar River

Scotland Neck

Tarboro

Wilson

Kilometers 0   20

Miles 0   20

Goldsboro

Neuse River

ers' Alliance sought were often expensive ones. They included better education, the return of self-government to the counties, more money in circulation, and higher prices. These were disliked by conservative members of the party. The Democrats, powerful as they were, could not afford to ignore the Alliance, to which so many voters belonged. In 1888, the party gave its approval for a commission to regulate railroads (and maybe hold down railroad rates). But the bill to create it was defeated by the legislature. The result was a revolt by farmers against Democratic leadership.

In 1890, the Farmers' Alliance went political. It backed many farmers as candidates to the General Assembly. To the surprise of Democratic leaders, many of these won. The legislature of 1891 became a "farmers' legislature" which spent money freely. Conservatives argued and criticized. However, the Assembly established a women's college for whites, an agricultural and normal school for blacks, and gave more funds to the university and public colleges. It increased taxes for public schools and created a railroad commission.

It was a fine display of independence by the farmers, but it failed in its main purpose. Agricultural prices kept going down, money remained scarce, and credit hard to obtain. There were cures the federal government might try—free coinage of silver, the provision of warehouses, and loans based on the amount of crops stored in them. But there was little the state could do. Since Republicans also opposed the main ideas of the Alliance, farm leaders proposed the formation of a third party. Leonidas Polk liked the suggestion, and with the more radical members of the farm community, left the Democratic party. The new Populist party thus split the Alliance, a setback from which it was not to recover.

The Populists entered North Carolina politics in the election campaign of 1892. They called for reform of the tax laws, economy in government, a limit on interest charges, and election reform. The Democrats struck back by nominating for governor Elias Carr, a former head of the Alliance but a conservative. What defeated the Populists, however, was the death of Polk, together with attacks for disloyalty to the Democrats. Political analysts saw hope for the future as far as challenging the strength of the Democrats. The votes cast by Populists and Republicans together exceeded those cast for Democrats. If the Populist and Republican parties could get together, the Democrats could soon be out of office.

What the Populists and Republicans found in common was hate for the Democrats. Spurred by a financial panic in 1893, the Populists joined the Republicans in 1894. This was called a fusion of the two parties. They agreed to support the

The Fusion party was formed by Republicans and Populists to beat the Democrats.

These early twentieth century photographs show washday (top left), home life (top right), spring plowing (lower left), and a mountaineer's cabin (lower right) in the North Carolina mountains, among the last areas of the United States to be changed by modern ways.

same candidates. They agreed to unite in calling for election reform, restoration of county self-government, and other measures. Carr still had two years to serve as governor. But the Fusion ticket won in nearly all the state and congressional races. The quarter-century stranglehold of the Democrats was broken at last.

In 1895, the Fusion legislature was bent on reform and to a large extent, accomplished it. Perhaps the major reform was the return of local self-government to the counties. This was the first time since the Democrats had seized state control of counties in 1868. The voters could now elect their county commissioners and justices of the peace. Candidates would have

Old people preserved songs, crafts, and folk stories of an age gone by. Their knowledge inspired the "Foxfire" project of preserving early ways and legends.

Aldermen are members of municipal legislative bodies.

to give itemized accounts of campaign expenses. Local election officials would be appointed equally from each political party. A new election law encouraged more registration and political activity by blacks. County self-government meant that black candidates were sometimes elected to office. When the General Assembly also voted a resolution in honor of Frederick Douglass, the great black journalist-orator who had recently died, Democrats groaned in dismay.

In addition to local self-government, there were other important reforms in 1895. More money was made available to the university and state-supported colleges as well as public schools. But the Populists and Republicans did not cooperate well as partners in government. They disagreed over the number of appointive offices to be given to each party. They quarrelled over legislative proposals. In the 1896 election campaign, they agreed on candidates for the state and national legislatures. But they supported different candidates for president, governor, lieutenant governor, and state auditor. Populists joined with Democrats to back William Jennings Bryan for president against William McKinley. The Republicans, with strong black support, did even better in 1896 than in 1894. But the Populists lost ground. It appeared that the days of the Populist party in North Carolina were numbered.

Hoping for better days to come, the Populists tried to cooperate with the Republicans and their governor, Daniel Russell. A law of 1897 required the voters of each school district to decide whether to levy local school taxes. Legislative allotments were made to all districts deciding favorably. The office of county superintendent of schools was instituted. County government was placed under a board of elected commissioners. Further efforts were made to assure the regulation of railroads. But the old suspicion of the Fusionists for one another soon reappeared. Ill feeling was increased by growing concern over the race issue.

Despite the good done by the Fusionists in education and self-government, Democrats said that the state was falling under black domination. The basis for the charge was the election of blacks to minor offices, especially in the East. There, they represented a large part of the population. Most black officeholders were justices of 'the peace, school committeemen and aldermen. However, Governor Russell appointed a few to state agencies. Some were named as postmasters by the federal government. This slight participation by blacks in their own government was blown out of proportion by Democratic leaders. By 1898, many whites feared that their state or community was becoming black-controlled.

The Democrats kept blacks from taking part in their 1898 program. They promised to rid the state of "black domination." Led by their new state chairman, Furnifold M. Simmons, they waged a vigorous campaign. It was devoted almost entirely to the supposed black menace. They encouraged the formation of White Men's Clubs and White Government Unions in the eastern counties. They pictured their own party as that of the white man against black Populists and Republicans. The "Red Shirts" appeared in the southeastern counties. They were bands of red-shirted horsemen who spread fear through black communities. In October, Governor Russell issued a proclamation warning against violence. He asked citizens to resist those who would appeal to their prejudices. But the violence of the campaign was mostly a matter of rash statements, made by white leaders for political gain.

Populists and Republicans tried in vain to show that the notion of black domination was nonsense. The Populists, in confusion and retreat, split. Some wanted to join with the onrushing Democrats. The offer was rejected and the Democratic party won easily in the November election. Between them, Populists and Republicans elected 36 members to the General Assembly; the other 134 were Democrats. Five of the nine new congressmen were also Democrats. To eastern Democrats, it seemed to be a question of whether civilization would survive. Many of them agreed with such editors as that of the Windsor *Ledger*. He headlined his front page in huge type:

Hurrah! Praise the Lord
North Carolina is Saved
From Further Mis-Rule and Corruption by
30,000
Democratic Majority!

Raleigh people dig out from "The Great Snow of 1899" (left).
This was the first train on the Elkin and Alleghany Railway,
July 4, 1911 (right).

Two days after the election a force of six hundred whites gathered at Wilmington and ushered in the new era by wrecking and burning the printing office where Alex Manly produced his *Daily Record,* a leading black newspaper. In the rioting that followed, ten blacks were reported killed and many others fled the city, including black city officials. A number of blacks were jailed for "starting a riot" and a new white administration took over Wilmington's government.

To a strong party member, the new Democratic majority in the state legislature meant a return of "responsible" government by resuming control of county government and "rescuing" railroads from the "perils" of close regulation. The railroad commission was abolished. A new corporate commission, appointed by the governor, was created. It was to regulate banks, telegraph and telephone companies, railroads, and other large enterprises. A new Democratic election law authorized the legislature to elect a state board of elections with power to select county election boards. The latter, in turn, chose county officials. An allotment of one hundred thousand dollars was made for public schools. But the public school law of 1869 was repealed.

The key item in the new legislative agenda, however, was the qualification of voters. Following the lead of Mississippi and other Southern states, the General Assembly began considering ways of disfranchising the black voter. New laws stated that a voter must have paid the poll tax. Also, one must be able to read and write any section of the Constitution in order to qualify. The white registrars were to decide whether

A few Raleigh girls gather around an oxcart near the governor's mansion, about 1900.

the reading or writing was satisfactory. The famous "grandfather clause" was proposed for the state Constitution. It exempted from the educational qualification any person who was entitled to vote at the beginning of 1867 or who was a direct descendent of such a person. Thus, illiterate whites would be able to register but not illiterate blacks. The new amendment was put before the voters and ratified by them in August 1900. It was the finishing touch to the long reign of "Jim Crow" over North Carolina. Many whites saw the disqualification of hundreds of thousands of voters as a step toward a more democratic society.

Jim Crow means discrimination against or segregation of blacks.

In the political campaign of 1900, the Populists were no longer an organized group. They joined the Republicans in denouncing the suffrage amendment. Charles B. Aycock, former schoolteacher, was the Democratic nominee for governor. He made use of the language of racial unrest as had his colleagues in the 1898 campaign. Because some feared the disqualification of poor whites under the new amendment, Aycock made a strong call for better public education as a means of overcoming illiteracy, especially among whites. Again the "Red Shirts" turned out in large numbers as had the Ku Klux Klan in earlier times.

The Democrats won a smashing victory. Republican leaders questioned the accuracy of voting figures. These showed that even counties with black majorities had voted heavily in favor of black disfranchisement. Blacks would not cease altogether to vote under the new laws. But both parties would hereafter reflect the views of white people and ignore the blacks. The process of segregating blacks in schools, transportation facilities, and public places was now complete. The Democratic party that entered the twentieth century was not so conservative as it appeared in 1900. [The race issue had been merely a political game. It was not an indication of political thought.] But the next half-century and more would be a long time of humiliation and despair for blacks.

The race issue dominated the closing years of the nineteenth century in North Carolina. Because of this, the public paid little attention to the war into which the country was carried in 1898. North Carolina raised three regiments for the Spanish-American War. One of them was black. Blacks were anxious to show their patriotism at a time when they were under attack. They supported the war effort warmly. Governor Russell appointed a black, James H. Young, as colonel of the black regiment. This angered the *News and Observer* and other Democratic journals. The black regiment was not sent to the war zone. Its fame was mainly its role as one more scapegoat in the campaign to discredit the foes of the Democrats. A white regiment from North Carolina fought in Cuba. Smaller units of blacks saw service in the Philippines, where Captain David J. Gilmer, a Greensboro black, won particular distinction. When he left the post where he had been military commandant, Captain Gilmer made a farewell speech to the Filipinos. In it he gave this heartfelt advice: "Teach your children," he said, "to judge men according to the deeds of the individual and not by the color of his skin."

Swan Song

The **swan song** is the last work or act of a person.

On a cold January morning in 1901, the Member from North Carolina's Second District rose to speak in the House of Representatives in Washington, D.C. The congressman proceeded to remind the House of some very recent history:

Persistent means constant.

> In the catalogue of members of Congress in this House perhaps none have been more persistent in their determination to bring the black man into disrepute . . . than my colleague from North Carolina, Mr. [William W.] Kitchin. During the first session . . . , while the Constitutional amendment was pending in North Carolina, he labored long and hard to show that the white race was at all times and under all circumstances superior to the negro . . . , and the excuse for his party supporting that amendment, . . . was that an illiterate negro was unfit to participate in making the laws . . . ; but an illiterate white man living by his side, with no more . . . exalted character, no higher thoughts of civilization, nor more knowledge of the handicraft of government, had . . . , because he was white, . . . some peculiar qualification. . . .

Exalted means high.

Since the elections of 1898, the congressman said, the Democrats had taken over state and local government in North Carolina. It was necessary, therefore, he continued,

Adieu means goodbye.

> that I bid adieu to these historic walls . . . , and that [Claude] the brother of Mr. Kitchin will succeed me. . . . In the town where this young gentleman was born, at the general election last August for the adoption of the constitutional amendment, and the general election for State and county officers, Scotland Neck had a registered white vote of 395, most of whom were Democrats, and a registered colored vote of 534, virtually if not all of whom

Claude Kitchin was a congressman for over 20 years and was the Democratic floor leader from 1915 to 1919.

Taunt means tease.

were Republicans, and so voted. When the count was announced, however, there were 831 Democrats to 75 Republicans. . . .

The figures were still more surprising for Halifax. Here was a town with 539 voters, more than half of whom were registered Republicans. There had been 1,031 votes cast, only 41 of which were Republican. Similar things had gone on throughout the South.

An excuse for these violations of the federal Constitution, said the congressman, was that some black officeholders of the Reconstruction era were wicked or ignorant men. But, in the 35 years since the Civil War, he pointed out, blacks had been able to reduce their illiteracy by 45 percent. "We have written," he added,

and published 500 books. We have nearly 300 newspapers. . . . We have now in practice over 2,000 lawyers and a corresponding number of doctors. We have accumulated over $12,000,000 worth of school property and about $40,000,000 worth of church property. We have about 140,000 farms and homes, valued in the neighborhood of $750,000,000, and personal property valued at about $170,000,000.

Blacks in the South had established banks, silk and cotton mills, five medical schools, five law schools, 25 theological seminaries, two thousand churches. They owned six hundred thousand acres of land and raised over eleven million bales of cotton a year.

All this we have done [he insisted] under the most adverse circumstances. We have done it in the face of lynching, burning at the stake, with the humiliation of "Jim Crow" cars, the disfranchisement of our male citizens, slander and degradation of our women, with the factories closed against us, no negro permitted to be conductor on the railway cars, . . . no negro permitted to run as engineer on a locomotive, most of the mines closed against us. Labor unions—carpenters, painters, brick masons, machinists, hackmen, and those supplying nearly every conceivable avocation for livelihood have banded themselves together to better their condition, but, with few exceptions, the black race has been left out.

The congressman thought it a matter of "ill grace" for the white man to "tie us and then taunt us for a lack of bravery," to "use our labor for two and a half centuries and then taunt us for our poverty," to "withhold even the knowledge of how to read God's Word" and "then taunt us for our ignorance. . . ."

William W. Kitchin served as a congressman as did his father and brother. He was the Governor of North Carolina from 1909 to 1913.

William W. and Claude Kitchin were the sons of William H. (Cap'n Buck) Kitchin.

In conclusion, the Second District congressman offered some advice with regard to the future. It concerned "the so-called American negro problem." The black citizen, said the speaker, asked for

> no special favors, but simply demands that he be given the same chance for existence, for earning a livelihood, for raising himself in the scales of manhood and woman-hood that are accorded to kindred nationalities. . . .
>
> Help him to overcome his weakness, punish the crime-committing class by the courts of the land, mea-sure the standard of the race by its best material, cease to mold prejudicial and unjust public sentiment against him, and my word for it, he will learn to support . . . that political party, that institution, . . . in every community where he lives, which is destined to do the greatest good for the greatest number.
>
> This Mr. Chairman, is perhaps the negroes' tempo-rary farewell to the American Congress; but let me say, Phoenix-like he will rise up some day and come again. These parting words are in behalf of an outraged, heart-broken, bruised and bleeding, but God-fearing people, faithful, industrious, loyal people, rising people, full of potential force. . . . [Loud applause.]

Shortly after giving this speech, George Henry White left Congress. For 27 years it would remain a place from which the American black was excluded. White also left the state of North Carolina, settling in New Jersey. There, he founded an all-black community known, in his honor, as Whitesboro. He later retired to Philadelphia and died there in 1918.

Cap'n Buck Kitchin died in the same month that White made his stirring farewell speech to Congress. But the Hon. Claude Kitchin, from 1915 to 1919, was Democratic majority leader in the House of Representatives. William W. Kitchin, from 1909 to 1913, was Governor of North Carolina.

Chapter Checkup

PEOPLE

William H. Kitchin
William W. Kitchin
Daniel Russell
Charles B. Aycock

James H. Young
Claude Kitchin
George Henry White

PLACES

Wilson   Tarboro
Scotland Neck   Rosindale

FACT

How did Cap'n Buck's religious beliefs help him justify "white supremacy"?
Why did mill workers join with farmers in 1890 to form the Populist party?
Who were the Fusionists? Why did Populists and Republicans unite in 1892?
How was George H. White defeated in the 1900 election?

INTERPRETATION

In what ways do you feel that newspapers could have played a more constructive role in the election of 1898?
Compare the "Red Shirts" of the 1890s with the Ku Klux Klan of the 1870s. How were they alike? Different?
Why did the Democratic party make use of the race issue in the 1898 election? Was it effective?
How close did North Carolina come to "black domination" in the 1890s? Explain.

VOCABULARY

Insolence   Bugaboo   Discord
Warrant   Disfranchise   Fusionists

ACTIVITY

Research the 1898 election in your community and the methods used by the winners.
Compare White's 1901 speech to Congress with Booker T. Washington's "Atlanta Address." How are they alike? Different?

SUGGESTED READING

Edmonds, Helen D. *The Negro and Fusion Politics in North Carolina 1894–1901.* Chapel Hill: UNC Press, 1951. Excellent survey by a black scholar of the rise and fall of fusionist politics.
Ingle, H. Larry. "A Southern Democrat at Large: William Hodge Kitchin and the Populist Party," *N.C. Historical Review* (Spring, 1968), pages 178–194. Scholarly and critical discussion of Kitchin as representing frustrations of Southern whites.

1891 Pinchot arrives
at Biltmore

1895 Biltmore completed
● Schenck arrives at Biltmore

1898 Schenck sets up Biltmore
School of Forestry

1898 Spanish-American War
begins *(Apr. 20)*

1900 Boxer revolt in China

1901 Aycock elected governor

1903 Wright brothers flight
at Kill Devil Hill

1904 Russo-Japanese War
begins *(Feb.)*
● Theodore Roosevelt elected
President *(Nov.)*

1907 Progressive gains
in General Assembly
1908 W. W. Kitchin elected
governor
1909 Schenck fired
by Vanderbilt
● Prohibition comes to North
Carolina
1912 Walter Clark defeated
in bid for governor's office

1912 Woodrow Wilson elected
President *(Nov.)*

1914 Panama Canal opens *(Aug.)*

1916 Thomas W. Bickett
elected governor
● Pisgah Forest donated to U.S.
by Mrs. Vanderbilt

1917 United States declares
war on Germany

18

THE PRUSSIAN PRIORITY

Biltmore

The **Rhine** is a river of western Europe.

Lorraine is a part of modern France.

For Dr. Schenck, his first glimpse of the fantastic house was like being thrown backward in time and space. Instead of the French Broad River in 1895, he seemed to be standing beside the Rhine River in 1385. Instead of Buncombe County in the time of Grover Cleveland, he imagined himself in the Duchy of Lorraine in the time of Philip IV. Nothing he had heard in Germany or New York had prepared him for what he saw in rural North Carolina. The great house loomed out of the bleak valley like a mirage in the desert. It was a dream castle in a land of log huts and poor dirt farmers.

His carriage stopped at the main entrance. The doctor's eyes widened at the mismatches of style everywhere. Here, at the right of the entrance was a pink marble fountain from twelfth-century Italy. There, at the entrance, lay a pair of sixteenth-century Italian lions. But this was only advance warning for what was found in the entrance hall. Here was a mix-

Carl Schenck, *an expert in forestry and plants*
George W. Vanderbilt, *a wealthy North Carolinian*
Gifford Pinchot, *a forestry expert*

Frederick Law Olmsted, *a landscape architect*
Furnifold M. Simmons, *a U.S. senator*
Walter Clark, *chief justice, North Carolina Supreme Court*

The ***Parthenon*** is a classic temple in Athens, Greece.

Jacobean refers to the period in England when James I was king.

Francis I, king of France, met Henry VIII, king of England, on the *Field of Cloth of Gold* to reach certain state agreements.

The ***Medicis*** were a wealthy family of Italy. ***Richelieu*** was a French cardinal and statesman.

Wedgwood is fine English pottery.

A ***chateau*** is a castle or handsome residence of Europe.

The ***Eurasian Continent*** is the land mass containing both Asia and Europe.

ture of conflicting styles and periods. There were tall wooden candlesticks from a seventeenth-century French church and wall reliefs copied from the Parthenon. There were old Chinese vases, a sixteenth-century Spanish treasure chest and a set of Jacobean black oak chairs. It was all very wonderful in a weird way. But the place was more a museum than a house.

Every door and archway led Schenck into a collection of priceless artpieces. The banquet room, with its 75-foot ceiling, boasted tapestries said to have decorated the tent of Francis I on the Field of the Cloth of Gold in 1515. The chess set and table in the Print Room had belonged to Napoleon. The settee on the first level of the main staircase had once been Marie de Medici's, the robes, Cardinal Richelieu's. There were fireplaces decorated with Wedgwood, paintings by Renoir and Whistler, carvings by Durer. The shelves of the library were under a ceiling from an old Italian castle. The library contained twenty thousand choice books. Not even a chateau of France, Schenck said, could equal the furnishings of the Buncombe County palace. It was as though Genghis Khan had returned from an expedition across the Eurasian Continent and left here the treasures of a hundred looted kingdoms.

It was not, however, with powerful armies that George W. Vanderbilt had looted the Old World. It was with silver and gold. "Biltmore" was the house three miles from Asheville that would protect his sickly body from winter's chill. It had cost him millions of dollars and six years' effort. He had hired a thousand workers including masons from Scotland and Ireland. He brought stone carvers from Italy and artists and finishers from France and Switzerland. Every brick—nearly three million of them—had been made in kilns on the grounds. Every limestone block in the walls had been brought from Indiana quarries.

Biltmore, when finished in 1895, was a gleaming monster of a house. It had two hundred fifty rooms, including 40 mas-

A **dynamo** is an electric generator.

Olmsted's book is titled *A Journey in the Seaboard Slave States with Remarks on Their Economy.*

ter bedrooms, each with private baths. It had billiard rooms and lounges, a bowling alley, and galleries. It had kitchens, servants' quarters, dining rooms, a dynamo room and a boiler room. There were 60 servants to keep up the house. The grounds had 20 miles of stone roadways snaking about the estate. No one doubted then, or now, that Biltmore was the grandest house ever built in North Carolina.

To lay out the grounds Vanderbilt hired America's foremost landscape architect, Frederick Law Olmsted. It had been almost half a century since Olmsted, then a young writer, had toured North Carolina and looked very carefully into its problems and its promise. Since then he had become famous. He was the designer of Central Park in New York City, the grounds of the national capital at Washington, and other outstanding places. He was the ideal man to turn the dreary Buncombe Valley into a millionaire's paradise.

Olmsted found a site for the house where those approaching it would get the most impressive view. From there, people inside would enjoy the grandest views of the mountains. He laid out gardens and walkways and little bridges. He directed the planting of groves of azalea and rhododendron. He placed the roads along the most beautiful streams. He even planned and laid out the model community for Vanderbilt's workers and servants.

But there was still something lacking. In talks with Vanderbilt, Olmsted complained about the estate's woodlands. Within the 7,280-acre grounds were a tangle of woods, dead and dying trees, burned-out patches of forests, and old, run-

George W. Vanderbilt spent millions in building his Buncombe County palace, Biltmore, still an architectural wonder.

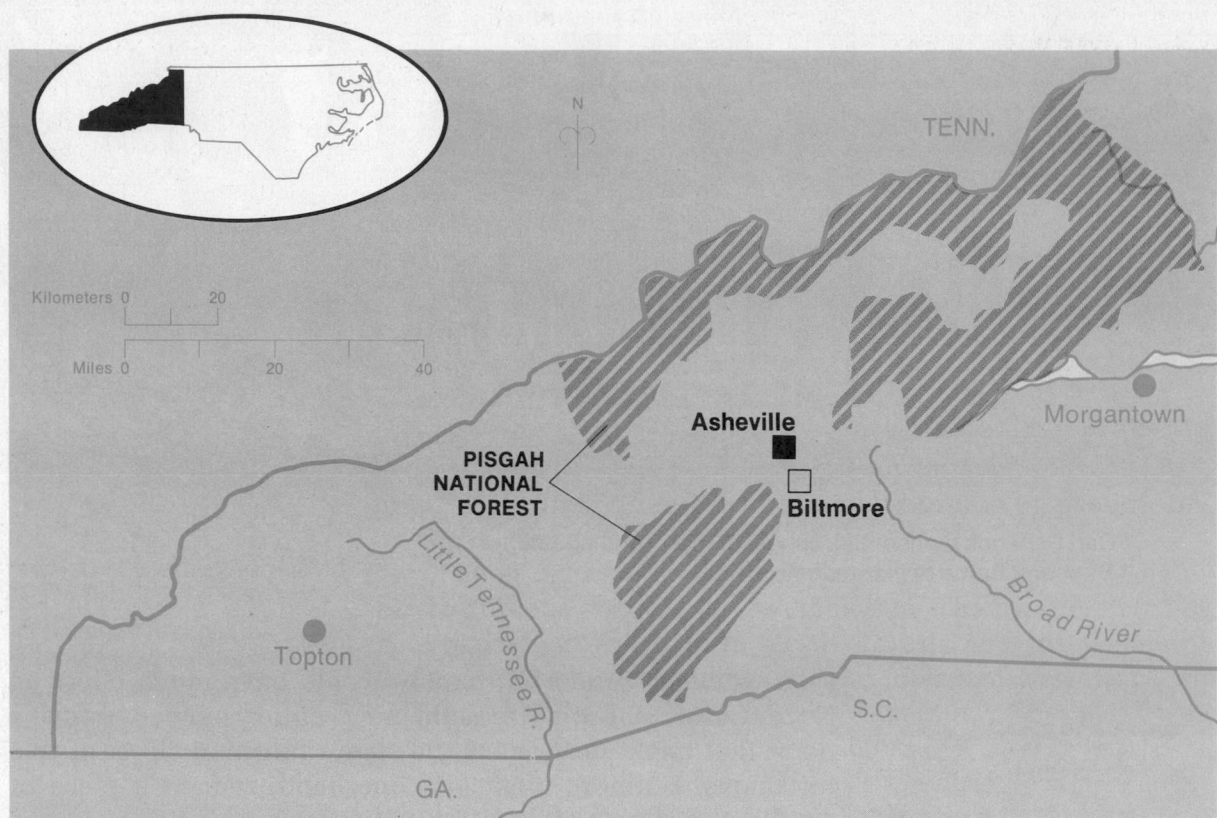

Western North Carolina, 1915

Prussia was the name of the dominant state of the German Empire, 1871–1919.

Kaiser was the title for the German emperor.

more and Pisgah Forest could mean for them. Schenck, with the views of a Prussian nobleman, was more concerned for the trees than the people.

It was two decades between Schenck's arrival at Biltmore and his departure for Germany on the eve of World War I. In that time, he had become a legend in the North Carolina mountains. He roamed the vast Pisgah Forest on horseback dressed in the uniform of the German forest service. It was complete with leather boots and spurs and a feathered Tyrolean hat. In the summers, he returned regularly to Germany to take part in exercises of the German horse artillery, in which he was an officer. Because of his dress and his large moustache, he was known among the people as "the Kaiser."

For his own part, Schenck looked on the natives as a nuisance to his work. He was annoyed that the mountaineers continued to use Pisgah Forest "for farming, pasturing, and hunting at their own pleasure," as he put it. "To my European feeling," he explained, such practices were ". . . equal to theft

Priorities are ranks in a scale of preferences.

Dr. Schenck's office.

Special-interest legislation is that which benefits or is demanded by only a small group.

and robbery." In a strict legal sense he was right. But Vanderbilt would soon need to decide on his priorities. The property could be developed with little or no thought for the people who lived nearby. Or the needs and the welfare of the people could guide its use and development. The first way was the democratic approach, the second, undemocratic. Many North Carolinians looked on with keen interest to see which path Vanderbilt would follow.

A New Century

North Carolina rid itself of nearly all black participation in government at the turn of the century. It now entered a period of one-party rule. It would be longer than the state had ever known. The line of Democratic governors began with Charles B. Aycock in 1901. It went on without a break until James Holshouser won for the Republicans in 1972. During this long period, the Democrats kept control of both houses of the state legislature and state delegations to both houses of Congress. The Republicans continued, as they usually had since 1861, to control the presidency and national government during most of the first third of the twentieth century.

Within North Carolina, the real political contests were between two wings of the Democratic party. One was conservative and the other, liberal. The former were stronger in the Piedmont and western industrial regions. The latter were stronger in the eastern agricultural country. Republicans contented themselves with federal offices such as postmasters, judges, and the like which fell to them through the power of their national party. They took little interest in state political affairs. They rarely made a serious campaign against Democratic rule. North Carolina, in short, had become a "safe" Democratic state. A candidate's victory in the Democratic primary meant election to office. For the time being, the two-party system ceased to operate effectively in North Carolina.

The state's Democratic party made a strong connection with the great corporations of the Piedmont and West. The owners of cotton mills, tobacco factories, banks, and the railroads could give the party campaign funds. The party could repay its debt in "special-interest" legislation. The railroad companies sought extensive state aid in building lines and supporting high freight rates. They were quite bold in their efforts to buy favor with Democratic leaders, through free passes and other handouts.

The path pointed out for North Carolina by the great corporations was somewhat similar to the experiences of the state before the Civil War. In the antebellum era, slave owners had dominated the state. The basis of that power—slavery—was now gone. But another was beginning to take its place. The oligarchy of the new century was based on mechanical, rather than human, slaves. Its leaders were the great factory owners instead of the great planters. Not in the plantation East, but in the industrial Piedmont, lay the main sources of its strength.

North Carolinians had been slow to detect the movement of their state into a new oligarchy. At first, public attention was drawn toward the benefits of the industrial age. Year by year, rail lines shortened the time and reduced the difficulty of transport and communication. There was also the rise of the tobacco industry and the development of banks and the textiles and furniture industries. These things profited the state in a thousand ways. Little Trinity College became an important university. This was only one of the ways in which big business was promoting cultural and economic progress.

Nevertheless, there were critics of North Carolina's new industrial order. Their criticisms were not simply aimed at

Oligarchy means rule by a privileged few.

Inventor Reginald Fessenden experimented with wireless telegraphy in Dare County, Outer Banks, in 1901-1902.

giants like Buck Duke. His very success was a threat to free enterprise. They criticized the way in which the new wealth was distributed. To these critics, it appeared unwholesome and dangerous that a democracy should allow a very small group of very wealthy people to exist among a mass of poor people. In particular, farmers and industrial workers feared the new industrial oligarchy. They questioned the ability of the state government to control it.

Perhaps the leading spokesman for corporate interests was Furnifold M. Simmons, leader of the conservative Democrats. For many years he was an outstanding member of the United States Senate. Simmons welcomed the rise of industry and big business. He wanted its help for himself and his party. Speaking of his role in gaining friends for his party in 1899, Simmons made this frank confession: "I promised the various denominational colleges, which were then rather hostile to state institutions, that I would not increase the appropriations for the latter during the session of 1899. . . . I also promised the large corporations that their taxes would not be increased . . ." It did not seem to occur to him that this bartering of public education and sound tax measures, in return for votes and money, was a blow at democratic government. Many others, however, shared his view of political power.

The victory of Simmons and his party at the end of the nineteenth century brought to power an all-white administration. It owed political debts to big business. Charles B. Aycock, the new governor, was a generally conservative leader—except in the area of public education, where he gained much for whites. But it soon became clear that the Democratic party now included an outspoken group of progressive and liberal leaders. They wanted reform in many areas of life. The most notable of these liberal Democrats was Walter Clark. He was the chief justice of the state Supreme Court from 1902 until his death 22 years later. A born fighter, he had been a Confederate lieutenant colonel at age 17. He was the youngest person in the Civil War to hold so high a rank. He was a practicing attorney before he was old enough to vote, a Superior Court judge in his 30s and an Associate Supreme Court Justice at 43.

The keynote of Walter Clark's liberalism was his view that "The public welfare is the supreme law." It meant that the law should be made by the people and not by the courts. Most lawyers and judges looked for answers to legal questions in the decisions of judges who had ruled before. Those earlier judges had been guided by still earlier ones. The result was that the courts and legal profession tended to be tradition-bound in outlook.

Big business found this legal system to their liking. The laws governing commerce had grown out of an age of small and local businesses. But giant corporations had developed in ways in which there was little control of their practices. Heartless competitive gouging and throat-cutting was tolerated. It was a mistaken idea that the good health of free enterprise demanded such actions. A legal system rooted in the economic conditions of the eighteenth century was not prepared to handle the corporate giants of modern capitalism.

Clark felt the main problem in the early days of democratic government in the United States was the establishment of political liberty. Now this goal was attained. However, the problem for his own time was to establish "socialized democracy." Means must be found, he declared, so that, "by the operation of just and wiser laws enacted by the people, a more just and equal distribution of wealth will follow and the enjoyment of material well-being will be more generally diffused among the masses." Even before the old century ended, this view brought Clark into legal battles with big business, particularly the railroads.

It followed from Clark's view of "socialized democracy" that the law ought to protect underprivileged and minority groups. He became a champion of the rights of women. He denounced laws that treated women in the same class with idiots and convicts. According to the principles of the common (court-made) law, a woman could not, he pointed out, own property or make a contract. A husband in North Carolina could sell all his property without his wife's consent. He could punish her with a switch—provided it was not larger than his thumb in thickness. Such laws did not come from legislative bodies of the peoples' representatives. They came from judge-made law handed down from generation to generation in the courts. The solution was for the people to get angry. Then they might make lawmakers enact legislation that was better related to modern life. They would overturn judge-made law. Clark also stressed the need for child labor laws. He denounced laws restricting the rights of racial and religious minorities.

Beginning about 1907, progressives began showing signs of strength. The progressive surge was seen by an act of the 1907 General Assembly. It reduced the rates that railroads could charge passengers. Later, conservative and liberal Democrats joined in an assault on the liquor trade in North Carolina. This resulted in the adoption of statewide prohibition of alcoholic beverages in 1909. Progressives rejoiced in 1908. William W. Kitchin, a mildly liberal candidate for governor, de-

"Get a horse!" was the usual remark to people in such a situation. This was a North Carolina road in 1920.

Interests means special groups seeking their own benefit.

An **omen** is a sign of some future event.

feated his conservative Democratic and Republican opponents. It was this victory that set the stage for the exciting state election campaign in 1912.

Walter Clark and his liberal allies chose 1912 to try to remove Senator Simmons from office. Simmons was the leading conservative among North Carolina Democrats, a very capable politician. Simmons had built a political organization so effective that it was criticized by his opponents as a "machine." He would be difficult to keep from being reelected. But Clark was convinced the time had come when "the contest for the control of the government must be fought out between the people and the interests." Kitchin also sought the Democratic nomination over Simmons.

Clark courted farmers and laborers and supported woman suffrage. He counted on the nationwide trend of Democrats toward progressive candidates and policies to sweep him to victory. Simmons recognized the trend as well as Clark. He portrayed himself as moderately progressive and a friend of farmers and laborers. At a critical point in the campaign, Josephus Daniels declared the neutrality of the *News and Observer*. It was the state's leading liberal newspaper. Simmons won the primary and election by a wide margin. Kitchin ran ahead of Clark for the Democratic nomination. Conservative Locke Craig was elected governor, an added ill-omen for progressives.

In 1912, North Carolinians elected conservatives to state offices. But they voted for Woodrow Wilson, the progressive Democrat, for President. Wilson's victory meant positions of prominence in his administration for Josephus Daniels, as Secretary of the Navy, and other leading North Carolina Democrats. Walter Hines Page of Cary became Ambassador to England. Simmons headed the powerful Senate Finance Committee. Lee S. Overman of Salisbury headed the Senate Rules Committee and Claude Kitchin led the Democratic majority in the House of Representatives. A number of Democrats from other Southern states held important offices under Wilson. This was the first time since the Civil War that Southerners had played key roles in Washington, D.C.

The sources of the liberal-progressive defeat in North Carolina might be found in Simmons' political leadership. There was also the generosity of business leaders toward conservative candidates and North Carolina's suspicions about "socialized democracy." The tradition of self-reliant individualism was less deeply felt than in earlier generations. But it was far from gone. If "socialized democracy" meant that people would no longer need to help themselves, but would be looked after by the state, North Carolinians wanted no part of it. Walter Clark and his allies did not mean this. However, there was a lack of communication between the social democrats and the voters.

By the early twentieth century, most conservatives accepted the need for some checks on competitive practices and

"Uncle Sam" and attendants appeared on the UNC campus during a World War I bond drive (left). Girls bid farewell to a troop train (right).

some public responsibility for those who were unable to do for themselves. Much still separated advocates of the opposing viewpoints. But the difference seemed less than in former times. The day had not yet come when complaint could be made that the opposing parties offered the voter no real choice. But Republicans and Democrats shared more in common than they disagreed upon.

The modest reform urge in North Carolina between 1907 and 1912 faded. World War I virtually destroyed it. Public concern over events in Europe accounted in part for the relatively quiet state elections in 1916. At that time, Thomas W. Bickett of Franklin County became governor. The war was soon to become a far graver concern. During the two years of American involvement (1917–1918), over a hundred thousand North Carolinians served in the armed forces. These included more than twenty thousand blacks. Nearly two hundred North Carolina women served as military nurses. While some two hundred North Carolinians lost their lives in combat, more than three times that number died of disease in the war.

The most glamorous service in the war by North Carolinians was probably performed by those who joined the Lafayette Escadrille, a famous air unit in France. Among the 38 Americans in it were Kiffin Rockwell of Asheville and James R. McConnell of Carthage. Rockwell was the first American to shoot down a German airplane. He was on his way to becoming one of the "aces" of the war when he was killed over Alsace. McConnell was also killed in action.

Alsace is a province of northeastern France.

In North Carolina, the war was experienced as recruiting drives as well as campaigns by the Red Cross and others to collect clothes and other supplies for the soldiers and sailors. "Liberty Loan Drives" were held. Training bases were established in the state. The largest were Camp Greene at Charlotte, Camp Polk at Raleigh, and Fort Bragg at Fayetteville. There was ship building at Wilmington, Morehead City, and Elizabeth City. But none of the ships constructed for the Navy in North Carolina was completed in time to take part in the fighting. Factories scattered about the state produced airplane propellers, gun shells, uniforms, and wagon wheels.

One of the new ideas of the war was the use of the airplane for scouting and fighting. Less than 11 years had passed since the first successful flight by the Wright brothers at Kitty Hawk in December 1903. But the invention had already made great strides. As far back as 1872, newspapers had reported the efforts of James Henry Gatling of Hertford County to build a powered airplane. (His brother, Richard Jordan Gatling, invented the first successful machine gun—the Gatling Gun.) But

The Wright brothers experimented with a glider (left) at Kitty Hawk before testing their first powered airplane. Orville and Wilbur Wright (right) made aviation history with their first powered flight on December 17, 1903.

Students' cabin.

Encroachment is trespassing on the rights or property of another.

James Henry did not live long enough to see his dream given reality by Wilbur and Orville Wright, the talented bicycle mechanics from Ohio.

Democracy in the Forest

For all his good work in forwarding the cause of conservation, Carl Schenck had never been able to see the forest in democratic terms. He did not like the encroachments of the people on the Biltmore woods and game animals. Their poverty and their needs were known to him. But he felt that the forest should be for the profit of the estate and its owners. He had disagreed with Pinchot over this. He continued to have the same difficulty with George Vanderbilt. Vanderbilt wanted a profit, but he remained mindful of the condition of the people. The last straw for Vanderbilt came in 1909. He learned that Schenck had leased exclusive hunting and fishing rights in Pisgah Forest to the Asheville and Chicago Hunting Club for ten thousand dollars. Vanderbilt dismissed his chief forester. But Schenck was able to keep his school open for a while.

A **constitutional monarchy** is a government in which the ruler is guided by the nation's constitution.

On the eve of World War I Schenck returned to Germany. He was satisfied that he had done a great deal in America. But he was puzzled by his experiences. "What I had seen of democracy in Asheville and in North Carolina," he later wrote, "did not impress me so favorably as to cause a preference for it over . . . constitutional monarchy. . . . And I admired Kaiser Wilhelm II as a Christian monarch and as the man who had maintained world peace from 1888, when he became emperor, to 1909—twenty-one years!"

Later events at Biltmore would puzzle Dr. Schenck still more. In 1916, following the death of her husband, Mrs. Vanderbilt gave more than half of the 160,000 acres then comprising Pisgah Forest to the United States Government. The public acquired the rest, along with several nearby tracts. The Pisgah National Forest was thus created. This forest is 100 miles long by about 40 wide. It was the first to be acquired from private owners and placed under federal protection. It was closed to hunters from 1916 to 1932 so its deer herds might grow. Hunts for bear, deer, and smaller animals have been held almost every year since 1932.

The **Pink Beds** referred to here are large areas of pink rhododendron.

Public use and enjoyment of the forest have expanded in many ways. The Appalachian Trail and the Blue Ridge Parkway bring hikers, campers, and motorists into the "Pink Beds" and other areas of natural beauty. Tennis, golf, swimming, and skiing are among favorite recreational uses of the forest. Timber is regularly harvested. The headwaters of rivers and other water sources are protected from harmful uses. Little of this could have been done without public ownership.

Dr. Schenck was a familiar figure in the forest areas as he developed the Biltmore forestry program.

Dr. Schenck (standing, center) is surrounded by some of his forestry students at Biltmore.

The Vanderbilt presence in Buncombe and nearby counties was also felt in the rising standard of living of families in the vicinity of Biltmore. Mrs. Vanderbilt got the Biltmore Industries to help preserve mountain crafts. Many craft shops were started at Asheville and elsewhere. The annual Craftsman's Fair at Asheville brings together hundreds of mountain people. Here, they demonstrate skill at wood carving, pottery, wrought iron, weaving, sewing, and various other crafts, often their main source of income. Others, profiting from the example of Biltmore Farm, learned better ways to raise crops and care for farm animals. The democratic ways of the Vanderbilt estate have been of great benefit to North Carolina.

Gaudy means flashy, overly showy.

For George Vanderbilt, the mansion he built was a gaudy waste of money, however breathtaking to see. His great gift was his enlightened attitude toward woodlands. He gave Pinchot, Schenck, and graduates of the Forest School the chance to increase respect for forest resources. It was Pinchot, with the support of Theodore Roosevelt, who laid the basis for a national forest policy. This broadened the scope of what was done at Biltmore. Walter Clark, with his ideas on "socialized democracy," would have approved of what was done at Biltmore and across the nation.

Chapter Checkup

PLACES

Biltmore   Fort Bragg
Pisgah National Forest   Kitty Hawk

PEOPLE

Carl Schenck
George W. Vanderbilt
Frederick Law Olmsted
Gifford Pinchot

Furnifold M. Simmons
Walter Clark
Walter Hines Page

FACT

How did Pinchot and Schenck differ in their attitudes toward the uses of Pisgah Forest?

Why were the Republicans able to dominate national politics in this period but not those of the Southern states?

What is meant by the term "socialized democracy"?

What did Walter Clark do for the rights of women in North Carolina?

INTERPRETATION

What does the Biltmore mansion indicate about its first owner?

Explain the difference between the aristocratic and democratic views about Pisgah Forest?

Would you say that the trend of national government has been more toward or away from Clark's conception of "socialized democracy"? Explain.

To what extent did the idea of "socialized democracy" conflict with North Carolina's heritage of free enterprise? Explain.

VOCABULARY

Liberal
Progressive

Chateau
Priority

Oligarchy
Cynical

ACTIVITY

Compare Biltmore with Tryon Palace as to style, size, cost, etc. How were their first owners apparently alike? Different?

SUGGESTED READING

Brooks, A. L. *Walter Clark: Fighting Judge* (pages 129–192). Chapel Hill: UNC Press, 1944. Full-length, sympathetic biography.

Daniels, Josephus. *Tar Heel Editor* (pages 1–544). Chapel Hill: UNC Press, 1938. Interesting commentary on opening years of 20th century by an active participant.

Lancaster, Lee S. "American Forestry Started Here," *The State*, June 1974, pages 8–12, 68. Illustrated article surveys the work of Pinchot, Olmsted, and Schenck; early days of the forest school.

PART SEVEN

A Reawakening

County Courthouse
at Marshall

1915-1940

1877 Fayetteville Colored Normal School founded

1880 James A. Garfield elected President *(Nov.)*

1889 State Agricultural and Mechanical College opened

1897 Local taxes first used to finance public libraries

1898 Spanish-American War begins *(Apr. 20)*

1903 State begins to lend money for school construction

1905 *The Clansman* published

1907 Compulsory school attendance started

1912 Woodrow Wilson elected President *(Nov.)*

1917 United States declares war on Germany

1918 Armistice signed *(Nov. 11)*

1920 Poteat attacked for teaching evolution at Wake Forest

1924 Ham preaches in Elizabeth City

1925 Poole Bill defeated in the General Assembly

1924 Calvin Coolidge elected President *(Nov.)*

19

THE CURSE OF HAM

The Independent *Man*

An *evangelist* is an enthusiastic preacher of the gospel.

The Ham-Ramsey Revival had not completed its first week. But W. O. Saunders was already starting to feel foolish. Now that he was joining the crowds for the twice-daily services, he had to admit that Mordecai Ham was worth hearing. The famed Kentucky evangelist started by telling the Elizabeth City folks on Tuesday that the results of his efforts here would not last long. "One bath," he said, "won't keep a fellow clean." And one revival wouldn't rid Pasquotank County of its sins. But it should help. The revival was also going to draw a lot of visitors and business to Elizabeth City. It would send a lot of sinners to church. Before he was finished, Ham promised, folks would pay their overdue store accounts and bootleggers would pack and move away. Church collections would improve. Local young people would have a more wholesome life. Even W. O. Saunders could make no quarrel with these goals.

Bootleggers are those who make or sell illegal liquor.

351

W. O. Saunders, *editor of the Independent*
Mordecai Ham, *a revival preacher*
Herbert Peele, *editor of the Daily Advance*
William Louis Poteat, *President of Wake Forest College*

Charles B. Aycock, *"education governor" of North Carolina*
D. Scott Poole, *sponsor of the anti-evolution bill*

Citations means references or quotations.

A *boob* means a fool.

A *tabernacle* is a church designed for a large congregation.

The editorials by Saunders in the *Independent* almost expressed regret for the sharp remarks he had made about the revival before it opened. A week ago he had predicted "a red-hot, rip-snorting, sin-busting carnival of evangelism." It would last for eight weeks or "as long as the town stands for it." After that, he predicted, Ham would pick up all "the bushels of loose change" and move on. But Ham had not turned out to be just another foot-stomping pulpit cut-up. He was tastefully dressed and a pleasant-voiced speaker. He used, observed Saunders, "an astounding array of citations and quotations that only a trained memory . . . could have handled," and he seemed to make good sense.

Elizabeth City's "good Christians" breathed a sigh of relief over Saunders' attitude. They had suffered the insults of the *Independent*'s free-thinking editor for many years. They had feared he would try to spoil the revival. Only in recent days he had referred to President Coolidge as a "timid, awkward, cringing boob." There was no guessing what awful things he might say about Mr. Ham. On the third day of the revival, Herbert Peele of the rival *Daily Advance* assured the town that Ham's opponents were now "in large measure converted, subdued, or at least, silenced." The revival would be "the greatest spiritual awakening" in the history of Elizabeth City.

It could scarcely be anything less. The pastors and congregation of all the town's churches had been preparing for this event for six months. Ham had put up a pinewood tabernacle to seat four thousand. His associates had recruited a local chorus of three hundred fifty voices and a platoon of ushers. Local business people agreed to close their doors every morning during the service. Plans were laid for businessmen's prayer-sessions and downtown services in stores

The Reverend Mordecai Ham created a great stir in Elizabeth City through his revival meetings.

Roger Williams was a 17th century English clergyman, founder of Rhode Island.

A cult is a group strongly devoted to a person or principle.

Liberalism, Bolshevism, and *evolutionism* were theories of the 19th century.

Bolshevism means communism.

and banks. There would be afternoon services for teen-aged girls, early evening services for women, and even a few special sessions for blacks. There were plans to include the high schools, the civic clubs, the Boy Scouts. The tabernacle had a roomy nursery for mothers who could not leave their infants at home.

By the third week of the revival, Elizabeth City had religion the way the Pasquotank River had bullfrogs. The *Daily Advance* summed up the progess so far in these words:

> The evangelist's grip on the city is almost breathtaking. The revival is the topic of conversation wherever one goes, whether he drops in at the barber shop, stops for a magazine at the newsstand, or greets a friend at the soda fountain. The barber at his chair, the salesman behind his counter, the executive at his desk, the worker at his bench, the laborer at his task are one and all thinking and talking about religion.

The creator of Elizabeth City's 1924 miracle was one of America's most effective pulpit speakers. During the 25 years of his ministry, he was said to have added seventy-five thousand people to the rolls of churches in the places he had visited. Seventy-two cities had voted dry after hearing him talk on the evils of alcohol. He was the seventh preacher in a family line going back to Roger Williams. He had probably saved more souls than all his forebears combined. His gifts included a personal charm that captivated audiences. He had, as one person put it, "the delivery of a Gatling gun."

The message of the Reverend Ham was not hard to grasp: the end of civilization was in sight. The time was short for those who still had not made peace with God. This fate had been marked out for people by the Fall of Adam. But it was being hastened to its end by the work of the living Devil, who kept as many souls from God as possible. The agents of the Devil's business were many. It was the evangelist's duty to try to warn people to their danger and to show the means of salvation.

The main tool of the Devil, according to Ham, might be described as the cult of modernism. Under this heading were many "evil" ideas, including liberalism, Bolshevism, and evolutionism. The specific forms taken by these ideas included jazz music, dancing, sports and games, woman's suffrage, wicked books and movies, and strikes by organized labor, among others. Those who spread such evils included, in general, the believers in any of these things. They also included actor Charlie Chaplin, historian H. G. Wells, Lord Byron,

Robert Burns, Oscar Wilde, the Jews, the president of Sears, Roebuck and Company, and many more.

The Devil's "favorite catch-phrase," said Ham, is "Liberty, Equality, Fraternity." One result was all "these feminine movements today trying to throw off [the] headship of man." Another was the Bolsheviks promoting "the liquor traffic, ... sports and games in colleges and high schools, ... the dance," and so on. The Soviets, in their campaign to destroy family life in America, sought to win converts to the creed of "universal suffrage, without regard for race, color, or intelligence. ..." Moreover, Ham claimed "President Harding was poisoned by agents of this [Bolshevik] organization."

There was reason, however, to hope that people were starting to see these dangers. Their awakening, Ham suggested, "was responsible for the election of President Coolidge. It was not that the country resented seriously the attacks of Davis [Coolidge's Democratic opponent] on the Ku Klux Klan. ..." It was simply that "the mass of the people have no use for the things that the Klan is fighting. ..." Perhaps it was not too late to turn back the tide of modernism and deny the Devil much of his harvest.

W. O. Saunders' surface calm began visibly to crack in the second week of the revival. So far he had taken only a few potshots at Ham while reporting with approval many sides of the revival's work. But the long days and nights of pious rubbish began to take their toll. The *Independent*'s good humor was strained by Ham's claim that many immoral girls "had admitted their downfall began with the dance." The paper flinched when the evangelist told a black congregation that the Ku Klux was the black's best friend. He said that the Klan had never bothered "a negro born in a Christian home. ..." But it was Ham's sermon on Friday evening, October 31, that finally broke Saunders' self-possession.

Up to that evening, Ham's fire had been directed mainly at general targets or familiar evils. On this Sunday evening, however, growing warm on the topic of Chicago's vice dens, he went further than usual. He said that officials in Chicago, "sickened by the horror of it,"

> put in charge of an investigation Julius Rosenwald, president of Sears, Roebuck & Company, but he was a party to the vice ring and the investigation resulted in a white washing.

Rosenwald was one of the country's most prominent Jews. He was also one of its foremost philanthropists. Pasquo-

Fraternity means brotherhood.

The exact cause of President Harding's death is not known.

William O. Saunders, an outspoken newspaper editor, wrote heated editorials about the Ham-Ramsey revivals.

Vice means evil or immoral practices.

Blacks often had to rely on primitive surroundings in order to have religious rites. Shown here is the washing of feet.

A **normal school** is one that provides two years of instruction for people preparing to become teachers.

tank County was one of many places in the South provided with "Rosenwald Schools" for the education of blacks. The town's normal school had also enjoyed his generosity. Saunders realized at once that the charge against Rosenwald was one that might be damaging to Ham. On November 7, the *Independent* carried a banner headline reading: "Believe the Prophet Ham has Lied." It was the beginning of one of North Carolina's most spectacular verbal battles.

Unlike the charges against liquor or dancing or jazz, Ham's claims against Rosenwald were subject to proof or disproof. Saunders sent telegrams to Chicago asking for proof. By November 14, he had statements in Rosenwald's behalf. These came from the mayor of Chicago, the U.S. District Attorney there, and the presidents of the University of Chicago and Northwestern University. He heard from pastors of the city's leading Baptist and Presbyterian churches. Letters and

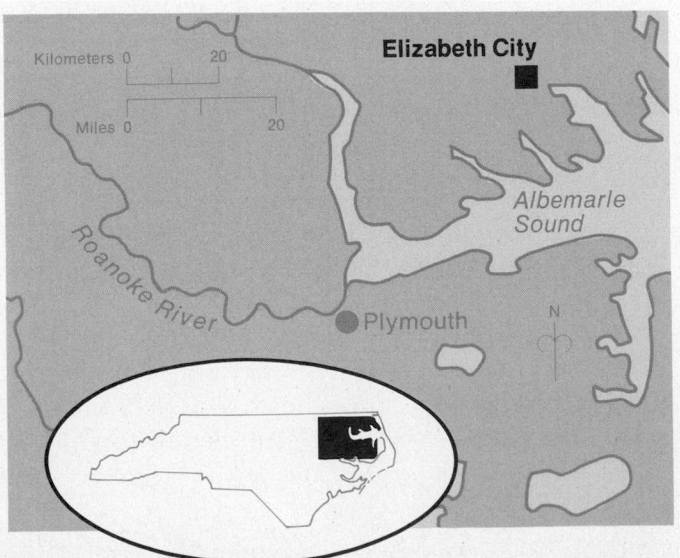

Elizabeth City Region, 1920

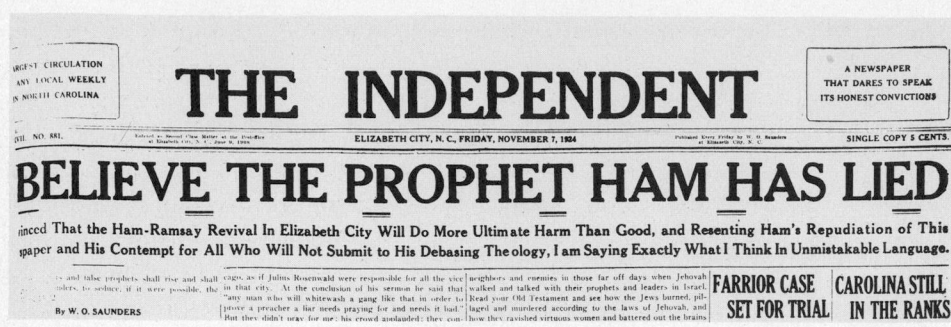

Editor Saunders accuses Ham of lying when the revivalist accused the president of Sears, Roebuck of misconduct.

telegrams poured in from North Carolina and elsewhere. The *Independent* dared Ham to back up his charges.

Ham answered Saunders by reading a clipping to his congregation. It was from Henry Ford's newspaper, the Dearborn *Independent*. It contained unproven claims against Rosenwald. There seemed to be no other foundation for Ham's statements. And all the proof remained on Saunders' (and Rosenwald's) side. But Ham's reply, according to the *Daily Advance,* was "warmly applauded by the congregation." The revival rolled on.

Ham blundered again a few nights later. He boasted of having discouraged some of his converts from their offer to kill those who criticized him. Saunders again saw the error and struck back hard:

Ultimate means last or highest.

Brazen means shameless.

> I have said that I believed Ham's theology was debasing and brutalizing and would do more ultimate harm than good. Do I need to submit more proof than Ham's own brazen boast that six or seven converts of his meetings are ready to kill some men in this town if he but says the word.
>
> What kind of religion is it that puts hate and murder into the hearts of so many men who listen to this preacher night after night? I ask you!

Ham blundered on. In a Sunday service, he showed, said the *Daily Advance,* that "every harvest of life in his meetings had been followed by a harvest of death of those who stubbornly resisted. . . ." From the "two consumptive ladies" who died just after the first meeting he ever held, Ham called the roll of many others who had met a similar fate. If he was turning the congregation into a lynch mob, he no doubt wished the deed to be done after he left town.

Nothing to Do But Fish

In this cartoon, the Devil has nothing to do but fish since the Ham-Ramsey revival "took his business away from him."

The evangelist and his party left Elizabeth City on November 23, after seven weeks. No one appears to have died during or after his visit in a way that would imply God's wrath. Otherwise, the results were hard to measure. The *Daily Advance* reported 125 persons added to the rolls of local churches. More were coming in every Sunday. It estimated conversions to Christ at two thousand or more. But it claimed that the real difference was not one of numbers. "Soul winners" were busy in the town as employers urged on their employees the importance of turning to Christ. Bootleggers and other criminals had publicly confessed their wrongs. They vowed to sin no more. Nearly every person had heard Ham at least once and about a third of them daily. Pastors and others agreed that Ham had done much good for Elizabeth City.

The *Daily Advance* had promoted the revival with every resource it had. Editor Herbert Peele had used more than one hundred fifty full-page columns to report the services. These did not count the editorials and his special issue of November 22. It was devoted entirely to the revival. His circulation increased rapidly. On August 28, he printed barely twenty-four hundred copies. On November 5, he printed three thousand. Curiously, circulation dropped in the closing weeks of the revival. It fell below twenty-four hundred by early December. The *Independent* increased from five to six thousand during the same period. Many local advertisers, however, had stopped using the columns of Saunders' paper.

Saunders claimed to have routed Ham. He published excerpts from the *Independent* in a small book called *The Book of Ham*. It sold many copies at 25 cents each. He felt sure the

North Carolina women often gathered together to can fruit, as shown in this photograph taken about 1910.

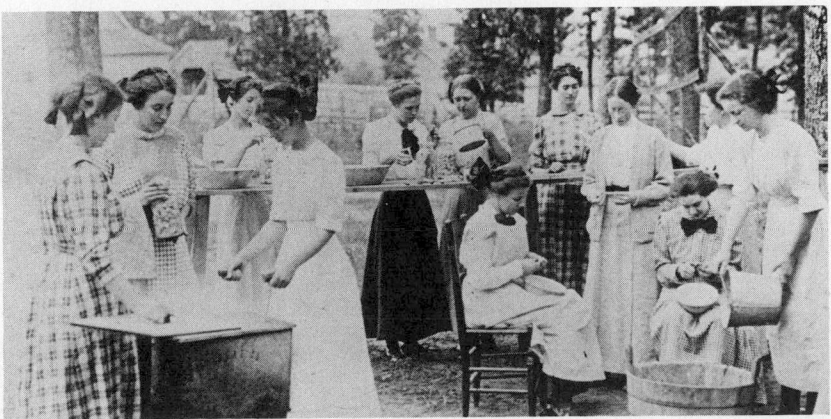

HEAR
EVANGELIST
M. F. HAM
AT THE

M. F. HAM, EVANGELIST

WM. J. RAMSAY, CHORISTER

Ham-Ramsay Tabernacle

SUNDAY SERVICES

3 P. M. Mr. Ham's Great Sermon-Lecture "THE SIGNS OF THE TIMES"

7:30 P. M. "Why I Believe There is a God; Why I Believe The Bible is His Book; Why I Believe Jesus Christ is His Son"

SERVICES EACH DAY EXCEPT MONDAY; 10 A. M. and 7:30 P. M.

This advertisement appeared in various newspapers throughout the area during the revival at Elizabeth City.

Evolutionism is the belief in the gradual development of life from lower to higher forms, especially as developed in the theories of Charles Darwin.

revival had left Elizabeth City with a feeling of hatred and ill-will. Ugly stares greeted Saunders on the streets. Old friends snubbed him. But the strong loyalty of well-wishers such as a Chapel Hill geology professor, a Goldsboro lawyer, and a Suffolk editor repaid him. If he had lost Elizabeth City, he had gained a national audience.

One of the more hotly-debated subjects between Ham and Saunders had been evolution. It was a part of Ham's teaching that the Bible was contrary to the theory of evolution. Nowhere in the Bible, he said, "do we find scripture to teach us that God by one act set certain forces at work and left them to develop themselves into what we see today." The savage cave man was a fiction of science. Men and women were created in the beginning exactly as they are today. History does not chart the forward progress of people from caves and monkeys but their decline from Eden. Human beings did not evolve from lower forms of life.

Saunders was an evolutionist and could see no conflict between Darwin and true religion. No doubt God had created life directly. But He had created man and woman indirectly. It was a result of a process He set in motion—the process of evolution. Human beings evolved slowly from lower animals. They passed through stages of primitive savagery before reaching their modern condition. Human beings were not on the way down but on the way up. Darwin had really saved religion by making it acceptable to intelligent people.

The sounds of the revival had not yet died at Elizabeth City. On December 26, 1924, the *Independent* reported that a bill was being drawn up for the next General Assembly. It would ban the teaching of evolution in North Carolina's public schools. Earlier in the year, Governor Cameron Morrison had forced the Textbook Commission to withdraw two biology books teaching evolution. Oklahoma had passed an anti-evolution bill in 1923. Other states were seriously thinking of doing so. In North Carolina, anti-evolution Baptists were pushing for the removal of Dr. William Louis Poteat from the presidency of Wake Forest College. He was a believer of Darwin. Many things combined to cause anti-evolutionists to feel that the time was right for the overthrow of Darwin. The year 1925 could determine the outcome of the struggle of the Old South against the New. Both sides braced for a showdown.

Mind Over Matter

For 25 years and more after the Civil War, the social and intellectual atmosphere of the old Confederate states stayed about the same as it had been in the antebellum era. The end of slavery did not greatly affect the status of blacks. The same classes of people still gave the Southern states their leadership. Old ways and old ideas lived on with surprising vigor. Economic changes were brought about by the war. But they were slow to change how people felt and behaved. Life went on very much as before.

In the 1880s, the rise of populism and other new forces began to have an effect on Southern society and thought. Within the next three decades, an important change took place. North Carolina was being drawn somewhat unwillingly into the mainstream of national life. It found itself adopting new ways and new beliefs. The automobile seemed a welcome thing until its effect on the social relations of young people became evident. Motion pictures seemed a welcome new form of entertainment until their use as a means of social and intellectual change were noted. There were scores of similar "Trojan Horse" benefits of the early twentieth century. They began to seem dangerous soon after they were introduced. Even the advance of North Carolina's educational system seemed to many a threat to old ways and values. Changes began to occur more rapidly. They seemed uncontrollable and, therefore, destructive.

When Charles B. Aycock became governor in 1901, he inherited perhaps the worst public school system in the nation. Policies begun by Calvin Wiley had not survived the Civil

The ***Trojan Horse*** is from Greek legend. Today it refers to a person or group seeking to attack an organization from within.

Many North Carolina women were active in the struggle to earn women the right to vote.

This is a typical 1910 schoolroom. Notice the small stove at the rear and the alarm clock on the teacher's desk.

Cornelia Spencer was a writer, an editor, and a strong supporter of education in post-Civil War North Carolina.

War and the economic suffering of the Reconstruction. The 1868 Constitution, providing free public schools for all children from six to twenty-one, had been ignored or violated. Only about one child in six was enrolled in school in the last years of the nineteenth century. And these were in racially segregated institutions. The public had been poorly led by its political and educational officers. It showed no interest in education. People had little concern about the state's backwardness. During the 1870s, North Carolina's illiteracy rate actually increased. Economic hardship was partly to blame. But the state passed up chances to change things when money was available.

A few people, friendly to education, got together at the end of the nineteenth century for a renewal of Calvin Wiley's policies. Presidents Kemp P. Battle and George T. Winston of the University of North Carolina, editor Walter Hines Page of Raleigh's *State Chronicle,* Cornelia Phillips Spencer of Chapel Hill, and Charles Duncan McIver of the State Normal and Industrial School led the movement. In 1889, McIver and Edwin A. Alderman, another president of the university, began conducting teachers' institutes in every county. This was a great boost to the morale of teachers and school officials. Rising prosperity in some sections of the state meant that poverty could no longer be an excuse for educational backwardness.

Governor Aycock stressed educational needs in his campaign for office. He proved to be as good as his word after he was elected. With James Y. Joyner, superintendent of public instruction, he opened a crusade in behalf of the schools. His first aim was to persuade thousands of citizens to vote for school taxes. He asked for the merging of school districts, better pay for teachers, and more schoolhouses. At his urging, a group of school leaders gathered and issued "A Declaration Against Illiteracy." Aycock and Joyner became members of a committee for promotion of public schools. Reconstruction-era court decisions limiting taxes that could be used for local school purposes were struck down.

Aycock's efforts succeeded. School districts responded by building almost three thousand schools in the first decade of the twentieth century. In 1903, the state began to lend money for building and improving schools. In 1907, a compulsory school attendance law was enacted. Illiteracy again began to go down. It was soon below 20 percent. Even black schools saw progress, though on a smaller scale than white schools. This was mostly through the generosity of agencies outside the state.

Agencies included the Rosenwald Foundation and other similar groups.

Public support for schools increased in the new century's second decade. The General Assembly increased taxes to al-

Domestic science (or home economics) is the art or science of homemaking.

low schools to remain open for six months a year instead of four. It strengthened attendance laws. It provided for the teaching of agriculture and domestic science. Steps were taken to examine and certify all applicants for teaching positions. The pay of school personnel continued to increase. Public education was still poor in many ways. But Aycock and his allies had begun a recovery from the disaster of the Civil War.

The state's university and colleges were also hurt by the Civil War. Most of them closed before the war ended. With few students and little money, some of those that reopened did not continue for long. Even the university was closed from 1870 to 1875. Its reopening brought little joy to the friends of higher education. It had only a small budget and a tiny student body. Private colleges, also deeply in trouble in this period, resented the spending of public money on the university. With college presidents struggling against one another, they had little energy left for a battle with hostile state legislatures.

The 1880s brought some improvement. In 1887, the campaign for the opening of a college of mechanics and farming finally ended. It resulted in the chartering of the State Agricultural and Mechanical College (later North Carolina State University). It opened two years later. As a land grant college, the funds came at first from the sale of public lands. A black teacher-training school, Fayetteville Colored Normal (now Fayetteville State University) was founded in 1877. Two more black colleges were founded in 1891. These were North Carolina Agricultural and Mechanical College (now North Carolina Agricultural and Technical University) at Greensboro, and Elizabeth City Colored Normal (now Elizabeth City State University).

The university and the colleges, both public and private, profited from the interest stirred up by Aycock and others. State money became available in larger amounts. Matching grants were made to the church-related colleges. The university greatly expanded its services to the people of the state. But the outstanding story of higher education in these years, as noted in Chapter 16, was the changing of little Trinity College—because of the Duke fortune—into Duke University. East Carolina Teacher's College (now East Carolina University) was established at Greenville in 1907. The Baptists opened Meredith (in 1899) and developed Wake Forest College. Local taxes were used to finance public libraries, beginning at Durham in 1897. The creation of the Library Commission to build new libraries and improve old ones was also important to the spread of public learning.

One result of the gains in education in North Carolina in the early twentieth century was the creation of a reading public large enough to support a few professional writers. In the last years before World War I, the important works of nonfiction by writers of the state were in the field of history. Judge Walter Clark's *Civil War Regiments,* in five volumes, appeared in 1901. At the same time his 16-volume *State Records of North Carolina* was being published. Samuel A'Court Ashe and Marshall de Lancey Haywood also produced valuable works of North Carolina history, as did Episcopal Bishop Joseph Blount Cheshire and educator Charles L. Coon. Trained scholars, including William K. Boyd of Duke, R. D. W. Connor, Stephen B. Weeks and J. G. DeRoulhac Hamilton of the University of North Carolina, shed light on the state's past.

The time was still far away when readers of history would support a magazine in North Carolina. But there were

The cakewalk (above) was very popular in the 1920s. The biological laboratory at A&M College (lower left) trained blacks for better opportunities. The North Carolina Mutual Life Insurance Company (lower right), founded in 1899, became one of America's largest black-owned businesses.

Frances Christine Fisher became a leading Southern novelist in the late 19th century. Her pen name was Christian Reid.

The Birth of a Nation (1915), the first major film epic, had its basis in the novel *The Clansman.*

Charles W. Chesnutt, a black novelist, short story writer, and teacher, lived for a time in Fayetteville.

several efforts to start magazines at the opening of the century. These included the *North Carolina Historical and Genealogical Register,* published at Edenton from 1900 to 1903. Another was the *North Carolina Booklet,* which struggled into the 1920s. There had been earlier attempts to build magazines of historical or general interest. These included the *South Atlantic* (1877–1881) and *Our Living and Our Dead* (1873–1876). But only the *North Carolina University Magazine,* because of its school backing, lasted long (1844–1920). The founding of Trinity College's *South Atlantic Quarterly* in 1902 was the first successful effort of its kind in the state.

In the field of fiction, North Carolina produced one of the world's outstanding short-story writers, William Sidney Porter from Guilford County. He was better known as O. Henry. Frances Christine Fisher (Christian Reid) of Salisbury and Charles Waddell Chesnutt, a Fayetteville black, were among the state's best novelists. None of North Carolina's writers, however, won the national recognition of Cleveland County's Thomas Dixon. Both of his first novels, *The Leopard's Spots* (1902) and *The Clansman* (1905), were best-sellers. Both were notable for deeply antiblack sentiments.

The War on the Professors

William Louis Poteat, president of Wake Forest College since 1905, was one of the best-educated persons in North Carolina. He had studied biology at leading schools in Europe and the United States. Like most educated people of his time, he accepted the theory of evolution as the best explanation of life on earth. It was not until 1920, however, that he was attacked for teaching evolution in biology classes at Wake Forest. His first critics were evangelist preachers. They claimed he taught beliefs that challenged the Bible. The dispute was reported in the *Biblical Recorder* and other papers in the spring of 1922. It was continued during the next several years by Mordecai Ham and other anti-evolutionists. James Larkin Pearson of Wilkes County, later North Carolina's poet laureate, was another of Poteat's critics.

In February 1925, D. Scott Poole, publisher of the *Hoke County Journal,* introduced a bill in the General Assembly to ban the teaching of evolution in the public schools of North Carolina. The House of Representatives referred the bill to its

At this time, D. Scott Poole was a representative in the General Assembly.

Propaganda is information spread to help or harm a cause, person, or nation.

William L. Poteat, President of Wake Forest College, was a controversial figure during the 1920s.

Education Committee. The committee announced an open hearing on the subject. It was held at the State House on February 19. Each side was given one hour to express its views. Mecklenburg Representative Julia Alexander and Concord Clergyman H. R. Pentuff were among the speakers in favor of the bill. Harry W. Chase, president of the University of North Carolina, and Zeno P. Metcalf, a science professor at State College, opposed it. The moment of decision, between the Old South, and the New, was at hand.

Some members of the General Assembly, like much of the general public, saw how hard it was to reconcile older beliefs with modern ones. Amid all the new gadgets and ideas, people tended to cling to what was familiar and comfortable instead of what was strange and challenging. It was not hard to believe that the new things of the age were somehow dangerous. World War I propaganda had played a role in shaping this view.

During the war, speeches and publications against the enemies of the United States included a strong emphasis on "Americanism." The concept was not new. But the war gave rise to the feeling that a True American was one who accepted certain views and rejected whatever was opposed to them. The True American, it was felt, believed in the truth of the Protestant religion and its holy scriptures. One believed in the superiority of the Anglo-Saxon race over the races of Africa, southern and eastern Europe, and Asia. One believed in capitalism and private enterprise and, up to a point, anyway, in the democratic form of government.

Threatening these beliefs of all True Americans, it was thought, were certain foreign (or minority) peoples and ideas. Any new practice or idea might be seen as a new way in which communists, Jews, blacks, or Roman Catholics were seeking to overthrow traditional American values. Simply put, what was old was usually regarded as good; what was new was usually regarded as bad.

Postwar speakers for this view found the main evil of the age in the theory of evolution. Here was a doctrine that seemed to go against well-known Biblical passages. It was also against the prevailing evangelical thought that human society was on its way down rather than up. People who said that humanity descended from, or was closely akin to, the ape led family opponents to attack the whole theory of Darwin.

But the focus of the anti-modernists on Darwin was a bad error. Each decade since *The Origin of Species* was published in 1859 had seen the build-up of more evidence to support Darwin's theory. Few scientists or well-informed people of

Baptisms often took place at a river or stream. The congregation gathered around as witnesses.

the 1920s had doubts about the theory of evolution. The reading public had accepted the main lines of Darwin's thought. Those against the theory might hope now and then to frighten a state legislature into passing a bill favorable to their views. But the battle for the mind of the thinking part of the public was already lost to them—whatever the law might require in the schools.

Following the presentation of both sides of the controversy on February 19, 1925, the Education Committee of the House voted a 17-to-17 tie on the Poole Bill. The tie was broken by Chairman Henry G. Connor, who opposed the bill. Later in the year at the Baptist State Convention, an effort was made to remove Dr. Poteat from the presidency of Wake Forest. The attempt was defeated. In the meantime, William Jennings Bryan labored through a long trial in the town of Dayton, Tennessee. He argued that schoolteacher John T. Scopes had corrupted children by teaching them about evolution. The outcome was a technical victory but a moral defeat for Bryan. His death followed a few days afterward. The trial symbolized the triumph of the modern over the traditional.

Though they were set back, the anti-modernists were far from finished. On a cool November evening in 1937, the Reverend Mordecai Ham thundered at a crowded congregation in rural Mecklenburg County. At the climax of his moving appeal, a trickle of people began moving forward down the sawdust aisle. They came to bow their heads in shame and relief and to accept the living Jesus into their hearts. Among those who made a "decision for Christ" that particular evening was a 16-year-old farmboy, a tall baseball player on the high school team. His name was William Franklin Graham. He was to become better known to the world in later years by his nickname, Billy. The modernists had acquired a dedicated foe.

Chapter Checkup

PEOPLE

W. O. Saunders   Edwin A. Alderman   William Louis Poteat
Mordecai Ham   William Sidney Porter Billy Graham
Herbert Peele   Thomas Dixon

PLACES

Elizabeth City   Wake Forest
Greenville   Cleveland County

FACT

What was the main theme of Ham's preaching?
How did the teachings of Ham conflict with those of evolution?
What did Charles B. Aycock accomplish for public education in North
    Carolina?

INTERPRETATION

If the theory of evolution contradicts the Bible, should it be taught in public
    schools anyway? Explain.
Which of Ham's preachings do you find still sound and valid today? Ex-
    plain.
Should editors be permitted to ridicule preachers of the Gospel? Explain.
Since Ham had such strong support in Elizabeth City and elsewhere, why
    do you suppose his ideas on evolution were not enacted into law?

VOCABULARY

Evangelist   Bolshevism
Evolutionism   Propaganda

ACTIVITY

Research the main ideas of evangelist Billy Graham and show how his
    views are similar to and different from those of Mordecai Ham.

SUGGESTED READING

Gatewood, Willard B. *Preachers, Pedagogues & Politicians: The Evolution
    Controversy in North Carolina, 1920–1927.* Chapel Hill: UNC Press,
    1966. Lively account of the matter during the period of crisis.
Linder, Suzanne Cameron. *William Louis Poteat: Prophet of Progress.*
    Chapel Hill: UNC Press, 1966. An admiring biography of Poteat.
Orr, Oliver H., Jr. *Charles Brantley Aycock.* Chapel Hill: UNC Press, 1961.
    Careful, scholarly biography of Governor Aycock.

1904 Duke Power Company founded

1904 Russo-Japanese War begins *(Feb.)*

1909 4-H clubs founded in Hertford County

1917 United States declares war on Germany

1927 Textile strike in Henderson

1929 Gastonia strike begins *(June 7)*

● Ella May Wiggins killed *(Sept. 14)*

1932 Franklin D. Roosevelt elected President *(Nov.)*

1933 Ehringhaus elected governor

1933 Prohibition repealed *(Dec.)*

1936 Franklin D. Roosevelt reelected President *(Nov.)*

1938 Fred Beal sent to prison

1939 Germany invades Poland *(Sept.)*

1942 Fred Beal paroled

20

THE HUNDRED DAYS OF ELLA MAY

Gastonia

The union had picked the night of Friday, June 7, to begin a "mass strike." It was pay night at the Loray Mill. Once the cash was in the hands of the workers, the bosses could not force them back to the looms. The secret plan called for the workers to be joined at the gate by the union people. From there, all would march to union headquarters for a mass meeting. The strike would be announced as having begun. At that point, the revolt would be a reality at last. "North Carolina," as George Pershing had said, "is the key to the South. Gaston County is the key to North Carolina. And the Loray Mill is the key to Gaston County."

The plan almost collapsed before it started. Vera Bush had just begun to explain to the crowd at the union lot how to form a picket line. An egg smashed into the wall behind her. There was a volley of eggs and rocks after that before the anti-union demonstrators could be subdued and kicked off the lot.

A *picket line* is a line of strikers to keep other workers from entering a place of work.

A *volley* is the hurling of many objects at the same time.

Subdued means overpowered.

369

Fred Beal, *a labor leader*
Chief Aderholt, *Chief of Police of Gastonia*
Ella May Wiggins, *a cotton mill worker*
Gordon A. Johnstone, *a mill production expert*

O. Max Gardner, *Governor of North Carolina*
J. C. B. Ehringhaus, *Governor of North Carolina*

It was only a little before 9 P.M.—quitting time at the mill— when the marchers finally got organized and set off for their meeting with the workers.

Union leader Fred Beal was still in his office a few minutes later. Several marchers rushed back and burst through his door. They were yelling about a fight at the railroad crossing between themselves and the police. Beal was trying to find out what happened when he glanced out the window. He saw some cars coming onto the union grounds. He watched while they stopped some distance from the union hall. Police Chief Aderholt and Officer Roach got out and walked toward the building. The police were stopped at the doorway by a union man who demanded a warrant. A scuffle started. Some shots rang out as the police and strikers began firing at one another. But the police left in a few minutes. An uneasy quiet settled over the union grounds. Striker Paul Harrison had been hit with shotgun pellets. But the gunplay had apparently caused

Attempts to assault the sheriff of Gaston County were stopped by National Guardsmen at a textile mill during a strike.

no further injury among the strikers. Some thought that one or more of the police had been hit too.

Toward midnight, a mob of about two thousand Gastonians gathered at the hospital. They had learned that Chief Aderholt and other police were shot. Anti-unionists shouted they had endured the Loray Mill strike for more than two months. It was time to put an end to the outrages of the strikers. Finally, the mob moved off in the direction of the union building and the tent city around it. When they reached the union grounds, the mob began to wreck the building and rip the tents. They chased the strikers off and destroyed their belongings. Before morning, police and deputies had arrested more than 70 strikers in connection with the shootings.

If tearing down the tent city was meant to end the fear and anger that had gripped Gastonia for ten weeks, it had failed. June 7 was but an early episode in the troubles of 1929. Next day, Chief Aderholt died of his wound. The hundred days of Ella May began.

That summer of 1929 was a time of hardship for the handful of workers who tried to keep the Loray Mill strike alive. The movement had started at the end of March. Nearly the whole work force walked off their jobs to protest the firing of some union members. The mill workers had many other complaints that went back a long time. Low pay, long hours, and poor treatment were some of the complaints. But only in recent months had the National Textile Workers Union (NTWU) come into the picture. With the NTWU leading the way, the Loray workers demanded a 40-hour, five-day week. They asked for a minimum weekly pay of 20 dollars, decent housing, and an end to the doubling-up of work loads.

The strike was only a few days old when the workers began to see that they were being drawn into a radical movement. It had not mattered at first that the NTWU was Communist-sponsored. But the speech made to them in the first week by Albert Weisbord, a Communist organizer, had changed things. "This strike," Weisbord said, "is the first shot in a battle which will be heard around the world." It would prove, he said, to be "as important in transforming the social and political life of the country as the Civil War itself." The strike seemed to be turning away from the needs of the workers toward the plans of the Communists. Within a few days, workers were flocking back to their jobs. By April 15, Loray was back in full operation.

The strike went on because several hundred refused to go back to work. A few of the strikers were Communists, but most were very poor people. They held grimly to the hope of

An *episode* is an incident.

Communist and other radical organizations pictured Gastonia citizens and mill owners persecuting the strikers.

Ella May Wiggins and a
friend are photographed
shortly before her tragic
death in 1929.

Super is short for
superintendent.

some improvement in their lives. Whatever the motives of the
Communists might be, it was true that Loray and other textile
mills paid starvation wages. They forced women and children
to work up to 12 hours a day. They took advantage of the
workers. Like hundreds of thousands across the South, Ella
May Wiggins had all she could take of the harshness of cotton
mill labor.

Much was written about Ella May that year. Now 29
years old, she had worked in textile mills since girlhood. Her
husband had run off, leaving her with five children, who survived from the nine born to her. "Four of them died with the
whooping cough," she told a reporter. "I asked the super to
put me on the day shift so's I could tend 'em, but he wouldn't.
So I had to quit my job and then there wasn't any money for
medicine, so they just died. . . . That's why I'm for the union,
so's I can do better for them."

Despite hard times, Ella May was a cheerful little woman.
With her youngest child in her arms, she would attend the
nightly meetings of the union. She composed ballads while
the others talked of demands and reforms. Before a meeting
ended, someone was sure to call on her for one of her "song
ballets," as she called them. Ella May would respond in her
clear, tuneful voice with her latest song. She understood little
of what the Communists or other speakers said, but they
talked of better days ahead for the workers. Ella May knew
she agreed with that.

The songs of Ella May helped hold the little band together when their spirits seemed to fade. When the mass arrests took place on the night of June 7, she wrote a song called "Chief Aderholt." It told of the police chief's death and ended:

> We're going to have a union all over the South,
> Where we can wear good clothen and live in a better house.
> Now we must stand together and to the boss reply,
> We'll never, no, we'll never let our leaders die.

Agitators are people who stir up others in order to strengthen a cause.

More than the speeches of the agitators, Ella May's songs voiced the needs of the mill people.

The death of Chief Aderholt on June 8 sent a shudder of fear through North Carolina. Might it be the signal for still greater acts of violence? The *Gastonia Gazette* fed this fear with its statement that the blood of the slain police chief "cries out for revenge. ... This display of gang law must not go unavenged." The union leaders were in jail, however, and others were in hiding. The tent city was wrecked. There were few targets left upon which vengeance might be taken. The city slowly returned to calm. Most of its citizens looked to the courts to deal with the accused murderers. It appeared that Fred Beal and his gang would go to the electric chair.

The trial of the 16 strikers charged with second-degree murder opened on August 26. On the morning of September 9,

Southcentral North Carolina, 1930

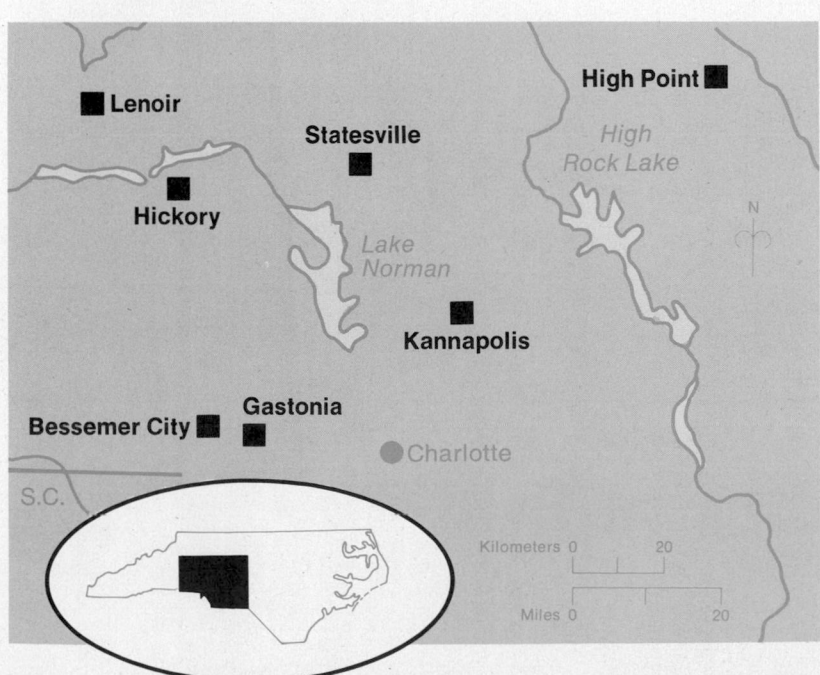

Strikers' children were seen by some as the main losers in the Gastonia labor dispute.

the prosecuting attorneys startled the courtroom. They wheeled in a life-sized wax dummy of Chief Aderholt. It was dressed in the officer's blood-stained clothing. The awful figure brought bug-eyed stares from the jurors. The judge demanded that it be removed. That night, one of the jurors had a nervous breakdown. Next day, the judge had to declare a mistrial. The case would have to be retried from the beginning.

During the summer, the Communists sent new organizers into Gaston County to replace those in jail. They set up a new tent city for the remaining strikers. Many Gastonians had grown more edgy about the renewed activity of the radicals. Now, with the mistrial of Beal and his followers, it appeared that the Communists had won a victory. The anger of the anti-unionists and anti-communists was growing. Gastonia was abruptly plunged into a ten-day reign of mob terror.

On the night the mistrial was announced, labor union headquarters was wrecked and labor leaders abused. A band of anti-unionists seized three NTWU leaders. They carried them into an adjoining county. There, they were beaten and left in a woods. The Communists called a mass meeting of workers in South Gastonia on Saturday, September 14. Mem-

These seven men were found guilty of murder in the second degree of Chief of Police Aderholt of Gastonia.

National publicity put the state of North Carolina in an unfavorable light for tolerating bad mill conditions.

A *martyr* is one who suffers or dies in behalf of a cause.

Beal had been a Communist for only a few months before coming to Gastonia in 1928. He soon gave up Marxism and returned to the United States. In 1938, he was arrested and sent to prison in North Carolina. He was paroled in 1942.

bers of Gastonia's anti-unionist "Committee of One Hundred" began to make plans for stopping the meeting.

In the afternoon of September 14, Ella May and 20 other strikers climbed on a small truck at Bessemer City, seven miles west of Gastonia. They set out for the mass meeting. Three days earlier, the *Gastonia Gazette* had stated that the Communists "have been warned to stay away. If they persist in coming, they do so at their own risk." Members of an American Legion post had been asked by the mayor to block all roads leading into South Gastonia. The truck, on reaching South Gastonia, was stopped by a roadblock. Its driver was told to return to Bessemer City. He turned around and headed back down Route 10. Ella May and the others were riding in the back. Several cars full of anti-unionists took off in pursuit.

As the truck approached the Southern Railway overpass two miles west of South Gastonia, one of the pursuing cars raced past. It braked to a stop in the road as it came around in front of the truck. The truck driver, unable to stop in time, slammed into the car. One of the workers heard a shot as the crash occurred. It was followed by Ella May's scream: "Lord a' mercy, they done shot and killed me!" She was caught by others as she fell, but Ella May was already dead.

As the trailing cars screeched to a halt, some of the workers began leaping off the truck. Others had been thrown off by the crash. Suddenly, men from the cars began shooting at the workers and chasing them across a field. Several were wounded, but police arrived to restore order. As night fell on Gaston County, the news was going out that the textile conflict had gained its first martyr.

The death of Ella May Wiggins was pictured in the Communist press and the liberal journals as a victory for greedy capitalists over hungry workers. Several citizens of Gastonia were arrested and tried for murder. But the evidence failed to prove who had fired the fatal shot. Communist leaders called for a general strike in the Gaston County area on the day of her funeral. They hoped to turn the event into a publicity stunt. But the funeral was just a quiet little Methodist affair on a muddy hillside.

In the retrial of suspects in connection with the death of Chief Aderholt, Fred Beal and three others were found guilty. They were sentenced to from 17 to 20 years in prison. Released on bond, they fled to the Soviet Union.

By late autumn 1929, order had been restored in Gastonia. The mill bosses were again in full control. The complaints

Ella May Wiggins' five orphaned children stand at her grave following the funeral.

that caused the trouble remained. By this time, however, the Wall Street stockmarket crash had begun. The textile industry faced an economic panic. The textile bosses now had less reason than ever to heed the important lesson arising from the Gastonia strike. That lesson, as a North Carolina editor put it, was that "The way to combat Communism is the simplest and the straightest—to prevent it. Communism never grows where industrial justice is done and a living wage is paid." Had the strike been a waste of lives and property? Had Ella May died in vain?

The Down and Out

North Carolina's industrial problems were the result, in part, of its farm problems. A population that had barely reached two million at the turn of the century had passed three million by 1920. As elsewhere, the state's urban population grew much faster than in rural areas. By the end of World War I, nearly a fifth of all "Tar Heels" lived in towns of twenty-five hundred or more.

The post-Civil War breakup of large farms into smaller ones continued. The number of small farms increased steadily. More and more of these were operated by tenant families who, by 1925, made up nearly half of all farm families. Most farm income came from tobacco, cotton, corn, hay, and peanuts. Tobacco replaced cotton as the state's leading cash crop. But peanuts boomed, especially after the invention of mechanical harvesters in North Carolina and Virginia in the early twentieth century.

The dramatic rise in tobacco and peanut production did not notably affect North Carolina's low farm profits. Farm leaders called again and again for the organization of farmers to promote their interests. The ill-success of the Grange, Farmers' Alliance, and similar groups did not inspire confidence in this approach. Beginning in 1905, a new effort was made. An organization known as the Farmers Union hoped to keep farmers from being used by railroad, tobacco, and other trusts. Again, however, the effort brought disappointing results. The 4-H club was founded in Hertford County in 1909. It brought improvements to the quality of rural life, as did the federally-aided vocational services of the Agricultural and Mechanical College. But the situation became worse with the coming of the Great Depression in 1929.

Tenants and small farmers fled to the cities in search of work. There they created a surplus of workers for industrial

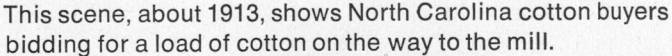

This scene, about 1913, shows North Carolina cotton buyers bidding for a load of cotton on the way to the mill.

growth. Factory owners in the South found that they could hire labor at wages far less than the national average. This was an important advantage to industries using mainly unskilled labor. In textiles, labor was the chief expense of production. The South also began getting New England textile bosses to move their factories southward. There seemed reason to hope that the growth of industry would take up the slack in North Carolina's worker surplus and restore prosperity.

But urban labor suffered from a drawback similar to that which had crippled many farmers. Farm workers who moved to the city still did not trust organization. A long tradition of individualism made the newly-arrived workers as suspicious of the American Federation of Labor (AFL) as they had been of the Grange. Without effective organization, factory hands were at the mercy of employers.

Studies had shown the results of the anti-organization feeling. One of these in 1920 showed that it took over 1,400 dollars to have a decent minimum standard of living in the Charlotte area. But the average textile worker in that year earned only 624 dollars. Average wages in the South were only about two-thirds of those for the nation as a whole. Workers in some industries, even in the South, managed to

Women and children were often hired to work in the textile mills because they could be paid less than men.

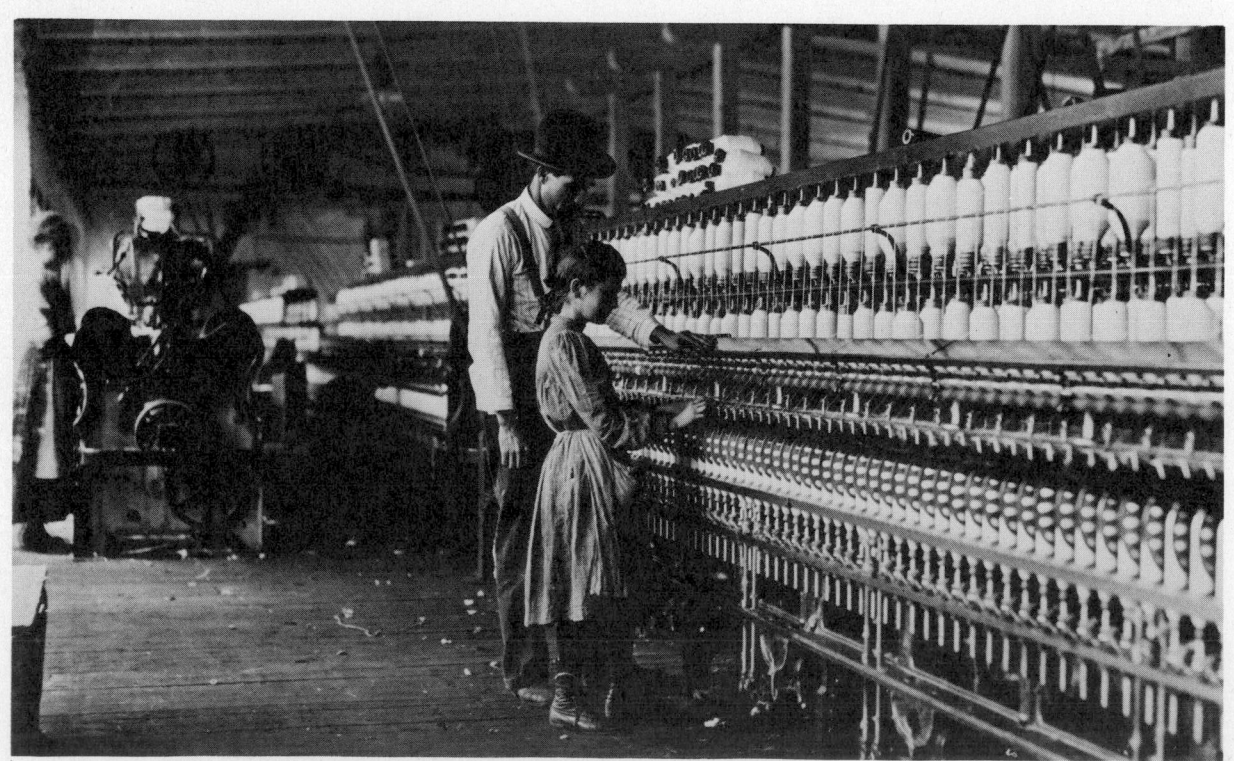

win the eight-hour day. But a working day of ten to twelve hours was far more common, especially in textiles. North Carolina forbade the employment of children under 14 in mills. But economic pressure caused laboring families to send their children into mill jobs as fast as they reached the minimum age. Women and girls made up more than a third of the South's textile workers.

Employers fought against the union movement in North Carolina. Many refused to bargain with unions. They insisted that they paid the best wages they could. But a stubborn group of workers and other advocates refused to give up. There had been a flurry of union-organized strikes in Durham, Fayetteville, and other towns as the century opened. All had failed and unionism nearly died. The federal government's Department of Labor in 1908 could find only one locality in the state with any union activity.

Although competition was intense, the profits of industry were better than owners liked to admit. The annual value of industrial goods had begun to pass that of farming as the nineteenth century closed. In the early decades of the new century, North Carolina rose to become the foremost industrial state in the Southeast. More cotton textiles, furniture, and tobacco products were produced here than in any other state in the Union. At this time, textiles were the leading product.

Denim is a heavy cloth used for jeans and work clothes.

Spurred by the growth of Duke Power Company (organized by Buck Duke in 1904), North Carolina's textile industry by 1930 was 15 times larger than in 1900. By the time of the Gastonia strike, there were almost six hundred mills in North Carolina. They employed over one hundred thousand workers. Most of the mills were small. They were scattered over a wide area of the Piedmont. But Kannapolis boasted the world's largest towel mill; Greensboro, the largest denim factory; and Winston-Salem, the biggest men's underwear factory.

Unionism in the textile industry grew from the labor shortages during World War I and the short boom that followed. The United Textile Workers claimed to have 43 local unions in the state in 1919. But a slump in business, beginning in late 1920, played havoc with both the industry and the unions. Mill owners began to cut back operations. They reduced wages by up to one half. Textile strikes in North Carolina in 1921 collapsed because the owners were under no pressure to reopen closed mills.

A tradition of personal interest on the part of owners in their workers now began to weaken. Up to the 1920s, employ-

ers prided themselves that they knew their workers' problems
and were willing to help solve them. But hard times brought
keener competition. Mill owners began to hire "efficiency experts" to find ways to reduce costs and increase production.
These experts often put the business ahead of human consid-
erations. Workers' complaints grew as the 1920s progressed.

A new wave of labor unrest in textiles was signaled by a
strike at Henderson in the summer of 1927. The discontent began to attract national headlines with an outburst of strikes
and violence at Elizabethton, Tennessee, in March 1929. The
Communist party had so far been unable to make headway
among Southern workers. Now it began to take advantage of
the unrest.

In 1929, Gastonia called itself "the combed yarn center of
America." Gaston was "the third county in America in cotton
manufacturing." Most of the town's twenty thousand people
made their living from its cotton mills. Most mill workers
lived in mill-owned communities on the outskirts of town.
They were mountain people. They had little in common with
the "up-town" people—the older families in the town itself.
The mill people attended schools and churches provided (at
least in part) by the mill owners. They kept mostly to themselves. The Loray Mill was one of the few in Gastonia owned
by a northern manufacturer. It had been purchased in 1923 by
the Manville-Jenckes Corporation of Rhode Island. Its workers lived mostly in Loray Village, a mill community on the
edge of Gastonia.

In the spring of 1929, there was agreement among many in
Gastonia that the trouble at Loray began in 1927. This was
when efficiency expert Gordon A. Johnstone was sent in to cut
costs and speed up production. Johnstone found that the tire
fabric produced by the mill was being threatened by the popularity of balloon tires. He began massive changes. He reduced the work force from 3,500 to 2,200 and made two wage
cuts. He switched the plant over to other fabrics. The change
that led to the most complaints was Johnstone's introduction
of the "stretch-out" system. This was an increase—often a
doubling—of the number of looms run by one weaver. By
these and other economies, Johnstone reduced costs by half a
million dollars in one year while increasing production. But
the morale of the employees at Loray declined sharply.

In late 1928, the Communist National Textile Workers
Union sent agents to the area. They had just begun to prepare
for a strike there when Manville-Jenckes learned of the anger
over Johnstone's measures. He was replaced with a new
supervisor, and plans were announced to correct some of

The work in the mills was hard for young boys. The hours were long and the pay was low.

Johnstone's policies. It was a welcome announcement, but it came too late to prevent trouble. Communist organizer Fred Beal found much sentiment for a strike. The Communists had not started the trouble, but they wanted to take advantage of it.

The strike brought to Gastonia an army of reporters, investigators, and trouble-makers. Most saw what they were prepared to see. The reporter for the conservative New York *World* found "a pretty little southern town" and a happy work force at the Loray Mill. He saw no child labor at Loray and found the mill workers' homes modern and comfortable. He compared Loray pay-scales favorably with those of competitors. Margaret Larkin, who covered the strike for the *Nation* magazine, a liberal publication, found none of this.

> The mill hands [said Margaret Larkin] live on cheap, bad food—"grits," field peas, beans, bread, corn meal, and "fatback"—a salt fat pork. They eat no fresh vegetables, no fruit, and very little fresh meat and milk. As a direct result of this diet, pellagra, a disease of malnutrition, rages among them. Deaths from this disease increased

fifty percent in North Carolina in the six months ending in September, 1929, according to the State Bureau of Health. It has decreased among textile workers whenever they have been able to buy the food they need.

A theme was touched upon by some of those investigating the Gastonia strike. It was the apparent willingness of mill owners to provide better for the workers if competitors would do likewise. A hard-pressed boss dared not consider granting a ten or eight-hour day unless the industry as a whole did the same. Higher wages, child-labor restrictions, good housing, and dozens of other reforms awaited similar joint action. But the textile industry, divided into thousands of small, competitive units, could form no such common policy. Close observers became convinced that the industry could not be reformed from within. It would take federal action to bring about these changes. But the conservative administration of Herbert Hoover was opposed to government "interference." Here was a dilemma to which there seemed to be no clear solution.

A *dilemma* is a difficult problem.

During the Loray strike, other strikes occurred in the South. These included the North Carolina towns of Marion, Pineville, Bessemer City, Leaksville, and Charlotte. As in Gastonia, all collapsed without attaining the ends sought by the workers. The strikers were defeated mainly by their own indi-

Members of several unions parade through the streets of Gastonia to demonstrate for better wages and conditions.

Apathy means without emotion or excitement.

vidualism, apathy, poverty, and suspicion of Northerners. Unionism, whether Communist or non-Communist, seemed only a means of expressing dissatisfaction. It did not seem a means of long-term bargaining with mill owners. As the urban-dwelling country-folk listened to radical speakers, they heard religion attacked, patriotism scorned, the equality of the races upheld. Such ideas were foreign even to city-dwellers in the South. But to rural people they were outrageous. Fred Beal had talked to the strikers in terms of their welfare. But the organizers who followed him killed the strike by talking of treason and atheism.

Atheism means disbelief in God.

The clash of new and old, of native and foreign ideas, was highlighted in studies among the clergy employed to work with the mill workers. A Methodist investigator talked with ministers in the mill villages in 1929. The investigator found them on the side of the owners against the workers. Some argued that children who worked in the mills were "better citizens and give less trouble than those who go to school." The investigator was told by the preachers that they had "a job which is to 'preach the Gospel' and to 'run a church' and they want nothing to interfere with that." It did not seem to them, the investigator concluded, that there was "any connection between the mind of Christ and low wages or night work for women or child labor."

Social gospel concerns a person's needs on earth rather than one's needs in the hereafter.

From a religious viewpoint, the issue at Gastonia was between a doctrine of personal salvation and a social gospel. Few of the clergy saw child labor and starvation wages as a concern of the church. The "Protestant Ethic" upon which the preachers had been brought up sought the salvation of the individual soul rather than the improvement of man's earthly lot. If the soul could be saved, evil could be conquered. No good could be obtained for a lost soul. The fact that some of the agitators denounced religion appeared to justify the hostility of the preachers to the strikers' movement.

The Legacy of Ella May

The Gastonia strike awakened some North Carolinians to the harsh conditions in the textile and other industries. Editors of the *Asheville Citizen, Greensboro Daily News,* and *Raleigh News and Observer* took up the cry for reform. At the University of North Carolina, history professor Frank Porter Graham drew up a petition. It was signed by more than four hundred citizens. It called for a recognition of the rights of laborers. It defended the workers' right to bargain collectively. It called for a reduction of the hours in their work day, an end to night work, and stronger child-labor laws. Governor O. Max Gardner, a textile manufacturer himself, joined in the call for better wages and shorter hours. But neither the industry nor the state could put the process in motion.

A new day for textile workers came with the election of Franklin D. Roosevelt as President in 1932. Roosevelt's National Industrial Recovery Act of June 1933 included a "code of fair practice" for the textile industry. It set minimum standards for the treatment of mill workers. Mill owners would have to hold maximum working hours to 40 hours a week. Fifty and more had prevailed in the industry. Minimum weekly wages were set at 12 dollars in the South (13 dollars elsewhere). Child labor under 16 years of age was banned. The right of the workers to join unions and bargain collectively was upheld. The legislation, as Roosevelt put it, allowed mill owners to "do by agreement that which none of them could do separately and live in competition." "I believe," said a Charleston editor about the mill owners, "that they are pleased that they have been driven to do what is sensible."

The National Industrial Recovery Act was struck down by the Supreme Court in 1935 as unconstitutional. Prodded by the Cotton Textile Institute, however, most mill owners agreed voluntarily to maintain the labor standards set by the act. Although conditions in the industry did not improve very much, the workers now had a right to band together to seek common ends. During the 1930s, the fear of unions began to disappear as a new generation of workers took over the looms from their parents. The new generation was less affected by the attitudes of the past. They were more willing to work together for their own good.

Yet, there was very little change in Gastonia. A report in late 1975 claimed that "although unions are somewhat on the rise in other parts of the South, they are growing much slower in Gaston County because of the memories of that strike." The Loray Mill, by this time under new ownership, still had no union. The question remained: had Ella May died in vain?

Faced with an economic depression, Roosevelt began his first term in 1933 with a long series of emergency acts. Among the earliest measures passed by Congress were the Civilian Conservation Corps (CCC), the Federal Emergency Relief Ad-

This cartoon attempts to show that the textile industry got a poor image through the inhumanity of some mill owners.

WHAT LABOR FACES IN THE SOUTH

ministration (FERA), and the Agricultural Adjustment Administration (AAA). All had important effects in North Carolina.

The CCC was designed to provide relief for the unemployed and to aid the conservation of natural resources. It established dozens of labor camps in North Carolina. By 1936, it had enrolled almost twenty-seven thousand members. The FERA provided both direct relief and work relief to the needy. In 1934, it gave help to an average of more than seventy-six thousand North Carolinians a month. The AAA made payments to farmers in return for limiting tobacco, cotton, wheat, and other crops as a means of soil conservation. The AAA was declared unconstitutional in 1936. But through this and other means, the federal government gave North Carolina farmers benefits totaling almost 100 million dollars.

The aid provided by Roosevelt's first "hundred days" in office came none too soon. Governor J. C. B. Ehringhaus took office in 1933. He found many farmers unable to pay either their taxes or their mortgages. Industrial wages were dropping rapidly and business was in decline. The failure of some 215 North Carolina banks added financial chaos to the dismal scene. Many county and municipal governments, unable to collect taxes, could not pay their debts. The state government itself was operating at a loss.

Ehringhaus sought economy by reorganizing and putting together state agencies (such as the State Highway and Prison Departments). He also sought other means. Pledged with the Democratic party to abolish the 15-cent *ad valorem* tax for the support of public schools, the governor made good his promise. But this made the search for new income urgent to help balance the budget. During a fight in the General Assembly over what to tax, the issue came down to a choice between a luxury tax and a general sales tax. The former would affect mainly the well-to-do. The latter would be paid by everybody. Over cries that it would be a "tax on poverty"—another blow against the poor people—the legislature adopted a sales tax of three percent. It proved to be the largest source of revenue for the state's general fund. It made balancing the budget possible. The state also took over almost total support of public schools. It extended the minimum school term from six to eight months to allow the lowering of local taxes.

An act of these same years was the repeal of Prohibition. North Carolina had adopted statewide prohibition in 1909. And the state also supported the adoption of the Eighteenth Amendment in 1919. But the victory of the "drys" over the "wets" didn't change people's minds or habits. Speaking in Raleigh, humorist Will Rogers observed that "North Carolina

Direct relief meant direct payments of cash; work relief meant payment for certain work done.

Mortgages involve the turning over of property to another as security for the repayment of a debt.

Ad valorem means goods taxed according to their value.

Poverty is the condition of having little or no property.

The Eighteenth Amendment to the Constitution (1920–1933) prohibited the manufacture, sale, or transportation of alcoholic beverages. The Volstead Act set up means to enforce the Amendment.

LABOR DEFENDER
Oct.1929   10¢

ELLA MAY—
MARTYR FOR AN ORGANIZED SOUTH

Ella May Wiggins became a martyr overnight when she died in Gaston County because of gunshot wounds.

voters would vote dry as long as they could stagger to the polls." Shortly after Franklin D. Roosevelt became President, the Eighteenth Amendment was repealed. But North Carolina held out against ending Prohibition. By 1935, however, special bills were passed to exempt individual counties from the ban on sales of alcoholic beverages. In that year, the first county-operated liquor store opened in Wilson. Today, the state liquor laws remain about the same as in 1935.

Federal and state measures reduced the hardships of the Depression and helped lay the basis for partial recovery. By 1935, the state was able to raise the salaries of teachers and other state employees. Steps were taken to restore curtailed state services. Speaking broadly, traditional attitudes toward the role of government were affected. Many North Carolinians had seen their state and national governments merely as the means of internal order and external defense. Now they saw them as a source of positive benefit. To this extent, the Roosevelt administration caused a great change in the minds of people across the state.

Chapter Checkup

PEOPLE

Fred Beal   Ella May Wiggins   O. Max Gardner
Chief Aderholt   Gordon A. Johnstone   J. C. B. Ehringhaus

PLACES

Gastonia   Statesville   Kannapolis
Reidsville   Hickory   Leaksville
High Point   Lenoir   Bessemer City

FACT

What factors in the early 1920s caused Southern mill owners to lose interest in their workers?

What factors account for the slow progress of unionism in North Carolina up to 1930?

Why were workers from rural areas harder to organize than those from urban areas?

INTERPRETATION

Which do you think helped the Communists at Gastonia more: bad conditions in the mills or the effectiveness of their organizers? Explain.

Do you think the ministers of the mill churches should have concerned themselves with the wages and conditions of mill workers? Explain.

Did competition among the textile mills help hurry or delay better conditions and pay for workers? How can you account for this?

Why do you think this chapter is called "The Hundred Days of Ella May"?

VOCABULARY

Picket line	Agitator	Efficiency
Martyr	Apathy	Prohibition

ACTIVITY

Conduct a poll of industrial workers in one or more firms near you. Find out whether their attitudes have changed since 1929. If so, in what ways? Can you discover reasons why North Carolina remains the least unionized state in the nation?

SUGGESTED READING

Cope, Robert F. and Manly Wade Wellman. *The County of Gaston: Two Centuries of a North Carolina Region.* Charlotte: Heritage Printers, Inc., 1961. A general survey of county history with an account of the strike.

Herring, Harriett. *The Passing of the Mill Village.* Chapel Hill: UNC Press, 1949. Deals with the transition of mill villages from corporate to private patterns of ownership.

Hobbs, S. H. *North Carolina, Economic and Social.* Chapel Hill: UNC Press, 1930. Good chapters on the textile and other industries.

1900 Birth of Thomas Wolfe
● Birth of Wilbur Cash

1898 Spanish-American War
begins *(Apr. 20)*

1918 Koch comes to Chapel Hill

1917 United States declares
war on Germany

1924 Stallings coauthors
What Price Glory?
1925 Boyd publishes *Drums*
1927 Green wins Pulitzer Prize
for *In Abraham's Bosom*
1928 Stringfield wins Pulitzer
Prize for ''From the Southern
Mountains''
1929 Wolfe publishes *Look
Homeward, Angel*

1932 Franklin D. Roosevelt
elected President *(Nov.)*

1933 Black Mountain College
founded
1935 Wolfe's *Of Time and the
River* published
1938 Wolfe's death
1939 Wolfe's *You Can't Go
Home Again* published
1941 Wolfe's *The Hills Beyond*
published
● Cash commits suicide

1936 Franklin D. Roosevelt
reelected President *(Nov.)*

1939 Germany invades Poland
(Sept.)
1941 Japanese attack
Pearl Harbor *(Dec.)*

21

SLEEPY JACK AND THE ASHEVILLE GIANT

The Rebels

Asheville took one look at Tom Wolfe's book and went into a sulking snit. The town had looked forward eagerly to a book about itself by a hometown boy. But *Look Homeward, Angel* laid bare Asheville's darkest secrets. It told of the genteel immorality of the old uptown families. It told of the vice dens of "Pigtail Alley" and "Niggertown." The writer had disguised names and incidents in the thinnest way. He gave old scandals new life and helped circulate new ones. Everybody snatched up the first copy they could find to see if they were in it. The most relieved were those who found they weren't.

People avoided the Wolfe family on the sidewalks. The public library refused to place any orders for the book. The reviewer for the *Asheville Times*, who had hoped for a pleasant description of the town that would help build the tourist trade, was keenly disappointed. Residents, he said, were going to be "severely annoyed," if not "shocked into chills," by Tom

Thomas Wolfe, *a novelist*   **Frederick Koch,** *a professor of drama*
Wilbur J. Cash, *a journalist*

Wolfe. "His life here," the reviewer concluded, "as he boldly sketches it, was crowded with pain, bitterness, and ugliness."

Other reviewers around the state agreed with the *Times.* It was not only Asheville that came in for a thrashing in *Look Homeward, Angel.* It was the entire South. Into Eugene Gant, a character representing Wolfe himself, the author had put a resentment caused, in the words of the novel,

Benevolent means characterized by good will.

Chivalrous means honorable and courteous.

Cavaliers are gallant gentlemen.

by the romantic halo that his school history cast over the section, by the whole fantastic distortion of that period where people were said to live in 'mansions,' and slavery was a benevolent institution, conducted to a constant banjo-strumming, . . . where all women were pure, gentle, and beautiful, all men chivalrous and brave, and the rebel hordes a company of . . . death-mocking cavaliers. Years later, . . . when their cheap mythology, their legend

The Wolfe family home in Asheville, birthplace of Thomas Wolfe, is now a State Historic Site.

This photograph shows Thomas Wolfe boarding a streetcar in Berlin, Germany.

To **writhe** is to squirm or twist about.

of the charm of their manners, the aristocratic culture of their lives, the quaint sweetness of their drawl, made him writhe—when he could no longer return to their life and its swarming superstition without weariness and horror . . . he still pretended the most fanatic devotion to them, excusing his Northern residence on grounds of necessity rather than desire.

Jonathan Daniels had known Wolfe while they were students at Chapel Hill. He was hurt by what he considered the anti-Southern tone of the book. "In *Look Homeward, Angel,*" he wrote in the *News and Observer,* "North Carolina, and the South are spat upon." The author, evidently "hurt by something he loved," had repaid his state and region "with a curse." He crowded his book with dope addicts, drunken doctors, and sick people. The novel, Daniels predicted, would "not give pleasure to the South in general and North Carolina in particular."

Addicts are people who are in the grip of a habit, such as drug-taking.

In the eyes of Daniels and many others, Tom Wolfe had gone to New York and turned traitor against his own home and heritage. In spirit, at least, he could not come home again.

Bolsheviks formed the Communist party in Russia after seizing power in the 1917 Revolution.

The awful news from Gastonia's cotton mills headlined newspapers from coast to coast in the fall of 1929. The book *Look Homeward, Angel* also appeared, critical of North Carolina and the South. The Bolsheviks and aliens could be ex-

Wilbur J. Cash's *Mind of the South* is still considered a major work for understanding that part of the country.

A *bigot* is a person who is intolerant of beliefs or opinions other than his own.

Veritable means truly, very much so.

Dubbed means named.

pected to write that way. But for a boy reared and educated right here in the Old North State, the book was seen as an act of treason. How could the state hope to overcome its critics if its own talented people joined in the mocking chorus? To make matters worse, Tom Wolfe was not the only native rebel writing for a national audience that autumn. In Boiling Springs, 50 miles southeast of Asheville, another brilliant young man was throwing scorn and accusations at his state and region. His name was "Jack" Cash.

Wilbur J. Cash, a Wake Forest graduate, was a part-time journalist. In July, he broke into the select columns of H. L. Mencken's *American Mercury*. It was the country's most exciting literary magazine. He wrote, what some people thought was a vicious attack on Senator Furnifold M. Simmons of New Bern, the "grand old man" of North Carolina politics. He belittled Simmons' 30 years of service to his state. Cash painted the senator as a racist and a religious bigot. He said the senator was sympathetic to Republicans but posed as a Democrat. The real horror, in Cash's view, was that Simmons was "the hero and veritable God of Hosts" of North Carolina Democrats. Cash dubbed him the "Jehovah of the Tar Heels."

Those who were displeased at what Cash said about the senior senator in July were to be even angrier in October. In that month's issue of the *American Mercury,* Cash wrote an article that was to have the effect of an earthquake on the way a whole generation of Americans saw the southern United States. The title of the article was "The Mind of the South."

Cash began his article by saying that people were becoming used to the term, "The New South." The modern image of the region was that of an emerging industrial empire, of railways and smokestacks, textile mills and blast furnaces. But, claimed the author, the image was little more than an illusion. The South, mentally and emotionally, was barely changed from a hundred or more years before. Its people still saw themselves in terms of cultured aristocrats and their loyal slaves. Like Thomas Wolfe in *Look Homeward, Angel,* Cash had no patience either with the so-called "New South's" vision of itself.

Warp and woof refers to the crisscrossed threads in weaving.

A *pretension* is the laying of a claim to something, usually unjustified.

The very legend of the Old South . . . is warp and woof of the Southern mind. The "plantation" which prevailed outside the tidewater and delta regions was actually no more than a farm; its owner was, properly, neither a planter nor an aristocrat, but a backwoods farmer; yet the pretension to aristocracy was universal. Every farmhouse became a Big House, every farm a baronial estate, every master of scant red acres and a few mangy blacks a

Haughty means proud, snobbish. *One-gallus* means poor, petty.

F.F.V. is the abbreviation for First Families of Virginia, the leading or oldest families of that state.

The *estuary* of a river is the place where its current meets the ocean's tides.

Fundamentalism means the belief that the Bible is entirely true and accurate in a literal sense.

Impervious means incapable of being influenced or affected.

feudal lord. The haughty pride of these one-gallus squires of the uplands was scarcely matched by that of the F.F.V.'s of the estuary of the James. Their pride and their legend, handed down to their descendants, are the basis of all social life in the South.

Cash tore into his fellow Southerners for their weaknesses. He attacked their acceptance of unreality more than reality. He criticized their narrow individualism and traditional ideals. He said they were indifferent to the fine arts. He mocked their Bible-thumping fundamentalism. These ideals were as typical in 1929 as they had been in 1829. Far from there being a New South, it was a region that was "almost impervious to change," successfully resisting the "pressure of industrialism, . . . continuing, in the main, to move through the old rhythms."

Editorial fire rained down for weeks upon the head of the young writer from Boiling Springs. Even *The New York Times* called the article superficial. The author received a letter from an old man named Cash in Nashville, Tennessee, who threw him out of the family. Some 50 columns were written against "The Mind of the South." Nearly all of them were by Southern writers. Few of the critics would have paid any attention if Mencken himself had written it. But Cash was a Southerner and, like Tom Wolfe, a traitor to his own. North Carolinians were especially embarrassed at the thought of having raised such a rebel. But two in the same year? That was a disaster never before known in the history of the state.

At first glance, two men could scarcely have been more completely different than Tom Wolfe and Jack Cash. Tom was a towering man, six feet five inches tall, who talked a blue

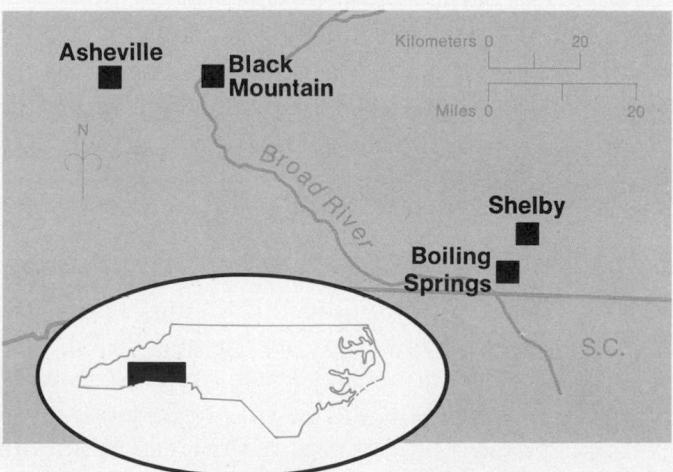

Asheville-Boiling Springs, 1940

A *perfectionist* is one who demands perfection in oneself and in all that one does.

streak and wrote the same way. Jack was shy and retiring, barely five feet ten, and spoke little except among close friends. They nicknamed him "Sleepy." He was such a perfectionist that the life he gave to writing resulted in only one book. It took him over ten years to finish it. In college, Wolfe had made A on nearly everything. Cash did well on only the subjects that really interested him. The outstanding North Carolina writers of their generation, they never met, and, it seems, never wrote to each other.

But Tom Wolfe and Jack Cash were very much the same in their lives and careers. Both were born in 1900 within a hundred miles of each other. Cash was born at Gaffney, South Carolina, and Wolfe, at Asheville. Both had been editors of their college newspapers. Both wrote for their campus magazines. Both became teachers in 1924, though neither found himself suited to it. Both soon turned to writing to support themselves. They both won Guggenheim scholarships in recognition of their writing abilities. And, as the next few years were to show, they would be great believers in Roosevelt's New Deal.

Along with other outstanding young men and women of the 1920s, Wolfe and Cash showed the influence being exerted by North Carolina's colleges. At Wake Forest, Cash boldly defended President Poteat from the attacks of the anti-evolutionists. He enjoyed a wide range of free expression. He even baited the *Biblical Recorder* when that paper got after President Harding for allowing social dancing at the White House. At the University of North Carolina, Wolfe was influenced by several of his teachers. These were drama teacher Frederick Koch, philosopher Horace Williams, and Dean Frank Porter Graham. Both writers were exposed, through their classmates, to the ideals of the "flaming youth" of the "roaring twenties." These helped create many rebels among the youth of that generation.

In 1929, North Carolinians saw a sameness between the two gifted new writers—their harsh criticisms of their state. In addition, they had violated a literary tradition of almost a hundred years standing.

What a contrast there was between 1929 and 1851! In the earlier year, John Hill Wheeler and Calvin H. Wiley had been attacked, in part, for praising North Carolina too much. But later writers had continued the theme. They built up North Carolina's good points and overlooked its faults. Even those, like Thomas Dixon in *The Clansman,* who showed the darker side of life in the state, did so only to boast of it. Clearly, however, by 1929, a rebellion was in progress. What did it mean?

Sallie W. Stockard was the first woman to graduate from the University of North Carolina. She was in the class of 1898.

In 1929, North Carolinians asked themselves why such a rebellion was taking place. They wondered why these bright young men had chosen to hurt the state and its people. They wondered, too, how much damage their harsh words would do to North Carolina. Not since Thomas Jefferson dismissed the "Mecklenburg Declaration" as a myth had North Carolinians felt so cruelly wounded. And, finally, along with many other Americans, they wondered whether Tom Wolfe and Jack Cash had given a true picture of the South. If they had, then nothing would ever seem quite the same again.

The ***Mecklenburg Declaration*** supposedly passed on May 20, 1775 declared that county's independence from Great Britain.

Literature's Greenhouse

A number of creative North Carolinians came to national attention in the 1920s, due in part to the rising standards at the state's own colleges. At the University of North Carolina, the arrival of Frederick Koch from North Dakota in 1918 was a major event in the school's history. In the first year, he founded the "Carolina Playmakers." Professor Koch taught his students that the way to write good plays was to begin by observing the world about them. It was a matter, he said, of studying the lives of those one knew best. Then one wrote about the comedy and tragedy of their lives. Kings and princes were not the concern of Koch and his students. The people and folkways of North Carolina and the South were. The Playmakers brought North Carolina a new era of native drama. It was based upon the lives of mill people, blacks, tenant farmers, fading Old South "aristocracy." One of the first folk plays produced by the Playmakers was called "The Return of Buck Gavin," by student Thomas Wolfe, in 1919.

Koch believed in learning by doing. He had each of his students write one or more plays for his course. These were discussed by the students as they progressed. The best six were chosen for an "author's reading" before the class. The best three were produced each year by the Playmakers. Paul Green of Lillington, Koch's most talented student playwright, won the Pulitzer Prize in 1927 for his play, *In Abraham's Bosom*. It was the first in a series of important and successful plays by Green. Others included his outdoor dramas, *The Lost Colony* and *The Common Glory*. Meanwhile, in 1924, Lawrence Stallings of Yanceyville coauthored *What Price Glory?* It was a gripping story about men in the heat of battle. It en-

Wolfe acts in his play, *The Return of Buck Gavin,* written while he was a student at the University of North Carolina.

Paul Green won the Pulitzer Prize for his outdoor drama *The Lost Colony.* He wrote several other similar works.

joyed nationwide popularity. Also in 1924, Hatcher Hughes of Polksville won the Pulitzer Prize for his *Hell Bent for Heaven,* another folk drama. Such recognition was a startling new development for North Carolina.

The most outstanding of several North Carolina novelists of those years was James Boyd of Southern Pines. A native of Pennsylvania, Boyd used the background of North Carolina as the basis for many fine novels. *Drums,* published by Boyd in 1925, quickly became a classic historical novel about the American Revolution. *Marching On* (1927) was an epic of a Cape Fear River boy in the Civil War. *The Long Hunt* (1930) was about an early nineteenth century trapper in North Carolina and Tennessee.

Conflict in the cotton mill towns was the subject of two novels by Olive Tilford Dargan. A native of Kentucky, she also wrote poetry and short stories after settling in North Carolina. Her novels were *Call Home the Heart* (1932) and *A Stone Came Rolling* (1935). Like the plays inspired by Koch at Chapel Hill, the best of these novels showed the concern for the writer's own world.

Realistic fiction about the South also profited from the research of Howard W. Odum of Chapel Hill. Through his Institute for Research in Social Science, Odum, a native Geor-

396

The **classes** referred to here are the poor and underprivileged people.

A **suite** is an ordered series of musical movements.

Olive Tilford Dargan, a native of Kentucky, wrote short stories, novels, and poetry after settling in North Carolina.

The **geodesic** dome is a type of light architectural structure.

gian, inspired studies of all-but-forgotten classes of Southerners. His *Southern Regions of the United States* (1936) was his major work. But he also produced others, including collections of black songs and folklore. His findings helped erase some of the myths about the quality and character of Southern life. Odum's work helped shape the thought of Wilbur J. Cash and many others.

It was not only in writing that North Carolinians excelled. Composer Lamar Stringfield of Raleigh won the Pulitzer Prize in music in 1928. This was for his suite entitled "From the Southern Mountains." Hunter Johnson won the *Prix de Rome* in 1938 for his musical compositions. History professor J. G. de Roulhac Hamilton founded the Southern Historical Collection of manuscripts at Chapel Hill. Law professor Albert Coates started the Institute of Government there. Duke University opened its Hospital and Medical School in 1930. Wake Forest received several large funds, the first of which led to the establishment in 1941 of Bowman Gray Medical School at Winston-Salem. Many of the state's smaller colleges also enjoyed strong gains prior to the Great Depression.

Between 1933 and 1936, the community of Black Mountain in Buncombe County was the site of an interesting educational experiment. In 1933, John Andrew Rice left his job as drama coach at Rollins College in Florida. Joined by some other Rollins teachers, he rented the summer quarters of the Blue Ridge Assembly. This was a church group at Black Mountain. There, Rice and his colleagues created Black Mountain College. It was to be a laboratory for offbeat and challenging ideas. These included a distaste for rules, complete freedom of behavior, and vague requirements. On the other hand, the school offered chances to the serious and mature student that were rare in higher education. Black Mountain was a place for breaking old rules in the hope of finding better ones.

Residents of the town of Black Mountain and the surrounding area looked on in wonder and, sometimes, suspicion at the school and its curious students. By mutual consent, the town and school had little to do with each other.

Before Black Mountain College ran out of students and money, it enjoyed, for a time, a reputation far out of proportion to its tiny size and budget. At one time or another, its faculty included architect Buckminster Fuller (designer of the geodesic dome), artist Josef Albers, and writers Paul Goodman and Eric Bentley. It boasted other world-renowned fig-

Photographs of Black Mountain College show the dining hall
and other buildings (above), Joseph Albers teaching a class
(lower left), and students performing a dance (lower right).

ures. Students enrolled in the school's lower level studied until they felt ready to take the exams for admission to the senior level. Examinations included some given to the students by outside examiners. Another set was given by the school's faculty. The questions by the faculty included such brain teasers as "What is good art?" and "How do you know the Philippine Islands exist?" No grades were given out and there were no course requirements.

Two Lives

Of the two young North Carolinians who burst upon the national scene in 1929, Tom Wolfe had far greater immediate fame. Asheville discovered early that it might have more to

Picturesque brochures are beautifully illustrated pamphlets.

gain from the brutally realistic picture of it painted by Wolfe than from any number of picturesque brochures and charming advertisements. Though the critical reaction around the country was somewhat mixed toward *Look Homeward, Angel,* it was soon apparent that the book might be considered one of the great American novels. Sinclair Lewis, regarded as the country's finest writer, hailed Wolfe while accepting the Nobel Prize in literature in 1930. With the whole world listening, Lewis, first American to receive the award, called the Wolfe novel one that was "worthy to be compared with the best in our literary production. . . ."

Many other famous writers and critics added their praise of Wolfe. North Carolinians awoke to the fact that the young giant from Asheville was a genius. The reading public eagerly awaited his second novel. When the second appeared, in 1935, it was greeted with critical and popular success. This novel, *Of Time and the River,* like Wolfe's first novel, was clearly autobiographical. It carried "Eugene Gant's" life forward from Asheville to New York, Europe, and the further adventures of Tom Wolfe. A third novel was far advanced when, on September 15, 1938, Wolfe died in Baltimore of an old illness. His death came as a stunning blow to the people of North Carolina and to the literary world.

Autobiographical means dealing with one's own life.

The legend of Thomas Wolfe grew more rapidly in death than it had in life. The huge manuscript upon which he had been working when he died was turned into three novels: *The Web and the Rock* (1939), *You Can't Go Home Again* (1939), and *The Hills Beyond* (1941). The publication of his short stories, poems, plays, and letters added new scope to the appreciation of Wolfe and his work.

A **manuscript** is the author's copy of a work.

In the years between 1929 and 1938, Jack Cash worked nearly in obscurity. Soon after "The Mind of the South" appeared in the *American Mercury,* publisher Alfred A. Knopf asked Cash to write a book on the same subject. Cash went to work on the manuscript. He had to support himself with small advances from Knopf and a small income as a magazine writer and book-page editor for the *Charlotte News.* He lived with his parents at Boiling Springs and, later, at Shelby. During much of the 1930s, Cash was never far from outright poverty. Poor health and failure in romance added to his woes.

The public was aware of Jack Cash during these years through his writings in the *American Mercury.* These included attacks on the mill owners of Gastonia, Governor Cameron Morrison, the city of Charlotte, and "Buck Duke's University," as he called it. These articles were full of ill-founded statements. But Cash had a lively style and a burning

This is a photograph of Thomas Wolfe and his mother. Asheville residents had mixed feelings about his first novel.

sense of justice. Despite criticisms of things Southern, the articles contained the beginnings of a brilliant new analysis of the South and its relation to the rest of the nation.

Cash had not thought much of *Look Homeward, Angel* when the book came out in 1929. (His attitude was mostly jealousy.) However, he soon became a great admirer of Wolfe and his work. Wolfe's early death was a source of deep, personal regret to him. Cash visited and wept over the novelist's grave in Asheville in the summer of 1939. Soon afterward, he wrote a moving and appreciative essay on the dead author's life and work. In early 1941, Jack Cash's own book, *The Mind of the South,* finally came out. It was an immediate success. However, the coming of World War II delayed full recognition of his work for several more years.

Unlike the article of the same title 12 years earlier, *The Mind of the South* was careful in its use of language and milder in tone. It began with a brief survey of early Southern history. It then moved quickly to the period from 1830 to 1860. At that time, according to Cash, the Old South had reached its full character. It was in this period, he claimed, that the "basic Southerner" emerged. This figure not only shaped the character of the Old South, but, in large degree the New South as well.

The two main traits of the "basic Southerner," in the old period and the new, were individualism and romanticism. The first, Cash maintained, was a result of the frontier. It had a thin population and a lack of social distinctions and effective law and government. Almost every person in a frontier society had to get along on his own. The result was increased individualism, guidance by personal whim, the "chip-on-the-shoulder swagger and brag of a boy. . . ." This led to the idea so characteristic of the Southerner, that "he would knock hell out of whoever dared to cross him." It accounted for the violence of the South, with its gouging and lynching, its fondness for fighting in wars.

By romanticism, Cash meant the "tendency toward unreality." It was the Southerner's habit of accepting what was pleasing and rejecting all else, rather than face the facts. Along with this trait was a tendency, furthered by a mild climate and the existence of slave labor, for the Southerner constantly to seek amusement. "To stand on his head in a bar, to toss down a pint of raw whiskey at a gulp, to fiddle and dance all night, . . . to be known eventually far and wide as a hell of a fellow, . . ." was the ideal.

A curious aspect of this society was its demand for "strait-jacket conformity" to its most precious ideas. The individualistic Southerner must not express any doubt over the need for slavery, the purity of Southern white women, and so on. Open and tolerant in some matters, the Southerner could swiftly become dangerous if this value system was threatened by criticism. For this reason, the Old South had not been truly free—even for whites. Though somewhat changed, Cash believed, the traits and ideals of the Old South had survived the Civil War, industrialization, and other powerful influences. They still had control over the behavior of millions of Southerners in the twentieth century.

These ideas led Cash to new ideas about the events at Gastonia in 1929. As a defense against continued Yankee domination after the Civil War, he said, the white South had invented the image of the arrogant black. This image helped create a tie between the poorest and the wealthiest white Southerners. The communists, Cash felt, were wrong to think that the upper and lower classes were always enemies of each other. The Gastonia strike had failed, he thought, because of the mill workers' gratitude to the mill owners for their jobs. So the Communist organizers had worn themselves out preaching a theory that was against the plain facts. Communists, Cash felt, simply did not understand human nature.

Cash admitted that the 1920s and 30s had brought a wave of educated rebels. They might destroy the Old South myth and its hold on twentieth century Southerners. But Tom

A ***strait jacket*** is a garment made to bind the arms of violent persons.

PART EIGHT

Entering the Mainstream

1925-

Downtown Charlotte at dusk

1921 Cameron Morrison elected governor

1925 Angus McLean elected governor

1929 O. Max Gardner elected governor

1932 Ehringhaus elected governor
● Reynolds elected to Senate

1937 Hoey becomes governor

1940 Broughton elected governor

1944 Cherry elected governor

1948 W. Kerr Scott elected governor

1951 Blacks admitted to UNC graduate schools
1953 Death of Willis Smith

1924 Calvin Coolidge elected President *(Nov.)*

1932 Franklin D. Roosevelt elected President *(Nov.)*
1933 Prohibition repealed *(Dec.)*

1939 Germany invades Poland *(Sept.)*
1941 Japanese attack Pearl Harbor *(Dec.)*
● United States declares war on Japan, Germany, and Italy

1945 Germany and Italy surrender *(May)*
● Japan surrenders *(Aug.)*

22

"LOOK AWAY, LOOK AWAY, DIXIELAND"

"Battling Bob" and Mr. Smith

Maybe Frank Graham could be elected to the United States Senate. But it was only going to be over the broken body of "Battling Bob" Thompson. On January 13, Thompson, the High Point editor, ran an editorial that was aimed at Graham and all his supporters. The candidate, in Thompson's estimate, was "pink-tinted." He must be exposed for his "radical following, his fronting for Communist organizations, ..." If Graham's friends felt this was mud slinging, then mud slinging they must put up with. Graham's social and political views were to be "the big issue in the coming campaign," Thompson warned. North Carolinians, he felt, must try to save their state from Communist influence.

The key to the defeat of Frank Graham was to find a strong anti-communist and conservative opponent. The names that were making the rounds were not well received. Charlotte realtor Manley R. Dunaway was unknown and inexper-

"Pink-tinted" meant extremely liberal, almost "red," or communistic.

called, had once defended a University of North Carolina professor for eating lunch with a black Communist. He defended a Chapel Hill pastor who permitted blacks to attend his services. He had been appointed to finish the term of deceased Senator J. Melville Broughton in 1949. During that time, Graham had sponsored a black to West Point. He was known to speak for a stronger United Nations. Many agreed with "Battling Bob" Thompson that Graham's record was that of "a stooge of Communist front organizations."

All this would become political ammunition for Bob Reynolds and Willis Smith in the 1950 campaign. But taking full advantage of Graham's political weaknesses would mean raising certain questions. Some would consider this unfair. It would take an opponent, said the *Fayetteville Observer,* who was "able and ruthless . . . of above average oratorical excellence, who is willing to exploit Graham's leftist tendencies to the point of muckraking." All of the signs pointed to a slashing contest.

The *News and Observer* and other papers backing Graham took quick offense at any statement by Smith or Reynolds that called attention to Graham's "leftist tendencies." At Scotland Neck, Smith warned against those who sought to "distort democracy into socialism." He hoped all good Democrats would "consider just where some of our leaders who have never been elected to public office are trying to lead us." It was hard to call this either "mudslinging" or "muckraking." But Smith made his point. If, however, the candidate himself was above name-calling, some of his backers were not. They ran a crude smear-campaign, showing Graham as an integrationist and a friend of Communism. Certain big business interests across the state took alarm at Graham's views, as did white supremacists and other groups.

In late April and May, the issue in the campaign seemed to shift. It moved from the merits of the candidates themselves to their relations with the administration of Governor Kerr Scott. The governor had won a stunning victory of his own in 1948. He had defeated North Carolina's "Shelby Dynasty," the Democratic group that had controlled the state since 1930. Scott had wrung a 200-million-dollar road building program from the General Assembly. He had set a precedent for the South by appointing a black to the State Board of Education. His selection of Graham to finish Broughton's term had come as a bombshell. He had given Graham strong support since the announcement that the senator would run in 1950. More than that of Frank Graham, conservative Democrats wanted the scalp of Kerr Scott. Graham's defeat would

A *stooge* is an assistant or helper, often used to achieve another person's purpose.

Muckraking means searching for scandal or corruption, especially in politics.

A *dynasty* is a succession of rulers from the same family, group, place, etc.

A *precedent* is a previous instance which serves as an example in later cases.

weaken Scott politically. It would raise the likelihood that the governor could be turned out of office in 1952.

As the May 25 primary neared, national attention was focused on the North Carolina senatorial campaign. Drew Pearson, Walter Winchell, and other experienced observers devoted many columns to the race. Senatorial colleagues of Graham rooted hotly for and against him. The North Carolina primary would be a test of popularity for Truman's "Fair Deal" policies. In the last days before the election, it became clear that Smith had a chance to unseat Graham. Could superpatriotic scare-tactics defeat a candidate of Graham's high standing? Graham's supporters throught it would be a sad day for the state if they could.

The Simmons Machine

For the first 30 years of the twentieth century, North Carolina's political life had been largely shaped by Senator Furnifold M. Simmons. The political "machine" built by Simmons turned back nearly every challenge from the Democratic party's liberal wing. It crushed all Republican opponents. Simmons and most of his supporters were conservatives. But they were not against using the government to promote material progress. As a result, North Carolina, particularly in the last years of Simmons' influence, enjoyed the benefits of growing prosperity. This period saw the election of three of the state's ablest governors. All of them were backed by Simmons.

Cameron Morrison (1921–1925), was known as the "Good Roads Governor." He sponsored the Highway Act of 1921. This added six thousand miles of improved roads to the state system. He was told that the cost could be made up from vehicle and gasoline taxes. Morrison promoted big bond issues for road building. He also got large increases for higher education. This secured the state university to attain national recognition for its social science and graduate programs.

E. C. Brooks was Morrison's Superintendent of Public Instruction. He secured increases in pay and certification requirements of teachers. He raised funds for vocational training and school building. Under Brooks and his successor, Arch T. Allen, the average school term increased from 134 to 154 days. A school bus system was started. Piedmont opposi-

Angus McLean was Governor of North Carolina, 1925-1929. He was also Secretary of the U.S. Treasury.

tion blocked Morrison's effort to improve state ports and water transportation. But citizens were learning to demand more and better services from the government and take advantage of its positive functions.

Despite continued farm depression, the state experienced further prosperity under Governor Angus McLean (1925–1929). McLean demanded more economy in government and helped create the Budget Bureau. This gave the governor more control over the expenses of government agencies. A Tax Commission was set up to study and classify all figures on state taxes. A County Government Advisory Commission was set up to promote better methods in county government. A State Board of Equalization was appointed to find the true value of taxable property. The board would see that each county received equal shares of school funds. In spite of McLean's economies, schools and roads continued to receive generous amounts of money.

O. Max Gardner (1929–1933) bore the burden of the Great Depression in North Carolina. Gardner decided to centralize

Central North Carolina, 1930

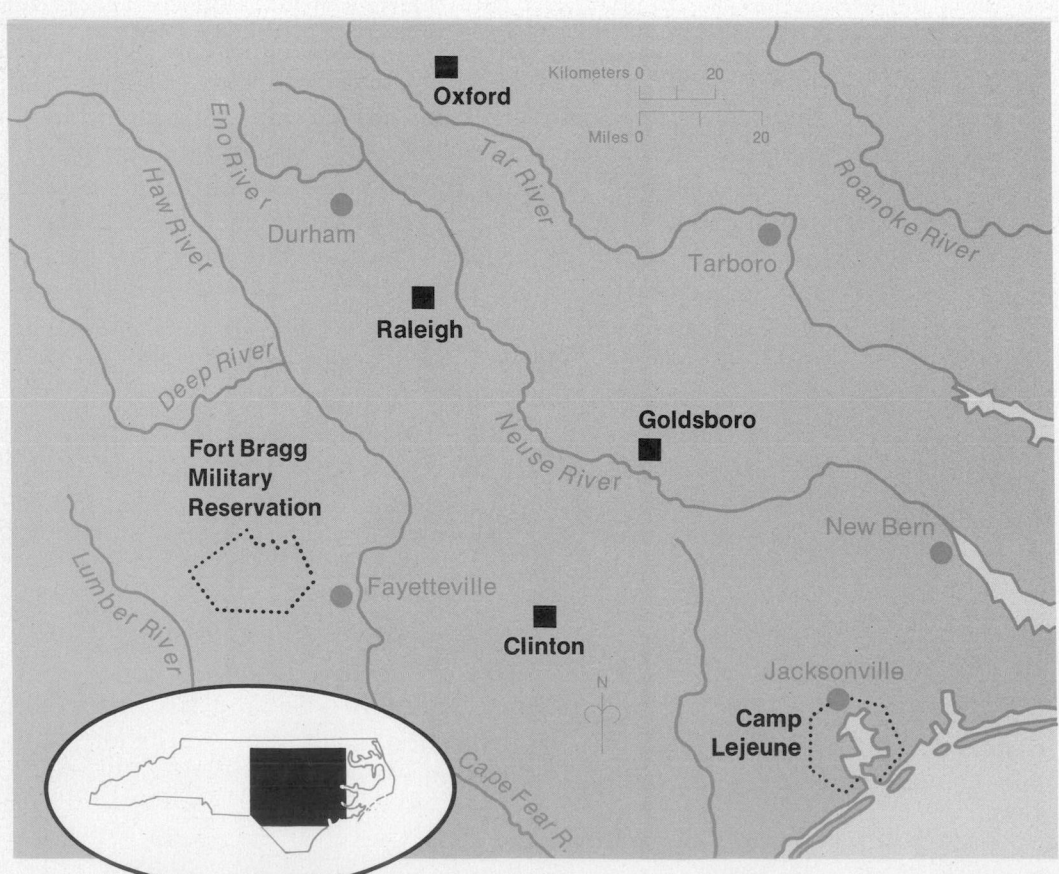

These photographs from the Depression era in North Carolina show a black cabin (upper left), a tobacco auction (upper right), a cafe scene (lower left), and a black barber shop (lower right). Notice the 1939 prices in the cafe.

things to meet the state's crisis. At his request, the General Assembly combined the University of North Carolina, State College, and Woman's College. It reorganized the state government. It cut the salaries of public officials. It raised gasoline and corporate income taxes, but reduced taxes on property. In 1931, Gardner announced that he had reduced the costs of government. He had lowered the burden of taxes on the distressed citizens of the state. The state now had the secret ballot. It had taken over road and school costs from local government.

In the 1928 election, Senator Simmons, long a champion of Democratic unity, had refused to support Alfred E. Smith.

(Smith was the Democratic candidate for president against Hoover and the Republicans.) Simmons cited several disputes with Smith. These included Smith's wanting changes in the Prohibition laws. But Smith's Roman Catholicism may also have been a factor. North Carolina Democrats were faced with a choice between a Republican and a Catholic. Many sided with Simmons and chose Hoover. Smith lost North Carolina and the election, but Simmons could not really claim a victory.

When Simmons split his own party to prevent Smith's election, he lost the support of many loyal Democrats. He tried to rebuild his organization during 1929 and 1930. But he found opposition too strong. Those who had stood by Simmons only to see Smith beaten had no more use for him after Smith's defeat. In 1930, Josiah W. Bailey, a former editor of the *Biblical Recorder,* trounced Simmons and the old political machine.

A new machine, similar to the old one, soon replaced that of Simmons. This was the "Shelby Dynasty," so known because two of its founders and leaders, Max Gardner and Clyde R. Hoey of Shelby, were brothers-in-law. This political group was strong enough in 1932 to insure the election of John C. B. Ehringhaus of Pasquotank as governor. Hoey then followed Ehringhaus in the governor's office. Except for the victories of Bob Reynolds in 1932 and J. Melville Broughton in 1940, the Dynasty controlled North Carolina's state and national politics for 20 years.

Despite the efforts of Governor Gardner, North Carolina was in financial difficulty when Ehringhaus began his term. The state was spending much more than it was taking in. Ehringhaus had promised the removal of the 15 percent ad valorem tax for public schools. He now faced a major task in balancing the budget. He was able to bring about other savings in the operation of government. But it soon became clear that sharp increases in taxes would also be needed—even though he had campaigned against them.

The tax question was fought out in the 1933 General Assembly. Some favored a tax on luxury items only. Others wanted a tax on general sales, i.e., all goods sold in the state. The *News and Observer* led the fight for the luxury tax. It argued that a luxury tax would fall mainly on those most able to pay. But a sales tax would hurt the poor as well. The legislature finally voted a general sales tax. However, it exempted a few items, such as bread, meat, and flour. The money brought in by this tax enabled the state to balance the budget. The state also took over the public schools from local government and extended the school term to eight months.

Ad valorem means that the amount of tax depends on the value of the article.

The prices in this store window in 1939 indicate the hard times present in the state.

Curtailed means stopped.

Clyde Hoey's term (1937–1941) saw the return of some prosperity to the state and nation. New Deal programs continued to pump large amounts of money into the depressed economy of North Carolina. By 1940, the war in Europe was creating orders for military and relief supplies from American farms and factories. Hoey was able to restore many curtailed state services and devote attention to improving conditions in industry. His administration raised the employment age of children in industry to 16. In dangerous occupations it was raised to 18. The hours women could work in factories were limited to 48 a week. Men were limited to 55 hours a week. Free textbooks were authorized for elementary schools and textbook rental for high schools. Also, the state-supported black colleges were finally permitted to establish graduate and professional schools in certain areas of study.

In the election of 1940, J. Melville Broughton of Raleigh defeated Robert H. McNeill, his Republican opponent, by a margin of three to one. This was the largest majority ever given a candidate for governor in the state's history. Roosevelt won easily in North Carolina on the way to his third term in office. The General Assembly was inspired by returning prosperity. It set aside large amounts for state agencies, public schools, teachers' salaries, colleges, state employees' pension and retirement plans, and vocational education. Steps were taken toward adding a twelfth year to the public school sys-

This tenant farmer's wife is stringing tobacco for drying. The photograph was taken in Granville County.

tem. An increase in population to three and a half million led to the creation of the state's twelfth Congressional district.

The coming of World War II had a major effect on the lives of nearly all North Carolinians. More than a hundred military bases were constructed in the state. The largest project was the expansion of Fort Bragg, near Fayetteville. It was to serve almost a hundred thousand troops. The nation's sec-

These rural children are enjoying some watermelon. They were among the many victims of the depressed economy of the 1930s.

ond largest marine base was established at Camp Lejeune. One of the largest marine air stations was built at Cherry Point. Greensboro, Goldsboro, Elizabeth City, Edenton, Wilmington and other places also had sizeable bases.

More than a million North Carolinians were registered by local draft boards during the war. But nearly 28 percent were rejected for military service due to physical causes. (The national average was 24 percent.) Others received deferments for farm or other essential labor services. Some 362,000 North Carolinians saw actual military service.

Deferments are postponements, temporary delays.

More than seven thousand of these lost their lives, besides many more thousands who suffered injuries and wounds. The state had its share of military heroes and winners of the Congressional Medal of Honor. But none of the leading figures of the war was a North Carolinian. Major General William C. Lee of Harnett County was North Carolina's highest ranking soldier.

Forty-one American naval vessels in the war bore North Carolina names. These included escort carriers, transports, gunboats, and tankers. The most famous was the battleship *North Carolina*. Already in service when the United States entered the war, the *North Carolina* saw much action in the Pacific. It survived a Japanese torpedo in late 1942. The ship is

The battleship *North Carolina* saw much action in World War II. It is now a memorial, berthed at Wilmington.

In World War II, members of North Carolina's 30th Infantry
Division cross a bridge in Europe (left) and stand in
formation in the square of a liberated Dutch town (right).

A **berth** is a space for
anchoring or docking a ship.

Delinquent means failing in a
duty or guilty of a misdeed.

now a floating museum of the war. Its permanent berth is in
Wilmington.

During the war, state politics was rather quiet. Senator
Bailey easily defeated Richard T. Fountain, Edgecombe Democrat, in 1942. Clyde Hoey, a senator since 1941, kept his seat
against Cameron Morrison in 1944. Gastonia's R. Gregg Cherry
defeated Dr. Ralph McDonald for governor in the 1944 Democratic primary. Roosevelt carried the state again that year by a
comfortable margin.

Extra effort was needed to ensure wartime preparedness.
However the Democratic state administrations were able to
extend the school term to nine months and create a school for
delinquent black girls. Funds were given to the North Carolina Art Society and the North Carolina Symphony Society
(organized in 1932). This was the first time either art or music
had received state aid. Public schools, institutions of higher
learning, and various state agencies received the largest
amounts of money in the state's history. Under Broughton, a
statewide medical care program was adopted. This provided
more doctors, hospitals, and insurance for the public.

Roosevelt's administration drew heavily upon North
Carolina talent, though not as heavily as Truman would do
later on. Robert L. Doughton of Laurel Springs was Chairman

Clyde R. Hoey served North Carolina as governor, congressman, senator, and editor. He was part of the "Shelby Dynasty."

W. Kerr Scott won a stunning victory in the race for governor in 1948 by defeating the "Shelby Dynasty."

Collective bargaining means discussions between workers and employers to reach agreement on wages, hours, and working conditions.

A ***referendum*** is the right of the people to vote directly on a law.

of the House Ways and Means Committee. Lindsay Warren of Washington was Comptroller General of the United States. Josephus Daniels served as ambassador to Mexico from 1933 to 1941. Historian R. D. W. Connor of the University of North Carolina was first Archivist of the United States (1934–1941).

Like the administrations of Broughton and Hoey, that of Governor Cherry (1945–1949) was blessed with continuing general prosperity and political harmony. State salaries and appropriations continued to rise. Some items were removed from the three percent general sales tax. Control of public school funds was placed under a new State Board of Education. A start was made toward increasing the medical school at the University of North Carolina from two to four years. A teaching hospital was created at the University medical school. A five-year hospital plan, begun in 1947, was aimed at adding five thousand new hospital beds in the state.

The machine Democrats inherited the organization created by Max Gardner in the 1930s. They approached the 1948 primary in the expectation of retaining power. State Treasurer Charles M. Johnson was picked to be the next governor. The machine geared up to insure the continuation of the dynasty. Not much concern was expressed over the statement of W. Kerr Scott, Alamance dairy farmer and Commissioner of Agriculture, that he would also seek the nomination. Conservative business and industrial interests felt confident that Scott could be beaten.

Kerr Scott's moderate liberalism made him unacceptable to most conservative Democrats. He was backed by farmers, industrial laborers, intellectuals, and dissatisfied Democrats. He claimed to be champion of what he called "the branch-head boys." They were the "little people" of North Carolina. A colorful, bushy-browed, tobacco-chewing campaigner, Scott talked of rural roads, electrification, and collective bargaining. Such things meant a spending program far above the former policy. After running close behind Johnson in the first primary, Scott carried the second. He was elected by almost triple the votes given to his Republican opponent, George M. Pritchard.

To the disappointment of conservatives, Scott pushed for a popular referendum. It endorsed his plan to raise a giant $200,000,000 in bonds for building secondary roads. He also raised the gasoline tax and gave $25,000,000 to the counties for school building and repair. He got the General Assembly to make appropriations for port facilities, salaries for teachers and other state employees, state agencies, and higher education. The legislature also authorized a dental school at Chapel

Hill in connection with the medical school. In four years, Scott's administration more than doubled the state's paved roads to 26,000 miles.

Among North Carolina blacks, Scott had almost unanimous support. He offered no program of progress in civil rights, but his campaign avoided slurs against the black population. Many of his projects would help blacks as much as whites. In 1951, federal court decisions led to the admission of blacks to the law, medical, and graduate schools of the University. This broke the school's long-standing policy of racial exclusion. It was also during this time that work began on what would be the new campus for Wake Forest College. This was the 400-acre estate just outside Winston-Salem. It had been given to the school by tobacco magnate R. J. Reynolds.

Damming the Liberal Tide

"Eggheads" means intellectual people.

Discouraged conservatives feared that Frank Graham, Scott's hand-picked Senator, would have little opposition in his bid for the Democratic nomination in 1950. The liberal Democrats were now in their eighteenth year of national power. The tide of liberalism seemed to favor further gains for them in North Carolina and elsewhere. But if Graham seemed only liberal to some, he seemed more than that to the Democrats of North Carolina. Organized labor and the university "eggheads" would stand by Graham. But it was less certain that Scott's "branch-head boys" would go along with the choice. Under the circumstances, many conservatives felt that Willis Smith would have a chance of unseating the "Fighting Half Pint" and inflicting revenge on Kerr Scott.

The plans of the Graham campaign called for strong and frequent denials by Graham that he was not the Communist or Socialist his critics labeled him. Newspapers carried regular headlines with some such statement as "Graham Strongly Denies that he is a Communist." The candidate told a Durham gathering that "Communism was a threat to capitalism and that capitalism must be kept free. He declared that capitalism was a great blessing to the people and should be shared by all." But even the denials helped keep the issue alive. They encourage opponents in their effort to raise suspicions about Graham.

"Willis Smith," declared his own campaign manager, "doesn't have to come out during a political campaign and

Fellow travelers are supporters of a political party or cause who are not actually members of the organization.

deny that he is a Communist or a Socialist. There are no shadows of suspicion about his head and no . . . records of association with fellow travelers that he will have to deny." It was gutter politics, but it was also effective. In the primary on May 27, Graham received 304,000 votes against Smith's 250,000. "Buncombe Bob" received 59,000. Smith called for a run-off. In the largest primary vote in the state's history, he beat Graham by 281,000 to 262,000. In the November election, Smith easily defeated Republican E. R. Gavin. It was "Battling Bob" Thompson's greatest victory. It was also the beginning for another of Graham's most well-spoken opponents, Jesse Helms of Raleigh.

Denied the major role he might have played in the senate, Frank Graham still continued to add to his career of public service. His earlier national offices included service as special advisor to the State Department on Indonesian affairs. He was the organizer and first president of the Oak Ridge Institute of Nuclear Studies. He held other prominent positions. But these roles were overshadowed by the important part he was to play in later years—that of an official of the United Nations. He was widely regarded as one of the greatest Americans of his time. As for Graham's rival, Senator Smith became a competent and dedicated member of the Senate. However, in June 1953, he died, only half way through his term of office.

The political fate of Frank Graham showed the distance that separated North Carolina's political views from those of the New Deal and Fair Deal era. Democratic liberalism had been welcomed in North Carolina in the 1930s. This was during a period of national distress. As long as the world war continued, it was not seriously challenged. But the post-war period, with its "cold war" tensions, saw a backlash against the rapid growth of big government and the welfare state. A mild form of liberalism, like that of Kerr Scott, was still acceptable. But Graham's more aggressive brand was mistrusted. Graham's patriotism and anti-communism should have been beyond question. But his social views were far in advance of those of most of his fellow North Carolinians.

Cold war is conflict between states or nations without actual warfare.

Graham stood higher in the eyes of national Democrats than with those of North Carolina. His views were closer to those of Roosevelt and Truman than to those of Hoey and Broughton. As a result, his opponents succeeded in driving a wedge between North Carolina's organized laborers and intellectuals, on the one hand, and the "branch-head boys," on the other. The Republican party could look forward to exploiting the split. They would find better times in the state than they had known in many years.

Graham was the most notable of many North Carolinians

who rose to positions of national significance during the Truman years. In 1947, Kenneth Royall of Goldsboro became Truman's Secretary of War. Later, he became Secretary of the Army. In 1949, Royall was succeeded in the latter post by Gordon Gray of Winston-Salem. Gray also succeeded Graham as president of the University of North Carolina. Max Gardner was named Under Secretary of the Navy in 1947. He died the next year as he was about to take up his new post as ambassador to England. James Webb of Oxford was Director of the Budget. Afterward, he was Under Secretary of the Treasury for Truman. John S. Graham of Winston-Salem, Dan Edwards, and George Allen of Durham, and Judges F. Donal Phillips of Rockingham and Richard Dillard Dixon of Edenton were among some three hundred other North Carolinians who held high office under Truman. A notable biography of Truman was written by Jonathan Daniels. He served for a time as Turman's press secretary. And not many years ahead lay the promise of a presidential candidate from North Carolina. The people of the state could be proud of its leaders in the state and national administrations.

Terry Sanford announced his candidacy for President in 1976. He withdrew, however, after defeat in the primaries.

Chapter Checkup

PEOPLE

"Battling Bob" Thompson	W. Kerr Scott	Clyde R. Hoey
Robert Rice Reynolds	E. C. Brooks	Kenneth Royall
Willis Smith	Angus McLean	James Webb
J. Melville Broughton		

PLACES

Clinton	Cherry Point	Goldsboro
Fort Bragg	Laurel Springs	Oxford
Camp Lejeune		

FACT

Why was Frank Graham considered by some people to be a dangerous radical?

What brought about the defeat of the Simmons machine?

In what ways did Kerr Scott depart from the policies of the Shelby Dynasty?

How did Graham's defeat help pave the way for later Republican victories in North Carolina?

INTERPRETATION

Were there sound reasons for fearing that Frank Graham might not be entirely loyal as a public servant? Explain.

Why do you think North Carolinians chose to put their faith in political machines and dynasties for so many years? Explain.

Is it clear that North Carolina was held back by the absence of a real two-party system for so much of the twentieth century? Explain.

VOCABULARY

Muckraking	"Eggheads"	"Branch-head boys"
Dynasty	Fellow travelers	"Pink-tinted"

ACTIVITY

Draw up a your own political platform as if you were to run for governor in North Carolina in the next election. Which planks in the platform would probably appeal to voters? Which would not? Do you think a candidate could win with this platform? Explain.

SUGGESTED READING

Fleer, Jack. *North Carolina Politics, An Introduction.* Chapel Hill: UNC Press, 1968. See especially Chapter V, "Interparty Competition."

Tindall, George B. *The Emergence of the New South, 1913–1943.* Baton Rouge: Louisiana State University Press, 1967. See North Carolina references in index. Highly authoritative scholarly survey of recent Southern history.

1952 Eisenhower elected
President *(Nov.)*

1956 Hodges elected governor
● Pearsall Plan adopted
1957 Partial integration
in some public schools

1960 Sanford elected governor
● Sit-ins begin at Greensboro

1961 Research Triangle Park
established

1960 J. F. Kennedy elected
President *(Nov.)*

1963 Civil rights demonstrations
begin at Chapel Hill
● Speaker Ban law enacted
1964 Moore elected governor

1965 Britt Commission
appointed

1963 Kennedy assassinated
(Nov.)

1964 Lyndon B. Johnson elected
President *(Nov.)*
1965 U.S. sends troops
to Viet Nam

1968 Speaker Ban law declared
unconstitutional

23

THE SPEAKER BAN AND THE PEARSALL PLAN

The Britt Commission

Representatives Godwin and Delamar were the sponsors of the bill.

A *scourge* is a disease that affects a large area.

Even the worst enemies of the Visiting Speakers Act had to admire the way the matter was handled. The bill had been introduced quietly on the floor of the General Assembly on June 25, 1963. It was the next-to-last day of the session. Some members had already gone home. In the shower of last-minute enactments, the bill was hardly noticed. Officials of the University of North Carolina and other likely opponents had not even heard of it beforehand. There was little discussion as it was passed in just 19 minutes. Representatives Godwin and Delamar were pleased with what seemed to be a fine day's work. The University of North Carolina was now protected against the scourge of Communism.

The Visiting Speakers Act, also known as the Speaker Ban Law, was simple and straightforward. From now on, all state-supported colleges and universities were closed to speakers that talked of the overthrow of the governments of

425

Dan K. Moore, *Governor of North Carolina*
David M. Britt, *commission chairman*
Luther H. Hodges, *Governor of North Carolina*

Thomas J. Pearsall, *a legislator*
Charles R. Jonas, *a U.S. Congressman*
Robert F. Williams, *a civil rights leader*

The Fifth Amendment to the Constitution states in part that no person ". . . shall be . . . a witness against himself . . ."

The American Legion is an organization composed of military veterans.

the United States or of North Carolina. This included all known Communists. It included also all persons who had pled the Fifth Amendment in response to questions concerning their loyalty. Enforcement would be the responsibility of the trustees or other officials of the schools.

Sponsors of the act expected some criticism but not the amount that came. Frank Graham didn't like it. The work of University Chancellors Aycock and Caldwell was supposed to be lightened by the law. But they labeled it a blow at academic freedom and university self-regulation. Television commentator David Brinkley and the Raleigh Ministerial Association joined in the attack. Terry Sanford, the liberal governor, declared he would have vetoed the bill if he could have. The liberal newspapers kept up a bombardment against the act. It soon became known to its opponents as the "Gag Law."

For months after its passage, opponents of the act were still issuing statements about it. Defenders of the act found it necessary to rally to its support. They tried to explain the reasoning behind it. The American Legion and Veterans of Foreign Wars issued statements of warm endorsement of the act. Senator Clarence Stone and Raleigh attorney Armistead Maupin spoke out. They thought the act offered protection to the university and to the young people of North Carolina. FBI Director J. Edgar Hoover and State Senator Robert Morgan, Chairman of the Board of Trustees of East Carolina College, called it a good bill. Various Republican groups indicated their support.

For the rest of 1963 and all during 1964 the debate continued. Each side said that the general public favored its position. Each side found respected Americans willing to say publicly that the Speaker Ban was either a blessing or a curse, as the case might be. The debate was deadlocked—but the ban remained in force.

Dan K. Moore succeeded Sanford as governor in 1965. It was becoming clear that the issue of the Speaker Ban must be

426

squarely faced and resolved. Either it was injuring the university or it was not. Opponents of the act, going beyond the question of academic freedom, were now arguing that state-supported institutions were being threatened with other dangers. A major accrediting agency said that it might withdraw the accreditation of the schools affected by the ban. This was followed by the announcement that some three hundred faculty members in the institutions concerned would resign if accreditation were lost. There was also worry about the loss of certain federal and private grants to the schools. There were hints that some faculty members were already resigning. They felt the intellectual climate of the schools had been damaged.

In June 1965, Governor Moore named Representative David M. Britt of Robeson County as chairman of a commission to study the Speaker Ban. He was to find out whether changes or even repeal might be in order. The Britt Commission decided the best way to handle the inquiry was to hold open hearings. At that time all sides might be heard. These hearings were held during four days in August and September at the new State Legislative Building in Raleigh. Newspaper, radio, and television coverage carried the hearings into almost every home in North Carolina. Never in the history of the state had a domestic matter had such wide exposure. The public was fully acquainted with the issues.

The Britt Commission found quickly that there was no convenient middle ground between those who favored the Speaker Ban and those who did not. State Senator Tom White of Kinston assured the commission that he did not believe "there's a Communist under every bush" at Chapel Hill. But he thought the people of the state needed the law for reassurance. He denied that there was any real danger of loss of the university's accreditation. He denied that the civil rights demonstrations at Chapel Hill had anything to do with passage of the act. If, however, it came to a matter of keeping accreditation or the ban, he favored the latter.

Legislator T. Henry Redding of Asheboro gave the commission three reasons why he opposed the act. First, the ban would apply to certain types of speakers no matter what their topic. They may, for example, be exchanging important scientific findings. Second, an act of 1941 denied the use of state property to persons advocating the overthrow of the government. It banned the same things as the Visiting Speakers Act. Finally, Redding said that he had three sons in college. He would not like to have them shielded in this way from intellectual challenges.

Supporters of the law made much of several Communist speakers who had visited the campus at Chapel Hill. An edi-

Accreditation means that a school must meet certain set standards.

Terry Sanford was Governor of North Carolina, 1961-1965, and later, President of Duke University.

Dan K. Moore was Governor of North Carolina, 1965-1969, and later, a justice of the North Carolina Supreme Court.

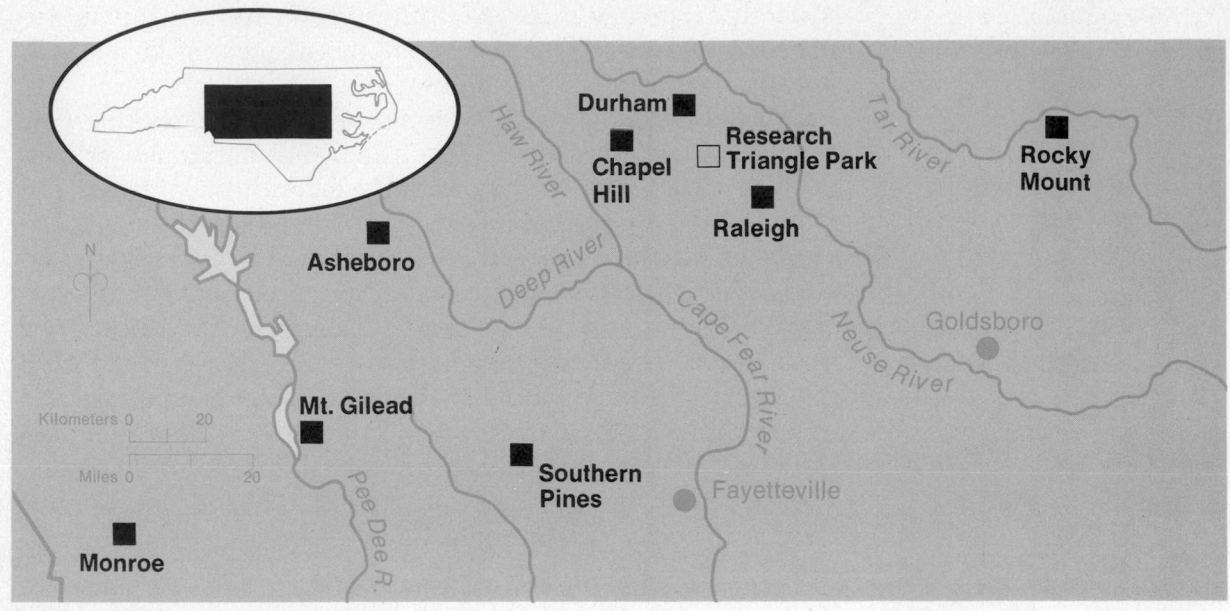

Central North Carolina, 1960

Inroads means hostile or unfriendly entry.

A **leftist tinge** means a liberal (left-wing) political viewpoint.

tor of the Communist newspaper, the *Daily Worker,* had spoken there in 1937. Four or five others had appeared in more recent years. Henry E. Royall, an American Legionnaire from Chapel Hill, described the "humiliation of seeing Communism making inroads into our great university." He said he could not name a Communist member of the present faculty or student body. But that was not his point. "I believe students there will tell you," said Royall, "that to pass their work and get good grades they have to take a leftist tinge." It was not certain, however, just what bearing this had on the need for a Speaker Ban.

Among the most effective presentations were those made in opposition to the act by two law professors. These were John P. Dawson of Harvard and William Van Alstyne of Duke. "Once we admit that speakers can be banned," warned Dawson, "no matter how peaceable, lawful, and politically neutral may be the themes that they discuss, we have taken a long step towards the thought control of which we hope to rid the world." Hearing all sides of issues, he observed, was vital to the process of education.

Professor Van Alstyne dealt with the question of whether the act was constitutional. He made a strong argument that it was not. He asserted that the Speaker Ban violated at least three separate clauses of the federal Constitution. Those

428

The *"due process"* clause of the Constitution requires fairness by the government in its dealings with citizens.

clauses provided for due process, free speech, and equal protection of the laws. He added that a similar Ohio law had been struck down by the courts.

The Britt Commission ended its hearings on September 9. It began preparing recommendations for Governor Moore. The Viet Nam War was now involving a growing number of Americans. It was an awkward moment to give even indirect comfort to the Communist enemy. Officials of the university had not shown that injury to the school had occurred or was even likely to occur. Although the big newspapers of the state were hostile to the ban, many smaller newspapers supported it. It might be easier for the commission to make a popular decision than an educationally sound one. At any rate, the two might well be different.

The Research Triangle

At the close of World War II, North Carolina's industry was several times larger than that of any other Southeastern state. But postwar growth proved to be very disappointing. Some growth continued, but not so rapidly as in other states of the region. Per capita income for North Carolinians fell. Farm income, high during the war years, leveled off. Citizens had learned to demand ever greater public services. But government tax revenues were not enough to provide them. Governor William B. Umstead died in November 1954, after less than two years in office. The challenge of these and other problems fell to his successor, former Lieutenant Governor Luther H. Hodges.

During Umstead's brief tenure, the General Assembly continued Kerr Scott's "Go Forward" program. The legislature passed bond issues for higher learning, charitable and correctional institutions, and for various departments of state government. In October 1953, every county in the state voted in favor of the General Assembly's large proposed bond issues. These were for school construction and the improvement of the state's mental institutions. But, if Hodges were to be successful, his administration would have to find new ways of bringing industry to North Carolina. It must also raise the wages of its workers.

Hodges' answers to the problems included a broad campaign of national advertising. This would acquaint businesses

The Burroughs-Wellcome research facility is one of many in Research Triangle Park, a major American research center.

with the advantages of North Carolina. He also sponsored new tax laws as a lure to industry. He led a trade mission to western Europe in search of more business from abroad. But the boldest effort Hodges made was developing the Research Triangle Park. The idea was to locate industrial and other research facilities near North Carolina's three leading academic institutions—UNC, Duke, and North Carolina State College. Hodges and others felt that this area would be attractive to industries. They could make use of the great number of scientists and research resources at the three schools. Headed by Robert M. Hanes of Winston-Salem, a Research Triangle Committee was formed. By 1961, a five-thousand-acre park was established in an area near the center of the triangle formed by the schools. Chemstrand and the U.S. Forest Service were the first to establish research laboratories there. Many others followed. In addition, the Research Triangle Institute was created to carry on research by contract with agencies and industries located elsewhere.

Following a national recession in 1957 and 1958, North Carolina had a swift recovery. This was due in large part to the success of Hodges' work in attracting industry. Hodges, elected governor in his own right in 1956, continued his program. The 1959 General Assembly adopted the largest budget in the state's history. North Carolina became the first state in the South to pass a minimum hourly wage of 75 cents. A Department of Water Resources was established. This was to coordinate the use and conservation of the state's water re-

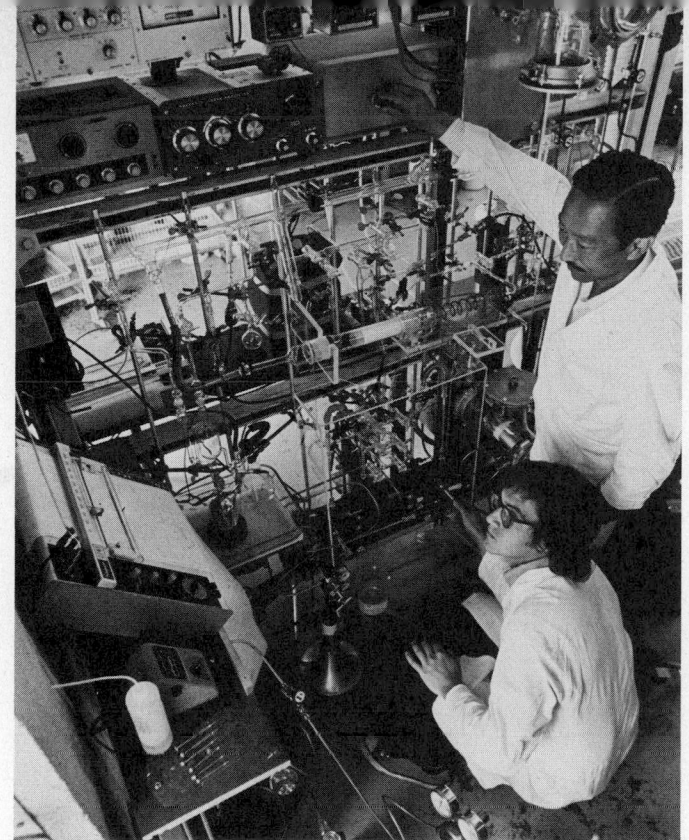

Research Triangle Park employs thousands of scientists who work closely with the nearby universities.

Research at the Park has resulted in many improvements in products and new ideas for American industry.

sources. The penalty-point system was adopted as a means of curbing the growing rate of highway deaths. Meanwhile, however, the question of desegregation was finally being faced by the nation. It would be up to Hodges to frame North Carolina's response.

On May 17, 1954, the United States Supreme Court made its historic decision. It ordered the desegregation of public schools "with all deliberate speed." The State Board of Education, with Lieutenant Governor Hodges as chairman, decided to continue segregation in North Carolina—at least for the coming school year. In early August, Governor Umstead appointed a committee, headed by Thomas J. Pearsall of Rocky Mount. The committee was to study legal aspects of the question. The General Assembly took up the issue in early 1955. It found that the "mixing of the races in the public schools . . . cannot be accomplished." It would threaten closing the schools if it could be. Acts were passed transferring authority over pupil assignment and school buses to local control. A special session of the legislature was held in the summer of 1956. An amendment to the state constitution was adopted. It was recommended by the "Pearsall Committee." The amendment allowed parents who did not wish to send their children to schools with children of another race to receive private tuition grants from the state.

The Hodges administration exerted no pressure for integration, and the process moved at a snail's pace throughout North Carolina. In 1957, school boards in Charlotte, Winston-Salem, and Greensboro admitted a few black students to formerly all-white schools. Craven and Wayne counties took similar action in 1959. Durham, Chapel Hill, and a few other towns followed in 1960; Asheville, in 1961. By the latter year, only a little over two hundred blacks were attending integrated classes. No whites had been assigned to black schools.

Despite this small effort, many North Carolinians congratulated themselves. They were avoiding the violence and disruptions that were occurring in states where "massive resistance" was practiced. North Carolina had few ugly incidents. The black population, so far, had not made a strong objection to the state's policy. Many people seemed to think that a policy of token compliance with the law of the nation might somehow go on forever.

As it had for many years past, North Carolina's senate delegation remained solidly Democratic. Charles R. Jonas was first elected in 1952. He was the state's only Republican delegate to the national House of Representatives in these years. But Democrat Adlai E. Stevenson barely edged Eisenhower

"Massive resistance" refers to the attempt by states or localities to block desegregation by refusal to keep schools open and other means.

for the North Carolina presidential vote in 1954. Eisenhower received the largest vote ever cast in the state for a member of his party.

Democrats also continued their hold on the governor's office. However, it was much less secure than in the past. The old lines between liberal and conservative factions faded quickly during the six years Hodges was governor. Hodges had won 85 percent of the vote in 1956, gaining favor with all factions. Terry Sanford of Fayetteville, in 1960, won a hard-fought primary victory over I. Beverly Lake. Sanford then defeated Robert L. Gavin, the Republican challenger. John F. Kennedy defeated Richard M. Nixon in the North Carolina presidential election that year. However, it was by a margin of only about 58,000 of well over 1,300,000 votes cast. In these elections, more appeared to depend on the personalities of the candidates rather than the factions which supported them.

Democratic General Assemblies tried to reorganize the state government in 1957. The 1959 legislature voted large funds for the erection of a new legislative building. There were also funds voted for higher education, ports, mental institutions, hospitals, and other capital improvements. By an act of 1959, North Carolina became the first state to require polio vaccination for children.

Polio is a serious nerve and muscular disease, most often affecting children.

These Durham residents are protesting the abuse of tenants in local housing in 1966.

Except for Jonas in the Tenth Congressional District, North Carolina, in 1960, still had no Republicans in major offices. People noted, however, that the state was gradually returning to the two-party system. Republican candidates came closer to success with each election. The Democratic reign seemed to be ending.

Governor Sanford endorsed both the "Go Forward" approach of Kerr Scott and the "New Frontier" program of President Kennedy. He made educational progress his main theme. The 1961 General Assembly voted almost half a billion dollars for public schools. This was by far the largest amount ever designated. To raise this huge sum, plus over sixty million for higher education, new taxes had to be imposed. The money was found by including food and other items in the three percent sales tax. These items had previously been exempt. The food tax was harshly criticized across the state.

People who supported increasing education money had good reasons why they thought it was necessary. Despite heavy spending for this purpose in the past, North Carolina public schools ranked forty-first among the 50 states in various measurements of quality. About four percent of the state's per capita income was going for education. But it was not enough. Less than half the white students and only about a third of the black students finishing high school were going on to further schooling. The proportion of North Carolinians in college was about half the national average.

Per capita means by or for the individual person.

In contrast to the plight of the public schools, North Carolina's colleges and universities were enjoying remarkable growth. The University at Chapel Hill had added library sci-

A laboratory worker at Triangle Park tests methods that can help solve major world problems.

ence and public health schools in the 1930s. It added departments of city and regional planning, radio, and religion in the 1940s. A communications center was opened in 1945. It gained Morehead Planetarium in 1949, and a department of astronomy and school of journalism in 1950. Chapel Hill had one of the largest graduate schools in the nation. It had the only schools of pharmacy, dentistry, and journalism of their kind in the Upper South.

State College's engineering school was one of the biggest in the nation. Its schools of agriculture, textiles, and design were among the country's best. It had the largest research forest in the world. This was its eighty-thousand-acre Hoffman Forest in Jones and Onslow Counties. The school had the world's first college-owned nuclear reactor. There were, in addition, nine other state-supported senior colleges besides those of the greater university. These were East Carolina in Greenville, North Carolina Central at Durham, Agricultural and Technical at Greensboro, Appalachian State Teachers at Boone, Western Carolina at Cullowhee, Fayetteville State, Elizabeth City State, Pembroke and Winston-Salem State Teachers. There were also five state-supported junior colleges including those at Charlotte, Wilmington, and Asheville. Besides all these, North Carolina had a total of 47 private junior and senior colleges in 1960.

In addition to funds for education, the General Assembly of 1961 approved bonds for improving mental institutions, ports, community colleges and correctional schools. Bonds were voted for a building to house the State Library and Department of Archives and History. More workers were brought under the Minimum Wage Act. The State Art Commission was abolished. Various other agencies were created or reorganized.

With farm income rising again and the state's general economic condition improved, Sanford continued Hodges' efforts to bring new industry to North Carolina. The Research Triangle Park developed greatly. The ports at Wilmington and Morehead City carried record quantities of shipments. The state was well represented in the Kennedy administration. Hodges became Secretary of Commerce. Voit Gilmore of Southern Pines was the first Director of the United States Travel Service. J. Spencer Bell of Charlotte was made Judge of the Fourth Circuit Court of Appeals. In late 1961, a general trend of prosperity and promise appeared to bless the directions taken by the state government.

In some respects, however, North Carolinians were showing signs of dissatisfaction with state and national events. A sign of voter displeasure was a rejection in 1961 of the legislature's proposed capital improvement bonds. It was the first time in almost 40 years that voters had defeated a state-wide bond issue. Were they reacting against Sanford's food tax and the general high cost of government? Or were they simply asserting their independence? The answer was not clear. But the "Go Forward" program seemed to be in trouble.

The Sanford administration faced an even greater challenge. This was in the rising national uproar over the civil rights of blacks. It included school desegregation and the integration of restaurants and theatres. North Carolina had been the first state in the Southeast to begin voluntary steps toward school integration. But its efforts had been only half-hearted.

The Lunch Counter Revolution

The signal for a radical new phase in the national struggle for civil rights came out of racial difficulties in the town of Monroe. During the trouble there in 1959, black leader Robert F. Williams of Monroe gave his fellow black citizens a warning. He said they could no longer depend on the protection of law-enforcement authorities. Blacks, he said, would have to buy their own arms and protect themselves. Williams fled to Cuba to avoid what some felt to be trumped-up charges against him. But he left behind the uneasy feeling that a race war might be in the making.

Trumped-up means false.

A race war of sorts did begin early in 1960. But it was fought with a new set of rules. They were unlike any that had governed previous conflicts. On February 1, 1960, four students at A. and T. College in Greensboro, a black institution, walked into a Woolworth store. They sat down at the segregated lunch counter. They were refused service. When they declined to leave, they were arrested. In the days that followed, students from A. and T. and other schools continued to fill the lunch counter seats. The demonstrations had broad meaning. The city ordinances they were protesting were the same as those long in force all over the South. If the movement won at Greensboro, it might be the beginning of the end for "Jim Crow" legislation.

This was the technique of the "sit-in" protest. It had been used from time to time in the past by black groups in Chicago, St. Louis, and other places. It had not, however, been used be-

A&T students at Greensboro launched a major national drive
for minority rights by refusing to leave seats reserved
for whites at a local lunch counter.

Picketing occurs when
people hold demonstrations
against government,
business, or other policies by
standing or marching in front
of a building or other area to
discourage people from
entering.

fore in the South or under the direction of young people. The
Greensboro protest was also different in that it did not remain
an isolated event. It was followed by similar incidents in other
towns. There were sit-ins and marches in the weeks that followed in many black college towns. These included Charlotte,
Durham, Salisbury, Winston-Salem, Fayetteville, Elizabeth
City, and Raleigh. Black high school students in Chapel Hill
used similar tactics during 1960. But they had no effect on the
town's "Jim Crow" statutes.

The civil rights movement finally struck Chapel Hill hard
in the spring of 1963. In April, a small number of white students, joined by some blacks, faculty members, and towns-
people, began picketing segregated businesses in Chapel Hill.
In January, Governor Sanford issued a public statement calling for an end to unfair practices in the hiring of blacks. He
had created a "Good Neighbor Council" to promote this aim.
The governor's method was to push for voluntary abolition of
discrimination rather than for government action. In Chapel
Hill, the picketers called themselves the "Committee for Open
Business." They soon began using sit-ins and other forms of

pressure to bring about the end of segregation in public places. Several unpleasant episodes between protestors and their critics led Sanford to ask that the demonstrations be stopped. But the Chapel Hill protesters thought this was a weakening of segregationist attitudes. They continued their activities into the summer of 1963. The university refused to crack down on student and faculty participants in the protest. This was resented by some who were watching the events at Chapel Hill. The "Gag Law" was in part the peevish response of the state legislature.

Peevish means cross, fretful.

The conservatives of the Democratic Party had had no strong influence since the death of Governor Umstead. In 1964, they rallied behind I. Beverly Lake, their choice for governor. A Wake Forest law professor, Lake was identified as a strong segregationist. He would stand for no nonsense from the civil rights demonstators. When the Sanford forces announced their support for L. Richardson Preyer of Greensboro, a wide gap of opinions was opened between the two candidates. Moderate Democrats put up Judge Dan K. Moore of Asheville, a respected mountain man. In the Democratic primary, Moore ran behind Preyer. But, in a run-off, he gained the support of Lake. He trounced the Preyer-Sanford faction. He also defeated Gavin, his Republican rival, by a little greater margin than Sanford had in 1960.

The June run-off among the Democrats featured the positions of the candidates over the 1964 Civil Rights Bill. That bill was sponsored by the Kennedy administration. Preyer announced that he was "against the Civil Rights Bill and for a calm approach to race relations." But Moore made much of Preyer's strong support in the black community. Lake's endorsement gave Moore a distinct edge in the competition.

Opponents of the Speaker Ban, as well as those favorable to racial integration, felt that Moore offered them little hope. In 1964, Moore repeated his earlier support for the ban. He said that he did not "believe we should dignify the Communist party by allowing its members or spokesmen to advocate the overthrow of our way of life at our public institutions." By mid-1965, however, Moore had second thoughts on the matter. He decided to have the charges of injury to the university investigated.

In November, the Britt Commission recommended to Moore that the act be amended. It was to return authority for the control of speakers to the trustees. The commission's report stressed that such laws tended to give glamor to the appearance of Communist speakers. It stated that many students would not continue to attend the eleven campuses if accreditation were lost. Faculty hiring and Reserve Officer Training programs would be hurt by such a loss. There was evidence of only five Communist students among the forty thousand graduated by the university in its long history. There were less than a dozen Communists among many thousands of persons who had spoken there.

Governor Moore immediately called a Special Session of the legislature. The body amended the Speaker Ban in the manner recommended by the Britt Commission. Students at the University, however, insisted that the law was still unconstitutional. They started a court challenge of the ban in 1966. In February 1968, a three-judge federal court struck down the ban as being "unconstitutional because of its vagueness."

Step by painful step, federal courts and civil rights legislation hacked away during the 1960s at the foundations of the "Jim Crow" system. The state of North Carolina professed good will toward its black citizens. But it backed down slowly before the federal onslaught. The retreat, however, was fast enough to preserve the state from the scenes of bitter violence and bloodshed that occurred elsewhere. By the beginning of the 1970s, great strides had been made in equalizing the opportunities of blacks. Much still remained to be done.

This protest was one of many that occurred in Chapel Hill in the 1960s as students and others fought to end discrimination.

The little band of integrationists who brought the racial strife to Chapel Hill in 1963 and perhaps inspired the Gag Law had as much grief as success from their efforts. On several occasions during their crusade, they were assaulted by restaurant owners and other opponents with fists, stones, and other weapons. In 1964, some of the demonstrators were tried on various charges of assault, trespass, and the like. A few of them were sentenced to active prison terms. By this time, however, businesses that had refused to serve blacks voluntarily were forced to do so by the new Civil Rights Act. It did not seem very probable that Chapel Hill would become the first sizeable Southern town to have a black mayor. But that event occurred when Howard Lee was elected in 1969.

In the course of the civil rights movement in North Carolina, a number of able black leaders emerged. They lent encouragement to fellow blacks and led them in the quest for social justice. These included Dr. Reginald A. Hawkins of Charlotte. He was the candidate for the Democratic nomination for governor in 1968 and 1972. Another was Floyd McKissick of Asheville, who became national chairman of the Congress of Racial Equality (CORE). Attorney Julius L. Chambers, a native of Mt. Gilead, was widely recognized for his work in civil rights cases. Golden A. Frinks became field secretary for the Southern Christian Leadership Conference (SCLC) in 1962. All over the nation, black men and women were finding the courage, inspiration, and resources to demand their full rights as citizens.

In 1977, Howard Lee became Secretary of Natural and Economic Resources in the Hunt administration, the highest position ever held by a black person in state government.

Chapter Checkup

PEOPLE

Terry Sanford	William B. Umstead	Robert F. Williams
Dan K. Moore	Luther H. Hodges	I. Beverly Lake
David M. Britt	Thomas J. Pearsall	Reginald A. Hawkins
William Van Alstyne	Charles R. Jonas	Floyd McKissick

PLACES

Asheboro	Cullowhee	Southern Pines
Research Triangle	Mt. Gilead	Monroe
Rocky Mount		

FACT

What were the terms of the Visiting Speakers Act of 1963?
What was the Pearsall Plan?
What role did North Carolina college students play in the civil rights protests and the Speaker Ban controversy?

INTERPRETATION

What parallels do you find between the Speaker Ban controversy and the evolution controversy of the 1920s?
How can you account for the widespread suspicions directed against the University of North Carolina in this and the previous chapter? To what extent, if any, were the suspicions valid?
How do you account for the significant role of young people in public issues during the 1960s?
Assess the short and long-range results of the Britt and Pearsall Commissions. Were their recommendations sound? Explain.

ACTIVITY

Take a poll among adult citizens as to their views on allowing Communists to speak on public property. See if you find differences in responses that can be related to the profession, place of residence, political party and age of the persons polled.

SUGGESTED READING

Ehle, John M. *The Free Men*. New York: Harper and Row, 1965. Recounts civil rights controversy and demonstrations at Chapel Hill.
Hodges, Luther H. *Businessman in the Statehouse: Six Years as Governor of North Carolina*. Chapel Hill: UNC Press, 1962. Former Governor Hodges' own account of his term of office.

1960   J. F. Kennedy elected
President *(Nov.)*

1961   Phosphate discovered
in Beaufort County

1963   Kennedy assassinated
(Nov.)

1964   Texas Gulf builds plant
in Beaufort County

1967   General Assembly passes
Water Use Act

1967   Arab-Israeli war

1969   U.S. astronauts land
on the moon

1976   Aurora adopts land use
plan

1976   James Carter elected
President *(Nov.)*

24

AURORA DAWN

Texas Gulf

Geologists are scientists who study the physical history of the earth and the rocks that compose it.

The first announcement of what was going on in Beaufort County came in late 1961. It had all the wallop of a snowflake on a roof. The *News and Observer* put the story on page ten. Having noted it, the newspaper said nothing more about it for more than two years. It may have interested geologists that the soil of Beaufort and nearby counties rested on top of ten billion tons of phosphate rock. But the public, along with newspaper editors, paid the matter little attention. Phosphate, after all, was not like gold or uranium ore. It was a lowly mineral used mostly in making fertilizer. Nobody seemed likely to get rich on it.

People concerned with the fertilizer and mining industries saw it as a major event. The Texas Gulf Sulfur Corporation had made a strike of major industrial and economic importance. The growth of the world's population was sharply increasing the demand for fertilizer. The Beaufort

Pesticides are chemicals used for destroying pests.

Detergents are synthetic cleansing agents.

County deposit was closer to major markets than any other in the world so far discovered. There was a rising demand for phosphate. It was used in pesticides and detergents, photographic supplies, dental cement, matches, and many other products. Such an industry could lead to investments of hundreds of millions of dollars in eastern North Carolina. This could be a boost such as that region had never known.

By the time the *News and Observer* again took note of the phosphate business in Beaufort County, Texas Gulf was about to make a major decision—whether to make an investment there. The corporation had dug a 15-acre hole at Lee's Creek on the Pamlico River. They had installed a three-story-tall drilling rig. On December 29, 1963, the drill struck phosphate slush 80 feet underground. If the phosphate ore were rich enough, the corporation would erect a processing plant and other facilities nearby. On April 3, 1964, the *News and Observer* flashed the news across North Carolina: "State Lands $45 Million Phosphate Mining Project." A state geologist startled many people with his observation that this was "the most exciting thing that's happened in my 40 years in the business." But what excited the specialist only baffled the public. Thirteen years after the first discovery of phosphate ore in Beaufort County, few North Carolinians had any idea what it was.

Many people got out their reference books that April. They learned that phosphate rock contains the calcium phosphate that once formed seashells, fish bones, and teeth. For

This is one section of the processing plant of Texasgulf Inc., near the town of Aurora.

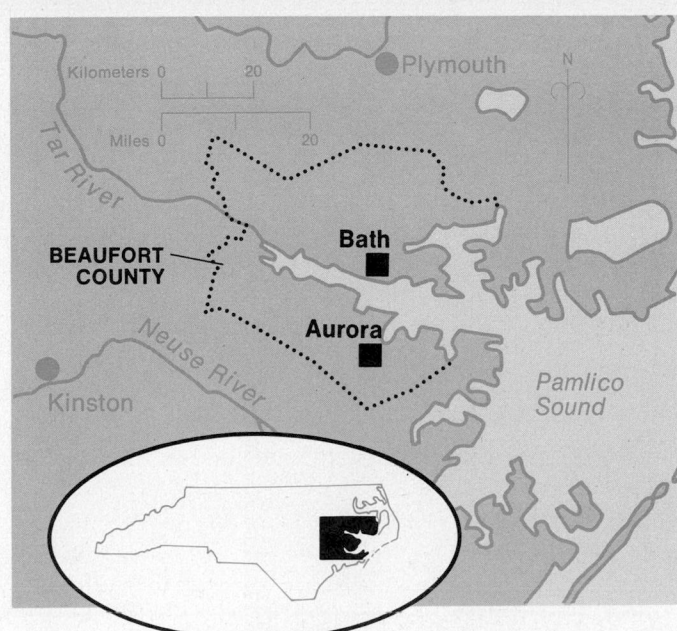

Beaufort County, 1965

millions of years the ocean covered eastern North Carolina. The death and decay of billions of sea creatures in that ocean had left phosphate layers up to 50 feet thick. This rock was now buried under deep layers of soil and clay. It could be found mainly in local concentrations. The people of Beaufort County had known since 1951 that there was phosphate rock beneath their soil. By 1964, they were beginning to understand just how large the deposit was. It stretched, they now learned, under seven nearby counties. If phosphate were truly valuable, then this eight-county deposit held a huge fortune.

The Texas Gulf Corporation worked quietly for as long as it could. This was to avoid excitement that would drive up land prices. The word, however, soon reached the lower Pamlico. Land prices leaped from fifty dollars an acre to as much as eight hundred. But this was only the first of a long series of important economic effects in the area. The corporation would need 35 miles of railroad lines for shipping their products northward. It would require new port facilities at Morehead City and elsewhere. Rivers would have to be deepened, creeks re-channeled, inlets enlarged. A considerable area of coastal North Carolina would have to be transformed. All this was needed to meet the growing demands of Texas Gulf's mining operations.

Week by week the plans of the Texas Gulf Corporation unfolded. North Carolinians began to appreciate the vastness

A huge dredge of Texasgulf Inc. pumps away earth and rock to get at the phosphate deposits below.

of what was taking place at Lee's Creek. The corporation would build five fertilizer plants in the vicinity of the town of Aurora. Aurora would have the world's largest plants to produce phosphoric acid, solid fertilizer, and sulfuric acid.

At later times, the corporation announced further additions. It raised its investment from 45 to 80 million dollars. It raised leases and purchases of land to thirty thousand acres.

Beaufort County hurried to adjust itself to the startling expansion of the phosphate business. It passed heavy bond issues for new schools for the children of construction crews and permanent workers. There would need to be new housing, many new school buses, more teachers, more power, sewer and water lines. The Texas Gulf management wanted to build a favorable public image for itself. It furnished the town of Bath with lighted all-weather tennis courts. It gave a great deal to community projects. Nearby, the Magnet Cove Barium Corporation and the North Carolina Phosphate Company were also growing. With the addition of related industries and services, no one could foretell just how great the total impact might become.

The economic effects of the phosphate business on eastern North Carolina were hard to judge. Its potential effects on

A *dike* is an embankment for holding back waters.

To *pollute* is to make dirty.

Monitoring means observing.

Aurora hoped for great growth and riches from the phosphate industry.

the physical environment were even harder. Throughout 1964 and the following years, Texas Gulf met with various state agencies about the environment question. Other groups also worried much about it. In 1964, the State Stream Sanitation Committee resisted the corporation's request to build a dike more than a mile long on the Pamlico River. It was to protect the fertilizer plant from floods. The committee finally agreed that the dike would be built from waste materials. It should not pollute the river to a dangerous degree. Later, the State Board of Water Resources objected to the huge amounts of ground water being pumped out of Lee's Creek.

By 1968, Texas Gulf was using 59 million gallons of fresh water a day. It came from the limestone beds containing Beaufort County's water supplies. The expected growth of Texas Gulf's plant, along with the North Carolina Phosphate Company, would almost triple water use. Much of the water was not returned to the gound. Some geologists predicted that the fresh water in the limestone beds would be replaced by salt water seeping from the ocean floor. The result would be a disaster. It might surpass in its effects any economic gains that the phosphate industry could bring to North Carolina.

In 1967, the General Assembly passed a Water Use Act. This was to preserve fresh water supplies in the affected area and elsewhere. The act required any industry using as much as 100,000 gallons of fresh water a day to have a state license for the purpose. Texas Gulf insisted that its own monitoring wells showed no contamination of Beaufort County's water. It announced that it would not be able to keep its plant open unless it were exempted from the act. Most of the fresh water was necessary for its drypit mining technique. The rest was needed for processing the rock after it was mined.

State agencies worried over the question of salt-water seepage. But new problems were arising at Lee's Creek. Hundreds of farmers and others in the vicinity of the phosphate mine began to find their own water pumps losing pressure. Some were even going dry. The mine agreed to help those affected. The mine would pay part of the cost of deeper wells or better pumps. But this failed to satisfy many of those who were being injured. Meanwhile, in the late 1960s, the world demand for phosphate fell sharply. This slowed the growth of the Texas Gulf plant. It caused other companies to delay plans for new mines nearby. But none of these hardships involved anything like the rage and despair that began to emerge in the town of Aurora.

The early 1960s had brought a glow of golden promise to the town of Aurora. It was the nearest community to the giant phosphate mine on Lee's Creek. Once the mine was in operation, everyone said allied industries would follow quickly. These would be detergent and pesticide producers. Aurora, a hamlet of less than four hundred people, would become a city of not less than ten thousand people. Very possibly it might grow to fifty thousand or more. Land values would skyrocket. Small businesses would become large ones. The tiny community would be known in a few years as the phosphate capital of the world. Aurora citizens and town officials loyally stood by the Texas Gulf Corporation in its disputes with the state. They defended the company from attacks upon it.

In the summer of 1974, North Carolina Phosphate announced that it would proceed with further plans. It would invest 220 million dollars in a Beaufort County plant. But the expected cheers from Aurora were not heard. Instead, residents of the town grumbled openly. They talked of fears over what the new development would do to the environment. Many outside the area were surprised. Aurora seemed to be inclined to bite the hand that fed it. In the coming months, however, newspaper reports gave support to the Aurora complaint. The reports showed that the fears were very real.

Boycotting means refusing to deal with.

The problem was not simple. The phosphate boom was now into its second decade. But Aurora had gained less than two hundred fifty in its population. Aurora citizens charged that Texasgulf Inc. was boycotting the town's businesses. They pointed to examples of local businesses whose incomes had fallen a great deal since the early 1960s. It seemed suspicious that executives of the corporation now served on local government agencies. These included one who was chairman of the county planning board. In the eyes of a growing number of residents, these and other signs added up to a secret plot on the part of the mine against the town.

In 1973, The Texas Gulf Sulfur Corporation changed its name to Texasgulf Inc.

A theory was put forth by many alarmed people of Aurora. It was that Texasgulf wanted to see the town die. Then the company could mine the precious rock below the surface. The corporation was quick to deny this idea. But it was perfectly true that the town sat squarely in the heart of the phosphate region. Texasgulf's operation had been creeping closer for years. The growth of a sprawling town would not serve the best interests of the phosphate miners. If mine people controlled the town's government, it was not hard to imagine how they would try to run it. It would be in a way most advantageous to Texasgulf. Aurorans had good reason to worry. Were they losing control over their own destiny?

The prosperity of an industry versus the life of a town was a symbol of the bigger worries of millions of North Caro-

A **habitat** is the native environment of a person, plant, or animal.

Posterity means future generations.

linians in the late 1970s and beyond. Elsewhere in the state there were other questions. Would an island wildlife habitat be turned over to private development? Would an ancient Indian townsite be sacrificed for the building of a dam? Would a handsome old building be replaced by a parking lot? Nearly every means of economic gain seemed to demand a brutal price. But it was in the form of some new outrage against the environment. Never before had North Carolinians seen such material progress or agonized so much over its coming. Would posterity bless or blast the decisions of the 1970s? This question was the heart of a thousand public conflicts.

Better Ways, Better Days

As the final quarter of the twentieth century opened, North Carolina was rapidly being changed from a farming state into an industrial one. This was especially the case in the Piedmont and mountain regions. There, cheap labor and hydroelectric power were plentiful. The Coastal Plain was still mainly a farming region. Even there, industry was growing at a startling pace. Textiles, tobacco, and furniture still led the advance. But the state's industrial economy was becoming more diverse than in the past.

In the 1970s, North Carolina had more textile mills than any other state in the nation. Many of these mills were the largest of their kind in the world. These included the towel factory at Kannapolis, the hosiery mill at Durham, and Greensboro's denim mill. There was Winston-Salem's men's underwear factory, Elkin's woolen blanket plant, and the damask mill at Roanoke Rapids. Cone Mills and Burlington Industries were among the giants of the business. In 1971, Burlington had one hundred thirty-two factories located in 15 states and 11 foreign countries. The School of Textile Design at North Carolina State University had the largest research department in the nation.

A major change in the industry was the passing of the mill village. These villages helped bring on the 1929 crisis at Gastonia. By the 1970s, most mills had sold the dwellings to the workers. Another significant change was that many smaller mills were taken over by larger firms. However, the industry continued to be one of many competing and widely scattered units.

A textile worker is placing yarn to be fed to the knitting machine behind her, which knits fabric for women's dresses.

Tobacco also remained a major North Carolina industry. R. J. Reynolds (Winston-Salem), Liggett and Myers (Durham), American (Reidsville), and P. Lorillard (Greensboro) were still dominant. There were periodic flurries of concern over links between smoking and cancer and other diseases. But the use of tobacco remained very nearly a world-wide habit. North Carolina farmers continued to grow nearly half the country's tobacco. The state's manufacturers made more than half the nation's cigarettes. But the industry was not safe against further evidence that smoking caused cancer. Also, someone might discover a suitable substitute for smoking tobacco. Either of these events might deal a crippling blow to North Carolina's economy.

The forest products industry was far behind textiles and tobacco. But it was still of major importance to the state. North Carolina remained the leading producer of wooden furniture. It was a major producer of paper and lumber. Other major industries were food products, chemicals, medicines, and cottonseed oil. Also included were electrical equipment, machinery, printing, publishing, and truck and bus bodies. More spectacular was the rise of many new industries. These were the manufacturing of surgical instruments, photographic

A ***commodity*** is an article of trade or commerce.

equipment, dental supplies, and clocks and watches. In the mountains, many new plants produced leather and rubber footwear. Plastics was now an important commodity in the state. Fayetteville had gained a large tire plant. Fabricated metals, such as hardware, machine screws, wire, pipe valves and fittings, and structural steel made large gains. Manufacturing had become North Carolina's leading employer and its main source of personal income.

Most labor unions gained from the policies of the New Deal and the Fair Deal. However, North Carolina labor was the least organized and lowest paid in the United States in 1976. It was one of only 18 states with a so-called "right to work" law. This outlawed compulsory unionization. It also discouraged the formation and growth of labor unions. It was in part the deliberate plan of the state government to create conditions that would attract new industry. Perhaps it was also the result of age-old attitudes of the state's workers themselves. Independent rural North Carolinians were still the backbone of the labor pool. They clung to the ideas that made their forebears so hesitant to join the federal union and the Southern Confederacy. But industry-dominated chambers of commerce also discouraged the introduction of unionized plants at various points across the state.

Apart from unionism, the state took a good deal of interest in the welfare of working people. This interest was shown mainly through the state Department of Labor. Since the 1930s, the agency had been making efforts to settle strikes, en-

A great deal of hand work goes into the making of fine wood furniture, a product for which North Carolina is famous.

force labor laws, and help the unemployed. It also found other ways to serve the needs of laborers. Through the state Industrial Commission, the Department administered the Workman's Compensation Act. This meant adjusting some forty thousand claims a year. But state policy still seemed aimed more toward the special interests of management than of labor.

Personal income levels had risen sharply in recent decades. But black workers still lagged behind whites in this respect. In 1970, only 32.5 percent of the black population of North Carolina was employed, as opposed to 40.9 percent of the whites. Blacks made up nearly 20 percent of the factory workers of the state. But they represented less than a tenth of the higher-skilled workers. For many years, the textile industry had refused to employ blacks. By 1970 it had a work force that was about 14 percent black. In the same year, nearly half the women over 16 of all races were employed outside their homes. This was a striking increase over earlier years. Critics of North Carolina's economic evolution argued that the state had been changed from a poor farming state into a poor industrial one.

Diversity means variety.

Even more than manufacturing, North Carolina agriculture in recent decades has been characterized by diversity. There was a tendency for larger farms to replace several smaller ones. In 1969, only six states had more farms than North Carolina. But the number in this state had dropped by seventy thousand from a decade earlier. And the number was still falling. The proportion of tenants dropped by half (to 15 percent) in the same period. Better jobs were found in other areas of the economy. Also, machines had replaced farm laborers. As the size and efficiency of farms increased, gross farm income also rose. It almost doubled between 1950 and 1971. Although the number of farmers was smaller, those farmers still in business were making far greater incomes. A slowing of the farm exodus seemed likely in the years ahead.

Exodus is going out or departure.

Flue-cured means dried or cured by warm air passing through heat ducts.

In the 1970s, tobacco led all other farm products in value, as it had for the past 40 years. Sales of flue-cured tobacco in 1972 amounted to more than half a billion dollars. This was because new insecticides and machines improved yields and quality. In 1971, there were almost 340,000 acres of flue-cured tobacco grown. Farmers grew more than a ton of tobacco per acre. In addition, sizeable amounts of burley tobacco were grown in the western third of the state. However, government quotas were much smaller for the flue-cured variety.

Corn was still a staple food crop. It was more and more in demand by the state's cattle and poultry producers. By the

North Carolina mountain farms not only are beautiful, but produce abundant crops. This is an autumn harvest.

1970s, corn became North Carolina's second most valuable farm crop. Soybean production almost doubled between 1962 and 1972. Soybeans had gained world-wide recognition as one of nature's finest sources of protein. Peanuts were the leading crop in ten northeastern counties. And North Carolina had taken the lead in the nation in sweet potatoes. But cotton had declined sharply from former times. It was dragged down in the second quarter of the century by world over-production and falling prices. Wheat, snap beans, apples (mainly in the west), peaches (in the sandhills), strawberries, and tomatoes were also among the state's leading farm products.

In 1971, livestock and poultry brought in more than six hundred million dollars to North Carolina farmers. The state was outranked in hog production by only ten others. In value of broiler production, only three other states were ahead. A large business in turkeys had grown up in the southeastern

Hanging Rock State Park, near Danbury, is one of the state's famous areas of natural beauty.

Uwharrie can also be spelled Uharie.

counties. But broiler production spanned the state from the mountains to the sea. North Carolina ranked third in the nation in the value of eggs sold. It did not rank high as a producer of beef or dairy products.

Federal and state governments improved the prospects of North Carolina farmers by providing aid. Since the 1930s, a great deal of federal money had gone into North Carolina State University's agricultural experiments and extension work. Large amounts went into vocational education throughout the state. Earlier, the New Deal had taken some of the sting out of the Depression years. It furnished loans and payments to farmers. This was for limiting the production of certain crops and for soil conservation. It was also to help raise prices. The state Rural Electrification Authority, created in 1935, helped bring electricity to most of rural North Carolina. The state Department of Agriculture operated test farms and furnished information on farm problems. It also sought pest control and gave other important services to the farming population. Gradually, North Carolina farmers learned the importance of fertilizer and machinery. They learned about careful seed selection, crop rotation, and other modern methods. A revolution in communication and transportation added to these advances.

North Carolina's Department of Conservation and Development (C and D) had its origin in 1925. But it would be many years before conservation ranked anywhere near development as a public concern. The New Deal had provided some assistance to farmers for soil conservation in the 1930s. But the benefits of the natural environment still seemed almost inexhaustible. Still, C and D operated fish hatcheries and enforced game and fish laws. It also operated game preserves and wildlife sanctuaries. Forest nurseries, state park supervision, and forest fire control also came under the responsibility of C and D. In addition, the state undertook studies of beach erosion, water pollution, and flood control. But it was not until after World War II that the environment became a major item in personal and administrative thinking.

There had been great success in bringing industry into North Carolina in the 1960s and 1970s. But now, the citizens of the state were confronted with some important choices. It had not been hard to establish the four National Forests (Pisgah, Nantahala, Uwharrie, and Croatan) in the state in earlier years. But now the growth of population began to squeeze all available living space. No longer were there large areas that might escape industrial and commercial development. Almost every new industrial gain would involve questions of further damage to the environment.

The rise of the tourist industry was an important factor in the growing assault on the natural environment. By 1962, North Carolina had twelve state parks scattered across the state from the ocean to the mountains. But many people were dismayed at the way private and commercial interests were taking over scenic natural areas. These areas were outside federal or state control. Wild areas, notably those on the Outer Banks and in the mountains, were shrinking year by year. The Great Smoky Mountains National Park was created by the federal government in 1962. The park covered half a million acres in North Carolina and Tennessee. It became one of the nation's most popular resort areas. On the coast, the Cape Hatteras National Seashore Recreational Area covered 28,500 acres. But the popularity of camping, boating, and other forms of outdoor recreation was straining the facilities of these parks. It was also boosting fast commercial buildup elsewhere.

Support began to grow in North Carolina during the 1970s for a Land Policy Act. Under this act, every county of the state would classify the land within its borders for future uses. Such plans would encourage long-term planning. Each county might have certain areas in which certain types of development could take place. Other areas would be set aside because of their scenic and natural beauty, or for other reasons.

It's fun to take a slide down Sliding Rock in Pisgah National Forest near Brevard, spilling into a pool of clear, cool water.

A potter (left) at Arden produces a small vase. A few of
the many products produced at Seagrove are shown at right.

The aim was to avoid the helter-skelter kind of development
that had marked industrial and commercial progress.

Could such broad-scale and long-range planning be
achieved? Industrial developers in growing numbers were
finding their plans blocked. The resistance came from envi-
ronmentalists or historical societies. They were trying to stop
the advance of the crane and the bulldozer. At the same time,
it was clear that new jobs and opportunities for people in
North Carolina were needed. Time and again, the public was
reminded that industrial development must not be crippled.
However, it needed regulation. Also, economic progress must
not result in the pollution and destruction of the environment.
The struggle to balance these opposing ends insured further
conflict as the twentieth century waned.

The ***aurora borealis,*** also
called northern lights, are
glowing streaks of natural
light seen in the northern
night sky.

Aurora Borealis

The town of Aurora was living in the shadow of a commercial
giant. Its fears were to be shared in the 1970s by a growing
number of North Carolinians. Not many miles northeast of
Aurora lay rural Washington, Hyde, Tyrrell, and Dare Coun-

ties. There, First Colony Farms had established a 375,000-acre agricultural giant. The forty-five-thousand-acre Open Grounds Farm was nearby in Carteret County. The possibility of uncontrolled pollution by these farms was staggering. The state's Environmental Management Commission tried to check on the farms. The commission felt that injury to surrounding areas was being caused by the huge amounts of pesticides, fertilizers, and animal wastes from these farms. Shellfishing was one of several major sources of coastal income. It was being affected badly by the giant farms and other sources of pollutants.

At Aurora and in nearby Bath (North Carolina's oldest town), worried residents organized the Pamlico-Bath Preservation Foundation. This was an effort to resist the growing influence of mining firms in local affairs. The group suspected Texasgulf, the North Carolina Phosphate Corporation, and FMC, Incorporated. They felt that industry was turning Beaufort County's land-use plan to the advantage of the mining interests. The foundation could quote an opinion of the state's Coastal Resources Commission. In late 1975, the commission stated that the county plan appeared to lean too heavily in favor of the phosphate producers. The county planning board was headed by a Texasgulf mining engineer. Recently, the board had stopped an effort to outlaw mining at the bottom of Pamlico River. Officials for Texasgulf said they had no plans for river-bottom mining until well into the twenty-first century.

Aurora's greatest fear was still for its future life. In the spring of 1976, Grace Bonner, Aurora's mayor, spoke to a newspaper correspondent. She said that Texasgulf wanted to have the town's high school—its "social hub"—moved to a site seven miles away. There was the likelihood that this would kill the town. It lent added suspicions to those already created against the firm.

The Aurora Planning Board was fighting to save the town from threatened death. It acted to throw an obstacle in the path of the advancing industry. It adopted a plan to prevent any mining within a mile of the town limits. But these limits contained thirty-seven hundred acres of Texasgulf property. It represented a direct challenge to the mining interest. Texasgulf and North Carolina Phosphate owned more than one hundred thousand acres in the county. Texasgulf could boast that 30 percent of the county's residents were its employees. These facts, beside Texasgulf's billion-dollar assets, appeared to be an impossible problem for the 671 residents of the little town.

Aurora also sought a zoning code to enforce its land-use plan. It got technical assistance from students of the School of

Mayor Grace Bonner fights to save Aurora and bring it to the prosperity it expected from the phosphate business.

A *zoning code* is a set of laws restricting the use of land in a certain area or zone.

Aurora's community pride is its best defense against forces that threaten its existence.

By-products are secondary products resulting from a process of manufacture.

Design at North Carolina State University. But it was expected that Texasgulf would challenge the zoning code. It would fight any other restrictions that might be made against its mining activities. The prospect was that Aurora would become a less and less desirable place to live in as the mining operations crept closer. But there were many other vicinities across the state where similar conflicts were going on. These would shape the destiny of North Carolina for years to come. If Aurora could manage to survive somehow and even prosper in the face of its trouble, it might yet become an inspiration for many other communities. It might become a light in the night sky of environmental decay, the aurora of a brighter day to come.

The problem in Aurora was symbolic of a national, even a world issue. The problem did not concern only the Pamlico River. The oceans of the world and the skies overhead were in danger. The entire world was being threatened by tons of polluting smoke, spray, and waste given off every hour by a growing world industry. Was humanity trying to poison itself with the by-products of its last natural resources? The great benefits of the past make a good argument for keeping the same pace or even going faster. But people who looked ahead as far as half a century were often troubled. Millions on every continent were not adequately clothed, housed, or fed. Two goals seemed to be fighting each other. One was to provide for people's basic needs. The other was to protect and preserve the environment. Could one goal be achieved without destroying the other? This conflict between two worthwhile and necessary goals seemed to haunt the future of humanity.

Chapter Checkup

PEOPLE

Grace Bonner

PLACES

Beaufort County	Croatan National Forest
Aurora	Nantahala National Forest
Morehead City	Uwharrie (Uharie) National Forest
Elkin	Great Smoky Mountains National Park
Roanoke Rapids	Cape Hatteras National Seashore
Burlington	

FACT

Why is phosphate valuable?
Why did some people feel that Texasgulf wanted to see Aurora disappear?
What is a "right to work" law?
What are North Carolina's leading farm crops?

INTERPRETATION

Do you think Aurora should cease to exist so the phosphate underneath it can be mined? Defend your answer.
Has the North Carolina government taken as large a role as it should in trying to control phosphate mining? Explain.
What do you see as the three leading problems caused by the industrial development of North Carolina? Why do you choose these three?
What do you see as the main reason why North Carolina's industrial laborers are the poorest paid in the country?

VOCABULARY

Geologist	Boycotting	Diversity
Pollute	Posterity	Zoning code
Monitoring		

ACTIVITY

Investigate an industry near you and find out whether it is careful not to injure the environment, how its wages compare with what is paid for similar work elsewhere in the country, whether and in what ways it tries to exert influence in community affairs. All things considered, is this industry an asset to the community or not?

SUGGESTED READING

Clay, James W. *et al. North Carolina Atlas: Portrait of a Changing Southern State.* Chapel Hill: UNC Press, 1975. See especially Part IV, "The Economy," for an up-to-date and forthright survey of North Carolina's economic gains and problems.

1967 North Carolina
Bicentennial planning
begins

1968 Martin Luther King
assassinated *(April)*
● Robert F. Kennedy assassinated
(June)

1969 Robert W. Scott
becomes governor

1969 Neil A. Armstrong,
first person to set foot
on the moon

1972 Bicentennial Commission
presents plans to
Governor Scott
● James E. Holshouser, Jr.
elected governor

1974 Richard M. Nixon,
first person to resign from
the Presidency

1975 Viet Nam War ends
(April 30)

1976 Bicentennial celebrations
(July)
● James B. Hunt, Jr. elected
governor

1976 Bicentennial year
of celebrations

1977 James E. Carter
inaugurated President

25

THE BICENTENNIAL AND BEYOND

The Spiriting Up

To some people, the issue seemed not how to celebrate the Bicentennial but why. Planning began in 1967 during the Viet Nam War. And final plans were being made as the war goal of "peace with honor" turned into military defeat. In the nine years before the Bicentennial year, Robert F. Kennedy and Martin Luther King had been assassinated. Violent civil rights and war protests had occurred. Vice President Spiro Agnew had resigned for taking bribes. President Richard Nixon had resigned over the Watergate scandal.

The situation in North Carolina was about as awkward as it was anywhere. Four people had served as director of the state Bicentennial Commission. Each person seemed less suited to the job than the one before. The holder of the title had been subject to the ups and downs of party politics and the whims of governors' wives. The commission had a lot of money to spend. But few could agree over how to spend it.

What should be the main concern? Should the Bicentennial honor the dead, aid the living, or provide for the yet-unborn? Should there be one grand celebration or many small ones?

A key question in planning the Bicentennial would be the role of local communities. Should the plans be made in Raleigh, and local groups directed from there? Or should the people themselves do the planning with help from the state commission? The second way seemed more democratic. But it conflicted with the way the government had been developing for many years. Decisions seemed to be made in Raleigh and Washington for everybody. People seemed to rely on the government to make up their minds for them. There might not be enough local pride and know-how to carry out a celebration even if people could decide what to celebrate.

That was the way the state legislature appeared to view the matter when it created the Bicentennial Commission in 1967. The law setting up the commission established two guidelines for its work. The commission was to plan and conduct the proper celebrations. It was also to acquaint citizens of the state and nation with "the major and leading role played by North Carolina in the American Revolution." The first of these goals suggested that the Bicentennial be handled by officials in Raleigh. The second was clearly impossible: North Carolina had played no leading role.

The Bicentennial Commission presented its plans to Governor Scott in 1972. It had paid little attention to the 1967 guidelines. The commission's view was that local communities should plan and carry out their own celebrations and get help from the commission staff. Communities would be asked to put emphasis on building for the future. They would be asked to identify problems affecting the quality of life of the people. Once this was done they would be encouraged to set priorities. They would go to work to solve their problems. In this way the celebration of the Revolution would become a continuing project. The hope would be to awaken the old idea of local initiative in problem-solving. It might not be too late to get people away from dependence on government. The commission wanted to launch a second American Revolution. It hoped it could bring forth the fresh spirit of the late eighteenth century.

There were some things that could not be accomplished through local groups. Some projects could best be handled by professional groups, others by the Bicentennial staff itself. Not much had ever been written about North Carolina's role in the Revolution. A series of scholarly pamphlets could help make up for this shortcoming. There were suggestions for films and TV shows. They could carry the message of the Bicentennial and its meaning to millions of people. The Bicentennial staff would have to spread itself thin. It would aid in all sorts of meetings for speakers, arrangements for festivals, re-enactments of battles. But its main purpose would be to encourage and support local groups.

The work went forward in spite of a thousand problems. These were mostly over what to do and when and how to do it. But many small problems appeared to some people as turning into one large one. The Bicentennial year, 1976, opened.

Ashland House, a restored plantation near Henderson, is one of thousands of early buildings being preserved.

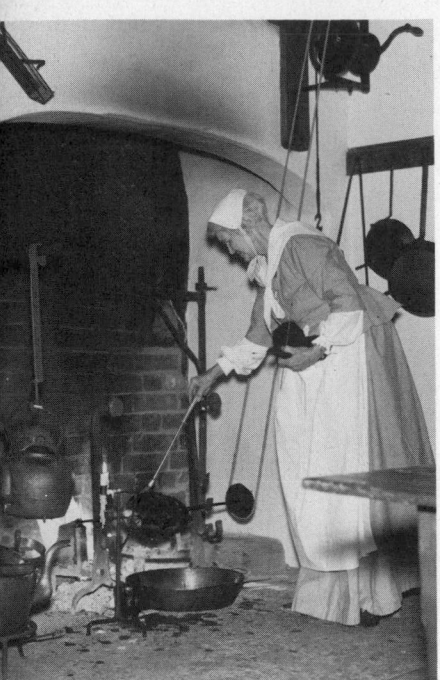

Old Salem, a restored 18th century Moravian community near Winston-Salem, recreates the life of early Piedmont settlers.

However, the program of activities was already well under way. In January, a former director of the state Bicentennial Commission reviewed the work done so far. The Bicentennial, he announced, had been betrayed. It had turned into a scene of backpatting for the country and state. The selling of cheap Bicentennial jewelry and knick-knacks had led many to refer to it scornfully as the "Buycentennial." The Fourth of July was still six months away. But many people were already sick and tired of the Bicentennial. They were ready to call the whole thing off. They could see no signs of any rebirth of public spirit, no reawakening of the revoluntionary feeling.

Had the celebration gone so terribly astray? Had the million dollars and more spent by the Bicentennial Commission in North Carolina been wasted? Some people argued that Americans no longer were able to do things in a revolutionary spirit. This spirit, it was said, belonged only to the have-nots of the world. America had become rich and powerful. It had lost sympathy for struggling young nations. It was fat and satisfied. It was not in a mood for heroism and self-sacrifice. The Bicentennial would be nothing more than a celebration of wealth and strength.

As the Fourth of July neared, the state government made an announcement. It said that the Bicentennial Commission would cease to exist at the end of 1976. There had been hopes from the first that it might continue to function until the end of 1989. Some felt that would be the proper time to end the celebration. It would be the 200th anniversary of North Carolina's ratification of the federal Constitution. Now the effort to rekindle the revolutionary spirit would have to be done in nine years instead of twenty-two. The grand dream had died—or so it seemed to some in the spring of 1976.

Sowing the Sahara

It was half a century before the Bicentennial year. At that time, critic H. L. Mencken referred to the South as a "Sahara" of the fine arts. He said that America's notable painting, sculpture, writing, music, and drama was mostly produced in other sections of the nation. Whether literature should have been included in Mencken's statement was a matter for debate. Writers such as Thomas Wolfe and Jack Cash were evidence against such a statement. But in other respects the charge

(Text continues on page 481.)

A cool clear stream high in the Great Smoky Mountains is one of North Carolina's great natural resources. A strong system of state parks protects wilderness areas like this and preserves them for future generations.

Each of the 35 state parks and many private recreation areas have special features. In summer the people of North Carolina can paddle over rapids on the Nantahala River (left). In winter they can ski down snowy mountain slopes near Banner Elk (right).

Nature created rivers for North Carolina but human hands—and human laws—built dams that made the state's lakes. Two Tar Heel sportsmen enjoy strong breezes on a lake in mountainous Henderson County.

Some of the state's best-known parkland is found along a 300-mile strip of sand—the Outer Banks. At Jockey Ridge State Park, a hang glider takes off from a giant sand dune more than 100 feet high. To conserve these windswept dunes requires constant care by park officials.

Conserving the state's wildlife is a fulltime job
for trained naturalists and park rangers. In swamplands
near the coast (upper left), a park ranger observes
the flight of birds, and then tries to rescue an injured
waterfowl (upper right). Another job of the park ranger
is to lead families and school groups through Fort Macon
State Park (below). Here he explains how the fort changed
hands twice during the Civil War.

These scientists are trying to learn how polluted water affects the growth of lobsters and crabs. They are working in one of the nation's most important centers of marine research—the Duke University Marine Laboratory at Beaufort.

Other pollution and environmental studies are carried out at another famous center of learning—Research Triangle Park. Here, one scientist (lower left) wants to find out what happens to quail eggs under special conditions. Another scientist wants to know how the human body adjusts to vigorous exercise (lower right).

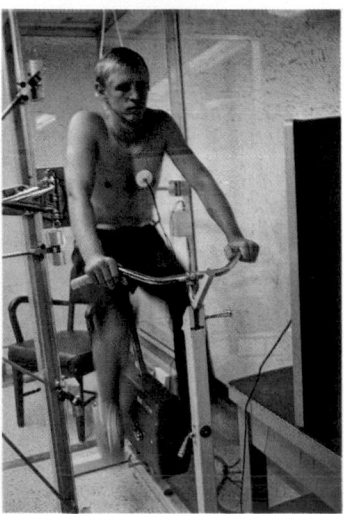

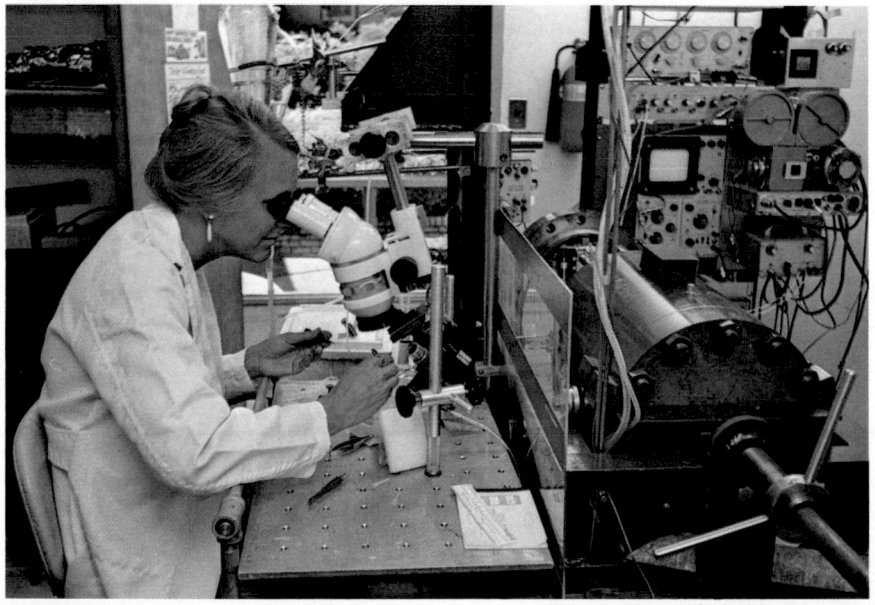

There are probably more doctors and scientists at work
in the Research Triangle than in any similar area in
the United States. The Burroughs Wellcome Company employs
hundreds of chemists and doctors in its gigantic Research
Triangle laboratory and its Greenville plant, shown here.
Some scientists (above) must wear special protective
clothing as they experiment with new kinds of medicines.
Other scientists (below) must be skilled in the use of
complex electronic equipment.

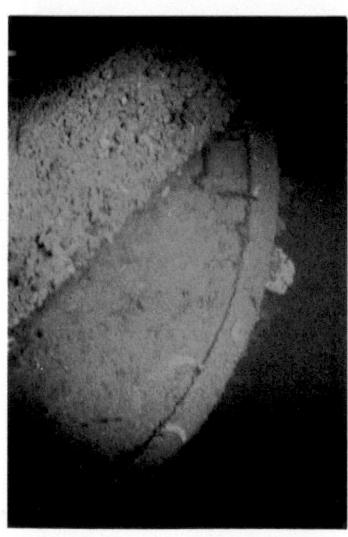

Scientific research can sometimes help to recover a
nation's past. The ship model on the desk of Project
Director John Newton (above) shows what the old Civil
War ship, the *Monitor,* looks like over a century after
it was shipwrecked off Cape Hatteras in 1862. Scientists
of the project are now at work trying to raise the ship
from the ocean floor. Compare the underwater photograph
of the *Monitor's* gun turret (lower left) with an old
Civil War photograph of the turret and the ship's crew
of Union sailors (lower right).

Scientists and research laboratories are changing North Carolina. So are workers in industry as they adopt new methods in farming, fishing, forestry, and manufacturing. For example, building boats for North Carolina's fishing industry requires great know-how and skill.

One result of better boat-building is a better haul of fish. Commercial fishing and sports fishing are both important sources of income for the people of coastal North Carolina.

The state's vast hardwood
forests are another source
of natural wealth. Using
powerful scissor-like
equipment, lumber companies
can snip off giant trees as
if they were toothpicks.

Knowing how to care for trees is as important as knowing
how to cut them down. Workers plant new trees and trim
young ones (lower left) so there will always be enough
mature trees to cut and turn into wood chips (lower right).

Small farmers still grow most of North Carolina's food and tobacco crops. But even this is changing. Huge corporations have entered the business of agriculture, or "agribusiness," as they call it. The huge tract of farmland (right) and harvesting machinery (lower right) belong to one corporation.

Making bricks the modern way is also big business in North Carolina.

North Carolina is also making progress in the arts. At the North Carolina Museum of Art in Raleigh, a painting by John Singleton Copley (upper left) is one of many masterpieces that the museum has purchased with funds voted by the legislature. The museum also displays a collection of rare Egyptian art, including a splendid gilded mummy case (upper right).

Tryon Palace, built for the British royal governor in New Bern in 1767, was once called "the most beautiful building in Colonial America." Destroyed by fire, the palace was carefully restored in the 1950s. Colonial laws were debated in the palace's council chamber (right).

Learning about art is what museums are for. A family learns about medieval painting in the North Carolina Museum of Art.

The performing arts—dance, music, drama—receive strong support from the people of the state. Both high school and college students can learn ballet (right) and costume design (lower right) at the North Carolina School of the Arts in Winston-Salem. Performances by student dancers and actors have impressed audiences throughout the United States.

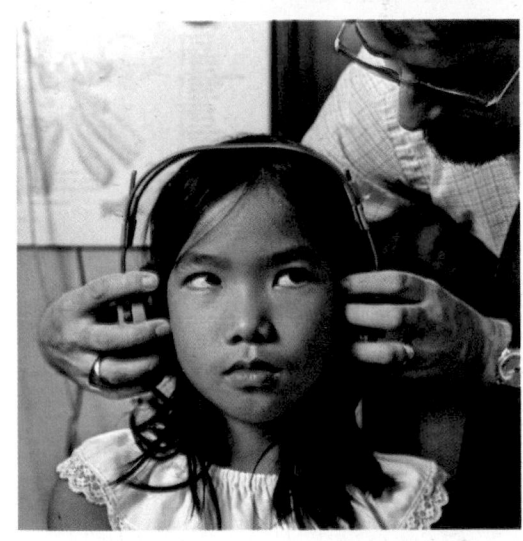
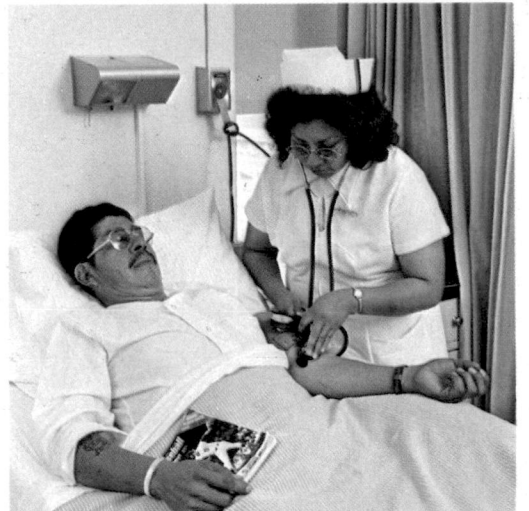

North Carolina's hospitals and health clinics are among the best in the country. They are especially well known for the help they give to handicapped people. At one clinic (above left), a handicapped child takes a hearing test. A nurse checks a patient's blood pressure (above right).

A blind person is being taught to read braille.

People in the mountain village of Cherokee are famous for their skills as basketweavers and handicraft workers. This woman employs weaving techniques practiced by her Cherokee ancestors for many generations.

The wooden figure (right) is another fine example of Cherokee art. The man who carved it, G. B. Chiltosky, (left) has been widely acclaimed for his work as a woodcarver.

Mountains. Beaches. Research. Industrial growth. Arts and crafts. The Tar Heel State is known for all of these. But there is more. Its folk music has long been known by music lovers outside the state. The North Carolina Symphony is beginning to be better known. In March 1977, North Carolina Governors Hunt, Sanford, Holshouser, and Scott (left to right) proudly attend the symphony's first performance in New York City's Carnegie Hall.

And then there is the game of basketball and Dean Smith, coach of the 1976 United States Olympic team.
The North Carolina Tar Heels, finalists in the 1977 NCAA championship game, have long been respected in the sports world for their exciting style of play.

seemed to be true. North Carolina appeared in some ways like a cultural desert.

To the world of the visual arts, for example, North Carolina had almost no claim to recognition. At the end of World War II, there were only a few small art museums and galleries. Charlotte's Mint Museum of Art, founded in 1936, had a small collection of excellent paintings. So did the Hickory Museum of Art, opened in 1944. But North Carolinians interested in fine art had to go to Richmond, Virginia, or places further north to see good collections. The state still had not given the nation an artist of first rank. It had never, in fact, been the home of one. The mother of James McNeill Whistler was a native of North Carolina. Whistler became a prominent artist. But his mother was almost the state's only claim to fame in the visual arts.

In 1925, a small group of art lovers created the North Carolina Art Society. Membership grew slowly. But the society hoped that it might someday put North Carolina on the map of the art world. This could be done if the state should ever have a major art collection. If that day came, more North Carolinians might become interested in art. They would seek professional training. In time, the state might even produce outstanding artists. Their work would serve to answer Mencken's criticism. No longer would North Carolina be a part of the cultural Sahara.

By 1929, the Art Society had acquired several small collections of fine paintings. A gift of paintings by Concord native Robert F. Phifer gave the society a good beginning. In that year the General Assembly agreed to take control of the society. It would provide annual funds for the support of the art collections. This meant the society could use space in state government buildings. There, it would exhibit its paintings and sketches. Soon afterward, North Carolina had the beginning of its art museum. It was in a spare room in the State Agriculture Building. It wasn't very much, but it was a start.

A major turning point for art lovers and students in North Carolina came in 1943. It was in the midst of World War II. State leaders began to think about a permanent State Art Gallery. The idea was to call it a memorial to North Carolinians who had served in both world wars. The appeal of patriotism might urge some legislators to vote for the project. A suggestion was made that the group first try to raise fifty thousand dollars from private sources. It would then ask the legislature to increase the amount. Robert Lee Humber, a well-known lawyer from Greenville, startled the group. He stated that it would take a million dollars to launch the project. Moreover, he added, he would try to find that much himself.

"Whistler's Mother" is a famous painting of Anna McNeill Whistler of Wilmington, mother of artist James McNeill Whistler.

The North Carolina Museum of Life and Science at Durham is
especially for children. Thousands of people visit it yearly.

Through contacts in New York, Humber began talks with
department store tycoon Samuel H. Kress. Those who were in
on the secret were astonished. Kress agreed to donate a million dollars to the North Carolina project! But the state must
match that amount or else it was "no deal." This seemed an
unlikely hope. But Humber came home and got the help of
key legislators. He went to work to try to sell the General Assembly on the idea. Representative John Kerr, Jr. of Warrenton made a stirring address in favor of the project to the 1947
legislature. Some, however, agreed with Representative Frank
Huskins of Yancey County. He said the people were more in
need of bread than this "diet of caviar." The bill squeaked
through by a vote of 45 to 43. The *High Point Enterprise* called
it "as foolish a piece of business as any the late legislature
enacted. . . ." Kress had refused to allow himself to be identified as the donor. Some wondered if Humber were not
dreaming.

The whole plan almost collapsed in 1951. Kress had become fatally ill and was unable to conduct business. The
Kress Foundation proposed that North Carolina accept a mil-

lion dollars worth of art instead of cash. This proposal came before the 1951 General Assembly. An attempt was made to kill the art museum idea. Some argued that a gift of paintings instead of money was not the agreement with Kress. Senator Alton Lennon of New Hanover spoke out. He said if the people could vote on this project, not ten percent would agree to it. But the legislators finally accepted the Kress plan. Backers of the art gallery went north to start selecting paintings that Kress would pay for. A series of lucky breaks occurred on the art market. These enabled the committee to buy a dazzling collection at reduced prices with the Kress and state funds. More hard work in the legislature brought another agreement. It was to spend another two hundred thousand dollars in state money to make the old Highway Building in Raleigh into an art museum. The North Carolina Museum of Art opened its doors in April 1956.

Later additions were made to the museum's collections. These increased its standing as one of the major art galleries in the country. In 1969, the General Assembly voted three million dollars toward putting up a museum building. In the meantime, important new museums had been established across the state. The Asheville Museum opened in 1948. The Statesville Arts and Science Museum opened in 1956 and the Ackland Art Center at Chapel Hill, in 1958. The growth of college art departments showed the new vitality of visual arts in North Carolina. Black artist Romare Bearden of Charlotte gained international acclaim for his work. Mabel Pugh of

Present-day North Carolina

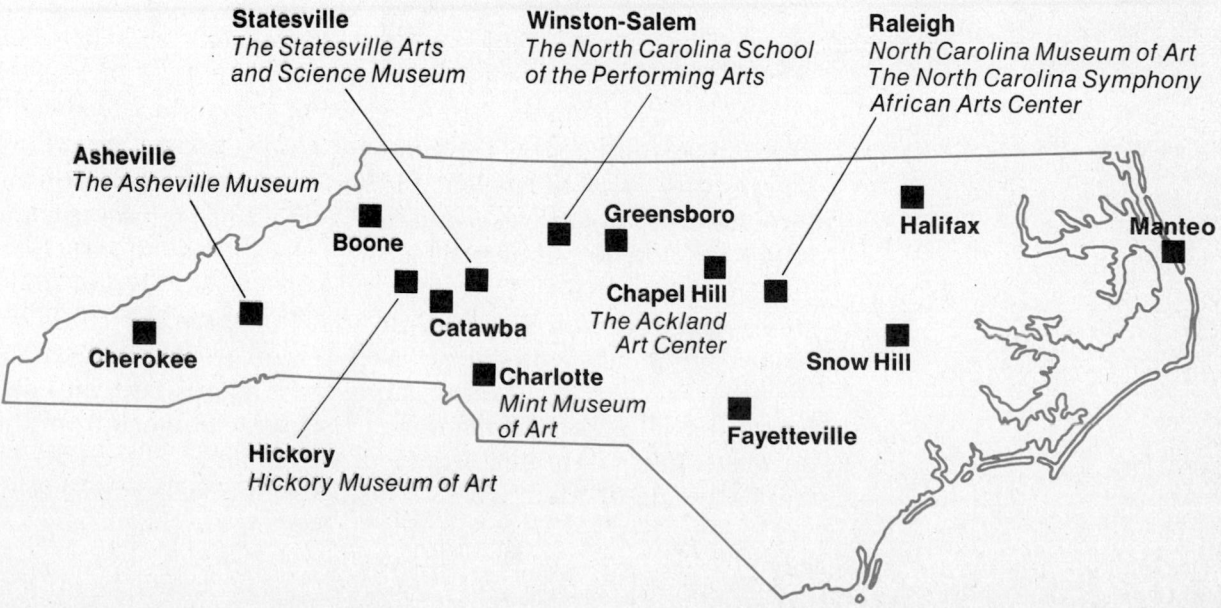

Statesville
The Statesville Arts and Science Museum

Winston-Salem
The North Carolina School of the Performing Arts

Raleigh
*North Carolina Museum of Art
The North Carolina Symphony
African Arts Center*

Asheville
The Asheville Museum

Boone

Greensboro

Halifax

Manteo

Catawba

Chapel Hill
The Ackland Art Center

Cherokee

Snow Hill

Charlotte
Mint Museum of Art

Fayetteville

Hickory
Hickory Museum of Art

Among the valuable collection in the Museum of Art at Raleigh are the African antelope headpiece from Mali (above) and the Jordaens painting "The Holy Family" (below).

Morrisville, Francis Speight of Bertie County, and Hobson Pittman of Epworth were among others whose works became widely known and honored.

Even now, North Carolina probably lagged behind other states as a center for the visual arts. But its effort could no longer be viewed with scorn. Well-known works by some of the great masters of world art hung from its museum and gallery walls. Hundreds of talented artists were at work from the ocean to the mountains. Many of them made a good living from the sale of their works. North Carolinians were gradu-

The International Festival Orchestra, North Carolina Symphony, performs in Italy in 1976.

ally acquiring a taste and a serious interest in art. This was unknown in earlier generations.

Other areas of the cultural arts were also showing the same kind of vitality. The North Carolina Symphony was founded in 1933. Funded by the General Assembly since 1943, it is the oldest state symphony in the United States. A performance by the symphony in New York's Carnegie Hall in 1977 was a step toward national recognition. By this time, eight North Carolina cities had symphony orchestras. Local groups sponsored a rich variety of music programs. These ranged from the Friends of the College series at North Carolina State University, with 20,000 paying members, to the Fiddler's Convention at Union Grove. Folk and country music conventions were held each year at various places around the state. The North Carolina School of the Performing Arts at Winston-Salem trained many talented young musicians.

James Ogle, Assistant Conductor of the North Carolina Symphony, demonstrates baton technique to an aspiring young conductor.

485

Community and college drama groups were building a large audience for drama. Among those offering original plays were the Frank Thompson Theatre at North Carolina State University, the Carolina Playmakers at Chapel Hill, and the Blue Masque at Catawba College. Little theatre troupes were active in many North Carolina towns and cities. The state's outdoor dramas were well known throughout the country: "The Lost Colony" at Manteo, "Horn in the West" at Boone, and "Unto these Hills" at Cherokee. But others, some of them inspired by the Bicentennial, were springing up at Halifax, Snow Hill, and other places. Television was not, after all, a danger to the desire for "live theatre."

Literature remained an important creative field in North Carolina. Another writer to rank with Thomas Wolfe had not appeared nor had an author with the literary gifts of Jack Cash. But in the 1970's there were larger numbers of serious writers and readers in the state than ever before. They supported poetry and short story magazines. These included such college publications as *The Carolina Quarterly* at UNC-Chapel Hill, the *St. Andrews Review* at Laurinburg, *The Pembroke Magazine*, and *The Greensboro Review*. Helen Bevington and Fred Chappell were among the state's finest poets. The novels of Reynolds Price, Guy Owen, Heather Miller, and others continued the state's fine literary reputa-

Students from the Brevard Music Center choose an outdoor setting for a rehearsal of brass instruments.

Cherokee Indians who refused to join the "Great Migration" preserve their crafts and heritage at Oconaluftee Village.

tion. In non-fiction, Jonathan Daniels, Gerald Johnson, and Harry Golden were among the state's nationally recognized writers. "Culture Week" was a unique event in North Carolina. It was the name for the week—late in each year—when cultural groups met in Raleigh to honor artistic achievements. They awarded prizes on excellence in the arts. Several college and commercial presses specialized in publishing North Carolina works.

The North Carolina Arts Council helped many cultural activities across the state. It set up local councils and helped them raise funds or add facilities and staff. It was a major benefit to the state. Funds from the National Endowment for the Arts came through the Arts Council. The funds went to a growing list of cultural projects. These included such groups as the Mount Airy Summer Theatre, Halifax County Arts and Crafts Association, and the African Art Center (Raleigh). Also included were the Jazz Merchants (Greensboro), the Lumbee Indian Arts and Crafts Association, and many others. The Arts Council was an idea that began in Winston-Salem. It spread rapidly across the nation.

There were few North Carolinians whose lives had not been touched by the rapid growth of cultural activities. Talent that might have gone unnoticed was being developed in every county. The lives of millions of citizens were being enriched by one or more of the artistic groups or movements. There

An *oasis* is a small, fertile spot in a desert, due to the presence of water.

was little evidence to uphold H. L. Mencken's criticisms of 50 years before. The "Sahara" had bloomed. North Carolina was a major oasis.

The Ongoing Quest

North Carolinians were invited to celebrate on July 4, 1976. This they did by the hundreds of thousands. But no one had told them exactly how to do so. Not everyone agreed on precisely what was being celebrated. At Pink Hill, the day was noted by a golf tournament, softball games, and fireworks. Miss Liberty 1976 and a Bicentennial Queen were chosen to reign over the festivities. At Kinston, American independence was celebrated with a dog show, sack races, a watermelon-eating contest, and other forms of hoopla. Chapel Hill had a pipe-smoking contest. Belhaven had shrimpboat and sailboat races. Bryson City held its "Ninth Annual Singing in the Smokies." A great deal of this had no relation to what took place in 1776. Most people just took the day off to have a good time.

The Bicentennial Plaza in Raleigh stands between the old capitol building and the legislative building. A four-hundred-thousand-dollar square, it was the most expensive project of its kind in the country. In the early afternoon of July 4, a small crowd—perhaps a thousand people gathered there. Bells were rung and the National Guard Band played "The Star-Spangled Banner." Politicians made speeches. A light rainfall was enough to drive off all but the most ardent patriots from this scene of doubtful merriment. Some waited to watch the unveiling of a plaque to the state's four governors during the Revolution. An added attraction was the rededication of the restored capitol building. Nothing much happened that seemed worth nine years' waiting. The celebration seemed lacking in spirit. A few onlookers thought the North Carolina celebration was in keeping with its role in the Revolution.

A *plaque* is an ornamental or commemorative plate made of metal or some other material.

The dreary program in 1976 in Raleigh was a kind of triumph of the Revolutionary spirit. The big Fourth of July parade was cancelled for lack of floats and participants. Most communities were too busy with their own celebrations to give any thought to Raleigh's. They did not send their expected entries for the parade. In other words, the celebration was happening about the way the planners hoped it would.

During a Bicentennial celebration, "Uncle Sam" talks with a little colonial miss.

Native American is the term by which American Indians prefer to be known.

Trivial means unimportant.

Hundreds of communities were celebrating as they chose. This was without direction from the center of government. For the moment, at least, people were not expecting the central government to do their thinking. If the attitude stuck, the Bicentennial might yet achieve its highest goals.

There were encouraging signs that the expected back-patting and self-congratulating was not all the celebration would amount to. A Bicentennial program was sponsored by the American Association of Nurserymen. This led many communities to start beautification efforts. Improvement of the environment by the planting of trees and shrubs was a part of the same program. Fayetteville started the idea of building a bicycle path along an old railroad bed. This led to a plan to create a statewide bicycle trail. The plan was aided by the Department of Transportation and the Department of Natural and Economic Resources. Backers of the project succeeded in their aim. They published a booklet called *Bicycling Through History.* This booklet showed how to set up a bike tour through a historic district. "Child Care '76" was a national program that enabled many communities in North Carolina to establish day-care centers.

The Bicentennial Commission produced a valuable pamphlet series on North Carolina and the Revolutionary era. A commission grant helped launch the first volumes of the *Dictionary of North Carolina Biography.* These are edited by Professor William S. Powell of UNC-Chapel Hill. This eight-volume series gives a brief, reliable biography of every prominent North Carolinian of the past. It includes information on thousands of people—female, male, black, white, and native American. Hundreds of people contributed to the project. A book by and about North Carolina blacks and native Americans, *Paths Toward Freedom,* was published in 1975. This was the largest Bicentennial project for minority groups in any of the 50 states. The Bicentennial Commission also sponsored a wide variety of other publications and projects.

As the commission had hoped from the first, many programs it aided were started by local groups. Some of these were trivial in meaning and slight in impact. But some were important in their long-range possibilities. They were often the seeds from which great progress might result. The Bicentennial Commission did not create this basic response. But it was able to help it along. As the various cultural activities of recent years had already shown, citizens were learning to take matters into their own hands. More and more, what they seemed to want from Raleigh and Washington was help in doing things their own way. In some ways, initiative seemed to be getting away from the centers of power. Local pride and self-respect were growing. It was too soon to say whether this showed a new kind of participation by citizens in the decisions that affected their lives. But the trend seemed hopeful.

Decade by decade, greater numbers of North Carolinians were joining the quest for "the good life." Blacks and native Americans were making progress in gaining their rights as citizens. Women were making great strides in the search for equality with men. Young adults between eighteen and twenty-one years were taking advantage of their new voting rights granted in the 1960s. A high school girl was one of North Carolina's presidential electors in 1976. In North Carolina as in the nation, democracy was becoming more democratic with each new generation.

Being a good citizen was becoming a more demanding responsibility. It was no longer enough to cast a vote every two years. Good citizenship meant taking part in groups seeking to make government serve the people. Some people were bringing pressure to bear on big business. They were demanding more concern for the quality of the environment, for the consumer, and for the laborer. Some people sought to end urban

The Theatre for Young People salutes the Bicentennial in "Tarheel Tales '76" featuring North Carolina tales and folksongs.

Ghettoes are sections of a city in which members of a minority group live.

ghettoes and to reduce the rates of crime. They wanted to preserve old houses, start museums, improve schools, and give aid and comfort to the aged. People demanded that the public's business not be held behind closed doors but in full view of public awareness.

The individualism that was so much a part of North Carolina's past was still a valuable trait. But individualism need not conflict with a sensitive concern for the well-being of others. People were depending on each other more and more—even around the world. Object lessons showed that a change in one place in the world could affect conditions everywhere. A frost in Brazil, a drought in the Midwest, a conference in Baghdad—any one could affect the lives of almost every American. It was clear that the state could not ignore the needs of others in the desire for self-fulfillment. Better than their forebears, people could appreciate that what does not benefit all does not truly benefit anyone. The lesson was not yet perfectly learned. But it was becoming very difficult to deny.

In three hundred years, North Carolinians had learned much. They had not completed their quest, but they seemed nearer to their goal. As the end of the century approached, people seemed more alert than ever to the fact that they were citizens of a country as well as a state. They sensed that they were also a part of a world community which they dared not ignore. The Bicentennial was history. It was now time to begin laying the foundations for a joyful Tricentennial. The third century could be more rewarding and fulfilling than the second.

Chapter Checkup

PEOPLE

Robert Lee Humber	Heather Miller	Gerald Johnson
Romare Bearden	Guy Owen	William S. Powell
Mabel Pugh		

PLACES

Morrisville	Cherokee	Southport
Epworth	Pembroke	Bryson City
Boone	Pink Hill	

FACT

How did the Bicentennial Commission alter its original instructions?
What were the chief criticisms of the plans and conduct of the Bicentennial in North Carolina?
How were the funds obtained to open the North Carolina Museum of Art?

INTERPRETATION

Do you feel that the question of whether to match the Kress offer with state funds should have been put to the people in a referendum? Defend your answer.
Can you list some reminders from the past year or so of how much we depend on people in other parts of the world?

VOCABULARY

Native American   Ghettoes

ACTIVITY

Plan a celebration by your school or class of the Bicentennial of some event of the Revolutionary period (up to 1789) associated with North Carolina. Decide what your goals will be and how you will try to reach them.

SUGGESTED READING

Foushee, Ola Mae. *Art in North Carolina: Episodes and Developments, 1585–1970.* Charlotte: Heritage Printers, Inc., 1972. The title is misleading since there is not much on developments before the twentieth century. Interesting on recent developments, however, including the establishment of the North Carolina Museum of Art.
Clay, James W. *et al. North Carolina Atlas: Portrait of a Changing Southern State.* Chapel Hill: UNC Press, 1975. See Part V on "Services and Amenities" for an up-to-date survey of cultural arts in the state.

CHIEF EXECUTIVES OF NORTH CAROLINA

- **Governors of the Original Virginia Colony**

1585-1586	Ralph Lane	Appointed by Walter Raleigh
1587	John White	Appointed by Walter Raleigh

- **Governors of Albemarle County under the Lords Proprietors**

1663-1667	William Drummond	
1667-1669	Samuel Stephens	
1670-1673	Peter Carteret	
1673-1676	John Jenkins	President of the Council
1676-1678	Thomas Eastchurch	
1677	Thomas Miller	Deputy
1677-1678	John Culpeper	Elected by "the rebels"
1678	Seth Sothel	
1679	John Harvey	Deputy
1679-1681	John Jenkins	President of the Council
1682-1689	Seth Sothel	

● **Governors under the Lords Proprietors of "That Part of the Province of Carolina That Lies North and East of Cape Fear"**

1689-1691	Philip Ludwell	
1691-1694	Thomas Jarvis	Deputy of the governor of Carolina
1694-1699	Thomas Harvey	Deputy of the governor of Carolina
1699-1704	Henderson Walker	President of the Council
1704-1705	Robert Daniel	Deputy of the governor of Carolina
1705-1706	Thomas Cary	Deputy of the governor of Carolina
1706-1708	William Glover	President of the Council
1708-1711	Thomas Cary	President of the Council
1711-1712	Edward Hyde	

● **Governors of North Carolina under the Lords Proprietors**

1712	Edward Hyde	
1712-1714	Thomas Pollock	President of the Council
1714-1722	Charles Eden	
1722	Thomas Pollock	President of the Council
1722-1724	William Reed	President of the Council
1724-1725	George Burrington	
1725-1729	Richard Everard	

● **Governors of North Carolina under the King**

1729-1731	Richard Everard	Held office until Burrington, the Royal Governor, arrived from England
1731-1734	George Burrington	
1734-1752	Gabriel Johnston	
1752-1753	Nathaniel Rice	President of the Council
1753-1754	Matthew Rowan	President of the Council
1754-1765	Arthur Dobbs	
1765-1771	William Tryon	
1771	James Hassell	President of the Council
1771-1775	Josiah Martin	

● **Presidents of the Council under the Revolutionary Government**

1775-1776	Cornelius Harnett
1776	Samuel Ashe
1776	Willie Jones

Governors of the State of North Carolina and Home Count

(Elected by joint ballot of the two houses of the General Assembly for
during the period 1776-1835; elected by the qualified voters for two-year
period 1836-1868; elected by the voters for four-year terms since 1868.)

1776-1780	Richard Caswell	Dobbs *(Lenoir)*
1780-1781	Abner Nash	Craven
1781-1782	Thomas Burke	Orange
1782-1784	Alexander Martin	Guilford
1784-1787	Richard Caswell	Dobbs *(Lenoir)*
1787-1789	Samuel Johnston	Chowan
1789-1792	Alexander Martin	Guilford
1792-1795	Richard Dobbs Spaight	Craven
1795-1798	Samuel Ashe	New Hanover
1798-1799	William R. Davie	Halifax
1799-1802	Benjamin Williams	Moore
1802-1805	James Turner	Warren
1805-1807	Nathaniel Alexander	Mecklenburg
1807-1808	Benjamin Williams	Moore
1808-1810	David Stone	Bertie
1810-1811	Benjamin Smith	Brunswick
1811-1814	William Hawkins	Warren
1814-1817	William Miller	Warren
1817-1820	John Branch	Halifax
1820-1821	Jesse Franklin	Surry
1821-1824	Gabriel Holmes	Sampson
1824-1827	Hutchins G. Burton	Halifax
1827-1828	James Iredell	Chowan
1828-1830	John Owen	Bladen
1830-1832	Montfort Stokes	Wilkes
1832-1835	David L. Swain	Buncombe
1835-1836	Richard Dobbs Spaight, Jr.	Craven
1836-1841	Edward B. Dudley	New Hanover
1841-1845	John M. Morehead	Guilford
1845-1849	William A. Graham	Orange
1849-1851	Charles Manly	Wake
1851-1854	David S. Reid	Rockingham
1854-1855	Warren Winslow	Cumberland
1855-1859	Thomas Bragg	Northampton
1859-1861	John W. Ellis	Rowan
	(Died in office)	
1861-1862	Henry T. Clark	Edgecombe
1862-1865	Zebulon B. Vance	Buncombe
1865	William W. Holden	Wake

(Appointed by Andrew Johnson, President of the United States)

Governors of the State of North Carolina and Home Counties
(cont.)

1865-1868	Jonathan Worth	Randolph
1868-1871	William W. Holden	Wake
	(Impeached and removed from office in 1871; succeeded by Lieutenant Governor Tod R. Caldwell)	
1871-1874	Tod R. Caldwell	Burke
	(Died in office)	
1874-1877	Curtis H. Brogden	Wayne
1877-1879	Zebulon B. Vance	Mecklenburg
	(Resigned to become U.S. Senator)	
1079-1885	Thomas J. Jarvis	Pitt
1885-1889	Alfred M. Scales	Rockingham
1889-1891	Daniel G. Fowle	Wake
	(Died in office)	
1891-1893	Thomas M. Holt	Alamance
1893-1897	Elias Carr	Edgecombe
1897-1901	Daniel L. Russell	Brunswick
1901-1905	Charles B. Aycock	Wayne
1905-1909	Robert B. Glenn	Forsyth
1909-1913	William W. Kitchin	Person
1913-1917	Locke Craig	Buncombe
1917-1921	Thomas W. Bickett	Franklin
1921-1925	Cameron Morrison	Mecklenburg
1925-1929	Angus W. McLean	Robeson
1929-1933	O. Max Gardner	Cleveland
1933-1937	J.C.B. Ehringhaus	Pasquotank
1937-1941	Clyde R. Hoey	Cleveland
1941-1945	J. Melville Broughton	Wake
1945-1949	R. Gregg Cherry	Gaston
1949-1953	W. Kerr Scott	Alamance
1953-1954	William B. Umstead	Durham
	(Died in office)	
1954-1961	Luther H. Hodges	Rockingham
1961-1965	Terry Sanford	Cumberland
1965-1969	Dan K. Moore	Haywood
1969-1973	Robert W. Scott	Alamance
1973-1977	James E. Holshouser, Jr.	Watauga
1977-	James B. Hunt, Jr.	Wilson

PEOPLE
IN THIS BOOK

INDEX

CREDITS

Cover Events Identification

Front cover, beginning top left, clockwise:
A textile mill, Ch. 20; The Revolutionary War, Ch. 8; The battleship *North Carolina*, Ch. 22; "A Lady of Quality," Ch. 7; Early settlement, Ch. 2; Biltmore, Ch. 18.

Back cover, beginning top left, clockwise:
The Civil War, Ch. 13, 14; A political speech, Ch. 9; Working the tobacco fields, Ch. 10; Science and education, Ch. 23; Early exploration, Ch. 1; A revival meeting, Ch. 19; Slaves plotting revolt, Ch. 10.

Photo Credits

Abbreviations:

Archives and History	State of North Carolina, Department of Cultural Resources, Division of Archives and History
NCC/UNC	North Carolina Collection, UNC Library, Chapel Hill
Duke	Manuscript Division, William R. Perkins Library Duke University
LOC	Library of Congress
Travel and Tourism	North Carolina Department of Commerce, Travel and Tourism Division

Page 12: *tl & r Archives and History; b*NCC/UNC. **13:** *tl, tr, cl Archives and History; cr Collection of Mrs. Frances Parker; b NCC/UNC.* **14:** *t & c NCC/UNC; bl & r Archives and History.* **15:** *t NCC/UNC; bl & r Archives and History.* **16:** *all Taylor Lewis.* **18:** *Bruce Roberts.* **25:** *LOC.* **26:** *New York Public Library.* **28:** *LOC.* **29, 31:** *Archives and History.* **32:** *LOC.* **34:**

510

Carolina Museum of Art, Raleigh; b Taylor Lewis. **477** all, **478** all, **479** all: Michal Heron. **480:** t North Carolina Symphony; b James Drake/SPORTS ILLUSTRATED^c Time, Inc. **482:** Travel and Tourism. **484:** both Collection of the North Carolina Museum of Art, Raleigh. **485:** t Winston-Salem School of the Arts; b North Carolina Symphony. **486, 487:** Travel and Tourism. **489, 490:** North Carolina Bicentennial Commission.

Bibliographic Citations

Page 23: Corbitt, David Leroy, editor. *Explorations, Descriptions, and Attempted Settlements of Carolina, 1584-1590*, p. 14. Raleigh: State Department of Archives and History, 1953. **45-46:** Powell, William S., editor. *Ye Countie of Albemarle in Carolina: A Collection of Documents, 1664-1675*, pp. 62-63. Raleigh: State Department of Archives and History, 1958. **57-58:** Lefler, Hugh Talmadge, editor. *A New Voyage to Carolina by John Lawson*, pp. 66-67. Chapel Hill: University of North Carolina Press, 1967. **107:** Fries, Adelaide L. et al, editors. *Records of the Moravians in North Carolina*, Vol. I, p. 323. Raleigh: North Carolina Historical Commission, 1922-1969. **121-122:** Letters and Papers of Elkanah Watson, Journal B., VI, page 346. Manuscript in the New York State Library, Albany. **131-132:** *Wilmington (N.C.) Journal*, February 28, 1853 **139-140:** *Wilmington (N.C.) Journal, February 28, 1853* **169:** *State Gazette of North Carolina* (New Bern), March 27, 1788 **173:** Morse, Jedediah. *The American Geography; or, A View of the Present Situation of the United States of America*, p. 418. Elizabethtown, Mass.: Shepard Kollock, 1789. **182:** Joseph Riddick to Willie Riddick, June 6, 1802. Manuscript in Perquimans County Slave Records (1802-1803). State Department of Archives and History, Raleigh. For original Colerain Letter, see Bertie County Slave Papers (1801-1805). State Department of Archives and History, Raleigh. **184t:** *The Mercury and New-England Palladium* (Boston), July 16, 1802. **184b:** *Raleigh (N.C.) Register*, July 27, 1802. **204:** "Journal of a Southern Tour—by an Unidentified Bostonian—May 1824." Typescript copy in "The Capitol." Miscellaneous Collections, State Department of Archives and History, Raleigh **214:** Polk, William Harrison. *Polk Family and Kinsmen*, p. 142. Louisville, Ky.: Bradley, 1912. **222:** *Raleigh (N.C.) Register*, December 20, 1851. **227-228:** Stokes, Durward T. "Five Letters from Jesse Holmes, the Fool Killer to the Editor of the *Milton Chronicle*," p. 311. *North Carolina Historcial Review*, Vol. L, Summer 1973. **242-243:** Quoted by *The Daily Journal* (Wilmington, N.C.), August 10, 1861. **248:** *Weekly Standard* (Raleigh, N.C.), January 3, 1861 **313:** *Wilson (N.C.) Advance*, October 20, 1898. **317:** *Wilson (N.C.) Advance*, September 15, 1898. **318:** *Goldsboro (N.C.) Daily Argus*, October 14, 1898. **323:** *Windsor (N.C.) Ledger*, November 10, 1898. **326t:** Frazier, Thomas R., editor. *Afro-American History: Primary Sources*, p. 200. New York: Harcourt Brace Jovanovich, Inc., 1970. **326b-327:** Frazier, Thomas R., editor. *Afro-American History: Primary Sources*, p. 201. New York: Harcourt Brace Jovanovich, Inc., 1970. **327c:** Frazier, Thomas R., editor. *Afro-American History: Primary Sources*, p. 206. New York: Harcourt Brace Jovanovich, Inc., 1970. **327b:** Frazier, Thomas R., editor. *Afro-American History: Primary Sources*, p. 206. New York: Harcourt Brace Jovanovich, Inc., 1970. **328:** Frazier, Thomas R., editor. *Afro-American History: Primary Sources*, p. 209-210. New York: Harcourt Brace Jovanovich, Inc., 1970 **353:** *The Daily Advance* (Elizabeth City, N.C.), October 24, 1924. **354:** *The Independent* (Elizabeth City, N.C.), November 1, 1924. **356:** *The Independent* (Elizabeth City, N.C.), November 14, 1924. **373:** Larkin, Margaret. "Ella May's Songs," p. 382. New York: *The Nation*. Vol. CXXIX, October 9, 1929. **381-382:** Larkin, Margaret. "Tragedy in North Carolina," p. 685. Cedar Falls, Ia.: *North American Review*, Vol. CCXXVIII, December 1929. **390-391:** Wolfe, Thomas. *Look Homeward, Angel: A Story of the Buried Life*, p. 155. New York: Random House, Inc., 1929. **392-393:** Cash, Wilbur J. *The Mind of the South*. New York: Doubleday & Company, Inc., 1941.